THE ECONOMY OF IRELAND

Policy and Performance

Fifth Edition

EDITED BY JOHN W. O'HAGAN

IRISH MANAGEMENT INSTITUTE

IRISH MANAGEMENT INSTITUTE
DUBLIN

First Published 1975

Second Edition 1978

Third Edition 1981

Fourth Edition 1984

Fifth Edition 1987

ISBN 0 903352 56 7 (soft cover)

Printed in Ireland by Mount Salus Press Limited, Dublin

Contents

Preface to Fifth Edition

Although it is twelve years since the preface to the first edition was written, the purpose and basic structure of the book have remained unchanged.

The central purpose of the book is to provide an account of the main features, performance and associated policy issues of the economy of Ireland in the 1980s. As such, it is an attempt to combine the functions of both the 'analytical' economist and the 'descriptive' economist in the confines of one book. I am sure it has been noticed, though, that since the early editions the analytical input to the book has grown enormously in relative importance.

Clearly economic performance cannot be properly assessed without well-articulated criteria for assessment. Part I of the book provides this background. In it a number of aims of Irish economic policy are defined and an attempt is made to rationalize these objectives. The next question that arises is how the economy is to be directed towards the attainment of these objectives, and, in this respect, Part II examines the government's role. Indeed, one could claim that it makes sense to discuss policy objectives in terms only of the government, since the word 'policy' implies a conscious decision rather than the acceptance of an outcome dictated by the 'invisible hand' of the market.

Part III follows on from this and looks at the extent to which the government has achieved its objectives of economic growth, full employment, balance in foreign payments and price stability. It also contains a lengthy analysis of the policy issues associated with the attainment of these objectives. Part IV extends this analysis considerably with its examination of the main sectors of the economy. It is argued in Chapter 7 that agriculture and manufacturing industry, the traded sectors, are the key focus for policy vis-à-vis GDP and employment growth: these sectors are discussed in Chapters 10 and 11 respectively. The counter-argument, that the non-traded sector should be the focus of policy for growth and employment, is presented in Chapter 12, where the services, and building and construction, industries are examined.

As the readings tend to concentrate on the recent past, it is thought important to provide a picture of the historical background to the present day economy, and for this reason the first chapter of the book is included.

While the overall *structure* of the book differs little from that of previous editions, the content and structure of individual chapters have been altered totally. Specifically, compared with the fourth edition, this book contains three new chapters, Chapters 1, 6 and 12 respectively. There has also been rewriting of substantial parts of Chapters 2, 5, 7 and 11 and all chapters have been revised and updated.

I would like to thank, on behalf of myself and the other contributors, the many people who have provided assistance in the preparation of this edition. The Irish Management Institute again financed and wholeheartedly supported the publication of the book. By doing this, as I have pointed out many times before, the Institute is catering for a market that might not, because of its small size, otherwise be accommodated. Trinity College Arts and ESS Benefactions Fund provided valuable finance for the administrative costs associated with the preparation of the book. Yvonne Scott assiduously read and checked the whole manuscript, prepared the index and charts, and made many suggestions regarding style and content. In this task she was ably assisted by Kevin Carey and Dermot Nolan. I would also like to thank the many students who pointed out errors in, and suggested improvements to, the earlier editions. The continuing high level of usage of the book in almost all third level institutions in Ireland not only makes the publication of the book commercially viable (almost!), but it also provides the motivation to the contributors to devote so much time, effort and enthusiasm to the writing and/or refining of their chapters. For this time, effort and enthusiasm may I thank sincerely the other contributors to the book.

John O'Hagan
University of Dublin
(Trinity College)

August 1987

Contributors

Chapter 1

Jonathan Haughton has a B.A.(Mod.) from the University of Dublin (Trinity College), and a Ph.D. from Harvard University. His current position is Assistant Professor of Economics, University of Maryland, Baltimore County.

Chapter 2

Andrew John has a B.A.(Mod.) from the University of Dublin (Trinity College), and an M.A. and M.Phil. from Yale University. His current position is Lecturer in Economics, Yale University, New Haven.

Chapters 3, 9

Dermot McAleese has a B.Comm. and M.Econ.Sc. from the National University of Ireland (University College Dublin), and an M.A. and Ph.D. from Johns Hopkin University. His current position is Whately Professor of Political Economy, and Fellow, University of Dublin (Trinity College). He is at present on leave of absence at the Economic Development Institute of the World Bank, Washington DC.

Chapters 4, 5

John W. O'Hagan has a B.A., B.E. and M.A. from the National University of Ireland (University College Dublin), and a Ph.D. from the University of Dublin (Trinity College). His current position is Associate Professor of Economics, and Fellow, University of Dublin (Trinity College).

Chapter 6

Brendan Walsh has a B.A. from the National University of Ireland (University College Dublin), an M.A. from the University of Tennessee, and a Ph.D. from Boston College. His current position is Professor of the National Economics of Ireland, National University of Ireland (University College Dublin).

Jim O'Leary has a B.A. and M.A. from the National University of Ireland (University College Dublin). His current position is Economist, Gilt Research Department, J. & E. Davy (Stockbrokers), Dublin.

Anthony Leddin has a B.A. and M.A. from Essex University. His current position is Lecturer in Economics, National Institute for Higher Education, Limerick.

Chapter 7

Sean Nolan has a B.A.(Mod.) from the University of Dublin (Trinity College), and an M.A., M.Phil. and Ph.D. from Yale University. His current position is Assistant Professor of Economics, Boston University.

Chapter 8

Kieran A. Kennedy has a B.Comm. and M.Econ.Sc. from the National University of Ireland (University College Dublin), a B.Phil. from Oxford University, and a Ph.D. from Harvard University. His current position is Director of the Economic and Social Research Institute, Dublin.

Thomas Giblin has a B.A. and M.A. from the National University of Ireland (University College Dublin). His current position is Research Assistant, Economic and Social Research Institute, Dublin.

Chapter 10

Alan Matthews has a B.A. (Mod.) from the University of Dublin (Trinity College), and an M.S. from Cornell University. His current position is Lecturer in Economics, and Fellow, University of Dublin (Trinity College).

Chapter 11

Frances Ruane has a B.A. and M.A. from the National University of Ireland (University College Dublin), and a B.Phil. and D.Phil from the University of Oxford (Nuffield College). Her current position is Lecturer in Economics, and Fellow, University of Dublin (Trinity College). She is at present Visiting Associate Professor, Queen's University, Kingston, Ontario.

Chapter 12

Kevin O'Rourke has a B.A.(Mod.) from the University of Dublin (Trinity College), and an M.A. from Harvard University. His current position is Assistant Senior Tutor, Harvard University, Boston.

1 The Historical Background

Jonathan Haughton

1 WHY ECONOMIC HISTORY?

WHY TAKE the trouble to study history, and particularly the economic history of a minor European island?

For economists, the most compelling reason is that history holds lessons for economics. Historical data can be valuable in testing economic theories; thus, for instance, Friedman's theories on the role of money have been, and continue to be, tested using historical data. A reading of history also generates ideas which seep into the thinking of economists. For example, a great deal of our understanding of the causes of famines comes from the study of historical instances of famine.

Historical events provide lessons for policy-makers. Those who favour protection as a means to foster industrialization would do well to examine the Irish experience. Recent efforts to curb hyperinflation in Brazil, Argentina and Bolivia have drawn heavily and explicitly on German experience in the 1920s. While it may be true that 'those who ignore history are condemned to repeat it', the study of history is not merely to avoid making mistakes, but also to learn what works well and is worth copying. The economic history of Ireland is of particular interest to most Less Developed Countries for, like Ireland, they typically are small open economies, have a colonial past, and today face many of the same dilemmas as Ireland did half a century ago.

A third reason for studying economic history is that it gives a long-run and global perspective, which serves as an antidote for the typically short-run and partial approach of standard economics textbooks or courses. The standard approach is excellent for studying the immediate effects of a change in demand or supply, or a devaluation or a monetary expansion, but it tends to lose sight of the 'big picture' — why some countries grow faster than others, or why growth sometimes goes hand in hand with greater equity and sometimes not. From economic history one gets a sense of the fragility of economic growth, and its intermittent nature. A look at

1

history also forces one to focus on how income is distributed; income distribution changes slowly over time, and the changes are only evident from looking at data over a longer period. It is no accident that modern economists have typically tended to undervalue economic history, and also to downplay questions of distribution, in contrast to the Classical economists such as Ricardo.

Economic history has an intrinsic interest, which is a valid reason for studying it, or almost anything. It does seem appropriate to be curious about our past, and what factors have made contemporary Ireland (or the world) the way it is.

Finally it is sometimes impossible to evaluate the arguments of ideologues without some knowledge of history. When nationalist writers argued that Ireland would be better off as an independent state rather than as a part of the UK they emphasized the ways in which the link with Britain has been historically harmful to Ireland. Without an independent knowledge of Irish history it is impossible to make an informed judgement about the empirical basis of such ideas.

Given the above, the main focus of this chapter is on how Ireland has developed economically. Crotty defines such development as 'a situation where (a) more people are better off than formerly and (b) fewer people are as badly off'.[1] By this yardstick it is necessary to look at population growth, since an economy which forces massive emigration has in some sense failed. To develop, incomes must rise (growth), including, or especially, those of the least well off (equality), and this is presumably facilitated by an efficient use of resources (notably full employment). These latter are the three primary objectives of an economy outlined in Chapter 2.

The material is approached chronologically, over long time periods. For each period we set out the main estimates of population, growth and equality, trace the principal effects on the structure of the economy, consider the possible causes of these trends, and comment on the links with political and social events. In practice it is not always possible first to present data and then follow with 'analysis', since the two are intertwined. Nor is it pretended that the approach is 'neutral', for the very way in which the 'facts' are presented represents the judgement of the writer as to what is important; clearly complete 'neutrality' is a chimera.

The starting point, arbitrarily chosen, is 1690, with the consolidation of the Protestant ascendancy. The subsequent years are divided into subperiods. The first phase stretches from 1690 to 1815, taking in a period of rapid expansion, a slowdown, and a steady period of growth and industrialization. The second phase is short, running from 1815 to 1850, during which time Ireland lagged seriously behind Britain, and culminating in the Famine period. The third phase covers 1850 to 1921, during which the economy provided rising living standards for a smaller number of people. The last phase, from 1921 to the present, is treated in most detail.

In the final section of the chapter an attempt is made to tease out some of the lessons for economists and policymakers from Irish history, notably in understanding the growth process.

2   1690 TO 1815

The Economy in 1690

At the time of the battle of the Boyne the Irish economy was predominantly rural, although it was no longer a 'woodland' society. Population stood at a little under two million, roughly double the level of a century before, and was growing at an historically high rate of at least half a per cent per year.[2] With the spread of population the forest cover was rapidly disappearing, giving way to both grazing and tillage. The largest town, Dublin, had about 60,000 inhabitants.

The country was an important trader, especially of grain, beef, butter, wool and, to a lesser extent, linen. Almost half of all exports went to Continental Europe, notably to France. The pattern of exports was strongly influenced by the Cattle Acts, passed by the English House of Commons in 1667, which forbade the importation of cattle, sheep, beef and pork from Ireland. Irish farmers and merchants responded by finding new markets for beef (mainly to provision ships plying the Atlantic, and to supply the Caribbean) and by exporting wool rather than sheep. Earnings from these exports were spent on items such as coal and tobacco, and a surplus on current account amounting to perhaps 10 per cent of exports allowed for the remittance of rents to absentee landlords. Between 1665 and 1686 tobacco imports almost doubled, and Cullen interprets this as evidence of rising prosperity over this period.[3] Petty, visiting the country in 1672, commented on the large number of people who rode horses, and the high standard of clothing relative to France and most of Europe. He also noted the shabbiness of the houses, of which he reckoned only a fifth had chimneys. The implication was that Ireland was not significantly poorer, and was perhaps better off, than most of Continental Europe at that time, although less affluent than most of England.

Income was distributed unevenly. Land was owned by perhaps

3

10,000 landlords, and six-sevenths of the land was held by Protestants. Much of this was let out to farmers, who in turn frequently sublet small plots to cottiers, or hired casual labour. By one estimate a little over half of the population constituted a rural proletariat, with minimal access to land, and close to the margin of subsistence. The potato had been introduced early in the seventeenth century, but was only an important part of the diet of the poor. Potatoes did not keep well, and were typically used from August to March to supplement the main staples of oats (consumed as porridge), milk and butter. Bread was rare. In a few areas peas and beans were still cultivated extensively, a throw-back to earlier dietary patterns.

Population
Ireland's population grew dramatically from a little more than a million people in 1600 to over eight million in 1841. Two turning points are of interest, notably the slowdown from 1725 to about 1750, and the particularly rapid growth from 1750 onwards, although the precise magnitudes of these changes have been much debated. Until recently most effort has been put into explaining the acceleration in population growth after 1750. The now conventional explanation, first offered by Connell, is that the marriage age fell. This, he suggested, was because it had become easier for young couples to find land on which to grow potatoes, so they could set up a separate family at an early age. High marital fertility (fecundity), coupled with earlier marriage, would together explain the rapid growth of population after 1750.

Drake argues that the evidence that the marriage age fell noticeably in the mid-eighteenth century is flimsy at best.[4] An alternative explanation is that death rates fell; there does indeed appear to be some evidence that the number of child burials fell at this time. Lower death rates may be attributed to an increased use of the potato, which was both nutritious and reliable; its use increased dramatically after the famine of 1740, about half a century before it came to be widely used in much of Europe. Better nutrition might also have increased fecundity. However a potato-based explanation is not entirely satisfactory, since at the same time the populations of England and Finland were growing even faster, but largely without the potato. This would suggest a role for public health measures, such as inoculation against smallpox, or a secular reduction (for unknown reasons) in the incidence of typhus or dysentery.

An alternative approach, due to Cullen, sees a steady increase in

4

population growth stretching back as far as 1600, in part due to the improvements in the diet of the poor, interrupted by famines in 1727-30 and 1740-41. The latter famine was extremely severe, and mainly attributable to a failure of the oat crop. By some estimates as many as 400,000, or over 10 per cent of the population, may have died as a result. Early in the century emigration from the north-east became standard and self-sustaining; in the difficult years of the 1770s the flow may have been as high as 12,000 annually.[5]

By the first half of the nineteenth century there is some evidence that the rate of population growth had slowed down, perhaps mainly because of quickened emigration.

Growth

The essential features of economic growth during the period 1690-1815 were a rapid recovery from the war, a period of relative stagnation (1700-1720), twenty-five years of crisis which included two famines (1720-1745), and a long period of sustained and relatively rapid economic growth (1745-1815). The evidence for these is indirect, since few economic statistics were collected at the time. Possibly the best source of information is trade statistics, recorded because trade was taxed, although data on other tax receipts have also proved to be useful. Some interesting trade figures are shown in Table 1.1. The figures for exports and imports are in nominal prices, but no price deflator is available; except for the period of the Napoleonic wars (1793-1815) prices were as likely to fall as to rise, so the nominal figures are of some use.

A growing economy might be expected to trade more, especially so as to import luxury items such as tobacco which could not be produced locally. The value of imports showed little increase until the 1740s, after which it rose fairly rapidly. One cause was lower exports due to the effect of the Woollen Acts, passed in 1699, which prohibited the export of wool from Ireland or England to other countries, and imposed a stiff duty on Irish wool entering England; this had the immediate effect of reducing Irish total exports by about 10 per cent.

On the basis of the stagnant trade figures for the first two decades of the century, it may be surmised that per capita incomes did not rise; since rents did rise during this period it follows that those who rented land became poorer. It is conceivable that rent increases reflected some population pressure on land.

The main setback to growth occurred during the 1720s, when there were several years of poor harvest, culminating in the famine of 1728-29. Recovery during the 1730s was halted by the terrible

Table 1.1

Value of Irish Exports and Imports
(£'000)

Year to March 25[1]	Exports	Imports	Imports/Exports %
1665	402		
1683	570		
1698	996		
1700	815	792	97
1701	670		
1710	712	554	78
1720	1,038	892	86
1730	993	930	94
1740	1,260	850	67
1750	1,863	1,532	82
1760	2,139	1,648	77
1770	3,160	2,567	81
1780	3,012	2,128	71
1790	4,855	3,830	79
1801	3,715	5,585	150[1]
1811	6,099	6,564	108[2]
1816	7,076	6,107	86

Sources: L. Cullen, *An Economic History of Ireland Since 1660,* Batsford, London 1972, p.54.
[1]1700 figures for year ending December 25. From 1801 figures are for year ending January 5.
[2]Exports are probably undervalued; official valuations did not account for price increases. Cullen believes that exports exceeded imports in these years too.

famine of 1740-41. It is only after this famine that the potato came to be relied on as the principal foodstuff (from August to April) by the bulk of the population, and it is noteworthy that for over a century thereafter the country did not suffer a serious famine. From mid-century onwards trade increased more rapidly.

Structural Change

In 1665 Ireland's main exports were cattle, sheep and butter. A century later the pattern had changed to beef, butter, pork and linen, while small amounts of grain were imported. By 1818 butter, pork and linen exports had risen further, cattle and beef remained important and, most surprisingly for a country with such rapid population growth, Ireland had become a major exporter of grain. The relevant figures are presented in Table 1.2. It is generally accepted that the changing pattern of exports mirrors the main changes which occurred in the economy domestically.

The first explanation for the changing economic structure is English laws. In 1667 the Cattle Act excluded Irish cattle, sheep,

Table 1.2

The Pattern of Irish Agricultural Exports, 1665-1818

Export		Mean of 5 years to:		
	1665	25/3/1758	25/3/1798	5/1/1818
Oxen (number)	57,545	22	12,143	35,634
Beef (cattle-equivalent)	14,632	81,724	60,065	52,137
Butter (cwt.)	26,413	197,552	300,160	422,189
Pigs (number)	1,446	0	4,273	59,107
Pig-meat (pig-equivalent)	3,134	60,004	321,758	563,240
Sheep (number)	99,564	0	0	21,990
Grain, net (tons)		– 17,900	36,738	111,527
of which oats		6,193	34,138	71,070
Flour and meal (tons)		– 3,631	3,106	6,627

Sources: R.C. Crotty, *Irish Agricultural Production,* Cork University Press, Cork 1966.

beef and pork from England. The country responded by exporting wool rather than sheep, and by searching for new markets for meat, notably the important provision trade, serving transatlantic ships and the West Indies, and the extensive French market. It also shifted resources from dry cattle to dairying, and butter exports grew rapidly. This process was speeded by the Woollen Acts of 1699 which made sheep rearing less profitable. The granting of duty-free access to England for linen helped that industry. In the course of the century most of the restrictions on Irish trade were removed or eased; the Navigation Acts were relaxed in 1731 and abolished in 1780, and the Cattle Acts ended in 1759.

The significance of English laws for Irish economic growth is a matter of controversy. Writers in the nationalist vein have typically stressed the ways in which English law has handicapped Irish growth.[6] Oddly enough the Cattle Acts have usually been interpreted as a blessing in disguise. By forcing the country away from ranching, which requires few labour inputs, and orienting it towards tillage and dairying the Acts forced the economy to provide more jobs than would otherwise have been the case. On the other hand the Woollen Acts are viewed as the key reason why Ireland, unlike Yorkshire, did not develop a thriving woollen industry. The Navigation Acts, limiting the extent of direct trade with British colonies were another source of grievance. 'Nationalist' writers also point to instances where the Irish Parliament took a lead in promoting economic development, as in the case of Foster's Corn

7

Law of 1784, which paid bounties for tillage.

In an important piece of historical revisionism, Cullen has called into question the negative impact of such laws on the Irish economy. He argues that in response to the Cattle Acts the country successfully developed other outlets for cattle, and switched to other activities. The Woollen Acts were not, he claims, regarded as unduly detrimental by contemporaries, although by the 1720s opinion had changed, and Molyneaux and others vehemently criticized the Woollen Acts; in any event they were passed against the wishes of the government of the day, and were a response to vested interests. As for the Navigation Acts, Cullen views them as 'a grievance to the Irish merchant rather than to the consumer'. Cullen's attacks on the 'nationalist view' are now widely accepted, although in his zeal to revise the 'nationalist' view he may have underrated the harm done by these laws.[7]

The second major influence on the structure of agriculture was a secular increase in agricultural prices relative to other prices. In part this was due to the increasing urbanization of Britain, and the resultant demand for food. The most dramatic price increases were during the Napoleonic wars, when Britain needed a secure source of food. Ireland continued to export grain until the late 1860s, when the falling costs of shipping, coupled with the opening up of the American mid-west, brought cheaper grain to Europe.

Agricultural structure was also influenced by the diffusion of the potato. It is well known that a relatively small acreage of potatoes suffices to feed a family. Rapid population growth, coupled with the subdivision of land, would tend to force relatively more people to depend on the potato. It has also been argued that causality runs the other way, with an abundant and nutritious potato fostering population growth. A third view sees the extension of the potato as largely the outcome of increasing commercialization; rather than eating butter or pigs or oats, cottiers increasingly turned to growing potatoes as a food crop, and selling their other produce. In this case the shift towards the potato was 'related to commercialization and the urge to increase cash incomes ... for luxuries'.[8]

Industrial change was dominated by the rise of the linen industry, 'perhaps the most remarkable instance in Europe of an export-based advance in the eighteenth century'.[9] From a low base in the 1690s linen exports rose rapidly, accounting for a quarter of all exports by 1731. The reasons for the rise of the industry, and its concentration in the north east, have been well documented.[10] The first linen weavers were mainly skilled immigrants, who were first attracted to the north east where land was more readily available; some of them

8

were Huguenots who fled France after 1685. Duty-free access to the English market helped. In 1711 the Irish Parliament set up the Linen Board to regulate the industry, spread information and subsidize projects. As the industry grew in volume it also expanded geographically, and by the end of the eighteenth century flax was grown and linen spun throughout Ulster, in most of Connaught and even in parts of Kerry. Based solidly in the rural areas — in contrast to wool spinning and weaving, which was urban based — the basic activities of flax growing, spinning and weaving could be undertaken at the household level. An elaborate network of merchants bought the raw linen and undertook the more capital-intensive activities of bleaching and finishing. By the early nineteenth century linen was increasingly spun and woven under the 'putting-out' system; cottiers would be provided with raw materials, and paid in cash for the amount they spun or wove.

Even as late as 1841 one person in five stated their occupation as being in textiles, and most of these were in rural areas. Fully a third of the counties reported in 1821 that more individuals were occupied in 'manufacture, trade and handicrafts' than in agriculture. It has sometimes been argued that this type of 'proto-industrialization' is usually a prelude to full (i.e. factory-based) industrialization, fostering as it does entrepreneurial skills, monetization of the economy, and commercial links. In the Irish case no such evolution occurred.

Other industries also expanded and modernized, notably those based on the processing of agricultural products, such as brewing, flour milling, and distilling. After 1800 the cotton industry flourished, albeit relatively briefly.

It is important to realize that the industrial revolution did in fact come to Ireland, initially. The organization of many industries was radically changed, with the establishment of breweries, textile factories, and glass works large enough to reap economies of scale. At first these factories were located where water power was available, but steam power was introduced early too. In the eighteenth century the road network was greatly improved and expanded, at first by private turnpikes and later by local government (the 'Grand Juries'). The first canals were built.

By 1785 Ireland was perceived as a viable competitor to English industry. When Pitt introduced his commercial propositions, which would have allowed Irish goods to enter England at low or zero tariffs, he was faced by a storm of protest from English industrialists, and the measures were quietly dropped. Irish industry was seen as having many of the same characteristics as British industry, but with

9

the advantage of cheaper labour. Even in 1800 many, including Pitt, believed that Ireland stood to benefit from access to British markets, and would be a strong industrial competitor. By then this was not the view in Ireland, and it is significant (and ironic) that the areas which most favoured union were Cork and the South, with their strong agricultural base; opposition was strongest in Dublin and the North.

Eighteenth-century Ireland experienced recessions from time to time. The most common cause was a poor harvest. This would reduce exports and create a balance-of-payments deficit which in turn would lead to an outflow of gold and coin, and with less money around credit would become tight. This would tend to depress prices and economic activity, thereby correcting the balance-of-payments imbalance and causing a recession.

Distribution

The benefits of economic growth in the late eighteenth century were not spread equally. Several divisions are discernible. The most evident was the rift between landowners and the large rural proletariat. Under the penal laws Catholic tenants were supposed to pay rent equal to two-thirds of the 'annual value of the land'. Although disregarded in practice, rents of a third of the gross output were probably normal. Thus a relatively few landlords, and the middlemen and farmers to whom they rented, and who in turn rented sub-plots to cottiers, extracted a large surplus from the poor majority. In 1687 Petty estimated rent payments at £1.2 million, of which £0.1 million was remitted to absentee landlords abroad. Rents thus came to approximately double the level of exports, and may have amounted to as much as a quarter of national income. It was this surplus, and tithes paid to the Church of Ireland, that financed the magnificent country houses, churches, Dublin squares, university buildings, paintings and follies that stand as monuments to the eighteenth century.

The burden of rents fluctuated, depending in large measure on how high agricultural prices were at the time the rents were due for renewal. Since agricultural prices were rising, on balance, during most of the eighteenth century, renters reaped a windfall between the time the price of their produce rose and when rents were adjusted upwards. This windfall gave rise to the interesting economic phenomenon of 'tenant right', whereby an outgoing tenant could extract a side-payment from the incoming tenant, presumably as compensation for access to a profitable asset. It is still a puzzle why landlords did not try to appropriate more of this

10

windfall for themselves, although by 1778, when Catholics were permitted to hold longer leases, landlords were tending to let land on shorter leases. Although prior to 1778 Catholics were barred from holding leases of more than 31 years, such leases were quite long, and not necessarily a major deterrent to investment.

Cottiers cultivated a small plot of land, and performed work for the farmers to which they were attached. Labourers did not have even the security implied by access to a plot of land. It is not always clear how these two groups fared during the century to 1815. Their position did not improve in the fifty years prior to 1745. There then appears to have been a period of rising real wages, which probably stopped in the 1770s, and may never have resumed.

A second divide was between Catholic and Protestant. The Penal Laws placed restrictions on the right of Catholics to purchase land, to worship, to run schools, to vote, to take public office, to enter the professions, to take long leases, and to bequeath property. Barred from the professions and politics, able Catholics often turned their energies towards commerce, and the expansion of trade helped create a significant Catholic middle class.[11] By 1800 the wealthiest Dubliner was Edward Byrne, a Catholic businessman. Presbyterians and Quakers, faced with similar disabilities, also turned to commerce and industry, with some success. Over time most of the restrictions were removed or fell into disuse, and by 1793 Catholics could vote, but could not stand for office or fill certain government positions.

The third divide was between town and country. Dublin grew to be the second town of the UK by 1800, with a population of about 200,000. Cork, basing its role on the profitable provision trade, had 80,000 inhabitants, or approximately the same population as a century later. The third town was Limerick, with a population of 20,000; Belfast was still a minor town. That the country was able to support such a significant urban population, and to export increasing quantities of food, reflected a growing agricultural surplus.

3   1815 to 1850

The period 1815 to 1850 was one of rural crisis, culminating in the disaster of the Famine. The crisis was reflected in rising emigration. This was also the period when Ireland most clearly failed to participate in the industrial revolution which was then in full spate in Britain. After outlining the elements of the rural crisis and documenting the failure of the country to industrialize, there follows a discussion of why this was so.

Population

During the period 1821-41 the population grew from 6.8 million to 8.2 million, or at an average of 0.9 per cent per annum.[12] Although rapid, this represented a slower rate of increase than in the preceding half century, during which annual population growth averaged 1.3 per cent. After 1845 the trend reversed, as population fell to 6.6 million in 1851, and continued to decline almost continuously for over a century.

Without emigration, the pre-Famine population would have grown more quickly thereafter, perhaps as fast as 1.7 per cent per annum. Such a high rate of natural increase was due to high marital fertility, i.e. to married women bearing many children, once married. The age at which women married, and the proportion of women who married, were in line with contemporary European experience. There is no entirely satisfactory explanation of the high marital fertility, but it is possible that it was due to a good diet, a weak tradition of birth control (despite a reference to it in Merriman's *Midnight Court*), or a desire to have children, whether for the pleasure they might bring or because in the absence of children and a Poor Law it would be difficult otherwise to face old age. The death rate was not especially high. Infant mortality, while well above the levels of England or France, was lower than in Austria or Germany.

Massive emigration predates the Famine, as Table 1.3 shows. The figures give only the numbers who went to North America. In addition perhaps half a million moved to Britain during the period 1815 to 1841. Once the flow of emigration became established, it created a momentum of its own, as early migrants sent back money to pay the way for other family members, and helped to get new migrants established in America.

Growth

On the eve of the Famine annual Irish income per capita has been reckoned to be less than 40 per cent of the British level, at between £9/-/- and £10/10/-,[13] about half of which was generated in agriculture. Contemporary visitors judged the country to be very poor, and were particularly struck by the shabbiness of clothing and the poor state of rural houses. It has been calculated that the per capita housing stock in England was worth between four and five times as much as in Ireland. In some areas poverty was extreme.

Table 1.3

Population and Emigration, 1815-50

	Population (millions)		Annual emigration to N. America ('000)
1821	6.8		
		1825-29	18
1831	7.8		
		1830-34	52
		1835-39	32
1841	8.2		
		1840-44	62
		1845-49	158
1851	6.6		
		1850-54	173[1]
		1855-59	85[1]
1861	5.8		

Sources: W.E. Vaughan and A.J. Fitzpatrick, *Irish Historical Statistics: Population 1821-1971.* Dublin 1978, pp.3, 259-261.
[1] All destinations, except UK.

Thus in 1837 'the worldly possessions of the inhabitants of Gweedore, Co. Donegal, included two feather and eight chaff beds, 16 harrows, one plough, 28 shovels, 32 rakes, seven table forks and 233 stools among a population of 9,000.'[14]

On the other hand it is worth noting that most of the population was relatively well fed, on grain, potatoes and dairy products. The exceptions were when the potato failed, as it did in the south-west in 1822, in Mayo in 1831 and in Donegal in 1836. Fuel in the form of peat was cheap and widely available. And observers generally thought that the Irish were healthy and strong; they grew taller than the typical Englishman or Belgian.

It has become common to consider the period as one of 'deindustrialization', whereby the importance of industry in the economy fell. This is only partly correct. For the island as a whole industrial output appears to have increased. Large scale and more efficient production methods were applied to milling, brewing, shipbuilding, rope-making and the manufacture of linen, iron, paper and glass. Despite these changes, *rural* industry declined. Thus, for instance, while Bandon boasted over 1,500 handloom weavers in 1829, the number had shrunk to about 150 by 1839.[15]

The first cause of rural deindustrialization was that the woollen and cotton industries wilted in the face of competition from Britain. After 1824, when the last tariffs on goods from Britain were removed, and especially after the crisis year of 1826 when British manufacturers dumped large amounts of textiles on the Irish market, these industries declined quickly. A number of writers see this as a case where Ireland would have been better served had it been able to maintain tariffs against goods from the outside. No less a person than Marx wrote that 'what the Irish need is ... *protective tariffs against England.*'[16]

A second blow to rural industry was the invention of a method for mechanically spinning flax which made hand-spinning redundant, thereby depriving large numbers of families of a supplementary source of income. It also led to a concentration of the linen industry in the north-east, where most of the spinning mills were already located. The weaving of linen was still done by hand, and was boosted by the development. In 1841 Armagh was the most densely populated county in Ireland, testimony to the importance of cottage-based textiles as a source of income.

Despite a rapid fall in prices after 1815, agricultural exports continued to rise, notably livestock and butter and, most dramatically, grain and flour. By the 1830s Ireland exported enough grain to feed about two million people annually.

The most traumatic event of the period was the Famine.[17] After a wet summer, blight arrived in September 1845 and spread over almost half the country. Peel's government provided funds for maize and meal; relief works were set up; and when these proved inadequate more funds were made available. Famine was largely avoided. The Corn Laws, which had kept foreign grain out of Britain were repealed in June 1846, and Peel's government fell, to be replaced by that of Russell. The potato crop failed completely in 1846, and by December about half a million people were working on relief works, at which stage they were ended. The winter was harsh. By August 1847 an estimated three million people were being supported by soup kitchens, including almost three-quarters of the population of some western counties. The 1847 harvest was somewhat better, but blight returned in 1848, and in 1849 over 900,000 people were in the workhouses at some time or another. After 1847 the responsibility for supporting the poor had increasingly been shifted from the government to the local landowners who, by and large, did not have sufficient resources to cope. Noting that a few years later Britain spent £69 million on the (futile) Crimean war, Mokyr argues that for half this sum 'there is no doubt that Britain could have saved Ireland'.[18]

As a direct result of the Famine over 1.1 million people died, and an approximately equal number emigrated. The effects were spread very unevenly. The worst hit areas were Mayo, Sligo, Roscommon,

Galway, Leitrim, and Cavan where the 'excess mortality' was at least four per cent per year. The eastern and north-eastern counties were less affected, and throughout the period some grain was exported from these areas. Cattle exports, which had grown by two per cent per annum from 1841 to 1847 actually grew faster, at four per cent per annum from 1847 to 1851.[19] Those most affected were labourers and small farmers. Between 1841 and 1851 the number of farms of between one and five acres in size fell from 310,000 to 88,000, while the number of larger farms rose. These unequal effects have led Cullen to argue that 'the Famine was less a national disaster than a social and regional one'.[20]

Blight struck other countries too. While the excess mortality in Ireland was about three per cent per annum, it was two per cent in the Netherlands, just over one per cent in Belgium and lower still in Scotland and England. The higher Irish (and Dutch) rate may represent, as Mokyr has suggested, 'the cost of failing to industrialize'; the more industrialized, and affluent, areas were more able and willing to sustain those whose lives were at risk because of the potato failure.

Distribution

According to the 1841 census, 63 per cent of the population had access to less than five acres of land, or were 'without capital, in either money, land or acquired knowledge'. A further 32 per cent were artisans, or had farms of between 5 and 49 acres. The remaining 3 per cent were professionals and rentiers. This gives a largely rural proletariat of somewhat over half the total population. There is some evidence that this class became worse off during the thirty years prior to the Famine. On balance, witnesses to the Poor Law Commission, which met in 1835, considered that the position of the poor had deteriorated since 1815.[21] Prior to the Famine landholding was highly unequal; a fifth of all farms had more than 30 acres and almost a quarter had between one and five acres; yet by 1851 the number of those small farms was halved, and made up one farm in six.

Rent, including payments in kind, accounted for about £15 million, or about 19 per cent of the national income of £80 million. Presumably the bulk of this rent accrued to the three per cent or so of the population who owned 50 acres or more, implying a very great degree of income inequality. Rough calculations suggest that the richest three per cent probably had per capita incomes averaging over £100 per annum, compared to a national average of £10, and an estimated £4 for poor households.

15

Why Did Ireland Remain Poor?

There is no shortage of hypotheses as to why Ireland remained poor, and hence uniquely vulnerable by European standards to the chance failure of the potato crop. Nor does any clear single cause emerge. Perhaps this should not be so surprising. Ireland is but one small region in Europe, and was not unique in undergoing rural deindustrialization and depopulation. It is possible that the appropriate question is why some areas *did* industrialize, for in the early nineteenth century this was the exception rather than the rule.

A Malthusian Explanation. 'The land of Ireland', wrote Malthus in 1817, 'is infinitely more peopled than in England; and to give full effect to the natural resources of the country a great part of the population should be swept from the soil'.[22] Although a popular view at the time, the Malthusian explanation has been sharply questioned. If the land was overpopulated then incomes should have risen rapidly after the Famine; yet between 1845 and 1854, when the male population on the land fell 24 per cent, output fell fully 17 per cent. While this implies an improvement in income per capita, it is weak evidence that population pressure severely depressed incomes in pre-Famine Ireland.

Even before the Famine Ireland had more cultivatable land per person (1.7 acres) than Belgium (1.0) or England and Wales (1.5), although less than France (1.9) or Denmark (4.8). In trying to explain differences in the average incomes among Irish counties, Mokyr has found that greater population density did not have the effect of depressing incomes. Indeed he even found some evidence to the contrary, and interprets this as strong evidence against the Malthusian view.[23]

Interestingly enough land reclamation occurred almost as fast as population grew during the period 1821-41, so that during this period there was very little deterioration in the amount of cultivatable land per capita.

Malthus himself later changed his view, and by 1836 considered that, given enough inputs, Ireland could develop 'prodigious' wealth, perhaps even surpassing England in income.

Insecurity of Land Tenure. In pre-Famine Ireland most farmers were tenants, and some of them had short leases. If they were to undertake fixed investment in their farms — drainage, reclamation, building outhouses, and so on — they ran the risk that the landlord would raise their rent. So, the argument goes, farmers invested too little in agriculture, except perhaps in Ulster. There an outgoing tenant could sell his or her 'tenant right' to the incoming tenant, thereby recouping some or all of the investment.

At first sight the argument appears plausible. At mid-century perhaps two-thirds of all farmers held short-term tenancies ('at will'), although these were typically the small farms, so that less than half of the land was held 'at will'. The systems of 'new husbandry', consisting largely of different crop rotations, were not taken up quickly, despite their apparent profitability. Potentially profitable investments in drainage and soil improvement also appear to have been ignored. While Mokyr considers that it was because farmers did not have adequate access to capital, it might in part be attributable to the tenure system; a tenant would have less collateral against which to borrow.

However one may also doubt the importance of insecurity of tenure in restraining incomes. Most annual tenancies were quite secure, and routinely renewed without significant rent increases. On theoretical grounds it would rarely pay a landlord to be 'predatory' and try to expropriate all the benefits from improvements undertaken by their tenants. Agricultural growth was not noticeably hampered in earlier or later periods because of the system of tenancies, and did not increase as a result of the shift to owner-occupancy in the later nineteenth century. Although there is some evidence of a movement to shorter leases from 1780 on, the shift was small, and there was 'no sudden aversion to long leases' which might explain rural stagnation in the pre-Famine decades.

Agrarian Violence. In certain areas rural unrest was common, especially in Munster, and generally 'pre-Famine Ireland was a remarkably violent country'. This may have deterred investors, notably landlords, provoking capital flight. It is widely agreed that the main source of this unrest was efforts by landlords to clear and consolidate their lands, thereby paving the way for a shift from tillage to grazing, although in Connaught the reluctance of farmers to grant conacre was also a major cause. One result of such violence may have been that rents were lower than they otherwise might have been.

Natural Resources. One of the most common explanations for Ireland's failure to industrialize is that it lacks extensive deposits of coal. In England 85 per cent of the textile industry was located in coal-mining areas, suggesting that the presence of coal was crucial. However while the absence of coal may have been a handicap, it does not seem to have been a major one. In England coal costs came to about four per cent of the total cost of manufacturing textiles; coal was perhaps two and a half times as expensive in Ireland, thereby increasing costs by six per cent. This was easily offset by lower wages in Ireland. The fact that some industries did succeed, such as the big

17

cotton mill in Portlaw which thrived until the 1870s, proves that coal was not the indispensable missing ingredient for industrialization.

Lack of Capital. It has sometimes been argued that Ireland lacked capital, and that this hampered its ability to industrialize. However in the aggregate, capital does not seem to have been lacking, particularly for infrastructure.[24] Thus, for instance, Dublin invested more in railways in the six years prior to 1850 than Belfast did in linen between 1800 and 1850. Irish roads were of high quality. In 1860 Irish residents held £40 million in British government stock, and £20 million in Irish banks, a total approaching the value of national income. Merchants do not appear to have been constrained from expanding their trade, and farmers were apparently able to increase the stock of cattle successfully.

Despite adequate amounts of savings, there may still have been shortages, because the system of intermediation, which matched savings with investors, may have been inadequate. Capital did not flow into the fishing industry; rotations were not quickly adopted in farming; housing remained poor. Many industrialists appear to have become landowners rather than reinvest in their businesses, victims of what Lee terms 'the aristocratic cult'. Thus there may have been a shortage of risk capital, although O'Malley cites Hobsbawm with approval when the latter wrote that a great deal of British capital 'was sunk into railways, and much of it was sunk without trace'.[25]

Human Resources. Some commentators have argued that Ireland did not industrialize because it lacked key human resources. In this view there were not enough entrepreneurs; the population lacked education; individuals were lazy; and emigration sucked out the best and the brightest.

The failure of entrepreneurship has been widely touted, most recently by Sinn Féin The Workers Party.[26] The problem here is one of endogeneity; do entrepreneurs lead development, or do they spring up when opportunities emerge? In some areas, including linen, banking and a number of industries, there were significant numbers of entrepreneurs, although not all of them were Irish. Mokyr has suggested a new twist, that the landlord class failed as entrepreneurs. He argues that they should have been a major force for change and improvement, but too often were absent from their estates to be effective.

In 1841, 54 per cent of men and 41 per cent of women could at least read. This represents a respectable level of literacy, given that all education was private before 1831, being somewhat higher than in Spain or Italy, but lower than in France. The establishment of the

18

National Board of Education in 1831 eventually boosted public education, and helped ensure almost universal literacy by the end of the nineteenth century, although the improvement was gradual.

There is a long, and not particularly respectable, intellectual tradition of accusing poor people of being 'lazy'. Even if true, which it frequently is not, taking more leisure may be a rational response to a lack of opportunities.

Seasonal unemployment was common among labourers in pre-Famine Ireland, but they appear to have been occupied for on average about forty weeks annually. Irish labourers abroad were often favoured because of their working abilities.

Emigration did impose a cost on the remaining population, since emigrants had to be fed, clothed and housed prior to leaving. The annual cost has been estimated at 1.5 per cent of personal income in the pre-Famine period. Those who emigrated appear to have been slightly less literate than the population at large, and to have come disproportionately from the poorest strata of society. It follows that those who remained were not necessarily the least enterprising or least educated, as has sometimes been supposed.

<u>Competition from Britain.</u> The industrial revolution in Britain made manufactured goods less expensive, and centralized production close to the main markets. Improvements in transport carried these goods to Ireland cheaply. Could Ireland have stood up to such competition? Not without the ability to impose tariffs on imports, say some, and this provides the main justification for an independent Ireland. Then, reply the critics, how did Scotland manage to industrialize so successfully? It is clear that the industrial revolution spelled an end to cottage production, but it is not obvious why this had to be due to competition from British, rather than Irish manufacturers. This is why a search for other, deeper explanations of the Irish failure to industrialize more fully is called for.

4   1850 TO 1921

The seventy years following the Famine witnessed enormous changes in Irish society and saw the emergence of the modern economy. Over this period per capita incomes more than doubled, and came closer to the British level, but the population fell by a third. A rural middle class emerged, replacing the landlords and squeezing out the rural labourers. Within agriculture tillage declined, and the production of dry cattle increased. The north-east became industrialized.

19

Population

The dominant demographic fact of the period is that population declined, from 6.6 million in 1851 to 4.2 million by 1926. Without emigration the population would have risen, by about one per cent annually in the 1860s, and by half a per cent annually at the turn of the century. This fall in the rate of natural increase was due to a fall in the birth rate, unaccompanied by any fall in the death rate. The lower birth rate was partly as a result of a falling marriage rate. By 1926 the median marriage age for women was 29, up from 24 in 1861, and a quarter of the population never married.

Rapid emigration continued, with almost two per cent of the population leaving annually in the 1850s; the pace slowed markedly, to under one per cent after 1890. The early emigrants were drawn from all areas of the country, since even for affluent families only the first son was likely to inherit the estate. In later years the bulk of the emigrants came from the poorer, mainly western, districts. After a poor harvest emigration typically rose.[27] Over the period 1820 to 1945 an estimated 4.5 million Irish emigrated to the US, comparable in magnitude to the flows from Italy, Austria and Britain.

Growth

The evidence, most of it indirect, suggests a period of substantial growth from 1850, giving way to a slump in the mid-1870s, when the world faced an industrial crisis in 1874, and a period of agricultural crises after 1877. By the 1890s growth had picked up again, and continued essentially uninterrupted until 1921. Between 1861 and 1909 gross agricultural output rose by a quarter;[28] since the rural population had fallen sharply, output per capita in agriculture more than doubled. Cullen reports that the agricultural wage doubled between 1852 and 1912, and concludes that 'rising rural prosperity was evident in post-Famine Ireland. The farmer gained; so too, to an extent, did the farm labourer.'[29]

Rising bank deposits also reflected growing affluence. Such deposits totalled £8 million in 1845, and rose to £17 million in 1865 and £33 million in 1891. By 1913 deposits had risen yet further, to £60 million, and they trebled again by 1920. The retail sector grew rapidly. Per capita consumption of tobacco approached English levels around 1870, and tea consumption approached such levels a decade later. In 1841 about forty per cent of all houses were classified as 'Class IV' cabins, made of perishable materials such as turf and mud. By 1901 this proportion had shrunk to 1.5 per cent. There is also some evidence of the growth of a middle class; in 1853 the amount of income subject to tax amounted to £21 million, whereas by 1886 it had risen to £26 million, despite the fact that prices had fallen by about a quarter.[30]

The *industrial sector* grew even more rapidly than agriculture. Between 1850 and 1875 employment in linen mills and factories rose from 21,000 to 60,000, of which about 70 per cent were women and children. Much of this reflected technological change in the industry, which led to the industry becoming more concentrated; with the introduction of power weaving the industry came to be almost entirely located in Belfast and the Lagan Valley. Linen output grew slowly, except for a spectacular expansion during the 'cotton famine' of the 1860s. Shipbuilding expanded rapidly after 1870.[31] As a result the population of Belfast, which had reached 75,000 by 1841, rose so fast that by 1901 it was larger than Dublin, with about 400,000 inhabitants. The industrial base of Belfast widened, to include rope making, textile machinery and other engineering activities. Londonderry became the centre of an important shirt-making industry, employing 18,000 full-time workers and a further 80,000 cottage workers at its height in 1902.

By 1907, when the first census of production was undertaken, industrial activity was half as large as agriculture, making Ireland a relatively industrialized country.[32] Half of all industrial output was exported, Ireland had a worldwide reputation in linen, shipbuilding, distilling, brewing and biscuits, and the volume of trade per capita was higher than for Britain. Hence Cullen's comment that 'along with its large foreign trade, its export-oriented industries and its highly developed infrastructure of banking, commerce and railways, extensive foreign investment yielding a sizeable income made Ireland comparable in some respects with a handful of highly developed countries'.[33]

These industrial changes did not occur painlessly. One major shock was the arrival of the railroads, which expanded rapidly from the 1840s onwards.[34] These made foreign goods cheaper in rural areas, and hastened the demise of the rural textile industry. In 1841 fully twenty per cent of the working population, or 696,000 people, gave textiles as their primary employment. By 1881 the number had fallen to 130,000, or five per cent of the labour force. Milling, brewing and distilling also became more concentrated.

It is sometimes wondered why Ireland did not become even more industrialized, more like Clydeside than East Anglia. And related to this question, why did the north-east industrialize while by and large the rest of the country did not?

There was no lack of capital, and indeed from the 1880s on Irish residents were net lenders of capital to the rest of the world, investing in British government stock, railways, and other ventures overseas. Interest and dividends from these investments, coupled with remittance receipts, enabled Ireland to run current account deficits on the balance of payments from the turn of the century onwards. The banks may have been cautious at lending, but in this they were no different from their counterparts in England, where industrial development was rapid. Nor is there evidence that skills were lacking. The primary school system expanded rapidly, enrolling 282,000 pupils in state-subsidized schools in 1841, and 1,072,000 by 1887. Whereas 53 per cent of the population was illiterate in 1841, this fraction had fallen to 25 per cent by 1881 and 16 per cent by 1901. Enterprise may have been lacking, although clearly not in the Lagan valley. The absence of coal probably had some effect, not because this raised costs of production unduly, but because coal itself was a big business; in 1914 a quarter of the British labour force was directly employed in coal or iron and steel.

Some ascribe the growth of industry in the north-east to the role of the Protestant ethic; however industrial development in Europe was not in general tied to Protestant areas. The Ulster custom of 'tenant right' has been given a role, but was neither as widespread in Ulster, nor as exclusive to the province, as was once thought. Government investment had a small role, although the efforts of the Belfast harbour board to clear a deepwater channel and reclaim dockland for industrial use turned out to be a key factor in attracting shipbuilders.

The structure of *agriculture* changed from crops to cattle. Between 1850 and 1921 the area devoted to the major crops — oats, wheat, barley and potatoes—fell dramatically from 4.0 million acres to 2.0 million acres.[35] Correspondingly the area under grass, or in meadow and clover, rose from 11.1 million acres in 1860 to 12.8 million acres by 1900. Cattle exports rose rapidly, from 196,000 in 1847-49 to 847,000 in 1907-09. Exports of sheep also rose, while grain exports fell. The reason is simple; the price of grain fell relative to the price of cattle. Over this period the number of cows hardly grew, as farmers came to concentrate on dry cattle, which were for the most part exported to Britain on the hoof. The dairy industry was reorganized, with the growth of private and then cooperative creameries.[36] This was partly in response to heightened competition in the British market from higher-quality butter from Denmark and New Zealand.

Farmers were not, as is sometimes supposed, slow to change or innovate. For instance, when circumstances demanded it they adapted the creamery system rapidly. Equally importantly, they responded fully to changes in relative prices. This was the basic conclusion of Barrington, in a famous paper delivered in 1926, when he argued that 'there is not a scintilla of evidence ... to suggest that the Irish farmer has regulated his productive activities otherwise than in accordance with the economic tendencies of his time.'[37] More recent research has supported this view. In 1951 Hans Staehl compared Irish with Danish agriculture over the period 1861 to 1909, and found that agricultural output per capita in Ireland grew as rapidly in Ireland as in Denmark, which was considered to have done exceptionally well over the same period. Faced with changing prices and technology 'the response of the Irish agriculturalist ... was rational and normal.'[38]

A more recent study of the 'rationality' of Irish farmers during this period was undertaken by Cormac Ó Gráda, and is worth reporting because it illustrates the more sophisticated quantitative methods used by the 'new economic historians'.[39] Ó Gráda aims to measure supply response elasticities for agriculture. Following a conventional approach he makes agricultural output (X_t) depend on the price which is expected in the coming season (P_t^*), giving

$$X_t = a + bP_t^* + u$$

where u is an error term. Farmers are assumed to adjust their price expectations on the basis of how much this year's actual prices (P_{t-1}) differed from this year's expected prices, giving

$$P_t^* - P_{t-1}^* = \beta(P_{t-1} - P_{t-1}^*)$$

Combining these two he forms the estimating equation

$$X_t = b_0 + b_1 X_{t-1} + b_2 P_{t-1} + v_t$$

With information on output and prices he is able to estimate this equation, and derive the response elasticities. His results are interesting. For the period 1850-1879 he finds a supply elasticity for wheat of 0.41, which means that for every 10 per cent increase in the price of wheat farmers will raise output by 4.1 per cent. By world standards this is a fairly rapid response. The response for mutton is smaller, which is to be expected for a 'crop' which must be planned some years ahead.

Ó Gráda's conclusions are clear. There is a 'significant, if slowish, supply response', which is not influenced by farm size or county.[40]

Thus farmers are 'economically rational'. It follows that the arguments that land tenancy, or ownership, inhibited the response to price changes, appear to be incorrect.

Moreover there is 'no strong, clearly discernible trend in responsiveness over time'. This is despite the fact that there was a revolution in land ownership during this period. It appears that those who argued that transferring ownership of land from landlords to tenants would boost Irish agriculture were substantially wrong, although of course the distributive effects were immensely important.

Distribution

The End of the Landlords. Between 1850 and 1925 the landed proprietors 'surrendered their power and property',[41] thereby effecting one of the most extensive land reforms in history. As a result of the Famine many landlords found themselves bankrupt, largely because of the tax burden of trying to provide for the poor. Under the Encumbered Estates Acts of 1848 and 1849 about a quarter of all the land in the country changed hands; nine-tenths was bought up by Irish residents, which reflects the large pool of savings which was available.[42]

When the Church of Ireland was disestablished in 1869, provision was made for tenants to buy out their holdings. However no major change occurred until the late 1870s. Falling prices coupled with fixed rents squeezed tenants; by now they felt confident enough to agitate for the 'three F's' — fair rent, fixity of tenure, and free sale of 'tenant right'. The Land League was founded by Michael Davitt, and forged a link with Parnell and the Irish party in parliament. Their efforts resulted in the Land Act of 1881, which established land courts to hear rent appeals. The courts reduced rents by an average of about 20 per cent, and later courts reduced rents by about another 20 per cent after 1887. In a formal sense this diluted the power of the landlord — Moody refers to it as 'dual ownership' — although it is noteworthy that during the same period real rents fell by comparable amounts in England.[43] In relative terms the landlord class was already in decline even before such rent reductions.

Further efforts prompted legislation which provided tenants with government loans with which to buy out their land, notably the Ashbourne Act of 1885 and the Wyndham Act of 1903. Laws for compulsory sale were passed in 1907 and 1909. The result was that 'by 1917 almost two-thirds of the tenants had acquired their holdings'. In 1923 the Free State passed a further law for compulsory purchase, and Northern Ireland did the same in 1925.

24

Apart from the change in land ownership, the pattern of land holdings changed significantly. The Famine almost halved the number of holdings under 15 acres. The proportion of farms of less than 5 acres continued to decline thereafter, from 24 per cent in 1841 to 12 per cent by 1901, although these tiny farms by no means disappeared.[44]

Disappearance of Landless Labourers. In 1841, 1.3 million people classified themselves as 'farm servants and labourers'; by 1911 the number had fallen to 0.3 million. Despite problems of definition, notably in classifying the adult sons and daughters of farmers, it is generally accepted that the period saw the 'virtual disappearance of the hired labourer from Irish agriculture'. Not only did many farm labourers die during the Famine, but they were particularly prone to emigrate. This is hardly surprising, for wages were better elsewhere. In 1900 an agricultural labourer made about ten shillings per week, compared to about sixteen shillings in England and eighteen shillings in Scotland. Agricultural wages also rose, slowly, by perhaps one per cent per annum in real terms. In large measure this was because the shift out of tillage to grazing reduced the demand for labour in agriculture. The change in land ownership had little effect on the labouring class, and the fact that the change took the form it did partly reflects the political impotence of the rapidly-shrinking body of farm labourers.

In a succinct summary of these changes, Lyons writes that 'the general effect of the economic changes of the second half of the nineteenth century was to substitute a rural bourgeoisie for a rural proletariat' although 'proletarian elements nevertheless remained'.[45] The number of paupers supported in workhouses remained steady, at just under one per cent of the population from 1860 to the end of the century, but this probably reflects more on the workhouse system than the level of poverty itself.

Other Divides. The distribution of income can be considered in other dimensions too. Thus, for instance, Protestants maintained their share of national income. This largely reflects the growth of the industrial north-east, which was dominated by Protestant interests, and the fact that Catholics were more likely to emigrate (and more died in the Famine). Catholics did come to fill an increasing proportion of government and professional jobs, although not in proportion to their numbers. The Catholic Church itself grew rapidly, with a spate of church building between 1860 and 1900. The number of Catholic priests, nuns and other religious rose from almost 5,000 in 1850 to over 14,000 by 1900, making it one of the fastest-growing professions during this period.

The small towns stagnated, and so did Dublin until late in the century. In 1861 a third of Dublin workers were 'skilled', but by 1911 the proportion had fallen to a fifth. Dublin's tenement slums were notorious, and probably contained a third of the inner-city population. For the decade 1901-11 the death rate in Dublin was 2.5 per cent per annum, compared to 1.7 per cent for the country as a whole. In 1910 the average weekly earnings of a family in Dublin amounted to £1/2/6, or between a quarter and a third less than in Britain. Housing was expensive however, perhaps double the cost of Belfast. The wages of skilled workers in Ireland were broadly comparable with Britain. In contrast to the rest of the country Belfast and Derry grew rapidly. By the early 1900s an unskilled builder's labourer could make £1 a week, and craftsmen twice as much. Real wages in Belfast trebled in the sixty years from 1850, although in years of recession unemployment was often a problem. The growth of Belfast was not confined to linen and ships. The city was also a major producer of agriculturally-based goods such as tobacco, whiskey, and maize flour. One explanation is that Belfast benefitted from 'external economies of foreign trade' — regular trade links with markets and suppliers, and a financial system geared towards supporting such links. The zenith of Belfast's prosperity came during and immediately after the First World War, with a boom in shipbuilding and engineering.

Another cleavage was apparent between the western fringe and the rest of the country. The west was clearly poorer. One measure is the amount of seasonal migration, largely to Scotland; for example, about half of the workers on the Dillon estates in Mayo/Roscommon routinely migrated for such work. Permanent emigration increased after 1890. In an effort to improve things the Congested Districts Board was established. The area covered by its brief contained a ninth of the total population. Between 1891 and 1926, when it was replaced by the Land Commission, the Board spent £9 million to purchase and consolidate over two million acres, affecting 59,000 farms. It also provided grants to foster local industry and farm improvements.

5   THE SOUTH SINCE 1921

Nation-Building and Free Trade

When it finally achieved independence, the Irish Free State could count some important assets. It had an extensive system of communications, a developed banking system, a vigorous wholesale and retail network, an efficient and honest administration, universal literacy, a large stock of houses, schools and hospitals, and enormous external assets.[46] By the standards of most of the world's countries the country was well off indeed.

On the other hand the new state faced some serious problems. It had to establish a new government, the civil war had been destructive, the dependency ratio was high,[47] and the post-war boom had run its course. Between 1920 and 1924 agricultural prices fell by 44 per cent, and this was particularly damaging for the Free State, whose agricultural exports accounted for the bulk of export earnings. The shock was moderated by the large net inflow of earnings from assets held abroad, which paid for about a quarter of all imports. The lowest point was reached in 1926, after which economic growth was fairly rapid.

The growth model pursued by the Cumann na nGaedheal government was based on the premise that what was good for agriculture was good for the country. Patrick Hogan, the Minister for Agriculture, saw the policy as one of 'helping the farmer who helped himself and letting the rest go to the devil'.[48] This emphasis on agriculture was not surprising. In 1926 agriculture generated 32 per cent of GDP and provided 54 per cent of all employment. The government relied heavily on the support of the larger farmers. The expectation was that not only would agricultural growth raise the demand for goods and services from the rest of the economy, but would also provide more inputs on which to base a more substantial processing sector. The three major industrial exporting sectors at the time — brewing, distilling and biscuit making — were all closely linked with agriculture.

The essential elements of the policy were free trade, low taxes and government spending, modest direct state intervention in industry and agriculture, and parity with sterling. Free trade was seen as essential if the cost of farm inputs was to be kept low.

The support for free trade was surprising given that Griffith had argued that one of the main benefits of independence would be that the country could grant protection to infant industries. On the other hand the government was cautious about making such changes, perhaps for fear of upsetting the financial community, whose opposition to protection was well known, or perhaps because they were, in the words of Kevin O'Higgins, 'the most conservative revolutionaries in history.' The government did in fact put tariffs on a number of items in 1924, and extended the list in 1925, so that by 1931 the average tariff rate was about 9 per cent.[49] However it deflected any pressure for stiffer protection by establishing the Tariff

Commission in 1926, and appointing members who were, in the main, in favour of free trade. The onus of proof was on any industry wishing to be protected, and the Commission moved slowly on requests, only granting tariffs in the cases of rosary beads and margarine.

Government spending was kept low, the budget was essentially balanced, and revenues came to just 15 per cent of GNP in 1931. As a result welfare spending remained low, and in the absence of major government assistance, housing for the less well off remained scarce.

Ideologically the government did not favour taking a very active role in promoting economic development. Despite this it intervened pragmatically in several ways. The Department of Agriculture was greatly expanded, although the impact of this on agricultural output has been questioned. The Congested Districts Board was replaced by the Land Commission, which transferred 3.6 million acres, involving 117,000 holdings, to annuity-paying freeholders during the period 1923-1937. At independence approximately a quarter of all farmers were still tenants. Laws were passed to improve the quality of agricultural output, by regulating the marketing of dairy produce (1924) and improving the quality of livestock breeding by registering bulls (1925). The Agricultural Credit Corporation (ACC) was set up to provide credit to farmers. The government subsidized a Belgian company to establish a sugar factory in Carlow, and provided incentives to grow sugar beet.

A major innovation was the establishment of the Electricity Supply Board (ESB) in 1927. This, along with the ACC, represented the first of the state-sponsored bodies which were established during the ensuing years.[50] The ESB successfully undertook the Árdnacrusha hydroelectric scheme, which boosted both its and the country's prestige, and was the most visible accomplishment of the first decade of independence. In due course state-sponsored bodies were set up in many fields — air, train and bus transport, sugar refining, industrial credit, insurance, peat development, trade promotion, industrial development, and so on. By the early 1960s, when the most important of these bodies had been established, they employed about 50,000 people, representing about seven per cent of the total labour force. The state-sponsored bodies were not the outgrowth of any particular ideology, but were rather 'individual responses to specific situations'. This, along with their ability to attract good managers, may help explain why they are generally considered to have been successful agents of economic development, especially in the first few decades after independence, when the private sector did not appear to be very enterprising.

Parity with sterling was the final ingredient in the development model pursued. Few countries at the time had floating exchange rates, and it seemed logical to peg the pound to sterling since 97 per cent of exports went to, and 76 per cent of imports came from, Britain.[51] The Currency Act of 1927 established an Irish currency, fully backed by British sterling securities; until 1961 Irish banknotes were inscribed 'payable in London'. By linking the currency with sterling the Free State gave up the possibility of any independent monetary policy, in return for greater predictability in trade. It followed that after the pound was returned to its pre-war parity with gold in 1925 the Irish currency became overvalued too, although since the bulk of trade was with Britain the biggest effect was due to the reduced demand resulting from the recession there.

The economic policy of the Free State in the 1920s was comparable to the typical prescription given by the World Bank to Less Developed Countries in the 1980s. Get the prices right, using world prices as a guide. Reduce budget deficits. Keep government 'interference' to a minimum. Follow a conservative monetary policy. Did it work?

The simple answer is 'in the circumstances, yes in most respects, eventually'. National income probably stagnated prior to 1926, and the population fell, partly as a result of the Civil War, which only ended in 1923, and the recession in the UK following the return to the gold standard. However between 1926 and 1931 real per capita GNP rose about three per cent per annum, or 16 per cent during those five years. Exports increased 20 per cent, reaching a peak of 35 per cent of GNP in 1929, and a volume which was not exceeded until 1960. Industrial employment rose by 8 per cent. On the other hand emigration continued at a high level, and the population fell by 1.3 per cent during this period. Agriculture, which was supposed to be the dynamo of growth, stagnated, as the area in tillage fell slightly, cattle numbers remained steady, and only sheep and poultry experienced marked growth.

By 1931 world conditions had changed so drastically that the growth model of the 1920s no longer looked appropriate even if, as Meenan has suggested, the policies pursued had been fundamentally sound. In the last few months of its term of office the Cumann na nGaedheal government raised tariffs sharply, symptomatic of a change in direction which it did not have the opportunity to pursue when Fianna Fáil came to power in early 1932.

Depression, Economic War and Self-Sufficiency

Three major features stand out in any discussion of the 1930s — the world depression, the 'economic war' with Britain, and the pursuit of self-sufficiency. The depression, which is typically traced back to the great crash on Wall Street in 1929, spread worldwide, and was accompanied by a spate of protectionism. Even Britain, long a bastion of free trade, erected tariffs; one result of importance to Ireland was that Guinness was prompted to establish a brewery at Park Lane near London, and Irish exports of beer fell as a consequence. By 1931 Ireland was one of the few countries which was substantially pursuing a policy of free trade.

As a reaction to this the government increased tariffs rapidly, and they rose from 9 per cent in 1931 to 45 per cent in 1936, dipping to 35 per cent by 1938. By world standards Irish tariffs were high, exceeded in Europe by Germany and Spain, but twice the level of the US and 50 per cent higher than the UK.[52] Since tariffs were introduced piecemeal they formed an untidy pattern and, in FitzGerald's view had 'no rational basis'; Meenan considers that they fell more heavily on finished goods, and so provided an incentive for domestic assembly using imported raw materials.

Apart from responding to a hostile world environment the government had another reason for desiring protection — it wanted to foster economic self-sufficiency. The nationalist logic tended to see the connection with Britain as the major impediment to Irish prosperity; it followed that severing this link would generate prosperity, of industry at least.[53] For some there was 'not so much an economic case as an intellectual and cultural case for protection. If the country lives almost altogether by a few industries its intellectual life will lack richness and variety ... because agriculture .. did not find employment for large numbers of engineers, electricians, chemists and bacteriologists.'[54] Keynes, lecturing at University College Dublin, in April 1933, supported this thrust. 'I sympathize', he said, 'with those who would minimize ... economic entanglement between nations. ... But let goods be homespun whenever it is reasonable and conveniently possible. ... If I were an Irishman I should find much to attract me in the economic outlook of your present government towards self-sufficiency.'

Most commentators have noted the apparent irony that it was Fianna Fáil, political opponents of Arthur Griffith, who implemented the protection he favoured. However there was a significant difference in outlook; Fianna Fáil were pursuing a policy of *self-sufficiency*, which implied broad and high tariffs, whereas Griffith favoured tariffs only on a temporary basis, to permit infant industries to grow. In this Griffith followed the ideas of the economist List, although, as McAleese has pointed out, List doubted that the infant industry argument would have much application to small open economies, since it risked protecting monopolies.

The pursuit of self-sufficiency did not merely involve the erection of tariffs and quotas, although this was an important element. In an effort to boost tillage, price support was introduced for wheat, and was instrumental in raising the acreage planted with wheat from 8,000 hectares in 1931 to 103,000 by 1936, although the total acreage tilled rose less spectacularly, from 428,000 hectares in 1931 to 832,000 hectares in 1936. Bounties were paid for exports of cattle, butter, bacon and other agricultural products in order to expand the volume of exports, and this resulted in a significant rise in the share of government spending in national income. To foster Irish involvement in industry the Control of Manufactures Act (1932) required majority Irish ownership, although in practice exceptions were always granted upon request. The Industrial Credit Corporation was set up to lend to industry, and issued £6.5 million in its first four years of operation. The Trade Loans Act provided further support for loans to industry.

The Housing Act injected money into housing, and was in effect a public works scheme. To avoid monopoly pricing by protected firms—the problem foreseen by List—the Control of Prices Act was passed in 1937, and set up the Prices Commission. Further state-sponsored bodies were founded, notably the Sugar Company, Irish Life (insurance), and the Turf Development Board, which later became Bord na Móna.

It is difficult to assess the effect of the policy of self-sufficiency because it became inextricably tangled with the effects of the 'economic war'. This began as a financial dispute between the Free State and Britain. In March 1931, on coming to office, de Valera refused to continue to pay land annuities to Britain. In July Britain retaliated by imposing special duties, initially at 20 per cent and later at 40 per cent, on imports of livestock, dairy products and meat, and also imposed quotas, including a halving of cattle permitted to enter Britain. The Free State countered with tariffs on British goods, including cement and coal. After these escalations tempers cooled. Under the Cattle Coal pacts Irish cattle had easier access to Britain, and Ireland agreed to buy British coal.[55] Initially agreed for 1935, the pact was extended and renewed in 1936 and 1937, and the Anglo-Irish Trade Agreement ended the 'war', with Ireland agreeing to pay a lump sum of £10 million and Britain ceding control of the treaty ports. The combined effects of protection and the economic war were initially dramatic. Industrial output rose 40 per cent between 1931 and 1936, and industrial employment increased from 111,000 to

154,000 over the same period. Population stabilized, standing at 2.933 million in 1931 and 2.937 million in 1938 — the first period since the Famine when there had not been a substantial decline — but the level of unemployment soared, almost quintupling between 1931 and 1934, and raising the unemployment rate sharply, to about 14 per cent of the labour force by 1935. In part this reflected reduced opportunities to emigrate to the United States. Despite rapid industrial growth, agriculture stagnated, as exports fell sharply. Where exports and imports together amounted to 75 per cent of GNP in 1926, they constituted 54 per cent in 1938. The existing manufacturing export industries also suffered some decline. By 1936, import-substituting industrialization had run its course, and industrial output only rose a further 4.5 per cent between 1936 and 1938. It is widely accepted that the slow growth of the economy in the 1950s was in large measure because of the inefficiency of the industrial sector which developed during the 1930s.

Was the drive for self-sufficiency a failure? A strong case can be made that it was not. Given that the rest of the world had turned protectionist it is difficult to see how Ireland could have avoided at least some measure of it too. Meenan argues that 'in the circumstances of the great depression it was necessary for any government to maintain, even to invent, employment at any cost'.[56] This may have been what was necessary for Ireland to preserve its democratic structure, which it did, in contrast to Italy, Germany or Spain. The expansion of the industrial sector may have provided experience in business management which was valuable in later years. On the other hand dependence on imports did not fall markedly. One may also wonder whether a policy of more selective protection might not have proven more durable.

The War and Rebound
Between 1938 and 1943 the volume of exports fell by a half, and imports fell even more. During this period industrial output fell 27 per cent, and industrial employment dropped from 167,000 to 144,000. The main reason was the scarcity of raw material inputs for industry, and the shortage of shipping capacity. Completely reliant on outside shippers until 1941, the government founded Irish Shipping, and moved rapidly to purchase ships, which soon proved their worth. The vulnerability of industry to outside constraints clearly underlined the limits of self-sufficiency for a small open economy. Because of the difficulty of obtaining imports, the country built up significant foreign reserves, but the increase was less dramatic than during the First World War, since price controls in

Britain were more effective in limiting the rise in the price of those goods which Ireland exported. By 1946 residents had external assets totalling £260 million, or approximately equivalent to GNP in that year.

The total value of agricultural output fell during the war period, but net agricultural output — i.e. total output less the cost of non-labour inputs—rose by 17 per cent between 1938-39 and 1945. This reflected the drastic fall in the use of fertilizers and other inputs, and is generally acknowledged to have exhausted the soil significantly. The structure of agriculture changed, as the area planted in grain and potatoes almost doubled. This was due to the introduction of compulsory tillage, initially set at an eighth and later at three-eighths of arable land. The stock of animals did not decline, with the exception of pigs, which prior to the war had been partly fed on inexpensive imported maize.

During the war real GNP fell, especially initially. Living standards fell further as households, unable to find the goods they wanted, were obliged to save more. The stock of capital in industry became run down. With emigration to the US blocked, population rose, by 18,000 between 1938 and 1946. The unemployment rate stood at over 15 per cent in 1939 and 1940, but declined thereafter to a little over 10 per cent in 1945. The decrease was due to a sharp rise in migration to Britain, reaching near-record levels in 1942, as people left to work in factories and enroll in the armed forces.

The war was followed by a rebound, and per capita real GDP rose by 4.1 per cent per annum between 1944 and 1950. The recovery was founded entirely on industrial expansion, since agricultural output stagnated, with gross volume falling between 1945 and 1950, and net output shrinking by 5 per cent; an exceptionally poor harvest in 1947 was enough to pull down GNP in that year. By way of contrast industrial production more than doubled during the same period.

Government spending rose far faster than national income during the postwar years, increasing its share of GNP from 23 per cent in 1945 to 39 per cent by 1951.[57] In large measure this increase occurred as Ireland sought to emulate the 'social investment' of the Labour Party in Britain, by expanding welfare spending. Alongside this increase was a striking change in the composition of public spending, towards devoting a larger share to capital rather than current spending. While just 5 per cent of government spending went to capital spending in 1945 this fraction rose to 24 per cent by 1950, to pay for housing, roads, hospitals, electricity and telephones. Much of the increased spending was financed by borrowing, which financed 6.5 per cent of the total public sector in 1947 and 29 per cent in 1951.

Stagnation and Growth

The essential fact of Irish economic life since 1950 is that stagnation in the 1950s gave way to sustained economic growth in the 1960s and 1970s. This growth was fuelled by export-led industrial expansion since 1958. Since then real per capita incomes have doubled, and population decline has been reversed, although by the mid-1980s there is some evidence that the pattern of the 1950s may be reasserting itself.

In the 1950s real GNP did not rise, although per capita income did increase since population declined, and 'those who had jobs in the fifties prospered quite nicely'.[58] By way of contrast, real GNP rose at an annual rate of 4.2 per cent between 1959 and 1979, interrupted briefly in 1966 and by the oil shock of 1974. During this time Gross Domestic Product per capita rose 92 per cent.

Growth was fuelled by the industrial sector, which expanded at 2.8 per cent per annum between 1950 and 1959, but by 6.1 per cent per annum in the following twenty years. Net agricultural output grew very slowly until the late 1960s, when it expanded substantially, reaching a new, and uneven, plateau thereafter.[59]

The Stagnant 1950s

Why did output stagnate in the 1950s? FitzGerald believes that the key problem was a 'failure to reorientate industry to export markets', considering that 'the naïveté of the philosophy that underlay the whole protection policy was not exposed until the process of introducing protection had come to an end'.[60] The quick benefits from protection had been reaped by industrial expansion in the 1930s; the war interrupted further growth, and the post-war boom was transient; by the 1950s Irish industry was supplying as much of the domestic market as it reasonably could, and in order to expand had no option but to seek markets overseas. But since much of the industrial sector could only survive because of protection, it was therefore too inefficient to export successfully.

To switch to exporting, new industries would have to be sought, or existing ones radically restructured; however local enterprise was timid (perhaps understandably so) and wary of initiating such change.

A more charitable view of the 1950s sees it is a period of *transition* rather than one of failure. It has been argued that the economy was in fact in the process of reorientating itself towards export markets, but that any such change was bound to be slow.[61] As J.J. McElligott put it in the 1920s, when warning of the dangers of protection, 'to revert to free trade from a protectionist regime is almost an economic impossibility'. Exports of manufactured goods rose quite rapidly, accounting for 6 per cent of all exports in 1950 but 17 per cent by 1960. Dramatic as this change was, the increase was from a very low base, and the export sector simply was not large enough to be a potent engine of growth.

A second explanation for the difference in growth between the 1950s and the 1960s is that the investment rate increased, from about 15 per cent of GNP in the 1950s to 18 per cent by the mid-1960s. By the late 1970s it had risen to close to 30 per cent. By the Harrod-Domar equation,

$$\text{GNP growth} = \text{Net investment rate}/\text{ICOR}$$

where ICOR is the Incremental Capital Output Ratio, or the amount of additional capital needed to generate an extra increment of output.[62] For a constant ICOR a higher investment rate generates higher growth. During the 1950s the ICOR was high, as Kennedy and Dowling find, and the more rapid growth in the 1960s was the result both of a higher investment rate (investment as a fraction of GNP) and a lower ICOR. Lowering the ICOR is of course a difficult business, and a strategy for doing that is at the root of efficient growth policy. Much of the investment undertaken during the 1950s was in infrastructure, and most notably housing; this contributes to a high ICOR as it has little immediate effect on output, although in the view of Kennedy and Dowling it provided a strong basis for subsequent growth.

Successive governments did try to foster growth, both by building up infrastructure, and by seeking to stimulate agriculture. Spending on agriculture absorbed 19 per cent of total state spending in 1962, up from 10 per cent in 1952. Agriculture did not respond much to this spending, with net output growing just 1.1 per cent per annum between 1950 and 1959, although output per farmer grew at a respectable 3.4 per cent. One problem was that tariffs which protected wheat and barley raised the cost of feed for pigs and poultry, and the latter both declined. In 1958 the Industrial Development Authority Act granted broader powers to the Industrial Development Authority (IDA), which had been set up in 1949, providing for tax holidays for export-orientated companies if they were to set up in the country.

An entirely different explanation for the anaemic growth of the 1950s comes from Kennedy and Dowling, who state baldly that 'the chief factor seems to us to be the failure to secure a satisfactory rate of expansion in aggregate demand'.[63] The main cause of insufficient aggregate demand was unduly restrictive fiscal policy. When balance-of-payments crises arose, as they did in 1951 and 1955, the government would seek to restrain total spending by trying to bring the budget more into balance. The intention was that this would reduce the demand for imports and help prevent prices from rising (or even reduce prices), thereby correcting the balance-of-payments problem. Kennedy and Dowling argue that the government overreacted to such crises, and could easily have borrowed enough to tide the country over. Indeed, by sustaining aggregate demand profit rates would have been higher, and the dependency ratio lower because emigration would have been reduced, and these would have increased savings; expansionary fiscal policy could thus have been largely internally financed. This argument provides an intellectual underpinning for the highly expansionary policy of the later 1970s and early 1980s; then it proved easy to borrow, but fiscal expansion was certainly not internally financed.

Whatever the causes, the poor economic performance created a feeling of pessimism, and this in turn probably deterred investors. As T.K. Whitaker, then Secretary of the Department of Finance, put it, 'the mood of despondency was palpable'.

In 1958, at the request of the government, T.K. Whitaker wrote the now celebrated report *Economic Development*. Recognizing the recent poor performance, characterizing agriculture as 'backward', noting the small scale of industry and diagnosing private capital as scarce and timid, the report called for a reorientation of government investment towards more 'productive' uses and away from a primary emphasis on 'social' investment (such as housing). It proposed that tariffs should be dismantled, unless a clear infant industry case existed, it favoured incentives to stimulate private industrial investment, and it proposed expanded spending on agriculture, notably for the eradication of bovine TB. On the other hand it warned against the dampening effects of high taxes. With such measures, it suggested, GNP could grow two per cent annually, although it stressed that this was not a firm target. What is most remembered about the report is that it struck an optimistic note in pessimistic times. These measures were incorporated in the *First Programme for Economic Expansion* which appeared in November 1958.

Economic growth during the period of the first plan exceeded anyone's wildest expectations, reaching four per cent per annum instead of the anticipated two per cent. At the time much of this increase was attributed directly to the impact of the First Programme, and support for such indicative planning increased.

The Second Programme, introduced in 1963 and designed to run to 1970, was far more detailed and ambitious, forecasting an annual increase in GNP of four per cent per annum; industry was to expand 50 per cent and exports 75 per cent during the plan period. When it appeared that these targets would not quite be met the Second Programme was allowed to lapse. A Third Programme was produced, but quickly sank into oblivion, along with most of the enthusiasm for indicative planning.

Since 1960

What sparked, and then sustained, Irish economic growth since 1958? The turning point coincided with the publication of *Economic Development*, but it is not clear how much the report *caused* growth. By generating an atmosphere of optimism it may have boosted investment, and this, as Keynes and others have argued, is a feature of considerable importance. On the other hand the Central Bank has pointed out that in the few years after 1958 Irish industry had significant levels of unused capacity, and external conditions were unusually good. This might start growth, but would hardly sustain it. Kennedy and Dowling argue that the foundations of growth had been laid in the 1950s, and that growth was sustained by the continued expansion of the industrial export sector, which was now becoming large and diverse enough to drive growth.

Once growth begins it is possible to get a virtuous circle, and this is emphasized by Kennedy.[64] He finds that labour productivity (i.e. output per worker) grew most quickly in those industries which expanded fastest. He hypothesized that faced with expanding sales, firms install new (and more productive) equipment more rapidly, and work harder to find ways of meeting the higher demand quickly, whether through organizational changes or the application of technical advances. This higher labour productivity in turn permits firms to raise wages faster than prices, or to restrain price increases and more easily expand to new markets.

A new economic strategy had emerged — *export-led growth*. The essential elements included trade liberalization, the provision of tax breaks and subsidies to companies, mostly branches of foreign corporations, which could export and grow, a higher investment rate, the provision of grants to restructure industry and retrain workers so that they might better face the increased competition resulting from free trade, and efforts to restrain wage increases which might erode competitiveness.

Trade liberalization was begun in the 1960s as Ireland unilaterally cut tariffs in 1963 and 1964, negotiated the Anglo-Irish Free Trade

Area Agreement in 1965 and subscribed to the General Agreement on Tariffs and Trade (GATT) in 1967. These moves to end protection were a recognition that it had not proved successful, and that in due course the country would have to join the European Community (EC) and should begin to adjust to that eventuality as soon as possible. Such a move was also motivated by the policy of export-led growth. Tariffs, by making inputs dearer and by sucking resources from other sectors of the economy, worked to inhibit exports. On the other hand it was recognized that tariff reductions would force some firms out of business, and this has indeed occurred, especially in those 'traditional' industries such as clothing and footwear where Ireland, as a relatively high-labour-cost country, cannot easily compete.

The IDA successfully induced foreign companies to set up branches in Ireland, and by 1974 new industry accounted for over 60 per cent of industrial output (see Chapter 11).[65]

The investment rate rose from 15 per cent of GNP in the 1950s to 20 per cent in the 1960s, financed mainly by domestic savings (13 per cent of GNP in the 1950s and 16 per cent in the 1960s), but also increasingly by foreign investment. By the late 1970s the investment rate briefly approached 30 per cent.

The government provided support for the restructuring of industry, to better prepare it to face foreign competition. In 1965 the Committee on Industrial Organization was set up, and reported that Irish industry was poorly equipped and managed. On the basis of its recommendations adaptation grants were provided to firms to help them modernize. In 1966 An Chómhairle Oiliúna (AnCO) was established to undertake and promote industrial training.

The final thrust of government policy was wage restraint, viewed as necessary, especially with a fixed exchange rate, to help keep industrial costs at a competitive level (see the growth model in Chapter 7). In the 1960s government efforts amounted to exhortation. In the 1970s wage bargaining was centralized, under the National Wage Agreements.

Ireland joined the EC on January 1, 1973.[66] The expectation was that Ireland would receive substantial transfers from the richer member states, and would become more 'European' in outlook. It was hoped that non-European firms would be more likely to set up in Ireland, as a point of entry into the EC, although it was also recognized that some existing industry would wither under the greater competition. Opponents of entry emphasized that consumers would be hurt by higher food costs, and were afraid that a return to conditions similar to those prior to Independence would suck skills and capital out of the country.

Neither all the hopes nor all the fears have been realized. By 1980 Ireland received net transfers from the EC equivalent to perhaps five per cent of national income (see Chapter 7); while significant, this is not an overwhelming amount, and probably has its largest effect on the balance of payments, pushing up the value of the Irish pound and thereby making Irish goods more expensive overseas and inhibiting the expansion of Irish exports. Trade has been reoriented away from extreme dependence on the UK market, and by 1981 almost a third of exports went to other EC countries. More foreign investment was attracted, notably from the US; while Irish GNP amounted to 0.7 per cent of the EC total in 1979, the country received 2.5 per cent of US manufacturing investment in the EC, although with the accession of Spain and Portugal to the EC, Ireland will face much greater competition in attracting this type of investment. Net agricultural output rose by 1.2 per cent per annum in the 1960s but 2.7 per cent per annum in the 1970s, although this rise has not been maintained. On the other hand indigenous industry has not responded well. Of the net increase in industrial jobs of 27,000 during the period 1973-80 just 5,000 were accounted for by indigenous industry, which has neither increased the share of output it exports nor reduced its dependence on the UK market. As economic growth in EC countries has faltered they risk becoming less generous in providing transfers to poorer areas. By 1977 the final tariffs with EC countries were removed. MacDonagh sees an irony in this, writing that 'thus the wheel was to come full circle by 1980. Sixty years after the treaty, the British Isles would once again become a free trade area; economically, the Act of Union would be restored!'.[67]

MacDonagh's words may have been premature, for in 1979 Ireland broke the link with sterling and joined the European Monetary System (EMS). This too was seen as a logical step to take to foster trade, since the share of exports going to the UK had declined to a third of the total, so parity with sterling was no longer so advantageous. Moreover sterling risked rising due to the development of North Sea oil.

Where does the Irish Economy Stand Now?
Population. In the decade up to 1984 the population grew by 1.3 per cent per annum. For the first time since the Famine emigration was reversed, and a net inflow of 109,000 occurred during the period 1971-79. Since then emigration has picked up again (see Chapter 8). The population remains relatively young, with a dependency ratio of 0.7.

Growth. Rapid economic growth was sustained until 1979, and has been more erratic since (see Chapter 7). During the years 1973-80 real GNP rose by 2.1 per cent per annum; after adjusting for the higher cost of imports, notably oil, the increase was just 0.3 per cent per annum. However real disposable personal incomes increased by 2.6 per cent per annum, and were maintained by increasing levels of international borrowing.

Since 1960 real consumption levels per capita have doubled, and this is evident in the increased number of cars and more consumer goods and better housing, along with some of the costs of increasing affluence such as more road accidents, congestion and pollution.[68] Levels of literacy, nutrition, health and life expectancy are high. Whether this adds up to a glass half empty or half full is a matter of opinion.

Growth in the 1980s has been uneven, sustained in large measure by substantial amounts of government borrowing. Net external debt amounted to about 37 per cent of GNP in 1981 and rose to 51 per cent in 1985, one of the highest ratios anywhere. Since much of this borrowing was not put into 'productive' uses, its servicing and repayment will eat into future income. The borrowing helped maintain the value of the Irish pound, and this may have contributed to slower industrial growth (and inflation). The economy is very open, has a high investment rate, and a relatively large government sector.

Distribution. Based on 1973 data the distribution of Irish income was found to be relatively equally distributed — less equal than Australia or the UK, but more equal than France or most less-developed countries (see Chapter 5).[69] There is some evidence of wage compression since then[70] although Blackwell considers that the distribution of income is 'not improving'.

The biggest change, and concern, is the dramatic increase in unemployment since 1979. In that year 90,000 individuals were registered as unemployed, or 7.3 per cent of the labour force. By 1983 this rate had doubled to 14.7 per cent, and by 1985 it reached 17.4 per cent, or 231,000 people. Faced with a rapidly increasing labour force the economy has been unable to raise the number of jobs. The need to support so many unemployed has been a major reason for recent government borrowing.

A New Growth Strategy. The growth strategy applied during the 1960s and 1970s served the country well. It geared the country towards free trade, and promoted export-led growth. Industrial investment from abroad was encouraged. Since about 1980 the strategy has performed less well, both in boosting output and, more clearly, in providing jobs. To maintain growth an ever-increasing absolute amount of foreign investment is needed, but this is probably unrealistic.

It is not easy to see what the growth strategy of the 1990s will look like. It will emphasize job creation, and will focus on vitalizing indigenous enterprise; moreover it will have to do this with a reduced reliance on increased foreign borrowing. Perhaps the focus will have to be on microeconomic issues, as Blackwell suggests — gearing society to produce entrepreneurs, evaluating public investment more thoroughly, introducing flexibility into the labour market, and reducing work disincentives to do unskilled jobs. Otherwise there will be a return to the experience of the period prior to the First World War, rising incomes, growing industry and increased exports, but for fewer and fewer people.

6   NORTHERN IRELAND SINCE 1921

In addition to cultural and historical reasons, there were good *economic* reasons for Northern Ireland to wish to remain within the UK. Its industrial sector, based on linen and textiles, shipbuilding, and engineering, was strongly orientated towards exporting, especially to Britain, and there was a widespread fear that access to that market would be more difficult if the north-east were to become part of a foreign country.

Population
Between 1891 and 1926 the population of the Six Counties hardly grew, with emigration almost exactly balancing any natural increase. Between 1926 and 1981 population grew at an annual rate of 0.4 per cent. Five-sixths of this increase occurred between 1937 and 1971, when the Six Counties experienced fairly rapid economic growth.

Growth
A long period of industrial expansion, stimulated towards the end by the First World War and the ensuing boom, came to an abrupt halt in 1921. Employment in *shipbuilding*, which stood at 15,000 in 1913 and rose to 29,000 in 1919, fell to just over 7,000 in 1924 and 2,000 in 1933.[71] In 1919 Harland and Wolff, and Workman Clark were respectively the largest and second largest shipyards in the UK. Yet in 1933 Harland and Wolff did not launch a single ship, and in 1935 Workman Clark was wound up. The principal reason was the fall in world demand for ships once the world shipping fleet had been

replenished after the First World War. Throughout the 1920s Belfast accounted for about 10 per cent of the merchant shipping tonnage launched in the UK, and in the 1930s this share rose substantially. Output in *linen*, which was far more important than shipbuilding, did not decline until after 1927, although employment had begun to fall before that, from a total of 74,000 in 1924 to 55,000 in 1930. Linen output amounted to 161 million square yards in 1924, but only 116 million in 1930, although it rose to 146 million in 1935 before gradually declining to 99 million in 1951. Here too the industry faced a declining market, as synthetic fibres and cotton provided greater competition. The linen industry increased its share of this declining market.

Agricultural change paralleled that of the Free State until 1932, after which it grew substantially while agriculture in the South stagnated. The clear explanation is that the British market remained open to Northern Ireland. Subsidies were also provided, and the output of pigs and poultry was particularly buoyant.

The net effect of these changes was high unemployment. In 1923 the unemployment rate stood at 18 per cent; it fell to 13 per cent in 1927, but this was the lowest rate of the decade. Throughout the 1930s the rate never fell below 22 per cent, and was 28 per cent in 1931. It is not surprising that Lyons concludes that 'the overwhelming problem of economic life in the Six Counties between the wars was the persistence at all times and in every sector of massive unemployment'.[72]

The government's reaction was to try to attract new industry to Northern Ireland, and to boost agriculture. The New Industries (Development) Acts of 1932 and 1937 allowed for incentives to be given to attract industry, including rent-free sites, rates relief, and interest-free loans. Apart from attracting the Short and Harland aircraft factory, which might have located in Belfast anyway, these incentives had a very marginal effect during the inter-war period. In agriculture the government introduced minimum standards for eggs and other products, compulsory marketing schemes, and a law to improve the breeding stock. Despite these efforts, the conclusion of one historian is that Northern Ireland 'lacked real power to regulate its economic life'.[73]

Industrial production rebounded with the Second World War, and agriculture benefitted from a high demand and, unlike the South, the availability of adequate fertilizer and equipment. The boom continued after the war, so that by 1949 a total of 222 firms, employing 22,000 people, had been established partly with the help of government assistance. Further grants to industry were provided in the 1950s, mainly for reequipment, and during the 1950s and 1960s GNP rose faster than in the South or in Britain. From a base of 100 in 1950 industrial output rose to 250 by 1973. Industrial employment peaked in 1970. This expansion was accompanied by a change in the structure of industry, as the relative role of textiles declined, to be replaced by a larger engineering sector, which had accounted for 15 per cent of industrial output in 1935 but produced 29 per cent of the total in 1957.

Since 1971 the economy of the Six Counties has stagnated. Total employment fell from 561,000 in 1971 to 524,000 in 1981, representing an annual growth rate of minus 0.7 per cent. Industrial employment fell far faster, by 3.4 per cent per annum, and between 1975 and 1981 industrial output dropped by 10 per cent. As a result, unemployment rates, which had been reduced during the boom years, have risen from 6.1 per cent in 1974 (the best performance of the decade) to 11.5 per cent in 1978 and 18.3 per cent in 1981. The structure of employment has also changed, with public administration, commerce and professional services taking a larger share. Between 1971 and 1981 the share of employment in the manufacturing sector fell from 32 per cent to 24 per cent, and is now somewhat below the level in the South.

Distribution

Incomes in Northern Ireland are only partly determined by the value of what is produced there. The other major component is the amount of resources transferred to or from the rest of the UK. In 1920 Northern Ireland was assessed an 'imperial contribution' of £7.9 million. This was subtracted from tax revenues raised in the Six Counties, and the residual provided the funds for the Northern Ireland government. However this assessment was regarded as excessive, and in 1923 the Colwyn Commission reversed the formula, so that the imperial contribution would be the residual after the revenue needs of the government of Northern Ireland had been deducted from total revenues. In 1934 the contribution amounted to a princely £24,000, although during the war the contribution increased significantly. Except for during the war, the Six Counties were thus provided with defence and consular services at a relatively trivial cost.

From the 1920s the Northern Ireland government was committed to ensuring essential parity with Britain in the level of welfare services — unemployment benefits and assistance, pensions, and so on. This strained the budget in the 1930s, but after 1945 Britain undertook to pay the necessary cost of such parity. As a result, transfers to Northern Ireland rose rapidly, and were probably a major cause of the solid growth in the 1950s, validating to some degree Kennedy and Dowling's claim that the missing ingredient in the South during the same period was sufficient aggregate demand. One study has estimated that by 1963 financial transfers from the British government were so large as to raise Northern Ireland Gross Domestic Income by 25 per cent.[74] Estimates for 1970 suggest a similar order of magnitude. One consequence of parity is that welfare benefits in Northern Ireland were generally higher than in the South; for 1969-70 FitzGerald has estimated that if the benefit levels of the North were to be applied to the Republic then welfare expenditures there would have to be more than doubled.[75] With far higher unemployment rates, the net effect of transfers on Northern Ireland incomes is probably even greater in the 1980s. However, the more rapid growth of incomes in the Republic since 1970 has brought income levels in the two areas more into line. Thus, for instance, while there was one licensed car for every 4.3 people in Northern Ireland in 1981, the figure for the Republic was almost identical, at 4.4.

7   CONCLUDING OBSERVATIONS

There is no shortage of possible ways to interpret Irish economic history. Perhaps the most influential approach has been the *nationalist interpretation*. This emphasizes the ways in which the links between the Irish economy and Great Britain have worked to Ireland's detriment. Writers in this vein have stressed the damage caused by the Plantations, the Navigation, Cattle and Woollen Acts, the solid growth during the years of Grattan's Parliament, the lowering of tariffs in the years after the Act of Union, the ineffectiveness of relief efforts during the Famine, and the costs of Ireland's inability to protect its industry from British goods during the second half of the nineteenth century. This approach has typically been used to lead to the conclusion that Ireland would be better off economically with independence. When independence did not bring a dramatic improvement in growth, and when the import-substitution policy of the 1930s created an inefficient industrial base which stagnated in the 1950s, the advantages of independence came to be seen as less obvious, especially as Northern Ireland appeared to be prospering.

However since about 1960, when growth in the Republic has been faster, and dependence on the British market curtailed, the nationalist view has become more respectable. Stripped of its political agenda, this view is comparable to the approach of *dependency theorists*, who emphasize the harmful results of links between peripheral areas and the major industrial powers.[76] The main weakness of this approach is that it has tended to neglect the potentially beneficial effects of links with Britain (or elsewhere).

A second approach to Irish economic history is essentially *Marxist*. This stresses the role of the conflict between different classes within the country. Thus, for instance, the Famine and subsequent emigration swept away the greater part of the rural proletariat, paving the way for the emergence of a rural bourgeoisie, which in due course wrested control over land from the aristocracy and provided the leaders of a conservative independent state. In this view the labouring class, whether agricultural or industrial, never achieved enough strength to effect significant social or economic change, and the indigenous capitalist class failed in its mission of creating a dynamic industrial base, thereby forfeiting its right to the perquisites which it continues to enjoy. The conclusion most commonly drawn is that the state needs to take a more active role in filling this entrepreneurial function. Foreign enterprise is seen as transient, having goals which may conflict with those of the populace at large. While the focus on class conflict can be useful, the Marxist approach is weaker at explaining how classes themselves grow and shrink, or why largely non-class conflicts, such as that in Northern Ireland, persist.

The third approach, followed by most recent writers, has tended to view economic events as having a significant life of their own, being 'substantially independent of political and constitutional issues'.[77] Hence the role of the Cattle Acts, or the Act of Union, or the replacement of tenant farmers by smallholders, are seen as minor. Economic actors are believed to redirect their energies fairly quickly, and seize the available opportunities. This perspective, epitomized in the large body of revisionist writings of Cullen, could be labelled the *classical economics* approach; it has been faulted for paying too little attention to the influence of political events. In the hands of a new generation of economists this approach to history has become increasingly quantitative.

The most interesting lessons from Irish economic history are about growth *strategies*. Economic growth comes from a multitude of sources such as new technology, capital investment, education and training, land reclamation, enterprise, shifting prices, higher aggregate demand and chance. However these are only the raw ingredients, and must be combined to sustain growth. It is easy to see these ingredients at work. The new technologies of the potato, railways, power weaving and computers have all been influential. Capital spending is essential at all times, and has increased in recent years. Higher levels of education and improved training have boosted labour productivity. Chance brought the potato blight and two world wars. Land reclamation helped fend off famine in the early nineteenth century. Enterprise was at the heart of the introduction of shipbuilding in Belfast. A secular increase in wheat prices radically changed agriculture in the eighteenth century. Low aggregate demand reined in growth in the 1950s.

Recognizing the role of these elements is important, but holds few lessons. The study of growth strategies is more illuminating. The policy of *laissez faire* need not guarantee growth, as experience from 1815 to 1850 demonstrates, and as economic liberals are sometimes slow to accept. Nor does a strategy of *import substitution* necessarily fare better, for while it may have been helpful in the short run in the 1930s, protection left a legacy of inefficient industry in the 1950s. An approach which favours *agriculture-led development*, such as followed by the Free State in the 1920s, may succeed in raising real incomes, but for fewer people, because the ability of a mature agriculture to expand is usually very limited. An *export-based-growth strategy* may work in a buoyant world market, but may require foreign skills and capital.

Other small open economies can take heart in the fact that the policies they implement can have important effects on growth, although they must recognize that economic growth is not a smooth process, and a success in one decade, like Belfast in the nineteen hundreds, can be a failure in the next. It also seems to be harder to find a strategy which provides employment than one which simply raises average incomes.

Footnotes

1 Raymond Crotty, *Ireland in Crisis*, Brandon Press, Dingle 1986, p.11.

2 There is considerable disagreement about the level and growth of the population in the seventeenth century. Petty estimated the population at 1.3 million in 1687, but this is widely considered to be a serious underestimate. Cullen reckons the population was about 1.4 million in 1600, doubled by 1712, and hence grew by 0.6 per cent per annum on average during the century (Louis Cullen, 'Population Growth and Diet, 1600-1850', in J.M. Goldstrom and L.A. Clarkson (editors), *Irish Population, Economy and Society*, Clarendon Press, Oxford 1981.). This would imply a population of perhaps 2.4 million in 1687. Clarkson believes that the population in 1600 was not more than 1.1 million, and had risen to 1.7 million by 1687 (L.A. Clarkson, 'Irish Population Revisited, 1687-1821', in Goldstrom and Clarkson (editors), *op. cit.* An intermediate figure of 2.2 million is given by K.H Connell in his classic, *The Population of Ireland, 1750-1845*, Clarendon Press,

Oxford 1950. These disagreements arise because it is possible to measure population only indirectly. The returns of the hearth tax collections are known. By adjusting these returns for the level of undercounting, and multiplying by the mean household size, it is possible to estimate the size of the total population. Disagreement centres on the extent to which the tax was evaded, and on the size of households at the time. Another useful source is M. Drake, 'Marriage and Population Growth in Ireland', *Economic History Review*, 1963, pp.301-313.

3 Tobacco imports amounted to 1.8 million lbs. in 1665, and rose to almost 2.4 million in the 1670s and 3.3 million by 1686. See L.M. Cullen, *An Economic History of Ireland Since 1660*, Batsford, London 1972, p.18. Many of the details in this chapter are drawn from Cullen's book.

4 Drake, *op. cit.* Following Ó Gráda, Cullen believes that the marriage age in Ireland was relatively low until the closing decades of the eighteenth century, when it probably rose sharply. See Cullen, *op. cit.,* 1981, p.94.

5 J.C. Beckett, *The Making of Modern Ireland 1603-1923*, Faber, London 1966, p.181.

6 See, for instance, George O'Brien, 'Historical Introduction', in E.J. Riordan, *Modern Irish Trade and Industry*, Methuen, London 1920; and R.C. Crotty, *Irish Agricultural Production*, Cork University Press, Cork 1966.

7 This point is made by H.D. Gribbon in his review of Cullen, *An Economic History of Ireland Since 1660, op. cit.,* in *Irish Historical Studies*, 1973.

8 Cullen, *op. cit.,* 1981, p.96.

9 Cullen, *op. cit.,* 1972, p.53.

10 See for instance Philip Ollerenshaw, 'Industry, 1820-1914' in Liam Kennedy and Philip Ollerenshaw (editors), *An Economic History of Ulster, 1820-1939*, Manchester University Press, Manchester 1985; and Beckett, *op. cit.*

11 Maureen Wall, 'The Rise of a Catholic Middle Class in Eighteenth Century Ireland', *Irish Historical Studies*, September 1958.

12 The 1821 and 1841 censuses may both have undercounted the population; however as long as the bias is proportionately the same they may be used to give a satisfactory growth rate. The 1831 count is too high, and has misled researchers into thinking that population growth fell more rapidly in the 1830s than in fact it did. For a good discussion see Joel Mokyr, *Why Ireland Starved*, Allen and Unwin, London 1983. This book is the culmination of a decade of work on the subject of pre-Famine Ireland, and is both important and controversial. Much of the detail in this section is drawn from this source.

13 Mokyr, *op. cit.,* Appendix to Chapter 1. This would put national income at about £80 million in 1841. Cormac Ó Gráda, 'Agricultural Head Rents, Pre-Famine and Post-Famine', *Economic and Social Review*, April 1974, estimates rents at about £15 million, if imputed conacre payments are included. If this represents a third of agricultural output, which is plausible, then agriculture accounted for just over half of national income.

14 Cited by Mary Daly, *Social and Economic History of Ireland Since 1800*, Educational Company, Dublin 1981, p.19. This book is a useful source of historical information on economic events.

15 E.R.R. Greene, 'Industrial Decline in the Nineteenth Century' in L.M. Cullen (editor), *The Formation of the Irish Economy*, Mercier Press, Cork 1969.

16 Cited in Eoin O'Malley, 'The Decline of Irish Industry in the Nineteenth Century', *Economic and Social Review*, October 1981, p.26. Marx's italics.

17 Much of what follows comes from E.R.R. Green, 'The Great Famine', in T.W. Moody and F.X. Martin (editors), *The Course of Irish History*, Mercier Press, Cork 1967.

18 Mokyr, *op. cit.,* p.291.

19 F.S.L. Lyons, *Ireland Since the Famine*, Weidenfeld and Nicolson, London 1971, p.40. This book is a valuable source of historical economic information. Cattle exports averaged 47,000 annually during 1821-25, rose to 98,000 in 1835, and to 202,000 annually during 1846-49.

20 Cullen, *op. cit.* 1972, p. 132.
21 The Poor Law Commission interviewed 1,590 witnesses throughout the country. One of the questions asked respondents to judge whether the position of the poor had worsened or improved. On a scale of – 2 (much worse) to + 2 (much improved) the average of the answers was .43. See Mokyr, *op. cit.,* p.12.
22 Cited by Mokyr, *op. cit.,* p.38.
23 *Ibid.,* Chapter 3. This test is embedded in an appropriate regression model. Mokyr's approach has been criticized by Barbara Solow in her review of his book in the *Journal of Economic History*, September 1984.
24 Joseph Lee, 'Capital in the Irish Economy', in Cullen (editor), *op. cit.*
25 Eoin O'Malley, *op. cit.,* p.40.
26 Sinn Féin The Workers' Party, *The Irish Industrial Revolution* , Reprol Publications, Dublin 1977. See also Lee, *op. cit.*
27 The harvest of 1879 was disastrous, yielding an output worth £23 million compared with a harvest worth £37 million in 1876. Emigration in 1880 rose to 96,000, in contrast to an annual average of 41,000 over the previous four years. Data from Cullen, *op. cit.* 1972, p.148. It may be a measure of rising incomes that Ireland did not starve at this time.
28 Hans Staehle, 'Statistical Notes on the Economic History of Irish Agriculture, 1847-1913', *Journal of the Statistical and Social Inquiry Society of Ireland*, 1950/51, puts the increase at 27 per cent. In his comments on this paper R.C. Geary notes that he had earlier estimated the rise at 23 per cent.
29 Cullen, *op. cit.,* p.137. His estimate that the wage doubled appears on p.156. P. Deane and W.A. Cole, *British Economic Growth 1688-1959* (second edition), Cambridge University Press, London 1967, p.23 report a wage index for Ireland which is a composite of average money wages in Dublin and average agricultural earnings. From a base of 100 in 1840 it evolves as follows: 1845, 100; 1850, 100; 1855, 129; 1860, 134. Adjusting for prices, *real* wages evolved as follows: 1840, 100; 1845, 119; 1850, 135; 1855, 132; 1860, 140. The price index used to deflate wages is the Statist Sauerbeck index given by Thomas Barrington, 'A Review of Irish Agricultural Prices', *Journal of the Statistical and Social Inquiry Society of Ireland,* 1926/27, pp.249-280.
30 T. Grimshaw, 'A Statistical Survey of Ireland from 1840 to 1888', *Journal of the Statistical and Social Inquiry Society of Ireland*, 1889. The price data come from Barrington, *op. cit.*
31 The company that later became Harland and Wolff was founded in 1853, and the other big shipbuilder, Workman, Clark and Co. was established in 1879. The rapid rise in output did not occur until the 1870s. Annual tonnage built between 1885 and 1888 came to 32,000, and rose to 158,000 per year during 1909-1912. Philip Ollerenshaw, *op. cit.*
32 According to the census of production, net industrial output in 1907 was £22.8 million, or about £79 per worker. Net output in agriculture came to £45 million, or about £46 per worker. Three-quarters of all industry was in Ulster. If the service sector was as large as the industrial sector, then industry generated a quarter of national income. Daly, *op. cit.,* pp.77-78, asserts that at this time Ireland was more industrialized than Denmark. Lyons, *op. cit.,* p.69, is less enthusiastic about the amount of industrial growth, commenting that 'by any standards this was a modest level of performance'.
33 Cullen, *op. cit.* 1972, p. 170.
34 See for instance Joseph Lee, 'The Railways in the Irish Economy', in Cullen (editor), *op. cit.* See also Cullen, *op. cit.* 1972, pp.143-144.
35 Interestingly enough Irish crop yields are typically high. For instance over the period 1912-16 Irish yields of wheat, oats and potatoes were, in cwts. per statute acre, 19.9, 17.6 and 107.7 respectively. These were higher than in France (10.6, 10.3 and 69.1) and Italy (8.1, 7.4 and 43.5). The higher Irish yields reflect the *difficulty* of growing such crops in Ireland; only when the yields are high enough, because the soil or site is favourable, are they worth the considerable effort and risk involved. The figures are from Riordan, *op. cit.,* p.59.

36 For an interesting discussion of Ó Gráda's work on the subject, see Liam Kennedy, 'Studies in Irish Econometric History', *Irish Historical Studies*, 1983.

37 Barrington, *op. cit.*, p.279.

38 Geary, commenting on Staehle, *op. cit.* Geary also called for the use of more rigorous statistical methods, a call which Ó Gráda clearly heeded.

39 Cormac Ó Gráda, 'Supply Responsiveness in Nineteenth Century Irish Agriculture', *Economic History Review*, 1975.

40 This and the next citation from Ó Gráda, *op. cit.*, pp.313 and 314. There are two arguments here. The traditional view blamed the woes of Irish agriculture on the 'high eviction rate, exorbitant rents, and tenant investment disincentives'. (James Donnelly, in his review of Barbara Solow's, *The Land Question and the Irish Economy*, Harvard University Press, Cambridge, Mass. 1971.) Solow effectively demolishes this view. Crotty, *op. cit.* 1966, stands the traditional view on its head, arguing that small farmer-owners were reluctant to buy and sell their land, and this delayed the removal of inefficient farmers from the land.

41 David Fitzpatrick, 'The Disappearance of the Irish Agricultural Labourer, 1841-1912', *Irish Economic and Social History*, 1980, p.66.

42 These new landlords have developed a reputation for being a hardheaded bunch; see for instance Beckett, *op. cit.*, p.353, for some typical comments. However during the post-Famine period rents rose no faster than in Britain, and the rate of evictions was low.

43 T.W. Moody, 'Fenianism, Home-rule and the Land War', in Moody and Martin (editors), *op. cit.* Donnelly, in his review of Solow's book, claims that between 1865 and 1880 real rents in Ireland rose 12 per cent, compared to 11.5 per cent in England and 12.5 per cent in Scotland. Despite the reduction in money rents the position of tenants did not improve immediately, because prices had fallen too. Solow has calculated that rents took about a quarter of a typical tenant's income in 1876; by 1881 the proportion was 28 per cent, and would have been a third but for the judicial rent reductions; as prices fell further, and rents did not, they came to absorb 36 per cent of tenant income in 1886. In this light the continued agitation for more reform is understandable. The Land League's slogan was 'The land for the people', but this meant different things to different individuals. To the tenantry it was interpreted as enabling them to become owners. For Davitt it meant the nationalization of land, to be rented out to tenants, so the rent would accrue to the population at large.

44 Emmet Larkin, 'Economic Growth, Capital Investment and the Roman Catholic Church in Ireland', *American Historical Review*, April 1967, data appendix. His figures for 1841 are suspect, and we have used the figures of Lyons, *op. cit.*, p.41.

45 Lyons, *op. cit.*, p.54.

46 Most of these points are made by Oliver MacDonagh, *Ireland, The Union and its Aftermath*, Allen and Unwin, London 1977, p.126. In 1926 Irish residents held approximately £100 million worth of British government stock. Daly, *op. cit.*, p.146.

47 The dependency ratio measures the proportion of young people (14 and younger) and old people (65 and older) to the rest of the population. In 1926 the dependency ratio stood at 0.62, and by 1966 it had risen to 0.74. See Kieran Kennedy, *Productivity and Industrial Growth*, Clarendon Press, Oxford 1971. Emigration tends to suck out 'prime age' men and women, thereby raising the dependency ratio.

48 Cited by James Meenan, 'From Free Trade to Self-sufficiency', in F. MacManus (editor), *The Years of the Great Test 1926-1939*, Mercier Press, Cork 1967, p.72.

49 W.J.L. Ryan, 'Measurement of Tariff Levels for Ireland, for 1931, 1936, 1938', *Journal of the Statistical and Social Inquiry Society of Ireland*, 1948/49. A full list of the items subjected to tariffs in 1924 and 1925 appears in Daly, *op. cit.*, p.143.

50 The most complete work on the subject is still Garret FitzGerald, *State Sponsored Bodies*, Institute of Public Administration, Dublin 1963.

51 Dara McCormack, 'Policy Making in a Small Open Economy: Some Aspects of Irish Experience', *Central Bank of Ireland Quarterly Bulletin*, Winter 1979.

52 *Ibid.* Based on a basket of goods which mirrored the trade patterns of the UK and the US, the (weighted) Irish tariff rate was between 79 per cent and 84 per cent (depending on the assumptions used) in 1937. The equivalent rate for Germany was 120 per cent, for the UK 51 per cent and for the US 42 per cent. Since the Irish pattern of trade was very different its actual tariff rate in 1938 was 35 per cent.

53 Dermot McAleese, 'Political Independence and Economic Performance — Ireland outside the United Kingdom', in E. Nevin (editor), *The Economics of Devolution,* University of Wales Press, Cardiff 1978.

54 AE, cited by Meenan, *op. cit.,* p.74.

55 An interesting side effect of British tariffs was the appearance of cattle smuggling into Northern Ireland. See D.S. Johnson, 'Cattle Smuggling on the Irish Border 1932-1938', *Irish Economic and Social History*, 1979.

56 Meenan, *op. cit.,* p.79.

57 Much of the information in this paragraph comes from Martin O'Donoghue and Alan Tait, 'The Growth of Public Revenue and Expenditure in Ireland', in J.A. Bristow and A.A. Tait (editors), *Economic Policy in Ireland,* Institute of Public Administration, Dublin 1968, p.188.

58 Dermot McAleese, in his review of Kieran Kennedy and Brendan Dowling, *Economic Growth in Ireland: The Experience since 1947*, Gill and Macmillan, Dublin 1975, in the *Irish Times.*

59 For a useful discussion, see Robert O'Connor and Philip Kelly, 'Agriculture: Medium-term Review and Outlook' in B.R. Dowling and J. Durkan (editors), *Irish Economic Policy: A Review of Major Issues*, Economic and Social Research Institute, Dublin 1978.

60 Garret FitzGerald, *Planning in Ireland*, Institute of Public Administration, Dublin 1968, p.10.

61 Kennedy and Dowling, *op. cit.,* make this case forcefully, and emphasize the role of learning (to export) by doing. They disagree strongly with FitzGerald's conclusion, *Planning in Ireland*, p.13., that 'what was achieved after 1958 could have been secured a decade earlier'. They minimize the differences between economic performance in the 1950s and 1960s. Between 1950 and 1961 GNP rose by 1.9 per cent per annum in real terms, compared to 4.1 per cent in the interval 1961 to 1968. Per capita GNP rose by 2.4 per cent, compared with 3.6 per cent; and GNP per worker increased at 3.2 per cent, compared to 3.9 per cent. Their results are very sensitive to the end points they choose. If one compares the period 1950-58 with 1958-68 we find the following. GNP growth: 1.0 per cent compared with 4.3 per cent. GNP per capita growth: 1.5 per cent compared with 4.1 per cent. GNP/worker growth: 2.7 per cent compared with 4.4 per cent. Admittedly 1958 was a depressed year, but by 1961 the economy had more than simply rebounded from recession.

62 The growth rate of income is given by dY/Y. Divide top and bottom by (dK) and rearrange to get dY/Y = (I/Y)/(dK/dY). Investment here is *net* of depreciation. If the net investment ratio is .15 and the ICOR is 5, then income can be expected to grow at three per cent per annum.

63 Kennedy and Dowling, *op. cit.,* p.246.

64 K. Kennedy, *op. cit.*

65 John Blackwell, 'Government, Economy and Society', in Frank Litton (editor), *Unequal Achievement: The Irish Experience 1957-1982*, Institute of Public Administration, Dublin 1982, p.51.

66 Much of this discussion draws on Alan Matthews, 'The Economic Consequences of EC Membership for Ireland', in David Coombes (editor), *Ireland and the European Communities: Ten Years of Membership*, Gill and Macmillan, Dublin 1983. According to Matthews, *ibid,*

p.123, net transfers from the EC to Ireland came to £481 million in 1980 and £439 million in 1981 These represent 5.4 per cent and 4.2 per cent of GNP respectively. GNP figures are from the *Statistical Abstract of Ireland 1981*, Stationery Office, Dublin 1985.

67 MacDonagh, *op. cit.*, p.139.

68 Blackwell, *op. cit.*, stresses this. Tobin and Nordhaus attempted to correct US GNP by subtracting the cost of the 'bads' associated with growth; their derived 'measure of economic welfare' was found to grow about half as fast as GNP as conventionally measured.

69 Brian Nolan, 'The Personal Distribution of Income in the Republic of Ireland', *Journal of the Statistical and Social Inquiry Society of Ireland*, 1977/78.

70 Kieran Kennedy, 'Summing up at Close of Conference', in *The Irish Economy and Society in the 1980s*, Economic and Social Research Institute, Dublin 1981.

71 Most of the data cited in this section come from Cullen, *op. cit.*, 1972; Daly, *op. cit.*; Lyons, *op. cit.*; and D.S. Johnson, 'The Northern Ireland Economy, 1914-1939', in Kennedy and Ollerenshaw, *op. cit.*, p.195.

72 Lyons, *op. cit.*, p.711.

73 Patrick Buckland, *A History of Northern Ireland*, Gill and Macmillan, Dublin 1981.

74 A.J. Brown, cited in Daly, *op. cit.*, p.210.

75 Cited in Lyons, *op. cit.*, p.742.

76 A recent variant on this theme, articulated by Crotty, *op. cit.*, 1986, argues that during the colonial era capitalist Britain imposed an alien set of values, notably respect for property, which was in some sense ill suited to the needs of the colony. That is why, he argues, no former colony has succeeded in becoming industrialized; he seems to imply that none are likely to do so.

77 L. Kennedy, *op. cit.*, 1983, p.213.

Part I

POLICY OBJECTIVES

2   Primary Policy Objectives

Andrew John*

1   INTRODUCTION

THIS CHAPTER provides a framework for a coherent analysis of economic policy objectives in Ireland.[1] The underlying argument is that the principal economic objectives of policy-makers can be usefully summarized in terms of three types of policy: policies to ensure optimal (efficient) use of economic resources at a point in time, policies that address allocation over time, and policies concerned with the distribution of output. These three aspects of economic decision-making can be discussed in terms of three measurable objectives: full employment, economic growth and economic equality.

These aims of policy may appear self-evident, yet half of the chapter is taken up with a relatively abstract discussion of policy and the derivation of these objectives from first principles. This might seem unduly pedantic; but, although the analysis does justify and explain some of the emphasis on unemployment, growth and equality in popular and political debate, it turns out that popular conceptions of these aims may be misleading in several respects. Informal intuition is not sufficient, and it is important to understand exactly why these are sensible objectives.

One aspect of the analysis is an examination of the role of markets in the allocation of economic resources and the achievement of policy aims. Economic thinking emphasizes that freely operating markets can play an important role in allocating goods and services in an efficient manner; this argument is considered in some detail.

Another important message of the chapter is that there are limitations upon policy. Neither economists nor politicians possess

*The author would like to thank John Clark and Maeve O'Higgins for many useful comments on this paper. His gratitude is also still extended to Tim Callan, Adrienne Cheasty, Isabel Harrison and Sean Nolan for discussions and comments on the version of this chapter that appeared in the previous edition of this book. All responsibility for remaining errors is his own.

the alchemist's stone, and not all policy goals that seem desirable may be feasible. (There is little point in suggesting that improving the weather should be a goal of policy.) Also, in designing policy, as elsewhere in economics, it is vital to recognize the existence of trade-offs: achievement of one policy goal may require the sacrifice of another. Full employment may be a desirable aim of policy; full employment at any cost is not.

Given the complexities of policy-making in practice, some simplifications are necessary in the development of an analytic framework. The arguments in this chapter are therefore based explicitly on assumptions about economic institutions and values. Considerable attention is paid both to the ways in which these assumptions enter the analysis, and to their deficiencies.

Section 2 presents the key assumptions of the chapter, and explains the relationship between these assumptions and economic efficiency. The possible role of markets in achieving efficiency is considered, and other arguments for a free market economy are evaluated. The role of economic policy in correcting deficiencies of the market is then discussed. Finally, the assumptions of the analysis are critically examined.

Section 3 argues that the criterion of economic efficiency, derived in Section 2, does not provide a sufficient basis for economic policy-making. Policy should also address distribution and intertemporal allocation. It is then argued that the policy-maker's problem can be usefully formulated in terms of proximate objectives that capture these different dimensions of policy. Full employment, economic growth and economic equality are proposed as suitable objectives.

The remainder of Section 3 is concerned with these objectives. For each aim, there is a discussion of measurement issues and the correspondence of the best available measure with the theoretical ideal. This is followed by consideration of whether or not policy intervention is desirable. This involves comparing the outcome in the absence of intervention (the free market outcome) with some ideal outcome. Economics can only make a limited contribution to the selection of this ideal, since it must ultimately depend upon the preferences and values of individuals. None the less, the methods of welfare economics may help to clarify the debate, so some of the important issues are discussed. Finally, there is discussion of what can be achieved by economic policy.

Section 4 emphasizes the trade-offs between different pairs of objectives, in order to highlight the choices faced by policy-makers. Section 5 contains some concluding comments.

2   ECONOMIC EFFICIENCY, ECONOMIC POLICY
AND THE MARKET MECHANISM

The first part of this section sets out some basic assumptions that are
maintained throughout the chapter. On the basis of these
assumptions, *Pareto-efficiency* is established as an important aim of
economic policy. Next, the case for a free market economy is
considered. The key point is that freely operating markets can play
an important role in achieving economic efficiency. Other
arguments for a market economy are also evaluated. Economic
theory also suggests that there are many occasions when free
markets will not achieve efficiency; these and the associated theory
of government intervention are discussed in the third subsection.
The final subsection considers criticisms of the assumptions and
methodology of this analysis.

Pareto-Efficiency
Four assumptions are central to the following analysis:
(i)   the aim of policy-makers is the maximization of social welfare;
(ii)   social welfare depends positively upon the welfare of individuals
       in society;
(iii) the welfare of individuals depends upon the goods and services
       that they consume;
(iv)   individuals are the best judges of their own welfare and act in
       their own self-interest.

For the present, these are simply taken as given; they are critically
evaluated at the end of Section 2. It is worth stressing at the outset,
though, that a theory may be useful even when its assumptions can
be criticized. Readers unhappy with these assumptions must decide
for themselves the extent to which their objections might alter the
analysis.

Now suppose that policy-makers can choose between two
situations (A and B) with the property that all individuals are at least
as well off (in terms of utility, or satisfaction) in B as in A, and at
least one individual is strictly better off. Then B is said to be Pareto-
superior to A. If, by contrast, some individuals are better off and
some are worse off, then the two situations are Pareto-non-
comparable. If a given situation has the property that there is no
feasible Pareto-superior outcome (so policy-makers cannot make
some people better off without making others worse off), then that
situation is said to be Pareto-efficient (or, for brevity, simply
efficient).

The first two assumptions, taken together, imply that efficiency is desirable. It is generally felt that the desirability of efficiency is a weak proposition that would be acceptable to most people as a guiding principle of policy. It underlies most welfare analyses undertaken in economics, and is probably the only normative proposition that commands general assent among economists.[2] As a guide to policy, though, Pareto-efficiency also has severe limitations, largely because it is such a weak proposition. This is discussed in detail in Section 3.

In economic analysis, Pareto-efficiency is decomposed into efficiency in production and efficiency in exchange. The third assumption above asserted that individuals derive satisfaction from the goods and services they consume. Since the production of goods and services requires resources, and since resources are limited, it follows that society should seek to make the best use of the limited resources at its disposal. In particular, it is desirable that it should not be possible to reallocate resources in such a way as to produce more of at least one desired commodity and at least as much of all other desired commodities; otherwise, social welfare can evidently be increased. Efficiency in production is achieved when no such reallocation is possible.

Efficiency in exchange concerns the allocation of goods and services. Given a fixed amount of goods to be distributed among consumers, an allocation is efficient if no Pareto-improving redistribution is available. If agents are the best judges of their own welfare (assumption (iv) above), then an efficient allocation can be achieved by voluntary exchange of goods. Put another way, an allocation is not efficient if there exist mutually beneficial trades. This observation underlies the argument, to be considered in detail in the next subsection, that freely-operating markets may be instrumental in the attainment of Pareto-efficiency.

The Role of Markets

One of the most fundamental results of economic theory is that efficiency in both the production and exchange of goods and services can be achieved in an economy characterized by perfectly competitive markets for all goods and services in all time periods. Further, any Pareto-efficient outcome could be attained in such an economy, by means of appropriate initial redistributions.[3] These 'general equilibrium' results (known as the first and second welfare theorems) are important and underlie a great deal of current economic thinking. In particular, they provide a rigorous theoretical justification for the belief that the price mechanism is an efficient allocator of resources.

Put a little more precisely, the argument runs as follows. Consider first efficiency in exchange. Suppose that individuals start off with a given quantity of goods and can buy and sell as much as they want of these goods and the goods of others, at prices that they take as given. It can then be shown that, at some set of prices, the desired transactions of everyone in the economy are mutually compatible. Furthermore, in carrying out these transactions, individuals effectively trade with one another up to the point where all benefits from exchange are exhausted. That is, they achieve an efficient point at which no further mutually beneficial trades exist; there is no conceivable swap of goods between any two individuals that both would favour.

Efficiency in production will be achieved under free markets given the additional assumption that producers maximize profits. (If producers are simply individuals, then this is not really an additional assumption, but rather an implication of assumption (iv).) Maximization of profits evidently entails productive efficiency: if a firm can obtain more output using the same quantity of inputs, then it can increase its profits. A more informal intuition is that any firm that uses resources inefficiently will be unable to compete in a free market. As an extension of the exchange efficiency argument, it can be shown that, with production, there is a set of prices such that everyone's transactions are mutually compatible.[4]

The import of these results is striking. If the transactions of agents are mediated by competitive markets, then individuals, *acting purely in their own self-interest*, arrive at an outcome with the desirable property of Pareto-efficiency. Freely operating markets provide the incentives for firms to produce the 'right' quantities of goods and services, and also provide the mechanism whereby individuals can carry out mutually beneficial exchanges.

As will be seen in the following subsection, these results actually need to be interpreted with a great deal of caution, and turn out to be less powerful than they might at first appear. None the less, they do suggest that a free market economy is the appropriate starting point for the systematic analysis of economic policy, and, from the perspective of economic theory, they provide the strongest argument in favour of the free market economy. Other less compelling justifications for free markets have also been proposed, though, and will be considered briefly here.

One argument for competitive markets is that they provide *consumer* sovereignty. This is the idea that, in a free market economy, production of commodities is designed to meet demand, with the function of producers being solely to respond to the wishes of consumers. Proponents of the consumer sovereignty argument like to describe it as 'economic democracy'.

A certain amount of mystique surrounds the consumer sovereignty proposition, given that it is really no more than a recognition of the fact that consumer preferences have an effect on the economic system; one could as easily speak of 'technology sovereignty'. But the idea does embody an important insight: if firms do respond to market pressures, the tastes and preferences of consumers matter. If consumers do not wish to purchase a good, it will not be produced; should demand for a good increase, production will respond. This stands in contrast, for example, to centrally-planned economies, where there is no such necessary link between consumer preferences and output.

Ireland is a small open economy, though, so consumer sovereignty does not imply that the preferences of Irish consumers give rise to the pattern of Irish output. Instead, as prices of traded goods in a small open economy are determined by world demand and supply, consumer sovereignty in the Irish context means that it is the preferences of American, British, European and other consumers that influence the pattern of output in Ireland. The emotional appeal of consumer sovereignty as economic democracy may be lessened somewhat. In any case, implicit in the consumer sovereignty principle is that the preferences of the rich are given much more weight than those of the poor; the idea would be better described as plutocracy.

A second argument for free markets derives from the possibility that the existence of choice may, in itself, be a source of welfare. In other words, it may be the case that competitive markets (as opposed to, say, monopolies or centrally-planned production) are not merely a mechanism whereby individuals can maximize their utility and achieve efficiency in exchange, but also are an independent source of welfare.

Suppose an individual is given a choice between two commodities — a loaf and a fish — and chooses the fish. Does this differ, in terms of the individual's welfare, from the situation where he or she is simply presented with the fish? If utility is derived purely from consumption, then the two situations must be identical in terms of welfare, yet intuition may suggest that having the chance to choose is preferable. Conversely, choosing may even be a source of disutility, if there are costs associated with decision-making. This argument has limited force, though, given that individuals are probably 'free not to choose'.

One final argument for a free market economy rests on the

assertion that economic freedom — the right to buy and sell goods and services in competitive markets — is a precondition for, or a part of, wider political freedoms, which are assumed to be desirable.[5] While this argument will not be discussed in detail here, one observation is worth making. A fundamental principle of a free market economy is the existence of property and private ownership, but there does not appear to be a good *prima facie* reason for associating freedom and private property. Private ownership implies an exclusive right to benefit from the flow of services from a good, which by definition restricts the freedom of others to benefit from that flow of services. It is certainly not self-evident that political freedom is automatically associated with a fully market-oriented economy. It would instead seem reasonable to suggest that, for some goods (say, wristwatches), freedom is well served by private ownership, while private ownership may imply undesirable and unnecessary restrictions on freedom in the case of other goods (such as beaches).[6]

Market Imperfections and Economic Policy
The theoretical results linking efficiency and competitive markets are based upon a set of restrictive assumptions that do not describe any actual economy. There are a number of reasons why free market economies in practice will not accord with the idealized abstraction of perfectly competitive markets. (Unrealistic assumptions, it is stressed again, do not imply that a theory provides no insights into real world economies; they do suggest that great care must be taken in interpreting and applying the theoretical results.) It is accordingly useful to consider why these assumptions may be violated in practice. Four possibilities are addressed here: externalities, public goods, information imperfections and non-competitive behaviour.

One crucial reservation about the efficiency of competitive markets in real economies arises from the presence of externalities. These are defined as costs or benefits that arise from production or consumption of a good, but accrue not to the producer or consumer, but to others. An example of a negative externality arising from production is pollution; by contrast, a positive externality might arise if advances in technology, due to the research of a particular firm, benefit other producers who did not pay for the research. A negative externality in consumption is 'second-hand' smoke from cigarettes. Conversely, if smoking makes someone less irritable and thus more pleasant company, then this is a positive consumption externality.

General equilibrium theory assumes that there are no (unpriced) external effects in consumption or production; markets are assumed to exist for all external effects in the general equilibrium framework. However, it is certainly the case that the market prices of goods in real economies frequently do not reflect their true (social) costs because of the presence of significant externalities; hence production and consumption will not be at their socially optimal levels.

A second problem with a free market economy in practice arises from the existence of public goods. These are goods which must be consumed in the same amount by all individuals (implying that no one can be excluded from the benefits), and which possess the characteristic that one person's consumption does not affect the consumption of others. The classic example of a public good is national defence. Individual welfare depends upon many such goods which cannot be directly purchased in the market. Hence social welfare cannot necessarily be equated with welfare arising from consumption of consumer goods only.

In developed economies, purchases made by consumers at the margin are generally of luxury goods rather than necessities. This might suggest a greater relative preference for public goods, since many public goods are, relatively speaking, luxury commodities; this implies in turn that the public good problem may be particularly serious in developed economies.[7] The market mechanism does not allow consumers to express a preference for better recreational, educational or health facilities, which again implies that free markets will not achieve efficiency in practice.

Another reason for expecting free markets to be deficient in real economies is that, contrary to the assumptions of general equilibrium theory, firms and consumers are not perfectly informed about the economy. Producers must make decisions based on incomplete knowledge of consumers' tastes, and consumers will in general lack information on both the prices and the quality of the goods they wish to purchase.

Lack of information on quality is particularly important in the case of goods that are technically complex, such as consumer durables. Because such goods tend to be relatively expensive and are bought infrequently, the price mechanism will be less efficient in allocating resources. The less frequently a good is bought, the less sensitive is the market mechanism, for there is no immediate way in which the dissatisfied consumer can convey this dissatisfaction in the market; this can only be done in the medium or long run, by which time the nature of the market may have changed. To put it another way, since market processes operate in real time and adjust over time, uninformed consumers may sometimes engage in inefficient out-of-equilibrium trades.

All of this suggests that information should be viewed as an economic good that is bought and sold like other commodities.[8] To a large extent this is true — think of *Which?* magazine — and may offset the problems just raised. But there are many reasons for expecting the markets for information to be imperfect. There may be substantial economies of scale in information gathering, implying that single individuals cannot acquire the information they need. Information also has many of the attributes of a public good. Finally, some information may be essentially impossible for individuals to acquire. Suppose, for example, that a worker wishes to know the safety record of the firm to which she is applying for a job. The firm may not have the incentive to tell the truth and the worker may be unable to verify the information received.

Perhaps the most obvious divergence between the theory and reality is that real-world markets are usually not characterized by perfect competition.[9] Even the classic textbook example of perfectly competitive markets — those for agricultural products — is not appropriate in Ireland, given the European Community and the Common Agricultural Policy. Prices in such markets are fixed by European Community agreement, not determined by demand and supply.

Furthermore, many markets in Ireland possess the characteristics of monopoly, oligopoly or imperfect (monopolistic) competition. In such cases agents possess market power; they are not price-takers but can influence the prices of goods they buy and sell. This means that firms will tend to reduce the quantity they produce in order to increase the price they receive for their output. The level of output that generates maximum profit for the firm will then be less than that required for an efficient equilibrium. This may in turn have repercussions beyond the market in question (as, for example, when the good in question is used as an input in the production of other commodities).

The weaknesses of a free market economy that have just been noted — externalities, public goods, information problems and market imperfections — can be interpreted as criticisms of the institutional assumptions of the competitive markets model. That is, they describe important problems that arise in real economies but are excluded by the assumptions of general equilibrium theory. Taken together, they amount to a powerful critique of the relevance of general equilibrium theory — and its welfare implications particularly — for real economies.

These arguments can also be viewed in a more constructive light, however, whereby they provide a basis for a systematic theory of policy intervention. When existing markets correspond closely to the competitive ideal, theory suggests that free operation of such markets will lead to efficient allocation. Intervention is then unnecessary. Conversely, when markets are characterized by one or more of the problems just noted, economic theory suggests that policy intervention is required, and should be designed to correct the 'distortion'. That is, policy-makers should intervene in such a manner as to make markets correspond as closely as possible to the competitive ideal, and hence bring about an efficient outcome.

The theory suggests, for example, that policy-makers should intervene to regulate monopolies and alter incentives (by means of taxes and subsidies) to adjust for externalities. Similarly, there may be a role for policy in the collection and dissemination of information, if imperfections are present in the markets for information. Policy-makers should also intervene to ensure the collective provision of public goods (alternatively, it may be possible to incorporate such goods into the market mechanism: national parks and toll motorways are examples).[10] The practical details of such policy-making evidently depend upon the tools that policy-makers have at their disposal, and will not be considered in detail here; these arguments are discussed in greater depth in Chapter 4.

This approach to policy-making is thus based on the idea of exploiting the known efficiency properties of competitive markets. In itself, the theory gives no indication of whether government policy should be highly interventionist or based principally on *laissez-faire;* that decision requires judgements on the empirical incidence of the different problems noted and of the costs of intervention. In this sense — but perhaps in this sense only — the argument is politically neutral.

Some significant reservations about this approach to policy should be noted. First, there is an important result, known as the theory of the 'second best', which indicates that if there is a distortion in one market (that cannot be corrected directly), then it may no longer be optimal for other markets to be perfectly competitive.[11] As an example of this, consider the case of a monopolist who imposes pollution externalities. If this monopolist is induced to produce the competitive level of output, then there will be an even worse pollution problem: the distortions associated with the externality will be increased.

From one perspective, this result is devastating, and suggests that this entire approach to policy-making is worthless. A more sanguine interpretation notes that the second-best argument requires that different distortions should be offsetting; hence it can be argued that the theory should be considered to be applicable unless the existence of offsetting distortions can be demonstrated explicitly.

Second, policies designed to correct distortions will in practice also have distributional implications, and may therefore not lead to Pareto improvements. (The introduction of toll motorways would make motorists financially worse off; the removal of the Common Agricultural Policy would make farmers worse off.) Traditionally, economic theory has sidestepped this problem by assuming that efficiency can be separated from the (political) problem of distribution. It is often posited, for example, that policy-makers have access to non-distortionary taxes and subsidies ('lump-sum transfers') which can be used to effect any desired redistribution without altering incentives. In practice, this assumption is not valid. The principal implication of this, as will be argued in Section 3, is that economic efficiency should not be the sole aim of policy, and efficiency gains may sometimes have to be sacrificed to achieve other objectives.

Note also that this approach to policy-making ignores many practical complications. Economists and politicians possess only an imperfect knowledge of the economy, so inefficiencies are not always easy to identify, effective policies may be hard to design, and the consequences of policy actions may be hard to predict. Recent work in economics also emphasizes the importance of expectations and credibility. Private agents form expectations about government policies, and these expectations influence the impact of policy. For example, the effect of a tax cut depends crucially on whether it is expected to be temporary or permanent. Policy-makers may therefore have more influence if they can credibly commit to policies in advance, but such credibility may be hard to acquire from a sceptical populace.[12]

In addition, the economic influence of policy-makers in Ireland is severely curtailed by the fact that the economy is 'open' (closely linked to the world economy through trade) and 'small' (so that economic events in Ireland have a negligible influence on the world economy). Much of what happens in the Irish economy is thus determined by developments in the outside world, beyond the realm of domestic policy. The importance of this observation will be apparent from the discussion here and in subsequent chapters.

Actual economies may also diverge from the competitive ideal in ways that cannot be corrected by policy-makers. For example, one notion underlying competitive markets is price flexibility. If prices are flexible, then they will respond to shocks in such a way as to ensure that demand and supply are always equal. If some prices are sticky, though, then demand and supply may not always be equal at the price prevailing in the market. Some mutually beneficial trades will then not be realized, suggesting inefficiency. Similarly, recall that general equilibrium theory assumes the existence of markets for all goods in all time periods. This assumption is palpably false: try and find someone willing to sell a promise to deliver kiwi fruit in Galway on February 16, 2060. Once again, certain mutually beneficial trades may therefore go unrealized.

Policy-makers, however, do not have it in their power to order prices to be more flexible. Similarly, policy-makers cannot simply establish markets that are missing.[13] Furthermore, there may be reasons why prices are rigid or markets missing; without understanding these, the consequences of economic policies cannot be predicted. These are among the deepest questions in economics, and it is not possible to do justice to them here; for current purposes, the important lesson is that there are substantial constraints upon policy. This observation arises again in Section 3.

Criticisms

This subsection represents a methodological digression from the main theme of the chapter. The line of argument that has been developed thus far represents orthodox economic reasoning, but is based on behavioural and ideological assumptions that some may dislike. A number of objections can be raised, most of which entail disagreement with the four assumptions set out at the start of Section 2.

Since the predilection of economists for making assumptions is frequently noted (and mocked!), it is worth emphasizing that it is simply not possible to discuss policy (or just about any other question in economics) without assumptions. The relevant questions concern what assumptions are most useful, not whether or not assumptions should be made at all. Condemning assumptions as unrealistic is easy, but worthless unless better alternatives are also proposed. Equally, it is important to recognize the weaknesses of the assumptions that are made, in order to make a judgement on the usefulness of the analysis.

There are certainly valid criticisms to be made of assumption (i) — that policy-makers seek to maximize social welfare. While this is a useful simplification, it ignores the fact that, in practice, governments may have many other aims, such as maximizing their probability of reelection, or maximizing the post-tax salaries of cabinet ministers! And the complexities of decision-making in the political process are hardly captured by an assumption that all political decisions are made by a benevolent government in the best interests of society. Indeed, some economists have argued that the political process should be evaluated in strict economic terms — that is, in terms of agents acting purely in their own self-interest.[14]

When carried to its limit, such an argument leaves little room for the more orthodox view that governments may act in society's interest. The view adopted in this chapter is that such criticisms are not sufficient to invalidate the orthodox approach, although they do raise an important caveat.

The second assumption set out above was that social welfare depends positively on the welfare of the individuals in society. In itself, this is hardly contentious; it is little more than a definition. This approach, however, suppresses the possibility that other (non-economic) objectives, such as human rights, may have a direct influence on social welfare. Sen has argued that an exclusive stress on the levels of the welfare of individuals is insufficient for policy purposes, and that other 'non-utility' information should also be used.[15] The emphasis on individual welfare in this chapter need not be interpreted as excluding the admission of non-utility information in policy-making; rather, such considerations are ignored for purposes of clarity and simplicity.

Criticisms of the third assumption — that individual welfare must always depend positively on the consumption of consumer goods — cut to the heart of the economic method. Critics of this assertion reject the consumerism that underpins the capitalist system. Consideration of such issues is beyond the scope of this chapter.

The fourth assumption asserted that individuals act in their own self-interest and are the best judges of their own welfare. This is essentially an assumption of rationality, and seems reasonable, at least on the surface. None the less, there are many criticisms of this assumption. First, there is evidently some question about the inclusion of certain individuals, such as children or the mentally ill. Second, although this argument is anathema to most economists, it is sometimes argued that policy-makers should be paternalist in certain cases. The validity of this is largely a question of personal value judgements, although it can certainly be argued that individuals may have a preference for a paternalist government.

Certain aspects of Irish law reflect such paternalism: examples that come to mind are the illegality of divorce and homosexuality. While these are moral judgements that are not easily explained in economic terms, other examples of apparent paternalism may perhaps be explained in terms of the earlier analysis. The illegality of hard drugs, for example, may stem from an information problem: drug-takers may not be fully aware of the consequences of their actions, and the cost of providing them with better information would be so great that legislation is a better option. Restrictions on the sale of offensive weapons, similarly, may simply be a way of dealing with a (potential) serious externality!

Another influential set of arguments countering assumption (iv) denies that the preferences of consumers can be viewed as a 'primitive' concept; rather, it is necessary to consider the ways in which consumers' preferences may be altered.[16] This may be particularly relevant if goods are bought, not because they satisfy a want themselves, but instead for purposes of conspicuous consumption (i.e., as status symbols), or because of a 'demonstration effect' (owning a good because it is fashionable, or to emulate others); in these cases consumer demand may be particularly susceptible to manipulation. The possibility of artificially created demands and desires was perhaps given its fullest exposition by Galbraith.[17] By means of advertising and other forms of sales promotion, Galbraith argues, wants may be actively created by producers. Certainly, if one accepts the premise that consumer demand can be manipulated, then producers will have an incentive to do so within a market system.

There are arguments to be advanced against this, however. First, advertising may play an important role in providing information to consumers. Second, firms may have other incentives to engage in advertising, such as a wish to create barriers to entry in a particular industry. Third, it is evidently not the case that Galbraithian arguments are applicable in all cases or to all goods. The public clearly cannot always be persuaded to behave as producers might wish: 'Guinness Light' is an example of an Irish product that failed dismally a few years ago, despite extensive promotion.

One final, fundamental objection questions the usefulness of the economic approach of studying society in terms of exchange relationships and individual self-interest. It is freely admitted that such criticisms imply that this chapter, and indeed this book, is of little interest.

3   PROXIMATE POLICY OBJECTIVES

Casual perusal of the newspapers indicates that popular discussion of economic policy is not usually cast in the language of Section 2.

This section therefore moves beyond that rather abstract analysis to consideration of more familiar objectives: full employment, economic growth and economic equality.

The first subsection argues that Pareto-efficiency, while a desirable aim of policy, is not a sufficient goal. This is primarily because it is a very weak principle, and hence not applicable in a large number of cases. Policy-makers need to address questions of equity and intertemporal allocation. The second subsection then considers the problem of specifying the policy-maker's problem to take account of these. The adoption of proximate objectives, embodying different aspects of policy, is proposed. The three proximate objectives of full employment, growth and equality are evaluated in three further subsections.

Beyond Pareto-Efficiency
It was suggested in Section 2 that most people would probably subscribe to the view that Pareto-efficiency is desirable. One reason why consensus on this aim is likely is that Pareto-efficiency is a very weak condition: a policy measure is justified, according to the Pareto criterion, only if nobody is hurt by it. But, as was also noted in Section 2, very few policy proposals will satisfy this condition in practice. So if policy-makers truly only considered Pareto-efficiency, the role of policy would be severely curtailed.

Put slightly differently, the Pareto criterion is of very limited value in practice because many potential allocations are Pareto-non-comparable. By implication, Pareto-efficiency provides no means of choosing among the (possibly infinite) set of efficient outcomes, and the Pareto criterion does not even imply that any efficient outcome is superior to any inefficient outcome. Hence policies that seem desirable on the basis of the reasoning in Section 2 may well not be mandated by Pareto-efficiency.

Another feature of the Pareto criterion is that it provides a basis for policy evaluation relative to some initial position; the set of acceptable outcomes is defined only with respect to this initial position. Pareto-efficiency can perhaps be criticized, therefore, for giving undue reference to the *status quo* as the appropriate reference point for policy decisions. The apparently laudable aim of minimizing the role of value judgements in economic analysis may give rise to a stress on current circumstances that is difficult to justify.

All of these observations essentially reduce to a simple point: efficiency takes no account of distributional issues. A society where millions are starving while its ruler lives in unimaginable luxury may be using and distributing its resources efficiently. Taking a pound from the richest person in society and giving it to the poorest cannot be justified on the grounds of economic efficiency, since even if the poorest person is saved from starvation, the other may be made worse off by having to consume champagne of an inferior vintage.

There are three responses to this problem. First, it can be argued that this weakness of the Pareto criterion is unfortunate, but that economic analysis simply has nothing to contribute in choosing among Pareto-non-comparable outcomes. Second, it is possible to consider *potential* Pareto-improvements — that is, cases where some are made better off by a policy and some worse off, but where the gainers could conceivably compensate the losers. Third, it is possible to include explicit consideration of distribution in formulating policy.

For some economists, it is almost self-evident that economic analysis should attempt to go beyond efficiency and consider questions of distribution. For others, the fact that such analysis requires the introduction of further value judgements makes it virtually worthless. One of the greatest strengths of economics is that it derives interesting and significant results on the basis of the single value judgement that economic efficiency is desirable. A certain reluctance among economists about the introduction of further values is understandable, but the desirability of efficiency is indeed a value judgement; furthermore, it is a value judgement *chosen by economists*. Despite the appeal of efficiency, it is not self-evident that all members of society would accept this judgement, never mind regard it as sufficient for policy analysis.

To put the point more forcefully, consider the extreme (and perhaps paradoxical) case where society contains an anarchic individual who is vehemently opposed to economic reasoning — so much so that any use of economic methods in policy evaluation drastically reduces this person's welfare. Then any economist who believes that Pareto-efficiency is the only basis for policy analysis would presumably be forced to conclude that economics could be of no assistance at all to policy-makers.

Potential Pareto-improvements have superficial appeal as a way out of the non-comparability dilemma. This idea underlies cost-benefit analyses: a policy is judged desirable if its benefits outweigh its costs, irrespective of who gains or loses. But this approach actually introduces an additional value judgement implicitly, by asserting, in essence, that distributional considerations should be irrelevant for economic policy (which is *not* the same as arguing that economics can say nothing about distribution). If a policy would make the richest person in society two pounds richer, and the poorest person one pound poorer, the policy is potentially Pareto-improving.

Alternatively, one can argue that economists can usefully identify potential Pareto-improvements without recommending them; the ultimate decision is then left to a policy-maker who takes account of distributional issues. This is then a restatement of the view that matters of distribution are outside the purview of economics.

The position adopted in this chapter is that the introduction of further value judgements is perfectly legitimate, provided these are made explicit. However, it must be recognized that, in moving beyond the Pareto-criterion, less consensus on policy aims is likely. Mainstream economic analysis also has less to contribute, since many economists concern themselves only with questions of efficiency. The discussion of proximate policy objectives in the following subsections therefore emphasizes critical analysis of the arguments for various objectives, rather than definite policy conclusions.

The foregoing discussion has emphasized that economic efficiency offers no guidance for choosing among reallocations of resources that improve the welfare of some and worsen that of others. There is a subtle aspect of this problem that deserves independent attention: intergenerational equity. Policies presumably need to be judged not only in terms of their effects on the distribution of resources today, but also in terms of the welfare of future generations.

This in turn raises an issue that has been ignored thus far: exactly which individuals should policy-makers care about? One extreme possibility is that policy-makers should concern themselves only with the welfare of those currently alive, and take no account at all of future generations. Alternatively, it may be felt that policy-makers should be concerned, to at least some extent, with the well-being of people in the indefinite future. Deciding between these is a matter for value judgements, but has important consequences for policy, as will be seen below.

The discussion in this section thus suggests that a complete analysis of economic policy should supplement the aim of efficiency with considerations of intragenerational and intergenerational equity. This forms the basis for the formulation of proximate policy objectives, which are discussed in the remainder of this section. It can be noted, finally, that the policy-maker's problem would be relatively simple if aims could be pursued in isolation. (If policy-makers really had access to the lump-sum transfers beloved of economic theory, for example, then the issue of distribution could more legitimately be separated from the pursuit of other goals.) Policy-making is complicated in practice by conflicts between objectives; this is considered in detail in Section 4.

Proximate Policy Objectives
In this and the following subsections a more complete analysis of economic policy is presented. The starting-point is the first two assumptions made in Section 2: that policy-makers seek to maximize social welfare, which in turn depends upon the welfare of individuals. To turn this into a well-defined policy aim, it is necessary to be more precise about how social and individual welfare are related. That is, it is necessary to *aggregate* the welfare of individuals.

One method of aggregation, to which welfare economists have paid much attention, is the formulation of *social welfare functions*. These presuppose that aggregate social welfare can be meaningfully described by some kind of 'summary statistic', or single variable that can be maximized. The simplest form of social welfare function expresses aggregate welfare, written as a number, as a function of the welfare (or utility) of all the different individuals in society.

This idea is conceptually straightforward and provides, from a theoretical perspective, an extremely useful way of thinking about the policy-maker's problem. Social preferences over distribution can be built directly into the form of the function, and policies can be judged by whether or not they increase the value of the function; but, from a practical point of view, social welfare functions have more limited appeal.

By considering the aggregation problem in stages, though, it is possible to make the maximization of a social welfare function more operational. Specifically, the idea is the following: social welfare is taken to depend upon a few target variables, which themselves represent aggregate indices of individual welfare. The usefulness of this approach depends upon the selection of appropriate aggregates. Ideally, the aggregates chosen should possess a number of characteristics: they should be well-defined, measurable, related to individual welfare, and they should offer a means of evaluating policies and assessing their overall impact on welfare.

One possibility would be to choose as aggregates groups of individuals with identifiable characteristics, and then consider social welfare as a function of the welfare of those groups. In practice government policies often take this form, and in many contexts this

71

seems sensible: resources might be devoted to provisions for the handicapped, for example. This method of aggregation might be particularly appropriate if distributional considerations were at the forefront of government policy.

This approach to aggregation has many disadvantages, though. Most importantly, it leaves the question of measurement of group welfare unanswered. In addition, there are no obvious criteria for the selection of groups, and it would be necessary to pay attention to the influence of particular groups upon policy. For these reasons, this is not the method of aggregation adopted in this chapter. None the less, policies aimed at different groups are still of interest, for they can be interpreted as policy *instruments* that may be used in the pursuit of other objectives. The discussion in Chapters 10 and 11 can in part be interpreted in such terms.

The aggregation proposed here is that of selecting proximate objectives of economic policy. These are aims that embody particular aspects of economic policy decisions. While there is some arbitrariness in the choice of proximate objectives, the prior discussion in this chapter suggests that, at a minimum, the aims should be chosen to take account of efficiency, intergenerational equity and intragenerational equity. The following subsections therefore consider objectives — full employment, growth and equality — which capture these elements of the policy-maker's problem.

Under this approach, measures of employment, growth and equality are selected that correspond as closely as possible to each dimension of policy. Policy-makers are then presumed to have some desired ('ideal') value of each of these measures, derived in some manner from individual preferences. The aim of policy is to get as close as possible to these ideal values. This entails a comparison of the ideal with the outcome that would occur in the absence of intervention — that is, in a free market economy possessing the distortions noted in Section 2. It is also important to consider the extent to which policy-makers can affect outcomes.

For each objective, therefore, the following questions are considered. First, drawing on the earlier assumptions about individual welfare, what is the best measure available for each objective? Second, how is the free market outcome likely to compare with the ideal value of the chosen measure? Third, what can the policy-maker achieve?

Before proceeding to this analysis, one final difficulty with the use of social welfare functions should be noted. In keeping with economists' preferences for minimizing value judgements, welfare economists were reluctant to assume that utility was measurable and that comparisons of utility across different individuals were possible. In the development of welfare economics, much attention was therefore given to the problem of formulating social welfare functions without making such assumptions. Ideally, one might wish to find a social welfare function that aggregates everybody's preferences over different possible social states.

Unfortunately, a very important result in social choice theory — Arrow's 'impossibility theorem' — indicates that there is no generally applicable way of deriving such a 'social preference ordering', if certain fairly weak assumptions are to be satisfied.[18] Specifically, Arrow's result implies that the use of social welfare functions requires both cardinal utility and the possibility of interpersonal utility comparisons. To proceed in welfare economics, 'the substantive issue is thus not *whether* interpersonal comparisons should be made, but *how*'.[19]

The main import of this theorem for the following discussion is as follows. The preferences of individuals in society are partially revealed by their market transactions. Market mechanisms, however, do not permit preferences to be articulated on all facets of economic policy. Arrow's theorem indicates that, unfortunately, it is difficult to use a consistent notion of social preferences. There is some difficulty in speaking of, say, a social preference for three per cent economic growth. With some apology, this chapter does not address these issues; to do so would require an extensive survey of the theory of social choice. Instead, it is taken as given that social preferences on certain matters can be articulated, albeit imperfectly, through the political process.

Full Employment
From the discussion in Section 2, it should be clear that many policies that are directed towards efficiency will be microeconomic in nature, since the emphasis of such policies is the correction of distortions in individual markets. An implication of this is that there are no simple measures of the extent to which efficiency is being achieved in practice; a case-by-case analysis of all interventions is required. There are still, however, useful indicators of efficiency for the economy as a whole. In particular, the definition of productive efficiency suggests that there are major inefficiencies present when economic resources are lying idle. Hence a necessary, though certainly not a sufficient, condition for efficiency would appear to be that all economic resources should be in use.

Given this, it is natural to consider the extent to which resources are employed as one indicator of economic efficiency. It is possible to consider the utilization of various resources; for example, the level of capacity utilization is an indicator of the efficient (or otherwise) use of the economy's stock of capital. The discussion here considers only the employment of labour in the economy. This can be justified both in terms of the popular interest in employment and the fact that employment of labour possesses many particular and important characteristics.

Many people probably feel that full employment does not require explicit justification as a policy objective: it seems obvious that unemployment is undesirable and inefficient. But, on the basis of the previous discussion, some subtle issues need to be considered. An obvious but important initial observation is that leisure is a desired commodity. In the labour market, workers exchange leisure for the ability to purchase other goods that they want. Efficiency therefore dictates that individuals should be able to work up to the point where the value of additional leisure equals the value (in terms of other commodities) of additional work. If this is the case for everyone, then all unemployment is *voluntary*, and does not signal inefficiency.

If, conversely, some individuals would like to work at the going wage, but are unable to do so, then they are said to be involuntarily unemployed. In this case, the supply of labour exceeds the demand for labour at the given wage. As will be discussed below, it is possible that economies may exhibit major coordination failures; that is, market failures of various types may give rise to considerable involuntary unemployment.

Given current levels of unemployment in Ireland, it may seem peculiar (and perhaps in poor taste) even to raise the distinction between voluntary and involuntary unemployment. Certainly, when large numbers state that they are unable to find work at the going wage, it seems perverse to deny the existence of involuntary unemployment. The distinction is important, though, because involuntary unemployment is the concept that ideally should be captured by an unemployment measure. Unfortunately (partly because of difficulties in defining involuntary unemployment precisely), it is not clear to what extent available measures capture this notion. The following paragraphs consider some of the difficulties of measuring unemployment and the deficiencies of the available measures.

Note immediately that, though employment and unemployment measures do provide information on the state of the economy, a concentration on employment at a point in time suppresses much information about employment and unemployment statistics over time. A more detailed and accurate evaluation of the data would also require consideration of quit rates, layoff rates, unemployment duration and labour force turnover.[20]

Some difficulties with the measurement of unemployment can be seen by considering the numerator and the denominator of possible unemployment measures. Consider the denominator first. The most obvious base for an employment measure is the labour force; this is indeed used in calculating unemployment rates. But this does not capture the fact that some unemployment may be represented by withdrawal from the labour force in times of recession (the 'discouraged worker' phenomenon). The tradition of emigration from Ireland reinforces this problem: Irish labour is internationally mobile. In other words, unemployment measures are suspect because the denominator is relatively volatile and is affected by factors which also influence the numerator. Choosing an appropriate numerator for an employment measure also presents some conceptual problems. For example, certain individuals, engaged in productive activity, are not registered as employed (or as members of the labour force); the obvious example is that of men and women doing unpaid housework.

Since labour is not homogeneous, aggregate unemployment measures may conceal marked divergences in unemployment rates for different sectors of the economy. This in turn makes the pursuit of full employment more difficult, for certain types of labour may be in excess demand while others are in excess supply. That is, there may be overemployment and unemployment in certain submarkets even if aggregate measures indicate relatively low unemployment. A similar divergence may apply across regions: in general, the unemployment rate will differ markedly across regions, but this will not be revealed by aggregate unemployment measures.

Another problem arises because inefficiencies may take the form of underemployment rather than unemployment. For example, if an individual has a job, but would like to work more hours and is unable to do so, then this is inefficient underemployment that will not find its way into official measures. Put differently, a redistribution of a fixed quantity of work across the labour force could have marked differences in measured unemployment.

Further difficulties arise with the choice of 'full employment' — that is, the ideal level of unemployment. Full employment should not be understood as meaning zero unemployment, for that would imply a static economy with no labour force turnover (assuming that changing jobs must sometimes imply some interruption in employment). It is reasonable to allow for a certain amount of unemployment associated with job search, turnover, and entry and exit from the labour force. This is known as frictional unemployment. Some frictional unemployment is necessary for the efficient functioning of the economy. The amount of frictional unemployment will not in general be constant over time. It will depend, among other factors, upon the microeconomic features of the labour market, such as the mechanisms which exist for matching supply and demand (employment agencies, etc.).

A second source of unemployment arises from the seasonality of certain occupations. Seasonal unemployment exists whenever there are sectors of the economy, such as construction, tourism or agriculture, that are influenced by seasonal factors; hence it is important in Ireland. Again, it is necessary to decide how much seasonal unemployment is acceptable.

The remaining issues to be considered are whether or not full employment would be achieved in the absence of policy interventions, and, if not, whether or not policy-makers can intervene to establish full employment. Active government intervention is justified only if there is involuntary unemployment and if government policies can be used to eliminate it.

The argument suggesting that policy-makers should intervene to achieve full employment is based on the proposition that important market failures result in large amounts of involuntary unemployment. For many years, the consensus among macroeconomists was that such 'Keynesian' unemployment was of considerable practical significance, and that active demand-management policies could be profitably used to achieve full employment. Since Ireland is a small open economy, though, the ability of Irish policy-makers to bring about full employment by means of aggregate demand management is extremely limited; this is discussed in Chapter 6. Microeconomic interventions to correct specific market failures may still be of great practical importance (see Chapter 8).

More recently, some economists have denied the existence of Keynesian unemployment, and have argued instead that markets do in general work efficiently. On this reasoning, unemployment is voluntary, arising solely because individuals value leisure, and hence policy-makers should not intervene to seek full employment. The *New* Classical macroeconomics asserts that the economy cannot be moved from full employment except transiently, as a result of unanticipated monetary shocks.[21] The basic implication of this reasoning is that there is no exploitable trade-off between unemployment and inflation (i.e., the 'Phillips Curve' is vertical). Thus, under this argument, policy-makers should not intervene to ensure full employment, cannot do so successfully anyway, and will only make matters worse if they try.

While this debate will not be discussed in detail, it should be noted that New Classical theory does not appear to provide a good explanation of short-run changes in employment, although macroeconomists doubt the existence of a long-run trade-off between inflation and unemployment. And, though these arguments are logically coherent, it must be stressed again that they rest on the *assumption* that markets are efficient, and so their relevance to real economies can be questioned. Above all, the conclusion that all unemployment is voluntary hardly corresponds with popular or political conceptions of current Irish unemployment.

Finally, very recent research has started to resurrect some elements of Keynesian economics, arguing that coordination failures may arise from imperfect competition and/or search externalities.[22] When such imperfections are present, economies may get stuck at inefficient levels of output and employment, and there may be a role for government policy. The implications — if any — of this for Irish policy-makers are difficult to infer as yet, but it seems likely that the openness of the Irish economy may again be a barrier to effective policy. A corollary of this is that coordinated economic policies (say, among the countries of the European Community) may be particularly desirable.

Economic Growth
As with full employment, the desirability of economic growth is apparently taken as self-evident by many commentators. But again, from the perspective of this chapter, it is not clear *a priori* that increased growth should be pursued by policy-makers. This is because the important feature of growth is that it embodies a choice or trade-off between consumption in the present and consumption in the future; in other words, decreased consumption today will permit increased consumption at some future date, and *vice versa*.

Growth should thus *not* be understood as referring to increased consumption in the future in conjunction with unchanged consumption in the present. Such a view of growth would imply that it is possible to get something for nothing, which will not be the case if resources are being used efficiently. The pursuit of efficiency as a separate objective precludes this view of growth. Consequently, if policies are designed to affect growth, they are ultimately concerned with the sacrifice of consumption at one time in order to consume more at some other time.

The selection of a desired growth rate for the economy therefore depends upon society's relative evaluation of current and future consumption, or, in technical terminology, the social discount rate. The choice of appropriate policies to influence the growth rate of the economy in turn depends upon the rate of growth in the absence of intervention relative to this desired rate. That is, increased growth is not an objective to be sought at any cost.

The discussion in this subsection is as follows. First, the choice of a measure of growth is considered. (This implicitly involves choosing a definition of growth also, for economic growth can really only be defined as a change in some economic variable.) The most important question concerns whether or not it is possible to find a measure that adequately captures intergenerational equity. In other words, can increased growth really be associated with higher welfare of future generations relative to those alive today? Whether or not policy-makers would wish actively to encourage growth is then considered; in particular, there is some discussion of whether freely operating markets might tend to lead to too much or too little growth, relative to the social optimum. The subsection concludes with a brief consideration of the ability of policy-makers to affect economic growth in Ireland.

As a first approximation, economic growth refers to an increase in the output of the economy. Output, in turn, is the production of goods and services in a given time period. An initial problem, therefore, is the choice of a more precise definition of output. The relationship between changes in output and individual welfare, meanwhile, also depends upon changes in the population and the population structure of the economy, as well as the way in which increased output is distributed. Changes in the population structure might have an effect to the extent that different age groups may have different needs and desires for goods and services, although the importance of this is difficult to assess.

Changes in population would certainly be expected to influence the extent to which increases in output can be associated with increases in individual welfare. This suggests that output *per capita* may be the most appropriate measure of economic growth. In fact this entails a further assumption about the relationship between social and individual welfare, to the effect that social welfare is increased when the general living standards of the population increase, and is not increased if living standards are unaltered, but the population increases. In some sense, that is, social welfare is measured by average utility. This apparently innocuous point might be considered to have important implications since, in the absence of other criteria, aggregate welfare would be increased by the death of any individual below the average! More seriously, it might be interpreted to imply a tacit assumption about the desirability of birth control in overpopulated regions or of abortion of damaged foetuses.

The next step is the selection of a measure of output that is a useful indicator of welfare. An initial observation is that, in practice, most measures of output tend to move together, so the choice may be of limited practical importance. At a theoretical level, though, it seems reasonable to exclude replacement investment and to include net factor income from abroad and net transfers from abroad. Also, welfare is presumably affected by real rather than nominal changes, so output should be expressed in real terms.

Given that economic growth can best be measured, in this context, by changes in real output *per capita*, the more fundamental question is whether or not it is appropriate to associate this variable with changes in aggregate welfare (that is, by assumption, with changes in individual welfare). In other words, does increased growth of real output *per capita* imply that future generations are relatively better off? To a large extent, this is simply equivalent to considering whether or not output *per capita* is a useful static measure of economic welfare.

The fundamental reason for believing that output *per capita* and economic welfare are related is assumption (iii) from Section 2: the welfare of individuals depends upon the goods and services that they consume. There are important qualifications to this argument, though. First, economic growth as measured will not include many factors that represent real welfare costs (and benefits) arising from growth; and, second, measured growth will include apparent increases in income that are in fact associated with decreases in welfare.

One example of the first reason might arise if economic growth is brought about by increased labour-force participation, which implies a decrease in leisure time; assuming that leisure is desired, this represents a cost that is neglected by the growth measure. It is certainly true that voluntary participation in the labour market would suggest that the increased real income more than compensates for the decreased leisure, but changes in output do not measure the *net* gain.[23] An even more important example arises from the presence of externalities: much consumption and production gives rise to costs and benefits that are associated with economic growth but are not included in measured economic growth. An example of the argument that measured economic growth may actually include welfare costs would be increased medical costs (i.e. output of hospitals) arising from, for example, pollution externalities or work-related accidents.

There is also a small but influential body of opinion that explicitly rejects growth as a policy aim. This is largely because of disagreement with assumption (iii), for the sort of reasons discussed in Section 2.[24] (Assumption (iii) asserted that individual welfare depends positively on the consumption of goods and services.) To date, this view seems to have been less popular in Ireland than in other European countries, where these issues have been brought into the political arena by (for example) the Ecology Party in Britain and the 'Greens' in Germany. Although these countries are richer than Ireland, it may be that such views will gain increasing importance in an Irish context.

A detailed consideration of this view is not possible here, but one observation may be in order. One subset of these arguments is concerned particularly with pollution of the environment and/or the rapid depletion of limited resources. While both of these are matters of importance that should be considered by policy-makers, they are problems that are best addressed directly; limiting growth, by contrast, is an extremely indirect and inefficient approach. As Solow has put it: 'what no-growth would accomplish, it would do by cutting off your face to spite your nose'.[25]

Despite these caveats, the desire of individuals for goods and services does still suggest that output *per capita* is an approximate indicator of welfare. So, if the growth rate increases, it is reasonable to conclude that the welfare of future generations relative to current generations is increasing. If policy-makers wish to address matters of intertemporal equity, then economic growth is a suitable proximate objective. The remaining question is then how the socially desired level of growth compares with the free market level.

The first point to recognize is that individuals in society do make intertemporal choices. Most obviously, people decide upon their present level of consumption and the amount they wish to save for future consumption. In a perfectly functioning economy, these saving decisions would generate the optimal amount of investment, from the point of view of the current generation. It would then not be appropriate for policy-makers to intervene and affect the rate of growth, as far as these individuals were concerned.

Further, since an individual's welfare may depend in part upon the welfare of her children (and, by implication, grandchildren, great-grandchildren, etc.), the interests of future generations are not completely excluded when decisions are made in the present. There is no immediate reason to conclude that intervention to encourage growth is socially desirable.

It is possible, though, to make the explicit value judgement that policy-makers should take direct account of the welfare of future generations. Such an opinion does in fact seem frequently to be expressed. In other words, individuals can decide to take collective action to ensure economic outcomes that need not arise as a result of individual behaviour. In this case, encouragement of economic growth (for example, by taxing current consumption to provide investment subsidies) may be an appropriate policy response.

There are also efficiency arguments for growth. That is, there may be massive market failures in those markets linking the present and the uncertain future, implying that policy-makers should target growth as a proxy for the infeasible task of correcting all the deficiencies of the market. The principal market failures are probably in capital markets and markets for insuring against risk, and it can be argued that the net effect of these is likely to be insufficient growth. Tobin has argued, for example, that market imperfections and externalities may imply that the social return to growth is in excess of that determined by private investment and may therefore exceed the social discount rate.[26]

A second argument would note that, historically, technical progress has been an important determinant of economic growth. Further, it can be maintained that there are substantial positive externalities associated with technological advances, since the returns to invention and innovation may not always accrue solely to the inventors and innovators. As a consequence, there may be insufficient investment, from a social point of view, in research and development, and so the growth rate of the economy may be suboptimal.

As is explained in Chapter 7, though, the rate of growth in Ireland is actually determined to a great extent by exogenous influences. Thus, while Irish policy-makers have some influence on growth rates, the impact of domestic policies is severely curtailed. Irish policy-makers cannot address market imperfections in other countries that may restrict economic growth in Ireland.

Finally, the expectation of continued growth, outside the influence of Irish policy, raises the provocative question of why current Irish consumption should be limited to promote growth. The appropriate redistribution may be from future generations to the present: 'why should we poor folk make any sacrifices for those who will in any case live in luxury in the future?'[27]

Equality

As was argued at length at the start of Section 3, the major limitation of economic efficiency as a policy aim is that it allows little consideration of distributional problems. Most importantly, the application of the Pareto-criterion implies that the initial distribution of society's resources is a principal determinant of the ultimate distribution. Discussion of equality is therefore motivated by the idea that society, and hence policy-makers, may have explicit distributional goals also. In this subsection, the definition of equality is considered more carefully, and some possible measures are discussed. Some of the arguments for and against equality are considered, paying particular attention to the underlying value judgements, and the free market outcome is also evaluated.

Two types of equality can be distinguished.[28] First, it is possible to embody principles of equality in the functioning or operation of the economic system. For example, legislation might be passed requiring that all employment pay the same hourly wage. A more relevant example is that of *equality of opportunity*, which states that the economic system should contain no biases that lead to any individual's having a greater or lesser chance than any other of profiting from the system. Second, equality can be defined in terms of the distribution of society's output after economic transactions have taken place. Examples of this are equality of incomes or equality of wealth.

The assumptions made about social and individual welfare in Section 2 suggest that welfare depends upon actual, not potential, consumption of goods and services. This in turn suggests that any evaluation of these different definitions of equality should be in terms of the distribution of output that they imply. For example, equality of hourly wages would imply that the resulting distribution of goods and services would be based upon work input.

Equality of opportunity suggests that the ultimate distribution of society's output would depend upon a number of different factors: most notably, ability, work input and chance. Equality of opportunity, in other words, implies a meritocratic distribution with a substantial random component. An individual's innate abilities are very important in determining distribution; similarly, the amount of work she does will have an impact. But exogenous shocks — chance factors — will also affect an individual's 'reward' from the system under equality of opportunity. Shifts in demand for an individual's product, for example, or shifts in the supply of close substitutes or important inputs, will have significant effects.

Definitions of equality that are expressed directly in terms of the ultimate distribution are therefore likely to be of greater use. Equality of incomes and equality of wealth are relatively straightforward concepts. The discussion in Section 2, though, might suggest that policies should ideally be cast in terms of equality of welfare. At the very least, it is important to ask how inequalities of welfare might be missed by income or wealth measures.

The most important element of this distinction is that equality of welfare takes explicit account of 'needs'; it is recognized, that is, that individuals who are disadvantaged — for example, handicapped persons — may in general require more income to bring them to the same level of welfare as those who are not. In its most direct form, this is Marx's proposal: 'from each according to his ability, to each according to his needs'.[29] A second point is that, because leisure is valued, labour input will have an effect on welfare: an individual who works a fifty-hour week for a given income will in general be at a lower level of welfare than someone who obtains the same income from working twenty-five hours a week.

Measurement of equality is considerably simpler when the definition chosen refers directly to the distribution of society's output, although there are still some difficulties, both conceptual and pragmatic.[30] For example, is it more appropriate to measure inequalities of income or wealth? As income includes earnings from wealth, it does seem that it better captures the idea that welfare results from consumption of goods and services. But this neglects the fact that wealth may also provide utility, either for its own sake, or through increased security or increased power. A more satisfactory (but less easily measurable) possibility is *permanent income:* current wealth plus the discounted value of expected future earnings. In any case, there are some difficulties associated with the precise definitions of income and wealth.[31]

There are also problems associated with the appropriate choice of unit; measurement in practice is often in terms of the individual, but policy measures designed to reduce inequality frequently relate to households. In some cases, the reduction of inequality between regions may also be an appropriate proximate objective. In addition, it is necessary to choose a suitable time period for comparison; this might be as short as a week, or as long as a lifetime. Finally, and perhaps most fundamentally, inequality is almost always considered at a national level, but there is no obvious logical reason why this should be the case. If Irish individuals subscribe to the objective of equality, then it would seem reasonable that this should apply globally as well as nationally. While efforts are often made to reduce inequality within a nation, aid from the Western industrialized nations to less developed economies is minimal, given the extent of inequality between them.[32]

Notwithstanding all these difficulties, there are a number of possible measures of inequality. The simplest of these are summary statistics on income distribution. For example, it is possible to examine the range of incomes (or wealth) in the population being studied, or the standard deviation, or the coefficient of variation. Statistical measures have also been designed specifically with inequality in mind, such as the (related) Lorenz curve and Gini coefficient, and other more sophisticated measures.[33]

It was noted earlier that equality of incomes and equality of welfare cannot be directly associated, and that the latter might be a preferable measure. The basic presumption that welfare and consumption are closely linked for any given individual does suggest that, at least over a significant and relevant range, inequalities of welfare and inequalities of income will be associated. More precisely, it can be argued that it is reasonable to assume that individuals have similar capacities for enjoyment, and thus similar welfare levels from the same income, unless there is particular evidence (in terms of, say, needs or work input) to the contrary.

A more rigorous defence of this argument is as follows. Suppose there is an ideal, but unknown, distribution of income corresponding to desired equality. Then total equality of income will minimize the maximum possible arithmetic divergence from this ideal; similarly, beginning from a position of inequality, measures to decrease inequality are more likely to move the distribution closer to the ideal than away from it. Put another way, equality of incomes maximizes *expected* social welfare.[34]

Having considered the problem of measurement of equality, it is now useful to consider some of the arguments that can be proposed for equality. These are the sort of questions that must be considered in the attempt to identify the 'ideal' degree of inequality. It must be stressed again that these arguments require the introduction of further value judgements or ethical principles.

The most basic such argument is probably that distribution according to needs may be ethically desirable. This is simply based on the following precept: if certain individuals in a society are disadvantaged (for example, handicapped, elderly, or involuntarily unemployed), then society should seek to help them or compensate them for this disadvantage, rather than hinder them. While measurement of needs obviously poses problems, it is likely that there is some consensus on such matters; Sen proposes the thought experiment of deciding whether one would prefer to be individual

A (say, a healthy person) with a given income or individual B (a handicapped person) with the same income, in order to make a judgement on relative needs.[35]

A number of influential arguments for equality are based on the idea that distribution should be determined according to principles that individuals would choose in an 'original position'; that is, prior to their being randomly allocated a place in society. One such argument is based on an assumption of risk-aversion: the idea that people, in general, attach a positive value to security.[36] Assume, for simplicity, that utility is measurable and that interpersonal comparisons are possible. Consider now the situation where, in the original position, an individual has to choose among possible states of the world, which differ in the distribution of utility across individuals but have the property that the (mathematical) expectation of utility is equal in all states. If the individual is risk-averse, then she will prefer a distribution where the utility of all individuals is equalized.

A closely-related argument is that of Rawls' 'Difference Principle'.[37] Rawls suggests that individuals in the original position would adopt a 'maximin' criterion, whereby the optimal social state is one in which the welfare (or income) of the worst-off individual is maximized. In terms of the above construct, this can be characterized by an assumption that individuals are infinitely risk-averse; the Rawlsian thought-experiment effectively removes the restriction that expected utility is constant in all states. For example, the Rawlsian principle would suggest that a social state where all individuals received an income of IR£10,000 would be preferred to a state where one individual received IR£9,999 and everyone else received IR£11,000. (Infinite risk-aversion implies here that an arbitrarily small probability of an arbitrarily small decrease in utility cannot be compensated for by an arbitrarily large probability of an arbitrarily large increase in utility.)

A related argument (which requires interpersonal comparability of utility) starts from an assumption that all individuals have equal capacity for enjoyment of commodities (identical utility functions), with the property that there is diminishing marginal utility of income. If the value judgment is made that society should seek to maximize total welfare (simple utilitarianism), then the optimal distribution of output will be egalitarian. This argument is subject to many objections, as utilitarianism of this form may imply distributions that are intuitively displeasing when the assumption of identical individuals is relaxed (for example, it may run contrary to the equality-of-welfare principle if needy individuals also obtain less utility from a given income).

One direct argument for a merit-oriented system of distribution derives from a consideration of historical factors. Nozick has suggested that distribution at any time should depend upon historical factors that determine individuals' entitlements, and that it is therefore invalid to consider distribution at a point of time, independent of these entitlements.[38] A welfare-economics approach, he argues, is inadequate because it cannot take account of such factors. It should be evident from the discussion in this chapter that this need not be so: the possibility of certain entitlements arising from work input, for example, is not in principle excluded in welfare economics. When this is recognized, Nozick's 'entitlements' differ little from the meritocratic rewards that have been discussed already. Nozick's argument does however highlight the fact that, under a meritocratic system, the initial distribution of economic resources is a crucial determinant of the final distribution.

The preceding arguments have suggested that both explicit welfare criteria and facility of measurement indicate that a useful definition of equality for policy purposes will be in terms of the final distribution of output. They also suggest that a socially-desired final distribution is unlikely to be obtained by the operation of market processes. The source of the conflict between such a socially-desired distribution and one implied by free markets is clear: the market mechanism represents — at best — equality of opportunity. The free operation of the market will thus lead to a distribution of output that depends upon the initial distribution of resources (i.e. initial inequalities), and meritocratic and chance factors. An implication of this is that those who are initially disadvantaged will, in addition to their handicap, receive less of society's output; market processes will thus tend to exacerbate existing inequalities, in contrast to, for example, a 'needs' principle of distribution.

This must be qualified in one important respect. People may have a *preference* for some redistribution.[39] This could be for altruistic or pragmatic reasons: marked inequalities may generate costs arising from social tensions. Inequalities between readily identifiable social groups may be particularly likely to lead to social unrest; examples of this might be Northern Ireland, South Africa, and, more generally, workers' revolutions and general strikes. In such cases the affluent may have a definite interest in redistribution. But the basic observation that the initial distribution affects the set of acceptable outcomes remains unaltered.

In practice, free markets are unlikely even to achieve equality of opportunity. There are a number of reasons for this. Perhaps most importantly, power structures within the economic and political system will tend to operate against equality of opportunity. To the extent that power and influence (through diverse channels such as personal contacts, control of economic resources, intergenerational transfers of wealth, etc.) do affect the workings of the economic system — and it is evident that they will do so for rational economic reasons, among others — the system will not operate in a manner that allows full equality of opportunity. In addition, inequalities in education, job opportunities and access to capital markets obstruct equality of opportunity in Ireland and other economies.[40]

Free markets in practice thus give rise to a distribution that is based on meritocratic and chance factors, and is further biased by the distribution of power and by major market imperfections. Furthermore, the ultimate distribution depends crucially upon the initial distribution of resources. The decision on whether greater or lesser equality would be socially preferred depends on the existing distribution of resources, but there are many reasons for believing that free markets will not achieve desired equality. To the extent that the arguments for equality presented here are accepted, it appears probable that greater equality might be desired. But, it must be stressed again, this decision depends ultimately on the value judgements of individuals in society.

Finally, there are few constraints in principle upon the ability of policy-makers to achieve redistributions by means of taxes and transfers. One possible difficulty is that higher tax rates may encourage tax avoidance and tax evasion, as is discussed in Chapter 5. The relevance of this is borne out by the undoubted importance of the underground economy in Ireland. The major barriers to redistribution, though, arise because of possible distortionary effects of taxes; these are considered in Section 4.

4   CONFLICTS AND COMPLEMENTS

The discussion in this section is concerned with the trade-offs between objectives — the fact that policy-makers cannot, in fact, pursue objectives in isolation. Although it may be the case that, other things being equal, efficiency, a given rate of growth, or a given degree of equality are desirable, policy-makers must recognize that gains in one area may entail sacrifices in another. Equivalently, objectives can sometimes be complementary. In either case, it follows that it is not possible to pursue economic aims in isolation; successful design of policy requires an understanding of these trade-offs. In particular, coherent policy decisions require that policy-makers know both their relative valuation of these aims and the extent to which these objectives are mutually feasible.[41] In the following subsections, the trade-offs between different pairs of objectives are considered.

Full Employment and Growth

If policy-makers wish to redistribute resources (either at a point in time or intertemporally), then they will have to levy taxes and pay out subsidies. Since (as was mentioned earlier) lump-sum taxes are not, in reality, available, these fiscal measures will in general have some distortionary effects. Redistributions, in other words, may imply some loss of efficiency. If increased growth is desirable because of market failures, conversely then, correction of these is also consistent with increased efficiency. A detailed discussion of all the trade-offs between growth and full employment that are relevant in Ireland is not possible here, for it would require a comprehensive and systematic analysis of all the relevant policies and constraints that apply to the Irish economy. Some examples must serve to illustrate the nature of these choices.

As one example, consider expansionary policies designed to promote full employment in the present. If these generate increased consumption and investment (and do not promote exports) then this will result in a balance-of-payments deficit, leading eventually to greater interest payments on the national debt. Such a policy, in other words, alters intertemporal choices by increasing current welfare at the expense of future welfare. Trade-offs may also arise because of market imperfections. In an economy characterized by Keynesian unemployment, increased investment may imply that capital displaces labour, and worsens unemployment. More generally, policies aimed at increasing Ireland's growth rate by improving its long-run competitive position in the world economy (see Chapter 7) will probably not be compatible with policies designed to reduce unemployment in the short run. Given limited resources, policy-makers therefore face a choice between correcting distortions that inhibit growth and correcting those that affect employment.

A rather different sort of trade-off between growth and full employment may arise because the appropriate definition of full employment will differ with the growth rate of the economy. Increased economic growth will in general require increased labour mobility and hence higher labour turnover. Frictional unemployment will therefore tend to increase if the economy grows more rapidly, implying that the 'full employment' rate of unemployment will be higher. Also, if growth is accompanied by increasing specialization and an increase in the size of firms, this effect may be exacerbated by a decrease in loyalty (on the part of both firms and workers) and hence increased quit rates and layoffs. Similarly, economic expansion will tend to induce movement into the labour force. Finally, a growing economy may face increased problems arising from the heterogeneity of labour; there may be bottlenecks and shortages of specific skills as new technologies render old skills less useful. This serves to increase frictional unemployment further.

There are also some reasons to expect that growth and full employment will be complementary. Increased demand for Irish goods is consistent with both reductions in Keynesian unemployment and increased growth. If the economy is characterized by positive search externalities, also, then increased economic activity may be consistent with greater efficiency. Further, when labour markets are tight (i.e. when unemployment is low), individuals will generally have more choice about their work and be able to change employment more freely, which may imply a more efficient allocation of resources.

Full Employment and Equality
The discussion in Sections 2 and 3 has indicated that there may be marked trade-offs between efficiency and equality. The nature of these can be seen most clearly by recalling the two types of equality distinguished in Section 3. Equality of opportunity is, in principle, highly compatible with the aim of economic efficiency. But, as already mentioned in the previous subsection, increases in equity may require divergences from the outcome of competitive market processes, and hence be inconsistent with economic efficiency.

The close connection between equality of opportunity and efficiency is readily apparent. Inequalities of opportunity imply that some individuals are excluded from trading in certain markets; this is an immediate source of inefficiency. Meritocratic distribution, furthermore, does not distort work incentives.

Equality in distribution may conflict with efficiency, however. First, there is the obvious point that redistribution will generally make some worse-off and hence violate the Pareto-criterion. Second, it may also be the case that policies designed to achieve redistribution will prevent resources from being used optimally, because of distortionary taxes; greater equality may therefore imply that the total output to be distributed will fall. The design of policies to achieve distributive goals must recognize that, in general, work incentives will be altered.

The disincentive effects of income taxation are actually unclear, since income and substitution effects have opposite effects on work incentives. If individuals wish to maintain a given standard of living, then increased marginal tax rates could conceivably increase work input. The importance of financial incentives is also lessened by the fact that well-paid jobs tend to be more pleasant, and yield greater job satisfaction, than low-paid work.[42]

Considering now the particular conflicts between equality and full employment, trade-offs are also apparent. In perfectly functioning labour markets, wages are simply supply- and demand-determined prices. Given that there are many different types of labour that are not perfect substitutes, and differing demands and supplies of each, it is evident that full employment in all these submarkets will probably involve large inequalities of income. In particular, when supply is relatively restricted and/or demand high, the equilibrium wage will be high, and conversely. Moves to increase equality will generally involve market distortions and an excess supply of labour in some markets. While this point is simple, it indicates the fundamental difficulty involved in increasing equality in a market economy.

It should also be remembered that the existence of unemployment has major distributional implications, implying that the pursuit of full employment and increased equality may be complementary. There can be little doubt that the unemployed bear the major costs of economic recessions (even though, in Ireland as in other developed economies, these distributional effects are partially offset by unemployment benefits). This is exacerbated by the fact that employment may yield non-monetary benefits (job satisfaction, self-esteem, social standing, or a desire to contribute to society, for example). Ireland is a society where status and identity are closely associated with employment, and so unemployment carries significant non-financial costs.

Even among the unemployed, the burden of unemployment is spread unequally. Much measured unemployment is accounted for by the long-term unemployed — that is, those who, once unemployed, remain out of work for long periods. In practice, the distributional impact of unemployment is probably one of the most important reasons for the pursuit of full employment.

Growth and Equality
In one sense, these objectives are perhaps the most complementary.

The reason for this is that growth, which implies relatively higher income in the future, may make intragenerational redistribution (in the future) possible with changes in *relative* incomes only. Increased equality may be possible without any reductions in the *absolute* standard of living of anyone, so it may be possible for redistribution to occur without violation of the Pareto principle. This is a persuasive argument for economic growth.

The validity of this reasoning strictly depends on whether the increased incomes from growth accrue to individuals or to policy-makers; if individuals receive the extra income, then redistribution still implies that some individuals benefit while others lose. In this case, the argument that increased growth facilitates redistribution must rest on a presumption that individuals are prepared to accept higher marginal tax rates as their incomes increase. While this is not obviously true, it does seem probable that it is easier to achieve redistributions when incomes are growing; people are probably more aware of a cut in their living standards than of the fact that their incomes are growing more slowly than they might otherwise be. And, in passing, it might be noted that even if growth does not lead to greater equality, it will still usually imply that the absolute standard of living of the poor will increase.

There is also an argument that suggests a trade-off between growth and equality, relating to savings and investment decisions in a capitalist society. On this reasoning, savings are necessary in a capitalist economy for investment in capital, which will in turn lead to increased future incomes; further, it is argued, the marginal propensity to save is higher at higher income levels. As a consequence, increased equality may imply a reduction in investment and hence a reduction in growth.

There are a number of points to note about this argument, both in general and in relation to the Irish economy. First, this reasoning merely suggests that some inequality of incomes may be necessary, and thus need have no logical connection to any particular distribution criterion. In particular, this argument does not of itself justify existing inequalities, nor does it necessarily favour distribution according to merit. Further, the argument does depend crucially on both its premises; and both of them are open to question.[43]

Most importantly of all, the argument has little — if any — relevance for policy decisions in Ireland. This is because, as explained in Chapter 7, there is no direct link between savings and investment in a small open economy, provided that financial markets operate efficiently. Thus one of the most common justifications for inequality in a capitalist society is probably wholly inapplicable in Ireland.

5   CONCLUSIONS

The discussion in this chapter has emphasized a number of aspects of the analysis of policy objectives. First, it has been argued that coherent economic policy-making requires that policies be directed towards three distinct aims: efficiency, intergenerational distribution and intragenerational distribution. Throughout the analysis, the value judgements and institutional assumptions needed for the arguments have been made as explicit as possible, and some attempt was made to indicate the weaknesses and deficiencies of them. Whether or not the violation of these assumptions in real economies leads to substantive differences in the conclusions drawn is partly an empirical matter, and partly a matter of individual judgement.

Second, detailed attention was paid to the problems of measuring the economy's performance in these three areas of policy, and it was suggested that measures of full employment, growth and equality can be utilized to this end. Third, some consideration was given to the extent to which pursuit of these aims is mutually feasible; that is, trade-offs between objectives of policy were discussed. Fourth, the discussion considered the extent to which explicit intervention by policy-makers might be required to achieve desired targets in terms of these objectives.

These factors were stressed because they are all essential for coherent policy decisions. Ideally, policy-makers should have an understanding of the ultimate aims of policy, of the relative social evaluation of these aims, and of the ways in which different policies interact and limit the policy decisions that can be made. Further, good policy decisions obviously require knowledge of the policy instruments that exist and the ways in which they can be used to achieve these aims. It is important to remember that, in Ireland, the effects of almost all policy instruments are influenced by the smallness and openness of the economy. The relevance of this for Irish economic policy will become even more apparent in subsequent chapters.

A major theme of this chapter is that Pareto-efficiency does not provide a sufficient basis for economic policy analysis, and that it is desirable to have well-defined aims in terms of other objectives. It therefore follows that policies should be directed both at efficiency and at these other aims; policies which are designed to achieve efficiency alone will not be sufficient to achieve the aims of policy-makers. If it were the case that the objectives discussed here could all be pursued independently of one another, then the existence of different objectives would not pose major difficulties for the design of economic policy. Unfortunately, the existence of trade-offs between objectives implies that policy aims do conflict.

One implication of policy trade-offs is that it is almost certainly undesirable to pursue one aim irrespective of the costs in terms of other objectives. For example, it is evident that it would not be optimal to direct all economic policy and economic resources to faster growth. This applies as much to the aim of economic efficiency as any other. If productive efficiency can only be achieved at a cost in terms of divergences from socially-desired redistributions, then complete productive efficiency is unlikely to be optimal. By implication, a system of perfectly competitive markets will also be suboptimal. Further, it may be the case that policies designed to correct market failures will have costs in terms of other objectives. The lesson of all this is that particular policies should be assessed in terms of their implications for all objectives, and no objective should be given absolute priority.

A corollary of this is that it is inappropriate to criticize a particular aim of policy on the grounds that it would be undesirable to exclude other considerations in practice. For example, economic efficiency should not be dismissed as an aim of policy because it implies no concern with distribution; similarly, increased economic equality should not be argued to be undesirable simply because it may generate some inefficiency. This point may seem obvious; it is mentioned only because it is frequently neglected in discussions of policy aims.

It is also worth noting that difficulties of measurement do not provide a good reason for dismissing an objective; it may be possible to make progress towards a policy goal even when the gains cannot be measured precisely. Equally, the fact that policy measures are sometimes crude and ineffective in practice does not imply that the aims of policy have been incorrectly selected; rather, failures of policies in practice are a source of information for the design of better policy in the future.

One unsatisfactory aspect of the pursuit of proximate objectives should also be stressed. They are useful as a means of defining and evaluating policy, but they represent, at best, an imperfect simplification of the policy-maker's problem. Because they are simple measures, they ignore a great deal. Measured equality might increase while some disadvantaged members of society are made even worse off. Unemployment might fall, despite increased inefficiencies.

Finally, it should be emphasized again that there are substantial problems in the articulation of social preferences over different objectives. But, while the derivation of social preferences is not straightforward, political mechanisms do exist, however imperfect they may be, to allow individuals to express such preferences. There is no particular reason why such opinions should be the same as those revealed in economic markets, and there is no reason to dismiss economic preferences voiced through the political process.

All individuals are entitled to their value judgements on the objectives considered here, and to express their preferences through all available mechanisms. This chapter has sought to clarify some of the strengths and weaknesses of various arguments for different objectives. But, ultimately, the appropriate choice of policy should depend upon the value judgements of individuals in society.

Footnotes
1 Some of the arguments presented here draw on readings by J.W. O'Hagan and M. Lipton in earlier editions of this book.
2 It by no means commands universal assent, however. One important reason for this is an intriguing result of A.K. Sen's, demonstrating a possible inconsistency between the Pareto principle and certain liberal, or libertarian, principles — in particular, the notion (which dates back at least to J.S. Mill) that there are certain decisions which should be the concern only of the individual who makes them. (See A.K. Sen, 'The Impossibility of a Paretian Liberal', *Journal of Political Economy*, 78, 1970, reprinted as Chapter 13 in A.K. Sen, *Choice, Welfare and Measurement*, Basil Blackwell, Oxford 1982.) This result essentially arises because, under the Pareto principle, whenever a person is permitted to have absolute control over one decision, he/she automatically has a potential influence on all decisions; hence it is not possible for two individuals to be in such a position (see A.K. Sen, 'Liberty, Unanimity and Rights', *Economica*, 43, 1976, reprinted as Chapter 14 in Sen, *op. cit.*). This 'Paretian Epidemic' leads to Sen's suggesting a weakened form of the Pareto principle which permits the possibility that individuals may not always wish all aspects of their preferences to be relevant for social choice. While Sen's result is of considerable interest in social choice theory, and has led to a large literature, it is neglected here because it has only limited significance for the following discussion, and because other problems are more severe in the current context.
3 See G. Debreu, *Theory of Value*, Yale University Press, New Haven 1959, K.J. Arrow and F.H. Hahn, *General Competitive Analysis*, Holden Day, San Francisco 1971, and F.M. Bator, 'The Simple Analytics of Welfare Maximization', *American Economic Review*, March 1957; see also the papers cited in these works.
4 Note that Pareto-efficiency in an economy also requires that efficiency in exchange and in production be 'linked'; technically, the marginal rate of substitution in consumption must equal the marginal rate of transformation in production. This is guaranteed by price-taking behaviour on the part of firms as well as consumers.
5 For this argument, see M. Friedman, *Capitalism and Freedom*, University of Chicago Press, London 1975, and F. Hayek, *The Road to Serfdom*, University of Chicago Press, Chicago

1944. For a discussion of freedom in an economic context and a critique of these arguments, see D. Heald, *Public Expenditure*, Martin Robertson, Oxford 1983.

6 See A.M. Okun, *Equality and Efficiency: The Big Trade-Off*, Brookings Institution, Washington 1975, pp. 35-40, for a discussion of this argument.

7 See T. Scitovsky, *Papers on Welfare and Growth*, Allen and Unwin, London 1965, p. 242.

8 Some aspects of this are discussed in G.J. Stigler, 'Economics of Information', *Journal of Political Economy*, June 1961.

9 As the theory is based on the notion that goods can be distinguished by their location in time and space, it can be argued that all commodities are essentially heterogeneous, implying in turn that the markets for most goods will be very thin. Perfect competition is correspondingly unlikely.

10 See Friedman, *op. cit.*, pp. 30-31.

11 See R.G. Lipsey and K. Lancaster, 'The General Theory of Second Best', *Review of Economic Studies*, 24, October 1956. See also P.A. Diamond and J.A. Mirrlees, 'Optimal Taxation and Public Production I: Production Efficiency', *American Economic Review*, 61, 1971, for the argument that the desirability of productive efficiency is fairly robust to this difficulty.

12 For a useful discussion of these matters, see W. Buiter, 'The Role of Economic Management', *Catalyst*, 1, Spring 1985.

13 Introducing one extra market when there are a number of markets missing also need not be welfare-improving, for second-best reasons.

14 See G. Stigler, 'The Theory of Economic Regulation', *Bell Journal of Economics and Management Science*, 2, Spring 1971, and S. Peltzman, 'Toward a More General Theory of Regulation', *Journal of Law and Economics*, 19, August 1976.

15 See A.K. Sen, 'Personal Utilities and Public Judgements: or What's Wrong with Welfare Economics?', *Economic Journal*, 89, 1979, reprinted as Chapter 15 in Sen, *op. cit.* A simple, though not fully satisfactory, way of circumventing this problem is to view non-economic objectives as constraints upon economic decisions. See also Okun, *op. cit.*

16 For some different critical perspectives on the economic theory of the consumer, see: T. Scitovsky, *The Joyless Economy*, Oxford University Press, Oxford 1976; A.K. Sen, 'Rational Fools: A Critique of the Behavioural Foundations of Economic Theory', in H. Harris (editor), *Scientific Models and Man*, Oxford University Publications, Oxford 1978; and J. Robinson, *Economic Philosophy*, Penguin Books, Harmondsworth 1978.

17 J.K. Galbraith, *The Affluent Society*, Penguin Books, Harmondsworth 1962. Galbraith also argues this case in *The New Industrial State*, Houghton Mifflin, Boston 1967.

18 See K.J. Arrow, *Social Choice and Individual Values*, Wiley, New York 1951. For some discussion of these issues, see A.K. Sen, *Collective Choice and Social Welfare*, Holden Day, San Francisco 1970, and A. Deaton and J. Muellbauer, *Economics and Consumer Behaviour*, Cambridge University Press, Cambridge 1980, Chapter 9.

19 Deaton and Muellbauer, *op.cit.*, p. 217. See also Sen, 'Personal Utilities...', *op. cit.*, and also A.K. Sen, 'On Weights and Measures: Informational Constraints in Social Welfare Analysis', *Econometrica*, 45, 1977, reprinted as Chapter 11 in Sen, *Choice, Welfare and Measurement*, *op. cit.*; see also the 'Introduction' in the latter volume.

20 For a consideration of some of these flows, see the papers in the 'Symposium on Unemployment and the Labour Market in Ireland', *Economic and Social Review*, 14, January 1983; in particular, see the paper by M. O'Mahony.

21 See, for example, T.J. Sargent and N. Wallace, 'Rational Expectations and the Theory of Economic Policy', *Journal of Monetary Economics*, 2, 1986. Strictly speaking, one can distinguish between full employment and the 'natural rate' of unemployment (which may differ from full employment because of microeconomic distortions); New Classical arguments refer to the natural rate. While New Classicals concede that the natural rate may move over time, it is difficult to interpret or analyze such movements. Most models in this

literature simply assume that a logical distinction can be made between movements around the natural rate and movements in the natural rate. Also, the emphasis of this literature is on monetary policies; other government policies will still affect employment.

22 Seminal papers are: P.A. Diamond, 'Aggregate Demand Management in Search Equilibrium', *Journal of Political Economy*, 90, 1982, and O. Hart, 'A Model of Imperfect Competition with Keynesian Features', *Quarterly Journal of Economics*, 97, 1982. This class of models is analyzed in R. Cooper and A. John, 'Coordinating Coordination Failures in Keynesian Models', *Cowles Foundation Discussion Paper* 745R, July 1985.

23 See Scitovsky, *The Joyless Economy, op. cit.*, pp. 140-145, for a more detailed discussion of this point. This book is also worth reading for a general critique of economic growth as a policy objective. Other useful critical evaluations of growth include: E.J. Mishan, *The Costs of Economic Growth*, Penguin, Harmondsworth 1979; and F. Hirsch, *Social Limits to Growth*, Routledge and Kegan Paul, London 1977.

24 See E.F. Schumacher, *Small is Beautiful*, Harper and Row, New York 1973, for one statement of this position.

25 R.M. Solow, 'Is the End of the World at Hand?', *Challenge*, 1973, reprinted in E. Mansfield (editor), *Principles of Macroeconomics: Readings, Issues, and Cases*, Norton, New York 1974.

26 J. Tobin, 'Economic Growth as an Objective of Government Policy', in W.W. Heller (editor), *Perspectives on Economic Growth*, Random House, New York 1968.

27 Solow, *op. cit.*, p.179.

28 The distinction here is close to that made by Friedman and Friedman, who differentiate between equality of opportunity and equality of outcome, although their definitions are probably too restrictive for a full consideration of equality as a policy objective. See M. Friedman and R. Friedman, *Free To Choose*, Penguin Books, Harmondsworth 1980, Chapter 5. This chapter is worth reading for an informal discussion of some arguments against equality, although many of these are considerably overstated. A similar distinction underlies Sen's useful discussion of 'needs' and 'desert' as principles of distribution. See A.K. Sen, *On Economic Inequality*, Clarendon Press, Oxford 1973. More generally, this book provides a concise and illuminating discussion of important issues of equality and welfare economics.

29 K. Marx, *A Critique of the Gotha Programme*, reprinted in R. Freedman (editor), *Marx on Economics*, Penguin Books, Harmondsworth 1978.

30 See A.B. Atkinson, *The Economics of Inequality* (second edition), Clarendon Press, Oxford 1983, Chapter 3, for an excellent discussion of these issues. More generally, this book provides a very thorough analysis of many economic aspects of equality, including detailed statistical evidence for Britain. It also contains an extensive set of references.

31 Atkinson discusses, in particular, issues of taxation, fringe benefits, production for home consumption, and imputed rent. See *ibid*, pp. 38-41.

32 In 1970, the United Nations recommended that by 1975 (or at latest 1980), industrialized countries should achieve an 'aid target' of 0.70 per cent of their Gross National Product. In 1980, the actual average was 0.35 per cent, while Ireland's contribution was 0.19 per cent of GNP.

33 See Atkinson, *op. cit.*, Chapters 2 and 3, and Sen, *On Economic Inequality, op. cit.*, Chapter 2. Atkinson has proposed a measure of inequality that depends explicitly on welfare. See A.B. Atkinson, 'On the Measurement of Inequality', *Journal of Economic Theory*, Vol. 2, 1970; see also the discussion of this measure in Sen. In particular, Sen notes the problem that a measure of inequality in terms of welfare alone may remove some of the descriptive meaning of the term.

34 This type of 'ignorance' argument was first propounded by Lerner; see A.P. Lerner, *The Economics of Control*, New York 1944. Sen, in *On Economic Inequality, op. cit.*, pp. 83-87, presents these types of 'maximin' arguments formally. See also Sen, 'On Ignorance and

Equal Distribution', *American Economic Review*, 63, 1973, reprinted as Chapter 10 in Sen, *Choice, Welfare and Measurement*, *op. cit.*

35 See Sen, *On Economic Inequality*, *op. cit.*, p. 78.

36 Technically, risk-aversion implies concavity of the expected-utility function; it is a common assumption in much economic theory. The fact that many individuals do engage in risky activities (such as gambling) does not imply that risk-aversion is an unrealistic assumption in general. In particular, it appears specious to argue that, because individuals sometimes choose to incur risk, they prefer greater risk in general. Arguments that seek to justify economic inequality on the basis of the existence of lotteries and gambling houses are correspondingly suspect.

37 See J. Rawls, *A Theory of Justice*, Harvard University Press, Cambridge 1971. This interpretation of Rawls is somewhat simplified, and does not exactly characterize the Rawlsian thought experiment. Note also that Rawls does not actually present his arguments in terms of utility, but rather in terms of access to social primary goods. See the discussion in A.K. Sen, 'Equality of What?', Chapter 16 in Sen, *Choice, Welfare and Measurement*, *op. cit.* Hence, the Rawlsian argument does not depend upon interpersonal comparisons of utility.

38 R. Nozick, *Anarchy, State and Utopia*, Basic Books, New York 1974. See H. Varian, 'Distributive Justice, Welfare Economics and the Theory of Fairness', *Philosophy and Public Affairs*, Vol. 4, 1974/75, reprinted in F. Hahn and M. Hollis (editors), *Philosophy and Economic Theory*, Oxford University Press, Oxford 1979, for a detailed critique of Nozick's arguments.

39 See A.J. Culyer, *The Economics of Social Policy*, Martin Robertson, London 1973. This book is also useful for a detailed discussion of the approach to policy-making outlined in Section 2, and for a strong statement of the view that economists should concern themselves only with efficiency.

40 See Okun, *op. cit.*, pp. 75-82, for a discussion of the effects of some of these.

41 Strictly speaking, the nature of trade-offs between objectives depends upon available policy options; hence this description is slightly misleading, because the trade-offs are not unique.

42 See Okun, *op. cit.*, Chapter 4, for a more detailed discussion of equity-efficiency trade-offs. As well as the sources of inefficiency noted here, Okun also discusses administrative and socioeconomic costs.

43 See *ibid.*, pp. 98-99.

3 Secondary Policy Objectives

Dermot McAleese*

POLITICIANS AND the media frequently advert to the balance of payments and price stability in such a way as to suggest that these factors are key components of economic welfare. Yet here they are being discussed as secondary policy objectives (i.e. not as ends in themselves). The significance of these secondary objectives, however, is that their attainment may be crucial to the achievement of primary objectives. In this light the importance accorded them is understandable.

This chapter begins with a description of the balance of payments, paying particular attention to its components and its various subheadings. The balance of payments always balances — in the same sense as saving 'always' equals investment — but it may not balance in a manner conducive to growth and free trade. The distinction between current account balances and capital account transactions is essential to keep in mind in balance-of-payments analysis. The reason for concern about the payments balance is that a smoothly functioning foreign payments system is a necessary precondition for the orderly and liberal exchange of goods, services and factors of production between countries. International trade and factor movements, in turn, exert a favourable impact on growth, employment, efficiency and choice.

Inflation is discussed in the second section. It is defined as a sustained increase in the general price level. The determinants of inflation are analyzed, distinguishing between the proximate causes (excessive increase in money supply or a slack exchange rate regime) and the ultimate causes (what makes governments acquiesce in a particular monetary or exchange rate policy). The adverse economic effects of inflation are surveyed. They arise chiefly but not exclusively because of the unpredictability of inflation and the uncertainty which is thereby created in economic transactions. Note is also taken of the depressive effects of policies designed to eradicate inflation. It is

*The author wishes to thank the editor for helpful comments on an earlier draft.

argued that the answer to a hangover is not another drink (the 'hair of the dog' principle) but to stay off alcohol. Inflation and deflation both bring problems — the solution is to maintain price stability. In this way the scene would be set for greater efficiency and less social disharmony.

1   THE BALANCE OF PAYMENTS

What is the Balance of Payments?

The balance of payments is, by definition, a record of all commercial transactions between residents of one country and residents of another. There are a number of ways of classifying these transactions but, for simplicity, only three basic concepts are considered here. First, there is the *balance of trade,* representing the difference between the value of merchandise exports and imports. Second, *the balance on current account* is obtained by adding 'invisible' items such as net tourism receipts, emigrants' remittances, repatriated profits, interest on foreign debt, transportation charges, etc. to the balance of trade. It is customary nowadays to divide invisibles into two groups: services and international transfers. Third, there is the *balance of autonomous transactions* which equals the current account balance plus net long-term capital inflows. Thus if the current account registers a deficit of IR£100m and net long-term capital inflow equals IR£150m, the balance of autonomous transactions is in surplus to the value of IR£50m. In deciding whether a country has a balance of payments 'problem' or not, the balance referred to ought, in most normal circumstances, to be the balance of autonomous transactions or, simply, the *basic balance.*

The remaining items on the balance of payments account include changes in external reserves and short-term capital movements. These are referred to in the literature as *accommodating* items on the grounds that they react passively to changes in the balance of autonomous items. Thus if a country has a deficit on the balance of autonomous payments, equality between supply and demand for foreign exchange can be brought about either by a reduction in the level of external reserves or by short-term foreign borrowing. The change in accommodating transactions is viewed as the direct consequence of the deficit in the balance of autonomous payments.

A country can be said to have a balance of payments *problem* when the basic balance is in deficit (or in surplus) for a sustained period of time in conditions of free trade and presumably 'full' employment. The time dimension is important since a transitory deficit (due to a dock strike or a bad agricultural harvest) presents fewer problems than one which is expected to persist. Free trade conditions must be insisted upon since it is always possible to rectify a deficit by a government decision to limit imports through tariffs or quotas or other administrative measures. Similarly a deficit can always be reduced by policies which restrain the growth of economic activity and the level of employment. Where protection or deflationary policies are used to correct a deficit, conflict appears between the primary policy objectives of growth and full employment and the secondary objective of balance-of-payments equilibrium. It is the task of economic policy to resolve this conflict to the utmost extent possible. The available policy instruments — competitiveness, the exchange rate and commercial policy — are discussed in Chapter 9.

It should be easy to state whether a country has or has not a balance of payments problem, but in practice this is not so. First, judgement has to be exercised in distinguishing transitory from permanent influences on the balance of payments. Second, opinions differ as to the precise definitions of 'free trade' and 'full employment'. Third, there are thorny statistical and conceptual problems in defining the basic balance.

An example of conceptual problems is the treatment of foreign borrowing by the Irish government. Some might interpret foreign borrowing as arising from the planned increase in public investment, most of the capital equipment for which was imported. The current account deficit on the balance of payments, therefore, was caused by the government's decision to borrow abroad in order to finance the public capital programme. A contrasting view would be that foreign borrowing was necessary in order to protect the official reserves from the consequences of a balance-of-payments deficit — which itself was caused by a number of specific factors, one of which was the upsurge in import-intensive investment expenditure. In the former instance, the foreign borrowing is autonomous; in the latter it is accommodating. An assessment of a country's balance-of-payments position, therefore, requires judgement and a knowledge of how the economy works.

Statistical limitations are a feature of most aggregates which economists deal with. Statistics on the capital account of the balance of payments are particularly prone to error. Mistakes on the capital account often entail consequential errors in the current account balance. For example, because of the incomplete coverage of data on repatriated dividends earned by overseas subsidiaries in Ireland, there is a suspicion that the current account deficit is underestimated. Since the overall balance of payments must always balance, an under-estimation of the current deficit implies that an item with the same sign on capital account (very likely residual capital flows) is overestimated. Discrepancies of considerable size can arise in this way. They pose problems not only for the Irish authorities but also for the International Monetary Fund which, in 1983, recorded a discrepancy of $89 billion in the world balance of payments on current account, due to statistical imperfections. 'A degree of caution', the Fund advises, 'is well warranted in interpreting current account developments as depicted by the available statistics'.[1]

Growth, Efficiency and the Balance of Payments

The balance of payments is relevant to growth because sustained imbalances tend to inhibit growth and to engender inflation. Imbalances include surpluses as well as deficits. But, for an Irish reader, the analysis of deficits must be the more interesting aspect. (A Japanese textbook might prefer to consider balance-of-payments surpluses.)

When a country runs a current account deficit this means that it is absorbing more goods and services from foreigners than it is earning from exports of goods and services to them. In this limited sense, a deficit signifies that a country is 'living beyond its means'. Suppose, however, that the deficit is being used to purchase capital equipment which will enhance the country's future earning capacity. In that case, running a deficit might make good economic sense. The deficit should then be financed by long-term capital inflows through the public or private sectors. The *basic balance* will be zero and there will be no balance-of-payments problem — or rather, in most normal circumstances, when there is a reasonable expectation of long-term capital inflow being used to productive effect, there should be no problem.

A problem arises, however, when: (a) the deficit is being used to finance excessive levels of consumption rather than investment; (b) there is difficulty in deciding how exactly the deficit is being deployed; or (c) the future earning capacity of the investment projects is doubtful. If that happens, the autonomous private capital inflows will decline, public sector foreign borrowing will become more expensive or may eventually have to cease because of the absence of lenders. This has happened to many less developed countries (LDCs) over the past decade and explains the concern over the Third World debt problem. The government of the borrowing country will, in these circumstances, have to cut back on public sector expenditure. This will mean lower growth (in the short run). The 'stop-go' policies of British governments throughout the 1960s is a case in point: reflation tended to be followed by balance-of-payments deficits which the government felt obliged to modify by deflationary policies. Another example is the Mitterand expansion of 1981-82 which was brought to an abrupt halt by a worsening balance of trade and an escalating government budget deficit.[2] For rather different reasons — and after a decade of 'go' — the Irish government is now being compelled to adopt 'stop' policies. In each case, the immediate effect on growth is negative, however necessary and worthwhile the corrective policies.

From a growth perspective, therefore, the objective must be to maintain a sound credit rating so that, in the event of unforeseen emergencies, a country can borrow abroad without the disruption of its investment plans which might otherwise be necessary. This can only be achieved if a sustainable basic balance position is maintained over time. Long-run current account deficits must therefore be matched by levels of profitable investment which will repay directly or indirectly the costs of financing them.

Efficiency and the balance of payments is another important link between primary and secondary policy objectives. A country in balance of payments difficulties will frequently feel it necessary to resort to protection. Protection, by inhibiting international trade, brings static and dynamic losses.

Every first-year textbook has a section on the law of comparative advantage. The law states that a country gains from trade by exporting the goods in which it has a comparative advantage and importing those in which it has a comparative disadvantage. The essential insight of Ricardo's law is as valid today as it was when first enunciated two hundred years ago. It is particularly relevant to small countries because small size poses obvious limitations on the number of products which can be manufactured efficiently at home. In addition to extending the market for domestic production, trade also brings substantial benefits through extending the range of product choice available to consumers.

The above 'static' gains from trade are complemented by 'dynamic' effects. Access to foreign markets, for example, makes it possible for a country to specialize to a vastly greater degree than if it were catering only for the domestic market. The resultant economies of scale are directly attributable to international trade. They help to explain why Ireland has become a major producer on a European scale of tennis balls, hospital disposable products, computer-related office equipment and cream liqueurs. Only a fraction of the output of the Irish plants producing these goods is absorbed on the domestic market. Large plants employing vast workforces are not needed to avail of scale economies. Horizontal specialization simply requires that moderate-sized plants (often in the 100-200 workers category) are allowed to specialize to a very high degree in a limited product range.

The second major dynamic gain arises from the stimulus to international competition given by exposure to foreign trade. Protection in a small state tends to foster monopoly — an argument stressed by Frederick List over a century ago and one which led him to describe the union of Britain and Ireland as 'a great and irrefragable example of the immeasurable efficacy of free trade between united nations'.[3] Firms exposed to external competition must keep up to date technically and have to operate at a high level of efficiency: otherwise they will not survive. The main beneficiary of this pressure on performance is the domestic consumer.

Although efficiency has been analyzed separately from growth, there is an interaction between them. More efficiency in the use of existing resources makes it easier to attain growth. A smoothly functioning world payments system makes it easier to attain both efficiency and growth. Adoption of a proper balance-of-payments policy by each country helps to ensure that the world payments system actually works smoothly. Balance-of-payments equilibrium is not desired for its own sake. People are concerned about it only because they are concerned that the benefits of trade and international factor movements should be maximized. Countries which have decided against availing of these benefits on a large scale — such as the Soviet Union, Albania and Vietnam — do not have balance-of-payments problems.

2   INFLATION

What Is Inflation?

Inflation is a rise in the cost of living resulting from a *persisting* rise in *money* prices.[4] Note the two words italicized and consider them in reverse order. It is prices expressed in *money* that have risen. Inflation affects most money prices to more or less the same extent. Some prices will rise more than others, which reflects a change in relative demands and supplies, i.e. relative prices are shifting as they would have even without inflation. Finally, inflation is a *persisting* rise in all money prices.

Inflation is defined by reference to the total money price of a particular *fixed* combination of consumer goods (sometimes called a basket of goods). This method of detecting inflation is based on the assumption that changes in quality and substitution among goods have significantly less effect on prices than inflation has. Three factors affect the accuracy of the figures. First, the number of goods in the sample basket is a far-from-complete inventory of the economy's goods.

Second, there may be changes in quality of goods. Third, people may make substitutions toward more lower-priced goods. A doubling in the price of potatoes, for example, would raise the Irish Consumer Price Index (CPI) by half of a percentage point (potatoes carry a weight of 0.8 per cent) but this takes no account of the availability of close substitutes such as rice and farinaceous foods. As time goes by, people switch their buying to products which have increased less in price: but the base weights (the CPI is a Laspeyres index) take no account of this switch.[5]

What Causes Inflation?

Inflation occurs when the growth of the money supply persistently exceeds the growth of real output. If each of us awoke today with twice as much money as yesterday and no less of any other goods and services, we would spend some of the new money on additional goods to reduce the excessive proportion of our wealth held as money. The demand for goods would rise. Prices — and wages — would be 'driven', 'pushed', 'pulled', or 'bid' up. Since spending does not reduce the *total* holding of money but merely transfers money from one person to another, nominal money stock remains at twice its original level. As prices rise, the real purchasing power of that money stock declines. Eventually equilibrium is reached when prices and income in money terms would be about twice as high as they were, because only then would we want to hold that doubled amount of money. This explains why inflation cannot continue without a sustained increase in the money stock relative to other goods and why continued excessive increases in the money stock are invariably followed by inflation. But how and why does the money stock increase so rapidly?

The issue has been debated for many years. Clearly the proximate cause is government action because only through such action — monetarily-financed budget deficits — can money supply be increased. But what causes the government (a) to run budget deficits and (b) to finance them by monetary means? Some argue that governments find it politically easier to print money to spend than to explicitly levy extra taxes to balance the budget. The ensuing inflation further eases the problem by enabling the government to increase the tax burden without explicit tax increases by the simple expedient of not indexing income tax bands to the inflation rate. Others argue that the reasons are more deep-seated: that governments validate inflation which arises because of inflationary wage demands (caused, for example, by dissatisfaction with the status quo) or because of supply-side shocks (for example, energy price increases). The government chooses to validate inflation because it believes that the short-run costs of not doing so in terms of civil strife, unemployment and disruption are greater than the economic costs of inflation itself (about which more later). A leading British sociologist, for example, concluded that inflation in the 1970s derived ultimately from changes in the form of social stratification, giving rise to more intense and more equally-matched social conflict than hitherto.[6]

Some modification of the analysis is required to explain inflation in small open economies (SOEs). These economies, being heavily dependent on trade, are exposed as much to external inflationary pressures as to internal pressures. The extent to which inflation is imported from the rest of the world, then, hinges crucially on the exchange-rate regime adopted by the small country. If the exchange rate is *fixed* relative to a weighted average of its major trading partners, inflation will be largely dependent on what happens in these countries. If they have high inflation, it will be transmitted to the small country; if they have low inflation, the small country will have low inflation. The *inflation-transmission mechanism* operates through a number of avenues. First, through international trade in goods and services — the SOE is a price taker which means that its export and import prices are fixed in foreign currency. If the dollar price of imported oil, raw materials and intermediate goods rises, and the exchange rate is fixed, the domestic price in the small country's currency must also rise. Second, if there is free movement of labour between markets (as is the case between Ireland and the UK), wage trends in the larger country will be followed in the small country. If they are not, labour will move towards the market with the higher wage so bidding up the price of labour. The transmission mechanism also works through capital markets. High inflation in the larger country means high nominal interest rates which, if a capital outflow is to be avoided, must be followed by interest rate increases in the small country. A third possible mechanism comes into operation if the higher inflation in the larger country leads to the generation of a balance-of-payments surplus in the small country. Insofar as this results in an increase in the latter's money supply, inflationary pressures are generated. The relevance of this third factor increases to the extent that price adjustment through the international trade mechanism is slow and interest rate adjustment rapid.

This explains why a small open economy with a fixed exchange rate might be expected to import inflation from its major trading partners. Ireland-UK inflation rates under the sterling parity system (see Chapter 1) was a classical example of this process. Another was Canada and the US during the period when the exchange rate between the two currencies was fixed. But there are many SOEs where the inflation rate is a good deal less, and others where it is considerably greater, than the weighted average of their main trading partners. Switzerland and Austria are examples of low inflators (3.9 per cent and 5.3 per cent respectively in the period 1973-84, appreciably below the industrialized countries' average of 7.9 per cent); countries such as Argentina, Israel, Peru and Uruguay would fall into the high inflation category. These countries all have *flexible exchange rates.* Thus, Switzerland has insulated itself from external inflationary pressure by periodic revaluations of the Swiss franc. Israel has exacerbated external inflationary pressures by frequent devaluations. In these instances, the causes of inflation must be discussed in the context of exchange rate policy as well as monetary policy. Why is it that a government in one country is able to revalue its way out of inflation while another adds fuel to inflation by devaluation? Again one reverts to considerations beyond the confines of economics, e.g. the public's attitude to inflation, the political power of the government, the degree of consensus in society and policy responses to adverse shocks to the economic system.

One frequently hears talk of the *inflationary spiral.* Inflation feeds on itself. Higher prices lead to higher wage demands which cause higher prices which result in even higher wage claims next round, and so on. Once caught in a spiral it is hard to escape, as the experience of inflation in Latin America testifies. It is a good reason for staying off the spiral in the first place. Israel is a salutary example of a country which had moderate inflation in the 1960s (6 per cent compared with Ireland's 5 per cent) but where inflation rose sevenfold to 45 per cent on average during the period 1970-81. Israeli prices in the early 1980s were rising at a rate in excess of 150 per cent per annum.

The proximate economic causes of inflation are comparatively easy to analyze. Its ultimate causes are more complex. Nobody believes any more that inflation is exclusively associated with excess aggregate demand — the prevalence of *stagflation,* i.e. recession combined with inflation, has seen to that. Nor can inflation be exclusively associated with poor countries. The 1970s have seen high rates of inflation prevailing in the developed as well as in the less developed economies.

Inflation and Primary Policy Objectives
Inflation has implications for efficiency, growth and income distribution. The precise dimension of these implications, however, is a matter of continuing debate. As Dara McCormack of the Central Bank observed:

It has been said, with some justice, that 'most people think that inflation is a bad thing for very bad reasons'. There is no consensus on the matter in the economics profession; some economists have seemed to suggest that since over time it will tend to be largely anticipated, inflation involves little more than, 'changing the unit of account' and has, therefore, negligible real economic effects. Others have argued that the layman's intuition is correct, that inflation is indeed a bad thing, and have sought to give cogent reasons as to why this is the case.[7]

In the conclusion of his chapter (much of which is reproduced in the following paragraphs), McCormack comes down firmly on the side of the anti-inflationists. The World Bank's assessment is also unambiguous:

Rapid and accelerating inflation undermines allocative efficiency because it increases uncertainty and induces savers to invest in unproductive 'inflation hedges' such as real estate, consumer durables, gems, and foreign currency deposits. Some countries have developed complex systems for indexing wages and prices to compensate for inflation, though this is administratively costly and tends to penalize those (mostly poor) people outside the indexation system. Where indexation does not exist, the 'inflation tax' contributes to a growing sense of social and economic injustice.[8]

Even if a debate of sorts exists about whether or not, or to what extent, inflation is damaging to economic 'health', no reputable economist has argued that high inflation is positively beneficial to efficiency and growth.

Modern analysis of the effects of inflation builds on a sharp distinction between inflation which is anticipated and that which is unanticipated or which comes as a 'surprise'. The principal welfare costs arise only when inflation is not fully anticipated. These effects would disappear if inflation were to continue at a steady (or otherwise predictable) rate which the public would learn to anticipate, and if institutions adapted fully to this anticipation. Perfectly anticipated inflation is a limiting case. By looking at the theoretical assumptions underlying it, and progressively relaxing them, light is thrown on the more fundamental effects of inflation.

Perfectly Anticipated Inflation. Inflation is fully anticipated when each and every transactor correctly forecasts what the rate of inflation turns out to be and can adjust his economic behaviour appropriately to the anticipated inflation. There are thus two main elements involved: first, the formation of correct expectations and, second, the absence of any institutional rigidities which would limit transactors' ability to allow for inflation. The latter would include any degree of official or unofficial price controls, ceilings on interest rates as well as institutional conventions and rigidities such as contracting in fixed nominal amounts (as in most insurance policies). There would have to be, in effect, a fully indexed economy implying, among other things, a comprehensive system of wage and salary indexation, indexing of tax brackets and allowances, taxation of real rather than nominal returns on assets, etc. In brief, all prices for goods and services, including labour services, would have to be perfectly adjustable. This would be an example of what has been called the 'flexprice' economy. In such an economy, when inflation is accurately anticipated there is only one welfare cost to inflation and this arises from the nature of money itself.

Cash balances yield an implicit social return by virtue of the convenience they afford in making transactions. Inflation can be regarded as a tax on cash balances; the negative yield on cash balances is equal to the rate of inflation. The higher the rate of inflation, the larger is the negative yield and the opportunity cost of holding cash. Holders of cash balances will, therefore, shift into less liquid and convenient but income-yielding assets. This substitution involves a further loss of efficiency insofar as cash balances, which are virtually costless to produce, are economized upon in favour of more frequent transactions in less liquid assets which do involve resource costs to effect.

The deadweight loss or excess burden of the inflation tax on cash balances, known as the shoe-leather cost of inflation, can be measured (subject, of course, to a daunting list of caveats) as the area of the triangle under a demand for narrow money or currency function. A number of estimates of the magnitude of this cost have been made for the United States. One study put the welfare cost of a 5 per cent rate of anticipated inflation on a par with that of the US corporate income tax and concluded generally:

> While this cost may be small in relation to the costs of redistributions of income and wealth when inflation is unanticipated, it is comparable to the welfare costs of other major components of the US tax system at levels of inflation as low as 5 per cent. Moreover, the size of the welfare costs of inflation increases rapidly with the size of the rate of inflation itself.[9]

On a similar basis of comparison, it was concluded in a recent article that the welfare cost of anticipated inflation was 'large in the distortions league'.[10]

In addition to this pure welfare cost, anticipated inflation will also attract the so-called 'menu-cost' of actually changing prices in what have been called 'customer markets', i.e., those markets in which prices are set and, in the normal course of events, kept unchanged for some time, such as labour markets, retail and wholesale trade, pay telephones and parking meters. Obviously, these menu costs are greater the higher the rate of inflation and, at some very high rate, nominal pricing would presumably be abandoned altogether in favour of some alternative indexation arrangements.

The welfare costs of anticipated inflation may appear arcane and insignificant. Yet, as mentioned, some studies have suggested that these costs are quantitatively quite significant relative to other distortions, even at relatively low rates of inflation. Thus, under ideal conditions, impossible to match in practice, there are non-trivial welfare costs associated with even a steady, fully anticipated inflation and these costs increase as the rate of inflation increases.

Accurate Expectations with Institutional Rigidities. In the theoretical long run, it is certainly inconceivable that, in the face of accurately predicted inflation, institutional rigidities based on transactions being conducted on a nominal basis would survive for very long. For such rigidities to survive, 'money illusion' would have to be widespread and there is little evidence of that being the case. However, if inflation were to proceed at, say, 5 per cent per annum over a number of years, this rate would come to be expected without there having to be any radical restructuring of payments habits, financial conventions, contract periods and so on. The reasons for this apparent inertia lie in the nature of most markets, other than some foreign exchange and commodities markets, where prices are not determined on a day-to-day basis by demand and supply. Most markets, notably labour markets, are what Hicks calls 'fixprice' markets where prices have to be 'made'; Okun's 'customer markets'[11] are essentially the same thing.

In such markets, it is easier to 'make' prices if, as Hicks puts it 'substantial use can be made of precedent; if one can at least start the bargaining from some presumption that what has been acceptable before will be acceptable again. When prices in general are fairly stable, that is often rather easy. The particular prices which result from such bargains may not be ideal from the point of view of the economist, but the time and trouble which would be involved in improving them is simply not worth the candle. To be obliged to make them anew, and to go on making them anew, as one is obliged to do in continuous inflation, involves direct economic loss and (very often) loss of temper as well!'[12] Costly information-gathering and research activities are reduced considerably by reliance on such precedents and conventions.

Unanticipated Inflation. Actual experience of the period from the late 1960s to the early 1980s was of inflation which was both historically high and extremely variable from year to year. The sharp acceleration in the rate of price increases from the late 1960s could not have been anticipated correctly by extrapolating past experience. Inflation has not proceeded at a steady pace. Rather it has been uneven and sporadic. From this feature springs the most serious welfare losses.

First, uncertainty about the inflation rate undermines the role played by money in economizing on transactions costs. Fixed-price orders, leases and other explicit long-term contracts, fixed-time schedules for price changes and the broad general commitment to continuity of offers by suppliers are important ways of abetting and aiding forward planning. Uncertainty about the future price level shortens the time horizons of such practices, thus imposing a welfare loss on society.

Second, uncertainty about the future price level results in a whole range of arbitrary redistributions of income and wealth. A faster-than-expected inflation rate, for instance, will tend to discriminate against creditors in favour of debtors; to redistribute income among various categories of asset holders from those whose incomes are either fixed in nominal money terms or which typically lag behind inflation (pensioners, annuity holders) to those whose incomes are more easily adjustable to inflation, such as unionized wage earners and owners of capital. Another, perhaps less familiar, redistribution is a probable redistribution of real wealth from the old (who have accumulated assets) to the young who are, in general, net debtors. Most of these redistributions reflect either a complete inability to adjust to a higher rate of inflation or, more likely, a lag in adjustment.

The haphazard nature of the income distribution effects can lead to social unrest and general discontent as people find it increasingly difficult to assess the progress in their real incomes and to predict what their real earnings will be in the future. Okun remarked that, 'people are not taught to store the consumer price index in their memory banks'! [13] In a period of 1 per cent inflation, people who received pay increases of 4 per cent recognize clearly that they have gained in real terms. In a world of 13 per cent inflation, those fortunate enough to receive pay increases of 16 per cent are likely to be much less confident about how they are faring. That loss of information is a genuine subtraction from welfare. A more graphic assessment is given by Keynes (who draws in turn on Lenin):

> There is no subtler, no surer means of overturning the existing basis of society than to debauch the currency .[14]

Third, inflation can have adverse consequences for economic growth, although the relationship 'is neither direct nor simple'.[15] The efficiency losses discussed above can be turned into growth losses indirectly. In addition, there are some potential direct effects. Inflation has a tendency to shorten time horizons diminishing the attractiveness of long-term commercial investments. There is, as the World Bank noted, a tendency to invest in 'inflation hedges' such as property to the neglect of long-term investment in industry. Uncertainty about inflation can lead to large unexpected losses in competitiveness, for example in instances where exchange rate changes do not reflect fully and promptly domestic price changes. It can also lead to damaging asymmetries in reaction to changes in a country's competitive position. An improvement in competitiveness resulting from a rise in foreign prices will quickly be eroded through compensating income claims. A deterioration in competitiveness arising from a fall in foreign prices relative to Irish prices may not, however, be offset as quickly through a compensatory fall in income claims. The tendency will be to wait and see if the price decline is permanent. During the interval, profitability will fall and firms will go out of business.

3   CONCLUSION

A clear link exists between the primary policy objectives and the secondary objectives of balance-of-payments equilibrium and price stability. Failure to maintain either or both of the secondary objectives has adverse consequences for efficiency, growth and income distribution. The nature of these effects has been outlined.

Rather more attention has been given to inflation because it has occupied the centre stage in economic discussion for many years. Inflation, however, has now become much less of a problem. Prices were increasing by only 5 per cent in the European Community in the period 1984-87 compared with 10 per cent in the period 1971-80. There has been a spectacular decline in the UK inflation rate from around 16 per cent in 1980 to under 4 per cent in 1986, in the process leaving many theories about Britain's intrinsic inflation proneness looking rather flat.

Has this decline in inflation been associated with a demonstrable improvement in economic efficiency and social stability? No clear answer is possible. Certainly the United States has made an impressive recovery but Europe remains dogged by slow growth and high unemployment. This does not invalidate the arguments about the adverse effects of inflation — had inflation continued, matters might have been even worse than they are now. What recent experience does is to draw attention to the painful withdrawal symptoms which accompany the breaking of the inflation habit. These occur because of slow adjustment in labour and commodity markets to the lower rate of inflation and to continuing uncertainty about whether this lower rate will be maintained. One consequence is inordinately high real interest rates which are scarcely encouraging for investment. Long-term Irish government securities in March 1987 yielded over 12 per cent compared with an end-year expected inflation rate of 3 per cent. Together these imply a real interest rate of 9 per cent. Writing sixty years ago, Keynes observed that 'each process, inflation and deflation alike, has inflicted great injuries. Each has an effect in altering the distribution of wealth between different classes. . . Each has an effect in overstimulating or retarding the production of wealth. . . *Both evils are to be shunned.*[16] Inflation creates problems; curbing inflation creates problems. The solution is for governments to ensure that price stability, once restored, is thereafter maintained. In a more stable price environment, increasing attention is likely to be focussed on balance-of-payments policy — automatic versus policy-induced adjustment mechanisms, foreign borrowing, the third-world debt problem, interdependencies between one country's balance of payments and others and international liquidity.

Footnotes

1 International Monetary Fund, *World Economic Outlook,* Washington DC 1983, p.161.

2 David Cobham, 'French Macroeconomic Policy Under President Mitterrand: An Assessment', *National Westminster Bank Quarterly Review*, February 1984.

3 The quote is from F. List, *National System of Political Economy* (translated S.S. Lloyd), Longmans, Green and Company, London 1904, p.100. Arthur Griffith once expressed the wish to see this book in the hands of every Irishman in the belief that arguments for protection addressed therein would support the Sinn Féin case. Had this wish been granted, the results might not have been as favourable to the protectionist cause as Griffith imagined.

4 A. Alchian and W. Allen, *Exchange and Production: Competition, Co-ordination and Control* (third edition), Wadsworth, California 1983.

5 Changes in the broad pattern of expenditure, however, tend to occur relatively slowly over time and the weighting basis has, in fact, been changed on five occasions since the foundation of the state, the most recent being November 1982 (see CSO, *Irish Statistical Bulletin,* Dublin, March 1983).

6 J. Goldthorpe, 'The Current Inflation: Towards a Sociological Account', in F. Hirsch and J. Goldthorpe (editors), *The Political Economy of Inflation,* Martin Robertson, Oxford 1978, p.210.

7 Dara McCormack, 'Inflation: Anticipated or Unanticipated', in D. McAleese and L. Ryan (editors), *Inflation in the Irish Economy: A Contemporary Perspective*, Helicon, Dublin 1982, p.31. This chapter draws extensively on McCormack's chapter.

8 World Bank, *World Development Report 1983,* Washington DC 1983. p.59.

9 John A.Tatom, 'The Welfare Cost of Inflation', *Federal Reserve Bank of St. Louis Review,* November 1976. Cited in McCormack, *op.cit.*

10 Stanley Fischer, 'Towards an Understanding of the Costs of Inflation: II', in Karl Brunner and Allan H. Meltzer (editors), *Carnegie-Rochester Conference Series on Public Policy*, Autumn 1981, pp. 5-42.

11 John Hicks, *The Crisis in Keynesian Economics,* Blackwell, Oxford 1974; and A.M. Okun, *Prices and Quantities: A Macroeconomic Analysis,* Blackwell, Oxford 1981.

12 Hicks, *op.cit.*, pp.78-79.

13 Okun, *op.cit.*, p.287.

14 J.M. Keynes, 'Economic Consequences of the Peace', in *Collected Economic Writings*, Vol.II, Macmillan, London 1971, p.149.

15 P.Neary and F. Ruane, 'Inflation and Growth', in McAleese and Ryan, *op.cit.*, p.38.

16 J.M. Keynes, 'The Social Consequences of Changes in the Value of Money', in *Collected Economic Writings*, Vol.IX., Macmillan, London 1971, p.6O.

Part II

POLICY
IMPLEMENTATION

4 Government Intervention

John W. O'Hagan

IN PART I economic aims have been explained and rationalized. Clearly the next question to be answered is how the economy is directed towards these objectives, and in particular one may ask what is the government's role, if any, in this respect. This issue has already been discussed in some detail in Chapter 2, and Section 1 below extends the discussion by examining the case in practice for government intervention in a traditional market economy such as Ireland's. Section 2 examines the *actual* level, nature and growth of government involvement in the Irish economy since the foundation of the state: the causes of this growth are also considered.

1 THE RATIONALE FOR GOVERNMENT INTERVENTION

Introduction

Any system, if it is to function in an orderly manner, requires a guiding and controlling mechanism. In the case of an economy, as mentioned in Chapter 2, this need would seem to be satisfied by the machinery of the market which appears capable of adequately solving the problems of production, distribution and exchange. Badly produced goods, and goods which are too expensive because of inefficient production or profiteering, will not sell. An employer who pays his/her employees too little will lose them to another employer, and one who pays them too much will soon be forced to close down. Exchange would be fair, for unless people benefited from it they would refuse to deal.

Despite this apparent efficiency of demand and supply in automatically regulating the economy, the total expenditure of the public sector in Ireland is now equivalent to over 50 per cent of GDP. The answer to this paradox lies in the general recognition of the market's many deficiencies as a controlling mechanism. In a number of ways it fails to allocate resources efficiently. Thus there are some goods which it fails to produce or will not produce in optimum quantities. Imperfections such as monopolies and other restrictive practices hinder the allocative influences of the market. Furthermore, the market is primarily concerned with the present allocation of resources and not with objectives like growth which are orientated towards the future. The market also fails to ensure adequate stability, for history has shown how great fluctuations in output and employment have been associated with *laissez-faire* economic policies. Finally, the market tends to maintain, and may intensify, inequalities in the distribution of income and wealth.

To compensate for these deficiencies, large-scale government intervention in the economy had, in the 1970s, become the norm in traditional market economies. In the case of Ireland this government involvement will be discussed in relation to five major areas: the provision of social and merit goods; the activities of state-sponsored bodies; the planning function of the government; stabilization or demand management policy; and redistribution.

Social Goods and Merit Goods

As C.M. Allan points out,[1] the price mechanism is based on two principles:

(i) the exclusion principle (i.e. a person not paying for a good or service will be excluded from the benefits of its consumption);

(ii) revealed preference (i.e. the market operates on information provided by people revealing their preferences through buying habits).

However, with some goods these principles cannot be effectively applied, thus resulting in the unsatisfactory provision of these goods in the market economy.

First, there are those goods which are characterized by the jointness of their consumption whereby a person cannot be excluded from the benefits provided. Clearly such goods are not suitable for market provision, for those people who do not reveal their preferences cannot be excluded from the benefits. Therefore these social or collective goods, sometimes called public goods, need to be provided collectively and, in most cases, the state has proven itself most suited to carry out this function. Common examples are defence, law and order, street cleaning and lighting.

Second, there are those goods which give rise to externalities, i.e. their costs or benefits are not confined exclusively to the individual producer or consumer. As a result, individual revealed preference will not reflect the true value of the good. For example, a person vaccinated against an infectious disease receives benefits, but benefits are also conferred on others as they will now be less likely to contract that disease. Similarly, a person driving a car will only take into

117

account his/her own operating costs. He/she will not usually consider the costs inflicted on society through the noise and pollution associated with his/her activity. Clearly, then, if externalities exist, the market will not ensure optimum consumption from the point of view of society, since *all* costs and benefits will not have been considered.

Finally, there is the question of ignorance. The efficient operation of the market system requires rational choice based on full appreciation of all factors involved. Even leaving aside the case of externalities, there are a number of instances in which this condition may not be fulfilled. Ignorance may arise from the separation in time of costs and benefits. Thus insurance and pension schemes may be underutilized. Ignorance may also arise from a lack of understanding of the nature of the costs or benefits themselves. For example, a heavy smoker may not be fully aware of the dangers to his/her health.

Goods to which externalities or ignorance apply are frequently known as merit or demerit goods, though they are sometimes also called quasi-public goods. As one would expect, merit goods tend to be underconsumed and demerit goods overconsumed in a free market economy. As a result, the state frequently intervenes to rectify the situation: sometimes it might provide the good itself (e.g. health and educational services), but more frequently it confines itself to encouraging or discouraging consumption of the good in question. Thus grants are provided towards house purchase; cigarette smoking is discouraged by advertizing and taxation; activities such as gambling are subject to strict licensing, and in other areas, e.g. pollution control, systems of fines exist.

Apart from increasing the welfare of society in general through these activities, the state can contribute significantly to the realization of two of the aims of economic policy. First, by its provision of social goods it corrects for the imperfections of the market, and thus economic efficiency is enhanced. Second, these activities can frequently provide a vehicle for redistributive policies. For example, some social welfare and health benefits are selectively provided, the less well-off receiving more.

State-Sponsored Bodies

The use of state-sponsored bodies as an instrument of economic policy has been a notable feature of the development of the Irish economy. This has not been based on any policy of state socialism, however. These bodies were essentially individual responses to specific situations, intentions being primarily pragmatic. Basically two traditional areas of intervention can be distinguished from the Irish experience.

First, there are those industries which, because of their technical circumstances, tend towards monopolistic production. Enormous economies of scale often make competition impracticable, as in the generation of electricity. This is particularly so in a country like Ireland with such a relatively small market. Often competition would also lead to chaos — imagine the confusion if two telephone companies were competing for the same custom! If these monopolies must exist, clearly some form of state regulation is necessary in view of the price-raising and output-restricting tendencies of private monopolies. This, in the view of many people, is sufficient reason to justify the establishment of state-sponsored bodies. There is, however, an even stronger case. Many of these industries are infrastructural industries — public utilities and transport — forming a direct part of the cost structure of most other economic activities. Thus, by ensuring that these services are efficiently provided in suitable quantities, the state can promote the economic welfare of the country as a whole. Furthermore, there is the added factor that the state can acquire a greater influence over the direction of the economy. Frequently this form of state activity is not only desirable but also essential to the formation or growth of the activity. This is particularly so where the capital investment required is so great as to preclude private interest. An example of this is the establishment of the ESB (Electricity Supply Board) in the 1920s. This form of intervention could grow considerably with the increasing complexity of modern technology. On other occasions, state intervention has occurred to eliminate what was seen as wasteful competition which the free market had given rise to. This has happened in the transport industries of many countries, as was the case in Ireland with CIE (Córas Iompair Éireann) being formed in the late 1940s in order to rationalize the public transport system.

The second area in which the use of public enterprise has been widespread is more associated with underdeveloped economies. Thus, in Ireland, the state became directly involved in the development of an industrial base, this need stemming from a number of factors. A poorly developed institutional structure, a low level of savings and the resulting lack of capital were important. It is also probable that prospects of profits in some cases were not great. Here the state could adopt a much broader perspective considering social benefits such as increased employment. Examples of this form of public enterprise are the Irish Sugar Company and Bord na Móna. As can be seen from the examples quoted, not only did many of these enterprises contribute directly to growth and employment but they also had considerable indirect impact through their linkage effects with the rest of the economy. Thus the Irish Sugar Company was based on home-grown beet, and Bord na Móna provided an important input for the electricity industry as well as using native resources. It should be noted that state activity in this field has been concentrated not only on directly productive enterprises: important steps have also been made on the institutional front to make up for the previous deficiencies in this area. Examples include the Agricultural Credit Corporation, the Industrial Credit Co., Bord Fáilte and Córas Tráchtála.

More recently, state-sponsored bodies have tended to provide the means for correcting the failures of the market as a device for locational planning. Here again one finds the tendency for individuals to take into account only private costs and benefits. However, a major aim of government policy is the development of poorer regions: thereby, interregional inequalities are diminished and economic choice is enhanced by making available a greater range of employment opportunities and reducing the amount of enforced migration. Frequently these social benefits will be judged to outweigh the costs of industrial dispersal. Thus, many state-sponsored bodies are situated away from industrial conglomerations, e.g. the Irish Sugar Company in Carlow and Mallow. More frequently, this policy has been pursued through the grant schemes of another state-sponsored body, the Industrial Development Authority (IDA).

Planning and Growth
As explained in Chapter 2, growth is now looked on by many as the most important of economic aims, particularly in a country like Ireland where the realization of other objectives such as employment and equality are so dependent on it. Here again one finds that government intervention is needed to supplement the market. It has already been seen how the establishment of many state-sponsored bodies was designed to foster growth in order to compensate for market deficiencies. However, the problem goes deeper, for growth is essentially a long-term objective, whereas the market is primarily concerned with static efficiency, i.e. efficiency at a point in time. Indeed, the case for government intervention here is similar to that for the provision of merit goods. Just as the market fails to take into account the externalities of particular goods, so too it fails to consider the benefits to society of allocating resources to achieve a greater level of growth — benefits such as greater income, employment and equality in the future. Similarly, ignorance can be said to be an important factor in that there is a lack of knowledge about future conditions, trends and opportunities due to market uncertainties. Clearly in such conditions the allocation of resources will not be optimal. (See Chapter 7 for a full discussion of this topic.)

In response to these problems, indicative planning was introduced. This is a form of national economic planning in which a target is set for the growth of national output over a series of years, usually about five. Quantitative estimates are made of what might happen to particular industries and sectors of the economy (e.g. private consumption, public consumption, investment) if the global expansion is achieved. The figures are accompanied by a list of policy measures intended to help fulfil the plan. The figures are thus an 'indication' of how the economy is expected to develop. The policy measures may include incentives or disincentives (such as subsidies or taxes) to promote the desired expansion, but these are not tied to the targets of the plan and there are no sanctions against industries or firms failing to achieve the output figures of the plan.

Indicative planning was introduced in Ireland in the late 1950s with the publication of the First Programme for Economic Expansion, 1959-63. The Second Programme for Economic Expansion covered the years 1964-70 but was abandoned in 1968. The Third Programme for Economic and Social Development was introduced in 1969 and officially ran until 1972. Between 1972 and 1977 there was no official programme, but in 1977 a new government department was formed — the Department of Economic Planning and Development. In early 1978 it published a White Paper on Economic and Social Development for the period 1977-80, but the department was abolished in 1979. A National Planning Board was established for a period in the mid-1980s and their report was used as an input to a government plan in late 1984 called *Building on Reality*. This document, according to one commentator, 'was probably the most sober planning document in the period since 1958'.[2] It was, however, seen as a political document and, as such, was the subject of much controversy.

Thus, indicative planning is still a 'live' issue in Ireland. However, many question its usefulness. First, it is argued that the statistical basis is not sufficiently comprehensive or up to date to allow meaningful national plans to be formulated. For example, some National Income and Expenditure data for 1985 were not available by mid-1987. Moreover, these data are often subject to significant revision a number of years after they are published. Second, it is argued, that a plan almost inevitably becomes politically 'tarnished', with a consequent in-built bias to overoptimistic growth targets. This in turn leads to a loss of confidence not only in planning, but in all aspects of government economic policy. Last, it is argued that given the small and open nature of the Irish economy, with its heavy dependence on conditions in the world economy, it is misguided to think that the government can do anything more than react to these conditions, rather than in any sense control them. As such, publishing overall targets for the economy is a misguided and wasteful use of resources.

The above is not to deny that a published plan for the *public sector*, setting out objectives for four or five years into the future, is not a potentially very useful exercise. Such a plan could provide much more certainty about future taxation and expenditure policies, it could greatly increase the coordination of decision making in the public sector and it could mean that the electorate at large has a useful check against which to measure government policy vis-à-vis the public sector. Besides, the fact remains that government intervention, to supplement the market, is needed if long-term economic growth is to be achieved (see Chapter 7 for a lengthy discussion of this issue) and a clear statement of the form and purpose of this intervention is needed from time to time.

Demand Management Policy
Before the 1930s, it was believed that the working of the market brought about a natural tendency towards equilibrium at full employment, and thus the government's main budgetary aim was to ensure that revenues would be sufficient to match planned expenditures. The historical sequences of trade cycles — alternate periods of boom and depression, inflation and unemployment which culminated in the Great Depression of the early 1930s — demonstrated the fallacy of this assumption. The 'Keynesian Revolution' showed that if governments were prepared to adopt a less conservative budgetary stance, the great waste and hardship brought about by these trade cycles could be largely averted. Thus was born the demand management function of the government. What is involved is ensuring that the aggregate level of *monetary* demand is just sufficient to sustain the projected level of output — not too great, causing inflation, nor too little, leading to unemployment. In recent years, however, there has been some disenchantment with this function of government.

As will be seen in Chapter 6, demand management suffers from many defects (especially in a small open economy like Ireland's), and is applicable only to a limited range of economic problems (i.e. those stemming from an inadequate level of monetary demand). Nevertheless, there is a great danger of over-stressing these weaknesses, since as a policy instrument it has been of major significance in the pursuit of economic aims, especially in the larger economies of the industrialized world. It enabled the maintenance of a much fuller level of employment than could otherwise have been envisaged. Furthermore, demand management policies were extremely important in creating the necessary environment for modern high growth economies.

Knowing of the government commitment to stability, investors were confident of a full level of demand and, furthermore, the absence of great fluctuations in the future improved the efficiency of investment, since it did not have to be made quite so flexible to cope with future uncertainties.

Redistribution

As pointed out in Chapter 2, there is much disagreement about exactly what constitutes equality; nevertheless, most people are committed to it in some form as an economic objective. Similarly, few would deny the market's inability to secure this aim.

Assuming perfect mobility and knowledge and equal abilities, the market will tend to lead to equality. However, mobility is not perfect, since it often involves great social as well as financial costs; information is not perfect; and not only do people have unequal abilities, but one has also to remember the plight of the old and the severely handicapped, both mentally and physically. Thus, relying totally on a market system causes gross inequalities to emerge.

Apart from the moral issues involved, inequalities also tend to produce alienation, tension and instability — conditions not conducive to economic welfare and progress. Much government intervention in the economy is therefore designed to reduce inequalities, either directly or indirectly. Direct transfers to the less well-off include pensions and unemployment benefits. The universal provision of social and merit goods can promote greater equality by making such goods available to all. Indeed, some merit goods such as health services are selectively provided, poorer people receiving greater benefits. Government stabilization policies can ensure greater equality than would occur under free market conditions, and other forms of government intervention are frequently designed to reduce interregional inequalities. Legislation has also been used to reduce discrimination on grounds of race, religion or sex.

One of the most obvious ways the government can alter the distribution of income and wealth is through the system of taxation (see Chapter 5). Consequently great stress is laid on the progressive nature of income taxes. However, since indirect taxes, which are largely regressive, have also to be extensively used, this tends to reduce the equalizing effects of the tax system.

A Tarnished Consensus? [3]

Until the 1970s, there appears to have been broad consensus among economists on the failures of the market system and the consequent need for large-scale government intervention in the areas outlined above. However, failure to analyze the operation of the state itself always constituted a weak link — a weakness that was obvious but yet not widely appreciated until the mid-1970s. The 'discovery' then that state and democratic political processes contain their own defects shifted the 'centre of gravity' of the economics profession, with a renewed distrust of the state emerging in the last decade or so. The consensus among economists on the Keynesian social democratic state has become 'tarnished'.

While market failure is a *necessary* condition for the state to intervene to improve resource allocation, it is not a *sufficient* condition. In a properly defined appraisal, it is argued, state action should be subjected to an analysis parallel to that of the market, thereby exposing its failures. As a result, before firm conclusions about the appropriate economic role of the state, either in general or in specific contexts, can be inferred, the costs of market failure must be weighed against those of state failure.

The two major failures associated with state activity, it is argued, are that the public sector will inevitably become 'overexpanded' and that the public sector is inherently wasteful of resources.

Overexpanded Public Sector. When the notion of the omniscient, altruistic public official — implicit in the market failure arguments for state intervention — is replaced by the reality of vote-seeking politicians and self-interested civil servants, distortions can arise.

First, it is claimed that the benefits and costs of public expenditure are inaccurately perceived, with a persistent and systematic fiscal illusion at work. Specifically, it is argued by some that public sector expenditure is overexpanded because much of it is designed to satisfy particular demands, whereas the costs of taxation are evenly spread and diverse. However, it is possible to argue the case in reverse, and claim that the benefits of public expenditure are diffuse whereas tax shares are keenly felt. Thus, even accepting the existence of fiscal illusion, it is not at all obvious whether it leads to an overexpanded or underexpanded public sector. Expenditure-raising policies may have captured votes in the 1960s and 1970s, but tax-reducing policies appear to be the 'vote-catchers' of the 1980s! There is also reason to doubt the existence of any systematic fiscal illusion. Economists always assume rationality on the part of consumers, but yet appear to suggest that the same person *qua* voter is consistently and systematically deceived. This, for reasons mentioned later, may be possible in the short run, but it is unlikely to persist over a longer period of time.

The second source of distortion arises from the fact that politicians cannot directly carry out the business of government, but rely for its execution upon civil servants. Niskanen[4] has suggested that the relationship between the politician and the civil servant is best viewed as one of bilateral monopoly: the politician is the sole supplier of money to the civil service department and the department is the sole provider of the output which the politician desires. However, because of the absence of a market valuation of output (e.g. health care), the politician cannot properly monitor the activities of the public servant. The public servant on the other hand is mainly concerned with maximizing the budget of his/her department and, in the absence of strict political constraint, will bring about an overexpanded public sector. As with the fiscal illusion argument, however, the reverse can be posited. For example, for ideological reasons, as perhaps in the UK in the 1980s, the political constraints on the funding of government departments may be over severe, leading to a suboptimal output of a public good. Thus, while distortions may arise, it is not obvious that these will necessarily lead to an overexpanded, rather than an under-expanded public sector. None the less, it has to be acknowledged that gaps between the level and composition of public output demanded by voters and what is actually provided can and do occur, and that this is a problem that must be kept under careful scrutiny.

Slow Productivity Growth. The growth of the public sector appears to have been accompanied by very slow productivity growth in the provision of public services. There are two polar explanations for this, with dramatically different implications for the future of public expenditure.

The first argues that there is a distinction between different types of economic activity in terms of the applicability of new technology. In broad terms, there are the technologically progressive sectors in which economies of scale, capital accumulation and innovation lead to continuous increases in output per person and the technologically non-progressive sectors in which none of this is possible. However, both sectors have to compete for labour in the same market and the non-progressive sector will also face trade union pressure to maintain 'comparability' with wages in the progressive sector. Thus, as real living standards rise, the unit costs of activities in the non-progressive sector will increase relative to those in the progressive sector. It is arguable that most publicly provided services (e.g. education, health care and policing) are technologically non-progressive in the sense described above and that slow or zero productivity growth in these sectors is an *inevitable* consequence of the nature of public sector activities.

The second argument, however, asserts that barriers to productivity growth are not technological, but institutional, and, as such, can be overcome. Three types of problem have been identified. First, the monitoring of goals in the public sector is removed from the discipline of the market and depends heavily upon the self-discipline of those running the government service. As mentioned earlier, goals other than maximizing the cost-effectiveness of the service may be chosen; for example, pioneering technical advance in hospital care even when it is economically unviable. Second, as output is difficult to define and measure, the monitoring of costs is often defective and can result in wasted resources. Third, public policies have unpredictable side effects, which often impose additional, and unaccounted for, costs on both public and private organizations, with the result that new programmes may sometimes be introduced to rectify the damage done by existing ones. The proposed solutions to many of these problems have varied from privatization of entire functions of government services, to the design of personal financial incentives for public servants, to tighter rules governing accountability. The theme common to all of these proposals, however, is the creation of greater competition, real or simulated, since the lack of it is seen as central to the problems of inefficiency and low productivity growth in the public sector.

Whether slow productivity growth in public sector provision arises from technological factors, or institutional barriers to change, or a combination of both, is still an unresolved issue. Likewise, the relative performance of public and private organizations is still a subject more characterized by strong assertion than systematic evidence. 'It is possible to cite "horror stories" about any organization but exceptionally difficult to assess either their accuracy or significance, never more so than when they relate to the state'.[5] What is true of any organization, though, be it private or public, is that a continuous review of procedures for control and accountability has to be undertaken in order to ensure its continued economic viability and effectiveness.

Apart from the above, a number of problems associated with state provision in practice have been identified. It is argued that the strategy of equality has failed, both on the expenditure and taxation fronts. It is also argued that the tax system used to fund public expenditure is complex and inequitable, leading to widespread dissatisfaction and dissent. Finally, from once being regarded 'as one of the few jewels in the crown of what was seen as a much-troubled system, public sector industrial relations have become its bed of thorns'.[6] Some of these problems will be looked at in later chapters.

Conclusion

Few would doubt that there is still an overwhelming case, on both economic and equity grounds, for continued large-scale government intervention along the lines mentioned earlier. As will be seen in the next section, almost half of government expenditure is in the form of transfers, such as unemployment benefit and old-age pensions, and no serious political grouping has suggested the abolition of these. Besides, there is no substantive body of opinion in Ireland proposing the phasing out of government provision of policing, defence, education or health (the large expenditure areas). Likewise, it is unlikely that there is any overwhelming economic argument for the privatization of, say, the Electricity Supply Board. However, what the events of the past decade or so have clearly demonstrated are: (i) that it is possible for the output of publicly produced services to exceed greatly the demand for such services, as evidenced by willingness to pay for such services (see next section), and (ii) that much stricter checks and controls on government provision are required to ensure greater cost-effectiveness in such provision. Reform, rather than abolition, of government intervention in the areas outlined earlier appears to be the only serious option.

2   THE EXTENT OF GOVERNMENT INTERVENTION

Expenditure
The foregoing section will have given some indication of the extent and diversity of government intervention in the economy. However, an even clearer appreciation of the importance of the government's role can be grasped by examining actual statistics relating to the public sector.

Although opinions differ as to what should be included in public sector expenditure, the general practice is to include both central and local government *total* expenditure (net of intergovernmental transfers), the latter being an important agent of government policy in areas such as health, housing and roadworks. The activities of semi-state bodies are excluded from this measure of public sector expenditure, even though, as shown in the previous section, such bodies are important instruments of government policy.

Turning to a somewhat different issue, the inclusion of transfer payments in a measure of public sector share may be queried, as transfers do not represent direct government control of resources. In most cases, the recipients of transfer payments, and not the state, determine what goods and services are bought (and hence produced). However, transfers are financed from general taxation, and expenditure on transfers is determined by political decisions about allocative as well as distributional objectives, decisions which are of equal importance to those relating to other aspects of public sector expenditure.

Last, it should be noted that absolute expenditure figures in isolation are not a sufficiently good measure of the extent of government involvement, since such a measure cannot be used for comparison over time and between countries due to differences in the levels of population, incomes and prices. For this reason, public sector expenditure expressed as a percentage of national product will be used.

No set of statistics, of course, can adequately convey the degree of control and influence that a government may have over an economy. In particular, if a government uses the method of *regulation*, rather than finance or direct provision, then it is possible that a small public sector, as measured above, could be compatible with overwhelming government control. On the other hand, the state may provide the full finance for areas such as education and health, and yet have little *effective* control. Much of government expenditure in these areas is on salaries and wages for people with virtual life tenure and, as such, governments in the short run have little room for manoeuvre in terms of altering expenditure. In this respect a government regulation, such as making the Irish language a compulsory examination subject, which involves little expenditure, could represent a much greater degree of control. Likewise, the monies allocated to the IDA, although small in the context of total expenditure, enable the government, through the IDA, to influence the whole process of industrial development in Ireland. With these important caveats in mind, the remainder of this chapter now concentrates on government expenditure as a proportion of domestic product as a measure of government control and involvement in the Irish economy.

The total expenditure of public authorities amounted to approximately 19 per cent of national product in 1926, the corresponding figure in 1987 being about 54 per cent. This clearly indicates the dramatic changes that have occurred in the economic involvement of the government since the foundation of the state. These changes, however, were not spread evenly throughout the period, but were concentrated into five basic subperiods: the early 1930s, the late 1940s, the 1960s, 1973-75 and 1978-82 respectively. Between 1931 and 1933 the public sector share rose by three or four percentage points, and by eight or nine points between 1947 and 1952.[7] Expansion in the public sector restarted about 1963, when it accounted for 30.8 per cent of GDP (about the same as that in 1952), and rose to 39.1 per cent in 1970. Between 1973 and 1975 there was a quite dramatic increase in public sector share, from 39.5 to 47.3 per cent of GDP, with a further huge increase between 1978 and 1982, from 45.3 to 55.6 per cent of GDP.

The public sector expansion that occurred between 1931 and 1933 can be largely explained by two related events — the accession to power of a government with much more radical and state-orientated economic policies, and the outbreak of the 'economic war' (see Chapter 1). As a result of the latter, a deficiency payment scheme was introduced to help farmers offset British import duties and thereby protect agricultural incomes. A major house-building drive led to a relative growth in capital expenditure on goods and services and there were large increases in capital subsidies, reflecting the government's drive for self-sufficiency and its attempt to influence the development of an industrial base.

In the second displacement period the orientation towards capital expansion was even more pronounced. This was largely attributable to increases in capital expenditure on goods and services, particularly in housing and health services. A major part of the immediate post-war expansion in public sector expenditure was social in character, and, in fact, public social expenditure doubled between 1947 and 1951. No doubt part of the explanation is accounted for by pressures to follow the lead of the Labour Government in Britain.

During the 1950s, against a background of a stagnated economic environment, the level of public expenditure remained fairly stable, but with the economic upsurge of the late 1950s and early 1960s, public sector expansion was renewed and continued until 1970. During this time there was an increase of about eight percentage points in the public sector share. The 1973-75 and 1978-82 expansions in public sector share were quite remarkable. As mentioned, the public sector share of GDP rose by more than fifteen percentage points in these two periods.

The rapid growth in the relative size of the public sector between the early 1960s and the early 1980s was not, of course, peculiar to Ireland. It occurred in all European Community (EC) countries (Table 4.1). The increase in Ireland and in the other small open economies of the Community was particularly pronounced though, especially between the mid-1970s and early 1980s. In marked contrast, the size of the public sector in Germany and the UK was kept broadly steady in the years between 1975 and 1982. Between 1982 and 1986 the share of the public sector in GDP stabilized or declined in most countries. The Netherlands has now the largest public sector (at around 60 per cent of GDP), followed by Belgium, Denmark, Ireland and Italy (all at around 55 per cent of GDP). Germany,

Table 4.1

Public Sector Expenditure as a Percentage of GDP in Selected EC Countries, 1960-86

	Bel.	Den.	Fr.	Ger.	Irl.[1]	It.	Sp.	Neth.	UK
1960	30.3	24.8	34.6	32.5	27.9	30.1	n.a.	33.7	32.4
1975	46.7	48.2	43.5	47.0	47.3	43.2	24.7	51.8	44.2
1982	58.1	61.1	51.1	49.4	55.6	54.8	36.9	61.3	45.0
1986[2]	55.1	56.4	51.7	46.6	53.7	56.7	38.6	60.2	44.0

Source: Commission of the European Communities, *European Economy,* Brussels, July 1986, Table 46.

[1]Derived from CSO, *National Income and Expenditure,* various issues. Public sector expenditure was defined as: public authorities' net current expenditure plus gross physical capital formation, plus subsidies, plus current transfers, plus capital transfers and payments to the rest of the world. This is almost identical to the definition used by the Commission.
[2]Estimates.

Greece, Portugal, Spain and the UK have public sector shares of about 45 per cent, and Spain has the smallest public sector share (under 40 per cent).

In most of the EC countries, current transfers accounted on average for about two-thirds of the increased public sector share, with current expenditure on goods and services accounting for the bulk of the remainder. The increased expenditures on transfers were largely for social security purposes, such as pensions, children's allowances, and sickness and unemployment benefit. The increased consumption expenditures were mostly allocated to education and health.[8] The position in Ireland was similar (Table 4.2). Between 1973 and 1986 expenditure on current transfers rose from 14.0 to 25.7 per cent of

Table 4.2

The Percentage Share of Public Sector Expenditure in GDP, Ireland, 1973-86

	Current goods and services	Capital formation	Current transfers	(of which national debt interest)	Other[1]	Total
1973	15.6	4.9	14.0	(3.7)	5.0	39.5
1978	17.1	4.8	17.6	(5.8)	5.8	45.3
1982	19.7	5.1	24.7	(9.0)	6.1	55.6
1984	19.1	3.8	26.1	(9.6)	4.9	53.9
1986[2]	20.0	3.7	25.7	(10.1)	4.3	53.7

Sources: CSO, *National Income and Expenditure,* various issues; and *Budget 1986,* Stationery Office, Dublin, January 1986.

[1]Subsidies, capital transfers and payments to the rest of the world.
[2]Estimates

GDP, i.e. they accounted for over four-fifths of the increase in the overall public sector share. The share of GDP devoted to current goods and services rose by over four percentage points, and the bulk of this was for increased expenditure on education, health, defence and police.

As mentioned previously, only expenditure on current goods and services and on capital formation represents direct government use of economic resources — the remainder simply results in a redistribution of resources. This is an important point, as it keeps the discussion of the level and growth of public sector share in Ireland in its proper perspective. Relating this expenditure to GDP (i.e. using the sum of the first two columns in Table 4.2), it can be seen that it accounted for only 23.7 per cent of GDP in 1986, a rise of just over three percentage points since 1973.

Table 4.3
Percentage Distribution of Public Sector Expenditure by Purpose of Expenditure, 1979 and 1983

	1979	1983
Social security and welfare	17.9	23.1
National debt interest	12.2	16.0
Health	13.4	12.6
Education	11.6	10.8
General government services (including defence)	11.5	10.5
Transport and communications	8.6	5.7
Housing	6.2	5.5
Agriculture, forestry and fishing	5.5	4.7
Mining, manufacturing and construction	5.7	4.1
Other economic services	4.4	4.2
Other	3.0	2.8
Total	100.0	100.0

Sources: CSO, *National Income and Expenditure 1985,* Stationery Office, July 1986.

Table 4.3 presents, mainly for informational reasons, the percentage breakdown of public sector expenditure by purpose of expenditure. As may be seen, social security and welfare now account for almost a quarter of total public sector expenditure. National debt interest accounts for a sixth, health for an eighth and education for a ninth. As may be seen also, social security and welfare and national debt interest together accounted for 30.1 per cent of the total in 1979, rising to 39.1 per cent in 1983 — the percentage for all other categories declined in the same period.

What were the causes of the increased public sector share in Ireland in the last twenty years? Looking at current consumption (goods and services) expenditure, a combination of factors may be posited. First, there was, as mentioned, greatly increased expenditure on education and health throughout the European Community, and, as a result, a strong 'demonstration effect' was probably in operation. Second, the rapid increase in living standards in Ireland in the same period (see Chapter 7) enabled the government to respond to the increased demand for these services, the demand being both autonomous and induced (via the demonstration effect). Last, and perhaps most important, the *relative* unit cost of providing public services, as mentioned earlier, increased in the last two decades. The scope for increased productivity in the provision of educational and health services in particular was very limited, yet the incomes of the providers of these services increased in line with, if not faster than, those in the high productivity growth sectors of the economy. As a result, the implicit price of public services increased relative to prices elsewhere. If the income elasticity of demand for these services was greater than the price elasticity, which empirical evidence indicates was clearly the case, then the public sector share would have increased automatically because of this fact.[9]

The greatly increased share of national expenditure devoted to transfers, likewise, has many causes. First, the demonstration effect and increased living standards were clearly important factors, especially for the very large increase in expenditure on old-age pensions that took place. Second, the recessions in 1974-75 and 1979-83 led to huge increases in unemployment-related transfers. Third, as will be seen in the next section, much of public expenditure in the last decade was financed by borrowing and the interest payments on this borrowing have emerged as a major component of current government transfers. For example, in 1973 interest on the national debt amounted to 3.7 per cent of GDP, rising to 9.0 per cent in 1982 and to 10.1 per cent by 1986 (see Table 4.2). Thus, between 1973 and 1986 more than half of the increased share of transfers in GDP was accounted for by national debt interest.

It is clear, then, that the way in which public expenditure was financed in the 1970s is influencing the extent of that expenditure into the 1980s. It is also believed by many economists that this was a major factor, over and above those already noted, in explaining the growth of expenditures, on both current goods and services and transfers, that took place in the 1970s. This issue is looked at in the next section.

Revenue

Government expenditures can be divided into current and capital, and these are financed by current and capital revenues respectively. When there is a current budget deficit this must be funded by capital revenues. Current revenues, which average about 75 per cent of total public sector receipts, consist predominantly of tax revenues, and some minor non-tax revenues. There are three major components of tax revenues:

(i)   taxes on income or direct taxes (income tax, social security contributions and corporation tax);

(ii) taxes on expenditure or indirect taxes (VAT, excise duties, customs duties, rates, motor vehicle duties, etc.);

(iii) taxes on capital (capital gains tax and capital acquisitions tax).

Capital revenues are made up almost totally of borrowing, the small residual being accounted for by interest on and repayment of loans made by the government. This borrowing has two components: normal exchequer resources (e.g. sales of securities, small savings) and residual borrowing from abroad and from domestic financial institutions.

The *trends* in receipts in relation to GDP are shown in Table 4.4. It is clear from this table that increased revenue from income tax, social security contributions, net borrowing and VAT provided the finance for the increased public sector share between 1973 and 1986. The increased revenue from VAT, though, has to be seen in the context of a declining share for other indirect taxes. As such, the increases in the first three forms of receipts are of most significance.

Table 4.4

The Percentage Share of Public Sector Receipts in GDP, Ireland, 1973-86

	1973	1978	1982	1984	1986[1]
Income tax	8.2	8.9	11.2	13.2	13.9
Soc. sec. conts.	3.6	4.3	5.6	5.8	5.8
Net borrowing	5.8	13.6	18.4	13.7	15.7
VAT[2]	5.1	6.1	6.6	7.9	8.2
Other	16.8	12.4	13.8	13.3	10.1
Total	39.5	45.3	55.6	53.9	53.7

Sources: as for Table 4.2.

[1] Estimates.

[2] Turnover tax was introduced in 1963/64 and wholesale tax in 1966/67. Both were replaced by VAT in 1972/73.

The increase in the share of income tax and social security contributions in GDP started from 1963, but it was not until after 1973 that the rapid escalation in the share of net borrowing in GDP took place. A broadly similar trend existed in all the EC countries, although no country relied on borrowing to the same extent as Ireland did to finance the increased public sector share.

It was these trends which led to the widely held view that the *cost* of the increased public sector expenditure was not visible, and therefore not realized by the electorate, at least at the time. This could have arisen from a subtle change in the system of taxation, or in the circumstances under which the taxation system operated. Was this the case in Ireland during the period of growth in the public sector share? Many economists argue that it was, and that the consequent 'illusion' that increased public output was 'free' was a powerful factor behind the increased public sector share in the period 1973 to 1982.

Personal income tax, as was seen in Table 4.4, was a major source of new revenue for the expansion of the public sector in Ireland for the period 1973-82. The argument about lack of visibility here is that with rapid increases in money incomes, due to increased real incomes and/or inflation, an increasing proportion of people's income automatically accrues, *ceteris paribus*, to the government in the form of income tax. This, in the absence of action to adjust tax allowances and bands, leads to an *automatic* increase in the average rate of taxation, an increase that to the vast majority of the electorate would initially be almost 'invisible'. Now while a decline in this form of tax illusion is nearly inevitable in the medium to long term, as evidenced by various events and developments since 1979, there is not likely to be a reduction in public sector share once the costs of previous rises in public sector share have been realized. Organizational pressure to protect public jobs is by then too well established.

The potential for 'fiscal drag', as it is called, has undoubtedly existed in Ireland, with very rapid increases in money incomes taking place. That fiscal drag has actually occurred is evidenced by the fact that the level of tax-free allowances has fallen sharply relative to earnings. As mentioned before, greater public awareness of fiscal drag is now in evidence. However, the main impact of the fiscal reform introduced in other countries to reflect this new awareness has been to keep the share of income taxes in GDP stable, rather than to decrease it. This confirms the point above: the impact of the phenomenon of fiscal drag on public sector share tends to be permanent. ·

The other main source of current revenue which increased its share of GDP, as was seen in Table 4.4, was social security contributions. These were clearly visible, but what could be argued is that it was not evident to many workers that social security contributions were for them a 'hidden' form of income tax. One of the reasons why the implementation of new social security taxes met with little resistance was that most workers may have believed that the benefits were highly individual, and thereby clearly visible. This belief was nurtured by the use of the term 'social *insurance* contributions', although it is well known by now that the social security schemes in existence in Ireland, or elsewhere, are not in any sense operated on a strict actuarial basis (see Chapter 5).

The final and major source of increased revenue share was borrowing. This form of revenue raising, at least temporarily, completely avoids the problem of raising visible taxes to meet the increased public sector share. In this case borrowing has to be seen as an appropriation of future taxation, both to service and to repay the debt. It could be argued that future generations should pay, and be prepared to pay, taxation for benefits received from capital equipment installed today. Even assuming, though, that additional public borrowing is used to finance investment-producing services, the well-known fundamental difficulty of ascertaining society's future preferences remains. Much more seriously, about half of the increased borrowing share was used to finance *current* expenditure (Table 4.5). Thus the government was able to increase visible benefits in the 1970s and early 1980s, whereas the costs would not become visible until later years. It could be strongly argued that most of the electorate were not, at least at the time, aware of the subtleties involved in this method of financing the increased public sector share, or else that they have not yet had to consider the costs. However, given what has been repeatedly argued above, public sector share may be flexible upwards only. Thus, when the costs of the increased public sector share eventually became evident to the electorate, it was too late to do anything without serious social conflict. This, indeed, is the case

Table 4.5
National Debt etc. as a Percentage of GDP at Market Prices for Selected Years, 1973-85

	Total debt	Foreign debt[1]	Debt service	Current budget deficit
1973[2]	60.0	6.2	5.6	0.4
1975	67.1	15.8	5.9	5.9
1982	86.2	39.7	9.1	7.4
1985	107.1	48.8	10.2	7.4

Sources: Central Bank of Ireland Quarterly Bulletin, various issues.
[1]Adjusted for exchange rate changes.
[2]Financial year 1973/74

that has been argued repeatedly by many economic commentators for some time.[10] The argument, then, that the electorate did not fully understand the costs of the increased public sector share in the 1970s and early 1980s and that, if they did, the expansion of the public sector would not have been nearly so rapid, is a forceful one.

National Debt
In 1922, at the foundation of the state, there was virtually no national debt, yet despite the fact that the country had no wars to fight, Ireland's national debt as a percentage of GDP is now the highest of all EC countries and interest payments and redemptions make up a major component of government current expenditure. In 1985, the value of the accumulated debt of the Irish central government exceeded the value of the country's GDP. This had risen considerably throughout the 1970s (Table 4.5) because of the increase in net borrowings noted earlier, and by 1985 was about twice the corresponding figure for most other EC countries. Belgium, however, had a higher debt/GDP ratio than Ireland (see *European Economy,* November 1986, Table 19).

The rapid increase in national debt in the last decade has alarmed most economic commentators, especially when the structure of the debt, and the uses to which it was put are examined. As may be seen in Table 4.5, the foreign portion of the debt rose dramatically, from 6.2 per cent of GDP in 1973 to almost 50 per cent of GDP by 1985. Such a reliance on foreign borrowing for an EC country is unusual and in this respect it puts Ireland firmly in line with some of the less (financially) stable Latin American and East European countries. As also may be seen in Table 4.5, Ireland ran a large current budget deficit between 1975 and 1985, implying that much of the increase in public expenditure was being used to finance *current* expenditure. Last, a point mentioned earlier, the cost of servicing this past borrowing has risen substantially and is usurping an increasing proportion of tax revenue. For example, the cost of debt service, expressed as a percentage of GDP, rose from 5.6 per cent in 1973 to 10.2 per cent in 1985. As a result, in the late 1980s, around 30 per cent of total tax revenue is going to service the national debt.

Borrowing to finance a deficit in the current budget only started on a large scale in Ireland in the mid-1970s and there are often sound economic reasons for doing so (see Chapter 6). Budget deficits can be important instruments of demand management policy and this may have been partly the case in Ireland in the last decade. However, 'the danger is that once a government incurs a current budgetary deficit, experience will show that a valuable psychological barrier against imprudence has been breached, current budget deficits will become the rule rather than the exception, and there will be a cumulatively increasing amount of debt ascribable to deficits in the current budget'.[11] Besides, budget deficits in Ireland appear to have just 'happened' rather than to have been planned. Moreover, in a demand management context, it is overall public sector borrowing (not just that incurred for current expenditure) and its funding that is of most importance. Thus, the general concern about the emergence of large current budget deficits in Ireland in the last decade appears to be very well founded. As a result, the elimination of such deficits by the end of the 1980s has been a major 'plank' of government economic policy.

Apart from the worry about incurring debt for current expenditure purposes, there has also been concern about the borrowing to finance some capital expenditure, especially where such expenditure held out little prospect of an economic return. However, this is an issue that will be returned to in later chapters.

The concern about the debt being foreign is that such debt is of a quite different character from that arising from domestic borrowing. First, the payment of interest and eventually the principal, entails a reduction in resources available to the country as well as a transfer problem in foreign exchange, problems that do not arise in the case of internal debt. The external obligations may require the government to reduce future public spending or to increase taxation at a future date, a problem that has already arisen. Second, the debt is subject to the uncertainty of exchange rate fluctuations. For example, the burden becomes greater when the currencies in which the borrowing took place appreciate in relation to the Irish pound. Third, in the case of domestic debt, the usual experience is that most of the debt is converted into new stock: 'in effect, the internal national debt can be regarded as permanent by consent'.[12] This is not the case with external debt, since whether this debt can be readily refinanced as it matures depends on the external lenders continuing to take a favourable view of the Irish economy's capacity to service and repay its obligations, i.e. on the economy's stability and growth and the country's capacity to run its affairs competently.

Foreign borrowing, or any borrowing for that matter, used for current or non-productive purposes does *not* directly increase a country's capacity to service or repay its debt: nor does it yield the foreign exchange that will be needed for those purposes. It is these twin problems of borrowing being foreign and large and expenditure being large and wasteful that have led to the national debt crisis in Ireland today.[13]

Conclusion

It is likely that the share of the public sector in GDP will remain at its very high levels of the 1980s until the end of the century. The continuing very high level of unemployment (see Chapter 8) will bring about increasing pressure on the government to alleviate the problem through more government intervention. There are also likely to be continuing strong pressures to maintain expenditure on education, health and social welfare (the large expenditure areas). Besides, as mentioned earlier, the low productivity growth in the provision of such services will automatically lead to an increase in the proportion of GDP needed to finance even present levels of these services.

The prospects of financing further increases in public expenditure out of taxation do not seem great: indirect taxes are already very high, and direct taxation is a considerable burden on the individual taxpayer, for effective rates of income tax are very high, despite the relatively low proportion of receipts collected in this form. The problem in both cases is partly due to the small base for each tax (see Chapter 5). The prospects, therefore, of decreasing the level of borrowing, without serious social conflict, do not look promising. The only real hope is for a very strong economic recovery to provide the revenue buoyancy needed to allow borrowing to be scaled down without any major cut-backs in services provided.

Footnotes

1 C.M. Allan, *The Theory of Taxation,* Penguin, Harmondsworth 1971.

2 John Bradley, 'Economic Planning: Lessons from the Past and Future Prospects' (paper read to the Dublin Economics Workshop, Ninth Annual Conference, Kenmare), October 1986, p.8.

3 This section draws extensively on David Heald, *Public Expenditure,* Martin Robertson, Oxford 1983.

4 See W.A. Niskanen, *Bureaucracy and Representative Government,* Aldine-Atherton, Chicago 1971.

5 Heald, *op. cit.,* p.118.

6 *Ibid.,* p.319.

7 See J.W. O'Hagan. 'An Analysis of the Relative Size of the Government Sector: Ireland 1926-52', *Economic and Social Review,* October 1980.

8 See J.W. O'Hagan, 'An Analysis of the Growth of the Public Sector in Ireland, 1953-77', *Journal of the Statistical and Social Inquiry Society of Ireland,* 1979/80.

9 See John O'Hagan and Morgan Kelly, 'Components of Growth in Current Public Expenditure on Education and Health', *Economic and Social Review,* January 1984, for a discussion of the above.

10 See NESC, *Report on Public Expenditure* (Report no. 21), Stationery Office, Dublin 1976, and articles in *Irish Times,* October 21 and 22, 1980.

11 T. O'Grady Walshe, 'The Growing National Debt: Implications', third edition of this book, p.123.

12 *Ibid.,* p.127.

13 See Jim O'Leary, 'The National Debt: Implications for Fiscal Policy' (paper read to Foundation for Fiscal Studies AGM, Dublin), April 1987, for further reading.

5   Taxation Policy

John W. O'Hagan

IT WAS mentioned in Chapter 4 that government involvement in the economy could be broken down into five broad areas: the provision of social and merit goods, the activities of semi-state bodies, planning, stabilization and redistribution. Alternatively, the discussion could have been conducted in terms of the three traditionally defined functions of government activity: allocation, distribution and stabilization. The allocational function refers to the government's role in influencing what is produced in an economy and, as such, broadly corresponds with the first three areas looked at in Chapter 4, Section 1. The other two functions correspond directly with the remaining areas looked at. This classification by function is particularly useful when discussing taxation policy.

As was also seen in Chapter 4, taxation is the principal means of transferring to the government the control of the resources needed to carry out its activities. However, a tax is rarely neutral and so it will have its own effects on the allocation of goods and services, on the distribution of incomes and wealth, and on stabilization. Thus the overall effect of government activity must be assessed in the light of both its revenue and expenditure pattern. The distributional and allocational effects of the important taxes in Ireland will be examined in this chapter.

To facilitate this, the chapter will look at taxation policy under three main headings: the taxation of income (including social security contributions), indirect, capital, and company taxation; and the overall distributional effects of taxation. The discussion throughout draws extensively on Kay and King's much lauded book, *The British Tax System.*[1]

Before embarking on the discussion of taxation policy, it is worthwhile to draw attention to the broad structure of taxation in Ireland. This is outlined in Table 5.1. As may be seen, income tax is the biggest source of tax revenue, and with social insurance contributions (effectively an income tax) added in, its primary importance is even more emphasized. Indeed, revenue from social insurance contributions amounts to 43 per cent of that from income tax. Excise duties and VAT are the other major revenue earners, with the combined receipts from both not much less than total receipts from income tax and social insurance contributions. The other sources of tax revenue are relatively insignificant when compared with the four major groupings, a fact that is often neglected in discussions on taxation, and frequently in economics textbooks as well. This applies in particular to the often grossly over-exaggerated emphasis put on corporation and capital taxation. In Ireland, as may be seen, the former only accounts for about four per cent, and the latter for as little as 0.6 per cent, of total receipts from taxation. A tax with a low revenue yield, though, may have significant allocational effects on an economy; capital taxes, perhaps, being a good example.

Table 5.1
Main Sources of Tax Revenue, 1985 and 1986

	1985 IR£million	1986 IR£million
Income tax[1]	2,260	2,472
Value added tax	1,402	1,509
Excise duties	1,313	1,361
Social insurance contributions	998	1,059
Corporation tax	217	245
Rates	144	142
Motor vehicle duties	122	126
Customs duties	97	104
Stamp duties	120	98
Capital taxes	33	35

Sources: Budget 1986, Stationery Office, Dublin, January 1986.
[1]Including income levy and youth employment levy.

1   THE TAXATION OF INCOME

How the System Works
Income tax is levied upon persons and the income to be taxed is determined by reference to a list of sources of income known as the 'schedules'. About 75 per cent of gross income assessable for income tax comes under Schedule E (wages, salaries and pensions) and almost all the remainder comes under Schedule D (mostly income from self-employment and other profit). Tax under Schedule D is collected in arrears,[2] whereas assessment is based on the current year's income for Schedule E. Nearly all of the income coming under Schedule E is subject to the withholding scheme, called Pay-

As-You-Earn (PAYE). This system requires an employer to deduct tax from the incomes of his/her employees according to certificates and tables issued by the Revenue Commissioners.

Self-employed people are assessed under Schedule E and the differential treatment implicit in this is a cause for some concern, especially to the PAYE sector. Apart from the fact that the self-employed pay their taxes in arrears, the expenses rule in relation to tax liability is significantly more liberal for Schedule E than for Schedule D income. Besides, being treated under Schedule E, it is felt, may confer 'a number of advantages on self-employed persons relating principally to the discretion which they enjoy in determining their tax liability, making their remittances of due taxes, and complying with the tax collection and enforcement agencies'.[3]

In assessing a person's liability for income tax, a wide array of allowances, reliefs and exemptions apply. There are also certain classes of income which are not included as income for tax purposes.

Allowances are fixed amounts of income which can be received free of tax and the most important is the *basic* personal allowance to which everyone is entitled. In 1987/88 this was IR£2,000 for single persons and double this for married couples. A further PAYE allowance (IR£700 in 1987/88) is granted to most people receiving taxable income under Schedule E (introduced in recognition of the more favourable tax treatment of the self-employed, outlined above). Additional *secondary* allowances are also granted, for example, to single parents, widowed parents and blind persons.

Income allocated to certain expenses is also 'relieved' from income tax. Reliefs relate to business expenses and non-business expenses, and by their nature are discretionary. Reliefs for business expenses are varied, and are difficult to define precisely. It is often impossible for the revenue authorities to draw a firm line between non-allowable personal expenses and allowable business expenses: meals out, cars, and travel abroad provide good illustrations of the difficulties. As mentioned, though, this is much more likely to be a problem with the self-employed than with the PAYE sector. Reliefs for non-business expenses are also heterogeneous. In some circumstances relief with respect to expenditure on a housekeeper can be claimed. Much more significantly, half of life assurance premiums, all premiums paid under permanent health insurance policies, and mortgage interest payments (up to IR£3,600 for a married couple in 1987/88), are tax deductible.

Certain income is completely exempt from income tax. Non-factor income such as gambling winnings (including those won under the National Lottery) and most social welfare benefits are exempt. Income from original and creative works, having cultural or artistic merit, retirement benefits, redundancy payments and so on are also exempt. Finally, low income (i.e. near or below the basic personal allowances) is exempted to eliminate the cost of dealing with such income.

Given the way that income is defined for tax purposes (see later), there are certain types of income which are not included for income tax purposes, but which should be, perhaps, if a comprehensive definition of income was adopted. There are two main categories in question, both in the form of investment income, namely capital gains and the imputed rental income from owner-occupation of a dwelling.

After all allowances, reliefs and exemptions have been deducted from income included for tax purposes, the remaining income (i.e. taxable income) is subject to income tax. A basic rate of 35 per cent applies to the first IR£4,700 (1987/88): income above this is charged at a rate of 48 per cent. When taxable income exceeds IR£7,500 the *marginal* rate rises to 58 per cent. For married couples the bands of income are doubled, the top rate therefore being paid on taxable income in excess of IR£15,000.

The discussion so far has not referred to social insurance contributions. These so-called 'contributions' are, however, simply another form of income taxation (see Chapter 4). Insurance implies a clear relationship between contributions and expected receipts, but the insurance element of the present social insurance system is almost totally illusory. Contributions are earnings-related and not risk-related and additional contributions produce no additional benefits. There are pay-related supplements payable with disability benefit, unemployment benefit and maternity allowance, but these are negligible in relation to total social insurance payments. Besides, people who have paid no contributions are eligible for social assistance, at rates not much lower than those under social insurance. On balance, then, the least misleading procedure is to view national insurance contributions as part of the income tax system. Indeed, as in Denmark, they could advantageously be incorporated in it.

For those whose incomes do not exceed a certain level (IR£15,000 in 1987/88), the rates of PRSI payable are 5.5 per cent by the employee and 12.33 per cent by the employer. A health contribution of 1.25 per cent is also applicable, as is a youth employment levy of 1.0 per cent. These levies and PRSI payments clearly make a marked difference to the income tax rate structure (see later).

The most important issue with regard to the basic personal allowances concerns the effect of inflation upon them and this will be discussed in a later section. Secondary allowances arise as a result of 'the perception that people with the same income but with different numbers of dependents, or who are disadvantaged on such grounds as physical incapacity or age, require special assistance'.[4] The main issue associated with these allowances is whether or not it is preferable to abolish them and replace them with *direct* payments to the people concerned.

The existence *per se* of reliefs for business expenses is not really a controversial matter, but what is, is the discretion they afford taxpayers to 'doctor' their accounts. This, as mentioned, is more a problem with the self-employed than with the PAYE sector. With regard to non-business expenses, their existence *is* questioned and they are often subject to considerable controversy, as they are seen by many simply as a convenient tax-avoidance mechanism, particularly for the better off. This issue also is discussed in a later section.

Each of the categories of income exempted raise important issues in their own right and the interested reader should consult the First Report of the Commission on Taxation for a discussion of these. The non-inclusion of certain types of income from the definition of income, for tax puposes, also raises important, and most interesting, illustrative case studies of the type of horizontal-equity issue that bedevils any tax system. For this reason, they are looked at in some detail in a later section.

Allowances, reliefs, exemptions, and the non-inclusion of certain types of income all reduce the tax base, i.e. the total income that is subject to tax. The smaller the base, the higher the *rates* of tax that must apply to yield a given total tax return. High marginal tax rates lead to two major problems, they provide disincentives to work effort and/or a marked incentive to avoid and evade tax, thereby probably reducing the tax base even further. For this reason, the widening of the tax base and the simultaneous reduction of tax rates is seen by many as the most pressing issue today with regard to income tax in Ireland.[5] The widening of the tax base is seen as essential not only in order to lower marginal tax rates, but also to render the income tax system more equitable (particularly in a horizontal sense). Some statistics on the erosion of the tax base and on actual tax rates are provided in the next section. Later sections examine the work effort and equity implications of these.

High Rates, Narrow Base
'The most striking feature of the present income tax system is the

143

fact that high marginal tax rates are reached at relatively low levels of income, especially by single people'.[6] Table 5.2 sets out the pattern of marginal tax rates (inclusive of income tax, PRSI and income levies) for both single and married people for 1986/87. As may be seen, a single person with an income level around average male earnings in manufacturing was paying a marginal tax rate of 65.5 per cent — this, by any standards, is a very high rate. The position with regard to a married person was not as marked, but none the less high marginal tax rates at relatively low income levels prevailed for married people. As a result, around 42 per cent of taxpayers were paying tax at rates above the standard rate in 1986/87. This compares with only 15 per cent in 1981/82 and one per cent in 1973/74, indicating clearly that the problem of high marginal tax rates only dates from the mid-1980s.

Table 5.2
Marginal Tax Rates for PAYE Employees by Income Range and Marital Status, 1986/87

Single		Married	
Income[1]	Marginal tax rate[2]	Income[1]	Marginal tax rate[2]
0.0- 26.9	5.5 (0.0)	0.0- 44.7	5.5 (0.0)
26.9- 31.1	40.5 (35.0)	44.7- 47.7	7.5 (0.0)
31.1- 69.2	42.5 (35.0)	47.7- 51.7	67.5 (60.0)
69.2- 94.4	55.5 (48.0)	51.7-126.1	42.5 (35.0)
94.4-126.1	65.5 (58.0)	126.1-129.5	41.5 (35.0)
126.1-132.4	64.5 (58.0)	129.5-132.4	54.5 (48.0)
132.4 +	59.0 (58.0)	132.4-180.0	49.0 (48.0)
		180.0 +	59.0 (58.0)

Sources: NESC, *A Stragegy for Development 1986-1990* (Report no. 83), Stationery Office, Dublin 1986, Table 4.6.
[1]As a per cent of average male earnings in manufacturing.
[2]Inclusive of income tax, PRSI and levies. Figures in brackets are marginal rates of income tax.

Table 5.2 also highlights a major anomaly in the structure of marginal tax rates, namely that they do not increase uniformly with income. For example, in the case of single persons the marginal tax rate declined over certain ranges of income: the position with regard to married persons is even more anomalous with large and sudden jumps in rates as a person enters a certain income range followed by equally large and sudden falls. These anomalies are caused by the following factors: (i) above a certain income level, health and PRSI contributions are not applicable; (ii) below a certain income level, the youth employment levy and the health contribution are not applicable; and (iii) the existence of the general exemption limit implies a very high marginal tax rate over a narrow range of income.

This complex and anomalous structure of marginal tax rates clearly inhibits an understanding of the tax system on the part of taxpayers and creates difficulties for the agencies responsible for collecting revenue. Furthermore, for low-income married persons with a large number of children they create a 'poverty trap', in that increases in gross income lead to *reductions* in post-tax income over certain ranges.

When one examines *average* tax rates (i.e. tax deductions as a proportion of pre-tax income) a somewhat different picture emerges. For a single person on mean industrial earnings, the average tax rate was 24.6 per cent in 1983 (22.4 per cent in the UK) and 14.0 per cent for married persons (18.1 per cent in the UK).[8]

Table 5.3
Estimates of Tax Foregone (IR£million) because of Allowances, Reliefs and Exemptions, 1985/86

Non-Discretionary		Discretionary	
Basic personal allowances	944	Interest relief	132
PAYE allowance	214	Medical insurance	30
General exemptions	186	Life assurance	28
PRSI allowance	82	Other	19
Others	47		
	1473		209

Sources: NESC, *op. cit.*, Table 4.12.

A *marginal* tax rate of 65 per cent and a relatively low *average* tax rate of 25 per cent for someone on average male industrial earnings can be largely explained by the fact that the tax base is so narrow. For 1986/87 it is estimated that the array of allowances, exemptions and reliefs taken together reduced the tax base by 43 per cent, compared to 39 per cent in 1981/82. Thus the tax base is greatly eroded, and has been increasingly so in recent years. As may be seen in Table 5.3, this erosion amounted to IR£1,682m in tax foregone in 1986/87. Discretionary reliefs are of particular interest, because of the equity, and indeed efficiency, considerations which they entail. Besides, income exempt on foot of them has increased much faster in the 1980s than that for non-discretionary items. As may be seen in Table 5.3, tax foregone because of discretionary reliefs amounted to IR£209m in 1986/87, mortgage interest relief, medical insurance and life assurance being the main categories. It is the higher income groups who are best positioned to take advantage of these reliefs: the deduction in tax liability which follows from a given deduction from taxable income also clearly increases with income in the presence of a progressive marginal tax structure. The available evidence suggests that the claims for tax deductions under these reliefs are heavily concentrated in the higher income groups in Ireland.

The Treatment of Investment Income and Savings
Implicit in the last section was that incomes from some investments and monies devoted to certain types of savings constitute major special categories in the Irish income tax system. For this reason, they are dealt with at some length here.

The Irish tax system has historically been inconsistent in its comparative treatment of investment, or 'unearned' income, and earned income. As mentioned in the last section, a PAYE allowance is granted to most people receiving taxable income under Schedule E (i.e. earned taxable income), but on the other hand the tax system has in most cases either exempted from any income tax, or taxed on favourable terms, a large portion of unearned income. The latter arises for a number of reasons.

First, capital gains are not taxed as income (see later). However, a comprehensive definition of income should *include* capital gains, as is the case in the US, and as such they should be added to one's income and taxed accordingly. For example, a person whose wealth increased in value (in real terms) by IR£4,000 during the year could have consumed IR£4,000 of goods and services and still have had the same real wealth as at the beginning of the year. However, under the present system the income arising from the increased real value of the person's wealth would, if it was realized, be treated more favourably than is ordinary income of the same value. Moreover, the benefits of this are likely to increase with income and wealth in that, as they rise, the proportion of total income accruing in the form of capital gains is also likely to rise.

A further objection against the separate treatment of capital gains is that it is relatively easy for certain people to turn high-taxed income into low-taxed capital gains. For example, company executives can be remunerated by means of stock options rather than salary, although the relatively strict benefits-in-kind legislation tends to curtail this. By exercising these options and selling at a profit, they reap what is taxed as a capital gain. Likewise, the shifting of one's money from a bank deposit (where interest is treated as income) to the purchase of a second house (where the increased value is treated as a capital gain) can reduce one's tax liability. There are, in fact, many forms of investment income that can be changed without difficulty into capital gains. Indeed, investment trusts exist whose main objective is to eliminate taxable income by turning it into capital gains, which are then favourably taxed.

A second major loophole in the taxation of investment, similar to the above, is the simplest and probably the most widespread. This is simply to buy durable goods. Since investment in shares, bank deposits, or investment property, can be very heavily taxed, it is not surprising that many rich people buy large houses, valuable pictures and furniture, cars and so on. Such purchases usually yield no *taxable* income, and they can be expected to maintain their real value in the long term. Moreover, increases in their value are unlikely to be subject to capital gains tax. 'Thus the tax system not only diverts private funds from productive purposes, but into forms which encourage the kind of conspicuous display of wealth which its architects were presumably hoping to reduce'.[7]

Owner-occupied housing is the category of durable good which receives most attention, because it is by far the biggest area of expenditure on durable goods, and because it receives special tax treatment. First, income which is derived from it is not subject to tax. This concept of income from owner-occupation puzzles most people, who view their houses as items of expenditure, not of income. However, if Mr. X rents a house from Mr. Y, the rent which is paid is (with some exceptions) taxable income in the hands of Mr. Y. But if Mr. X and Mr. Y happen to be the same person — i.e. the owner occupies the house — no money actually changes hands and so the tax liability disappears. There is therefore a marked incentive in favour of owner-occupation as against renting.

This may not be considered on important issue in practice, but it does provide an excellent textbook illustration of the problem of horizontal inequity in a tax system (see later) and it is worth looking at a little more closely. Consider three people, each with IR£40,000 to invest and wishing to live in a IR£40,000 house.[8] Assume zero inflation, that the return on *all* assets (including housing) is 5 per cent and that the tax rate is 35 per cent. Ms. R. decides to rent (at IR£2,000 per annum) and puts her money in shares, receiving IR£2,000 in dividends and paying tax of IR£700 on this. Ms. O.

decides to buy her house outright and pays IR£40,000 in cash, receiving no dividends, but saving herself rent of IR£2,000, i.e. she benefits from an imputed rent of IR£2,000. Since this is not counted as taxable income, she pays no tax. Ms. M. buys a IR£40,000 residence by taking out a mortgage, while using the IR£40,000 to buy shares. She receives IR£2,000 in dividends, but since the IR£2,000 she pays on her mortgage is tax deductible, she has no *net* addition to her taxable income. Her imputed rental income of IR£2,000 is also tax-free. Thus, here are three people, all with the same money to invest and living in similar houses, but one is paying IR£700 in tax and the others are paying no tax. The problem is to determine how the three can be placed in an equal position for tax purposes. Removal of the interest deduction makes Ms. M. liable for a tax of IR£700 and brings her into line with Ms. R., but Ms. O. would still pay no tax. Allowing payments of rent as a deduction in computing taxable income means that none of them would pay tax, thereby ensuring equal tax treatment for all three. However, this solution provides a tax incentive in favour of expenditure on housing, as opposed to other forms of expenditure. The best solution, perhaps, is to make imputed rent chargeable to tax, leaving interest as a tax-deductible expense. All three would then pay IR£700 in tax, making the tax system neutral both between the various types of housing tenure and between expenditure on housing and other expenditure.

Apart from the exemption of imputed rental income and the allowing of mortgage interest as a deductible expense, any capital gains that accrue from owner-occupation are exempt from Capital Gains Tax. Thus, unquestionably, investment in housing for owner-occupation is very favourably treated relative to investment in other kinds of asset. However — and this is the major argument against removing such favoured treatment — these tax concessions may mean that house prices are higher than they would otherwise be. If this happens, the tax privilege is said to have been 'capitalized'. In this event, the interest and capital repayments being made by current house buyers are substantially greater than they would be if there were no tax concessions, and as such the concessions are of little *net* assistance to them. However, they would lose financially if, for example, relief on mortgage interest was now to be withdrawn: apart from having to pay more in tax every year, the anticipated capital gains on their house would fail to materialize and might, in fact, be turned into a loss if house prices declined as a result of removing the relief. 'In other words, tax capitalization is a trap. In such a situation, almost everyone could agree that it would be better if the concession had never been given in the first place, but once it has been given, it is inequitable to withdraw it, and such a course is likely to cause real hardship'.[9]

A third major area where there is favourable tax treatment for investment relates to life assurance and private superannuation schemes. As regards life assurance, one half of the premia paid on life assurance policies is a deductible expense, subject to some restrictions. Besides, an employee whose employer runs a pension scheme approved by the Revenue Commissioners can claim all his contributions as a deductible expense. Furthermore, the employer's contribution to such a scheme is not regarded as part of the taxable income of the employee. In effect, then, the Revenue Commissioners are paying a proportion of the premia and/or pension contributions on behalf of the individual, thereby increasing the effective rate of return on his investment.

The real objection to these concessions is that they do not apply to all types of investments/savings. For example, money invested in shares, or a building society, is not tax deductible, and thus the scheme is inequitable. Second, it may be inefficient in that it may encourage the wrong type of investment, as noted in the following remarks:

> These privileged assets all have certain characteristics in common. They are all what one might loosely describe as civil servants' assets rather than entrepreneurs' assets. They are all well suited to people who have conventional intentions and predictable career prospects, but not to those who have no settled plans, who wish to take risks, or who have uncertain incomes. They are all highly illiquid: none of them can readily be realized in an emergency . . . Two of them significantly reduce mobility between locations and between occupations.[10]

The tax-induced money channelled into assurance companies and pension funds, though, is spent on the stock market and on property. Even so, there is little evidence that the switch to institutional investors has contributed anything positive to the efficient working of the capital market.

The special treatment of some types of investment income and savings probably has marked effects, therefore, on the structure and composition of personal wealth in Ireland. Data for the UK indicate that housing accounted for 43.3 per cent of personal wealth in 1979, as against a figure of only 19.1 per cent in 1957. The share of pension funds in the total also increased dramatically, whereas that of equities declined very considerably. It is likely that similar trends existed in Ireland. There were also likely to have been marked distributional implications resulting from the tax concessions above. In particular, it is probable that the actual progressivity of income tax was greatly reduced; this topic is returned to later. However, in this respect it is worth emphasizing that certain investments in the past offered *negative* real rates of return, thereby having marked, and unintentional, redistributive effects. This is dealt with in the next section.

Income Tax and Inflation[11]

In some respects, inflation was as potent an influence for change in the structure of Irish taxation in the 1970s and early 1980s as any *explicit* reform. The reason is that income tax has been subject to a phenomenon called 'fiscal drag' (see Chapter 4). This arises from the effect of an *unchanged* and *progressive* tax structure in an inflationary environment. In these circumstances, tax brackets are fixed in terms of *money* incomes and increasingly higher levels of money income correspond to fixed levels of *real* income. Thus someone who is no better off after adjustment for price changes finds himself paying higher and higher *effective* rates of tax — i.e. a higher *proportion* of his income is *automatically* accruing to the government. This is precisely what happened in Ireland. The first result of this was mentioned in Chapter 4 — it probably led to a higher public sector share than otherwise would have been the case. Second, it substantially shifted the balance between direct and indirect taxation. Last, it affected certain income groups more than others, with those on below average and those on fairly high incomes worst hit.

There is only one way of ensuring that inflation does not alter things without the Oireachtas having to condone it, and that is indexation. Measures of this kind have been adopted in Canada, Denmark, Holland and Sweden. The nominal value of allowances and rate thresholds would be linked, in the absence of amending legislation, to the general price level. Governments could, of course, still alter income tax rates if they so wished, but they would now have to do this by an explicit, and voted-upon, decision in the legislature.

The problems which inflation raises for an income tax are not confined to fiscal drag. Inflation poses problems for the definition of income itself. When prices are stable, an investor who earns 10 per cent on IR£1,000 deposited in a bank is better off by IR£100 at the end of the year, i.e. his income increases by IR£100. When inflation is at 20 per cent, then the position is very different. The interest he receives now is significantly short of what he requires simply to stay as well off as when the money was deposited in the first place. In fact, his *real* income is *negative,* and not positive. Nevertheless, the taxman will present him with an income tax bill for IR£35 (if he is on the basic rate), and thereby he will suffer an even greater decline in wealth. In effect, wealth, and not income, is being taxed.

The taxation of capital gains is the only aspect of taxation in Ireland that explicitly recognizes the existence of inflation (see later). However, the indexation of interest payments which are tax deductible poses a major problem. If only *real* interest payments can be taxed, then only *real* interest payments can be allowed as a deduction. This clearly would have dramatic implications for some home owners. Take a young couple who had a mortgage of IR£15,000 at an interest rate of 12 per cent. As matters stand now, they would receive a tax allowance of IR£1,800 a year for mortgage interest. However, if indexation was introduced, and the inflation rate was 20 per cent, then the *real* rate of interest is *minus* 8 per cent. Instead of receiving an increased tax allowance of IR£1,800 their allowances would be *reduced* by IR£1,200. At the basic rate of income tax, this means they would be IR£1,050 per annum worse off. This is not to argue against indexation, but simply to draw attention to one of the many problems its implementation would involve.

Drawing the findings of this and the last section together, it has been shown that the effective rates of tax on some investment income are much lower than on earned income. On the other hand it has been shown that the concept of investment income which is subject to tax described a tax base which, in inflationary conditions, is much higher than it ought to be. It could be argued that a kind of rough justice operates in which the two anomalies described cancel out. This may have some validity in the *aggregate,* but at an *individual* level the effects are arbitrary, and may be reinforcing rather than cancelling.

Income Tax and Work Behaviour

The potentially most important allocative effect of income tax is that on work effort and work patterns through the taxation of earnings. Unfortunately, this is an area where it is difficult to disentangle rhetoric from hard evidence.

In assessing the effect on work effort resulting from an increase in taxation there are two conflicting pressures to consider. First, an increase in taxation would reduce a person's post-tax income, and thereby provide an incentive to work harder to maintain post-tax income at its previous level. This is the *income effect* of the tax change and it depends on the *average* rate of tax, i.e. on the *total* tax bill faced by an individual. Second, an increase in taxation reduces the amount of additional consumption which can be enjoyed as a result of additional work, and thereby provides an incentive to work less. Put differently, an hour of leisure substituted for an hour of work would now involve less of a loss of income than previously. This is the *substitution effect* and it depends on the *marginal* rate of tax, i.e. on the proportion of any *additional* earnings which are absorbed in tax. The *net* impact of the tax change on work effort clearly depends on the balance of these two effects.

Although there is no empirical evidence relating to the effects of taxation on work effort in Ireland,[12] a number of international studies have been carried out; most attention in these has been given to those income groups where disincentive effects are expected to be strongest.[13] First, there are econometric studies of the effect of wage changes on the number of hours worked; since taxation alters the effective wage, its effects can be inferred from these. Overall these studies suggest that the incentive/disincentive effects of taxation are not very strong. This finding is generally supported by the second group of studies, namely the *experimental* studies undertaken in the late 1960s in the US. There have also been some carefully designed questionnaire surveys of the impact of taxation, the results of which also confirm the findings above.

The general advantage of the questionnaire approach is that one generates one's own data and, as such, the effects of taxation can be identified in greater detail. A study of British solicitors and accountants was published in 1957; this work was replicated in 1968 and the results published in 1971. Although solicitors and accountants are likely to be relatively well informed about the tax system, and are also in a better position than most to vary their effort and hours of work, both surveys showed remarkably high percentages (77 and 70 per cent) stating that taxation had *no* effect on work effort. Among those for whom taxation effects did exist, disincentive and incentive effects almost balanced out. The results of a survey of blue-collar workers in Britain were published in 1976. Almost 70 per cent stated that income tax had no effect upon work effort, 20 per cent that it had an incentive effect, and 10 per cent that it had a disincentive effect. The results of a different kind of interview study appeared in 1980.[14] A selection of companies in Britain was approached and asked what difficulties they had experienced as a result of the impact of taxation on their senior executives. It was particularly concerned with cases where, because of income tax, managers emigrated, or refused to return from overseas postings, or where suitable candidates were reluctant to accept senior positions. It was found that the incidence of such problems was negligible.

The discussion above relates to the amount of work which people do, given that they are already at work in a particular occupation. But the effects of taxation on whether they choose that occupation at all may be of more significance. First, there is the question of whether people choose to live in Ireland rather than in some more lightly taxed jurisdiction. Second, given that people live in Ireland, there is the issue of whether or not they choose to work at all. Married women are the most important group in this category, but retirement is also a decision which may be postponed or brought forward because of taxation considerations. Third, there is the possibility that taxation may affect the choice between jobs by substantially reducing post-tax differentials in incomes between different occupations and thereby distorting the workings of the labour market.

Another possible consequence of high marginal rates of income tax is that they have led to income being sought and given in untaxed or lightly taxed forms. There is evidence that well-paid workers in the private sector in Ireland, Britain and elsewhere are offered a 'total remuneration package', which will include a salary and a range of fringe benefits. The latter were estimated to have amounted to 37 per cent of the basic salary for 'general managers' in the UK in 1978. There is also evidence that tax evasion is significant, with the 'black economy' possibly accounting for ten per cent of GDP.

The question is: what can be done about tax avoidance and tax evasion? They are clearly the inevitable consequence of high marginal rates and a complex system of exemptions. Indeed, in many respects it is ironic that the latter may have diverted money that otherwise would have been paid in salary into conspicuous items of consumption, such as expensive company cars and lavish expense accounts, which only increase rather than decrease the visibility of differentials and the extent to which they are resented. Given this, many people consider a significant reduction in the progressivity of income tax to be the solution. This, however, would clearly conflict with the government's distribution objective (see later). Another course of action is to tighten the legislation governing tax avoidance and to introduce new measures for the detection of evasion. Both of these steps have been taken by Irish governments in recent years, although no tax authority can ever hope to eliminate such practices. In this regard, it should be stressed that the present 'benefits in kind' tax legislation in Ireland does *not* leave much scope for tax *avoidance* in this direction. Tax evasion, though, is still possible.

In conclusion, there is little evidence of any strong relationship between income tax and work effort. However, none of the studies related either to Ireland or to a situation such as that pertaining in Ireland in the late 1980s — namely where an extraordinarily high proportion of taxpayers face marginal tax rates above the standard rate. In this situation it is far more likely that income tax *does* affect work *effort*. It will almost certainly also affect work *patterns* in that high marginal rates affect the choice of occupation and lead to substantial tax avoidance and tax evasion.

Conclusion

It is clear from the foregoing that many of the weaknesses of the Irish income tax system derive from the absence of a coherent view as to what should constitute the appropriate tax base. The current legal definition of income for tax purposes has been arrived at over the years by a process of piecemeal statutory revision and judicial interpretation of the tax acts. There is little doubt that this definition is neither clear nor consistent.

The definition of income which is accepted as being the most comprehensive implies making an estimate of: (i) the amount by which the value of property rights would have increased between the beginning and the end of a period; and (ii) the market value of rights which have been exercised. In other words, comprehensive income is measured by the change in the value of a person's wealth plus the value of what that person consumes. Thus, capital gains, bequests and gifts received, lottery winnings, compensation payments for loss of work and all non-money income would be chargeable for income tax using this definition. The inclusion of these receipts in the income tax base would, of course, remove the need for the capital taxes at present in existence in Ireland.

The application of the comprehensive definition of income, though, runs into a number of potentially serious problems. First, treating capital gains as income for tax purposes would introduce substantial anomalies and administrative problems (see later). Second, there are certain forms of non-money income 'which cannot reasonably be brought within the scope of taxation because their control and enforcement is beyond the power of any efficient tax administration'.[15] Third, the adjustment of income measurement to account for inflation poses very serious difficulties, one of which was seen earlier. There are other problems, but perhaps all of these difficulties can be overstated, as it is generally accepted that even a partial movement in the direction of a comprehensive income tax would make the system less complex and inequitable.

2   INDIRECT TAXATION AND COMPANY AND CAPITAL TAXATION

Indirect Taxation: Structure and Issues

An examination of the structure of commodity taxes in Ireland reveals one general sales tax — VAT — and heavy duties on three products — tobacco, alcoholic drinks and petrol. The revenue from these taxes, as mentioned, exceeds the total revenue from income tax. The fact that so much revenue is derived from these sources is readily understood when the tax element in the price of tobacco products, alcoholic drinks and petrol is disclosed. In 1987, around 76 per cent of the price paid for cigarettes was due to tax. The equivalent figures for a 'pint', a bottle of whiskey and a gallon of petrol were approximately 50, 70 and 45 per cent respectively.

The main advantage of VAT is that it is a method of levying a tax on all commodities that enter consumption, while effectively exempting all intermediate goods — those who buy goods for further production get a refund of the tax which they have been charged and only those who are the final consumers of the goods actually pay it. This meets one of the key principles of the economics of taxation — that the burden of commodity taxation should be confined to final goods. However, it is a very expensive tax to administer. Not only is the collection cost to the Revenue Commissioners high, but so also are the compliance costs. VAT is a self-assessed tax and for small retailers the costs (in lost time) of filling in forms, etc. can at times amount to a substantial proportion of the actual VAT revenue being collected. None the less, for large organizations with sophisticated accounting systems, the compliance costs are probably small.

The implementation of VAT in Ireland in 1973 was part of the process of EC harmonization. However, such harmonization was very limited in that the tax base and rates of VAT were *not* harmonized. In Ireland three main rates are applied — zero, ten and a standard 25 per cent.

While VAT is the only major tax in Ireland for which inflation poses no problems, the opposite is true with excise duties on tobacco, alcohol and petrol. The base for VAT is simply current transactions and the tax is proportional, so receipts rise automatically with, and no faster than, prices in general. However, excise duties are *fixed* monetary amounts, so unless they are regularly increased in line with increased prices their *real* value will steadily decline. This is the exact opposite situation to that looked at earlier in relation to income tax, where *real* revenue will increase automatically if no government action is taken. In Ireland, in fact, there has been little, if any, change over the last decade in the *real* excise duty charged on cigarettes, beer and whiskey, with an actual decline in the *real* duty charged on petrol — all of this despite the, by now, annual 'doomsday' predictions following on each budget increase in the *nominal* value of these duties.

Another advantage of VAT is that it causes a minimum of price distortion, i.e. it need not alter the structure of *relative* prices to a great extent. This is clearly not the case with excise duties. The prices of commodities subject to excise duty (as seen) are wildly different from what they would be if no duty was imposed. These taxes on alcohol and tobacco, of course, are not imposed for reasons which are primarily economic (i.e. for allocation purposes). 'The real reason these taxes exist is that it is rather easy to induce feelings of guilt about these forms of consumption: and as a result it is more acceptable to raise revenue in this way than in others'.[16] The inelastic demand for these commodities also ensures that these taxes can form a substantial proportion of the retail price without affecting demand for, and therefore tax revenue from, these products.[17]

The fact that the consumption of alcohol and tobacco has unpleasant consequences (i.e. diseconomies) for others is sometimes cited as an argument for these taxes. However, 'smokers make reduced demands on public services by dying prematurely and alcohol as a social lubricant has beneficial as well as adverse external effects'.[18] A common view, anyway, is that the government simply could not 'afford' to discourage smoking or alcohol consumption because of the loss of tax revenue which would result. However, this needs some qualification. If consumption of these items was discouraged, there would be a reduction in medical costs and in claims for sickness. Against this, as mentioned above, people would live longer and thereby increase government expenditure on state pensions. However, increased life expectancy in turn may increase welfare, although this would not appear in the calculus of balancing government revenue and expenditure. Whatever the balance of these arguments, however, it is unlikely to persuade the Irish government in the foreseeable future to attempt to alter radically drinking and smoking habits through the taxation 'weapon'.

It has almost become part of the conventional wisdom for some groups that the tax structure in Ireland should rely even more than it does on indirect taxation. However, some of the reasoning underlying this viewpoint is misplaced. A typically erroneous argument is that the disincentive effects of high rates of direct taxation can be reduced or avoided by a move to indirect taxes. Assume that a 25 per cent tax on all income exists and that it is to be replaced by a tax on expenditure, yielding the *same* tax revenue. Now a person earning IR£20 a week extra in overtime under the old system would be left with a post-tax income of IR£15, and thereby be in a position to purchase goods and services to this value. Under the new system the post-tax income is raised to IR£20, but in order to acquire the IR£5 lost in income tax, a tax on expenditure of 33.3 per cent has to be imposed. This implies that for every IR£15 spent on goods and services, a person must 'give' a further IR£5 to the government. Thus one cannot, in the long run at least, remove the effects of taxes by disguising them under a different name. The 'ordinary' person now clearly realizes that what matters is the *relationship* between take-home pay and prices in the shops. An increase in the former, accompanied by a consequential increase in the latter, does *not* significantly alter the disincentive effects of taxation.

There is, however, at least one grain of truth in the argument above. In the case of income tax the marginal rate is generally significantly higher than the average rate, while for commodity taxes they differ little. In other words, direct taxes are much more progressive than indirect taxes, and given that disincentive effects depend on marginal rates, then these effects would be reduced when switching from direct to indirect taxes. However, this argument rests on the reduction in progressivity, *not* on the shift in the structure of taxation, and 'this reduction could be equally well — and more honestly — achieved by altering the rates of direct tax than by changes to different kinds of tax'.[19]

A second erroneous argument for preferring indirect to direct taxes suggests that the latter are not voluntary in the same sense that the former are. It is true that, for example, excise duty on beer can be avoided by any *particular* individual who chooses not to consume beer. However, given that a certain amount of tax revenue is needed, it is also true that indirect taxes in general cannot be avoided by individuals *in general*. Thus an 'escapable' tax, if many people choose to escape it, simply makes others worse off, since it requires a higher rate of tax on those who continue to consume the good in question. A switch to taxes with such arbitrary distributional implications could hardly be considered desirable, as they would very seriously violate the principle of horizontal equity in taxation.

It is extremely difficult to quantify the extent of horizontal inequity of excise duties using available data and no such study appears to have been attempted. However, it is probably correct to say that the higher the level of the duties, the more marked will be the effects on the horizontal distribution of income. To illustrate how pronounced these effects could be, an example will be looked at using data on excise duties on alcohol. Table 5.4 shows the percentage of a person's income that would have been paid in 1986 in excise duties on alcohol consumption for three income levels — half the average industrial wage, the average industrial wage and twice this level — and for various levels of alcohol consumption. (It should be noted that the lower and upper limits of alcohol consumption are not extreme cases. Around 30 per cent of the adult

Table 5.4

Implicit Percentage Excise Tax Rate[1] for various Income and Beer Consumption Levels, 1986

Income	0 pints	Average daily consumption			
		½ pint	1 pint	2 pints	4 pints
Half average industrial wage	0.0	1.8	3.6	7.3	14.6
Average industrial wage	0.0	0.9	1.8	3.6	7.3
Twice average industrial wage	0.0	0.5	0.9	1.8	3.6

Sources: J. O'Hagan and Y. Scott, 'The Consumption and Taxation of Alcoholic Beverages in Ireland, (unpublished paper, Department of Economics, University of Dublin (Trinity College)), 1987.
[1]Including the VAT payable on the excise.

population in Ireland effectively are alcohol abstainers while a substantial proportion of the population consumes four pints or more a day.) The data in the table clearly demonstrate the inequity of alcohol duty as a revenue source. For example, a person on the average industrial wage, who drinks four pints a day on average, would pay 7.3 per cent of his/her income (as a proportion of *disposable* income it would, of course, be much higher) on alcohol excise duties alone, whereas a non-drinker no matter how high his/her income would pay nothing.

There are some valid arguments, though, for taxes on *particular* commodities. As mentioned in Chapter 4, they may be imposed to reduce the consumption, for example, of alcohol.[20] Likewise, a tax is often imposed on energy consumption to stop excessive use of this scarce commodity. Thus taxes on particular commodities to account for 'external effects' can be justified. A further reason for such taxes may be to act as a tariff (see Chapter 9), although the role of such taxes has been limited by Ireland's membership of the EC.

Indirect Taxation: EC Harmonization
The goal of establishing a single, unified market in the EC has never been achieved. The White Paper of the Commission of the European Communities in 1985, *Completing the Internal Market,* was a landmark, though, in that it was the first major initiative in this regard for well over a decade. The document set 1992 as the target date for completion of the internal market and three broad targets were identified: (i) the removal of physical barriers (e.g. customs posts, immigration controls); (ii) the removal of technical barriers (e.g. differences in product standards); (iii) the removal of fiscal barriers, mainly by the harmonization of VAT and excise rates. It is the last mentioned that is of interest here.

Detailed proposals concerning, for example, the value of the standarized excise rates have yet to be negotiated and agreed by the member states. Indeed it could be said that little progress has been made since 1985 and that the target date of 1992 for completion of the internal market is already unattainable. None the less, fiscal harmonization is likely to become a major issue in years to come.

Fiscal harmonization would have major tax-revenue implications for a number of countries, Ireland in particular. First, as may be seen in Table 5.5, Ireland has the highest standard rate of VAT in the Community and harmonization would almost certainly imply a substantial reduction in this rate. Also, as VAT is applied to a very narrow *base*, many goods and services at present zero-rated or exempt would be subject to VAT if harmonization was to take place. Second, Ireland relies to an extraordinary extent on excise duties as a source of tax revenue. Excise receipts amounted to 8.9 per cent of GDP in Ireland in 1985 compared to a Community average of 3.6 per cent. This difference arises largely from the fact that the excise duty on beer (expenditure on which constitutes a significant proportion of total consumer expenditure) in Ireland is so high compared to the other member states.

As may be seen in Table 5.6, Ireland has by far the highest level of excise duty on beer in the Community and it is more than ten times that in France, Germany, Greece, Italy, Luxembourg, Portugal and Spain. Clearly, then, harmonized excise duties would imply huge reductions in beer duty in Ireland, with a consequential huge drop in tax revenues to the government from this source. There would probably also be a large fall in duty levels on spirits and wine, and to a much lesser extent on cigarettes and petrol, but the revenue implications would not be nearly as significant as in the case of beer.

Table 5.5

Percentage Rates of VAT in EC Member States,[1] 1986

	Zero	Reduced	Standard	Higher
Belgium	✓	1 and 6	19	25 and 33
Denmark	✓	—	22	—
France	—	5.5 and 7	18.6	33.3
Germany	—	7	14	—
Ireland	✓	10	25	—
Italy	✓	2 and 9	18	38
Luxembourg	—	3 and 6	12	—
Netherlands	—	5	19	—
Portugal	✓	8	16	30
Spain	—	6	12	33
UK	✓	—	15	—

Sources: F. O'Dwyer, 'Fiscal Harmonization in the European Community' (unpublished M.Litt. thesis, University of Dublin (Trinity College)), 1987.
[1]No VAT was levied in Greece in 1986.

Table 5.6

Index of Excise Duty Rates on Selected Products in EC Countries, 1986: Ireland = 100

	Petrol	Beer	Spirits
Belgium	65	11	46
Denmark	121	63	129
France	98	3	42
Germany	64	6	43
Greece	103	9	2
Ireland	100	100	100
Italy	140	5	9
Luxembourg	52	5	31
Netherlands	76	21	48
Portugal	105	8	9
Spain	53	2	11
UK	80	60	91

Sources: as for Table 5.5.

The fall in excise revenue would be the strongest grounds by far for objection that Ireland would have to any harmonization proposals. However, in the longer term other sources of revenue could be tapped. This is the most obvious and practical solution, as given a reasonable period of adoption there is no reason why changes in the tax base should reduce the overall taxable capacity of a given economy. In other words, what people gain in one hand (through lower indirect taxes) they should be prepared to give up with the other (domestic rates, the abolition of certain allowances, or whatever). There may, of course, be major administrative and political difficulties with altering the tax system in this way, but this must be set against the advantages of harmonization.

The main perceived economic advantage resulting from the establishment of a single market is an increase in competition and efficiency. It is argued that, with regard to competition, it will be 'intensified among businesses that can take advantage of a large area without frontiers, which will favour economies of scale and make investment in advanced technology profitable'.[21] Similarly, one could expect the volume of trade to grow between member states and the precedent of the abolition of internal customs duties is cited by the Commission in support of this assertion. As fiscal harmonization is viewed as a *sine qua non* of a single market, in this sense it would contribute to increased efficiency.

Fiscal harmonization, if it led to a single rate of VAT applied to most goods and services in all member states, would also lead to other efficiency gains. It is generally accepted that a tax system should be neutral with respect to consumer choice. In the present context, this simply means that in choosing between two similar goods in two different locations, the amount of tax attached to each good should not be a significant factor in the choice — otherwise efficiency is lost (as evidenced by smuggling and large cross-border purchasing). A similar argument applies to the choice between two goods in the same location. It was this type of efficiency loss that the Commission on Taxation had in mind when it proposed the adoption of a single rate of VAT applied to all goods and services supplied in the state. The Third Report (p. 62) states that:

> Exempt and low-rated goods and services result in discrimination against those persons who have relatively low preferences for such goods and services. Closely related to this is the distortion in the demand for and supply of goods and services caused by exemptions and differential rating. Generally speaking, changes in relative prices resulting from taxation alter the allocation of resources among various possible uses. Unless these changes

compensate for market imperfections, the allocation of resources is distorted and Irish people are poorer as a result.

It is extremely difficult to quantify in any way the magnitude of the efficiency gain for Ireland resulting from the removal of distortionary indirect taxation both within the country and between member states. This would involve estimating a vast and complex array of demand and supply effects resulting from the changes. The important point, though, is that it can be safely argued that harmonization could create *conditions* conducive to large efficiency gains.

It could be argued that there are also other important effects associated with harmonization.[22] Excise duties, as pointed out above, are a very inequitable form of taxation and any reduction in reliance on them as a revenue source would be desirable from an equity point of view. The imposition of VAT on food, though, would partly offset this advantage. Harmonization would also involve the loss of some fiscal manoeuvrability on the part of the Irish government, but this may be more illusory than real given the present restrictions in this regard resulting from the large common land border with the UK and the freedom of movement between the two countries. There is also, of course, an important ideological dimension to the debate on fiscal harmonization, a person's stance in the debate being largely influenced by how he/she views eventual European union. For those in favour of a single economic and political 'space' in Europe, the real question is not 'whether' but 'how' harmonization can be brought about: for those opposed to such a concept, harmonization may be an irrelevancy.

Company Taxation

Since 1975 company taxation in Ireland has been based on the imputation system. This system gives shareholders credit for tax paid by the company, this credit being usable to offset their income tax liability. Part of the company's tax liability, in other words, is 'imputed' to the shareholders and regarded as a prepayment of their income tax on dividends. The company pays tax on its profits at the rate of corporation tax, and all profits distributed are regarded as having had income tax deducted at a certain rate, which is sometimes called the 'imputation rate'. Shareholders have to pay additional income tax on their dividends only if their marginal rates of income tax exceed the imputation rate, while if their marginal rates are less than the imputation rate they actually receive a tax refund.

The main argument in favour of the imputation system is that under this system profits are taxed at the same rate, regardless of whether they are retained or distributed. However, this only applies if the imputation rate is the same as the weighted mean of the marginal rates of income tax that shareholders are liable for. In Ireland, if the imputation rate was 35 per cent, it would be unlikely that, on balance, shareholders would have to pay much further income tax on dividends received. The actual imputation rate is 30 per cent, where the corporation tax rate is 45 per cent. However, the treatment of profits from manufacturing industry has always differed from this. Prior to January 1981 no corporation tax had to be paid on profits from export sales, with rates varying between 35 and 45 per cent being applied on profits from domestic sales. From January 1981 a ten per cent scheme of corporation tax for *all* manufacturing industry is in operation, with an imputation rate of just over 5 per cent. If profits are retained there is no further tax to be paid. Conversely, if they are distributed the shareholders will have to pay a large income tax bill on their dividends. As a result, the main argument for the imputation system of company taxation does not apply in Ireland — quite the contrary, as the present arrangements clearly favour retention.

Given the system of company taxation in Ireland, with its favourable treatment of profits on exports and generous depreciation allowances, it has been found that the *effective* rate of company taxation was very low, even prior to 1981. Fifty-nine per cent of a large sample of firms that had positive taxable profits in 1979 paid less than 10 per cent of taxable profits in 'current cash tax payments'. The corresponding figure in 1964 was only 12 per cent of firms. This trend towards a declining effective tax rate is likely to continue, with the state already possibly a net provider of funds to the corporate sector. 'One important implication is that additional fiscal incentives which directly affect post-tax profits may have little effect, as many firms already pay little or no Irish corporate tax'.[23]

Capital Taxation[24]
Taxes on capital have a longer history than taxes on companies or taxes on income. 'This may seem surprising to those people who regard the idea of a wealth tax as a recent left-wing idea, but rulers found it easier to measure their subjects' wealth than to perform the more sophisticated calculations necessary to compute their income'.[25]

Capital taxes are defined as those taxes whose base is the value of a *stock* of assets at a given time and so they differ from taxes on income, expenditure and sales whose base is the value of a *flow* measured over a period of time. Given this, Capital Gains Tax (CGT) is unambiguously a tax on income and not a tax on wealth. It is discussed in this section for two reasons: it operates in practice quite separately from income tax and it has been regarded by Irish legislators as part of a general package of taxes on capital as opposed to income. Capital Acquisitions Tax (CAT) and Annual Wealth Tax (AWT), the other two taxes considered,[26] clearly qualify as taxes on capital.

The Irish CGT was enacted by the Capital Gains Tax Act, 1975 (which was substantially amended in later years), and is applied to gains arising from assets disposed of after April 6, 1974. Subject to certain exceptions, a taxable gain arises whenever an asset is disposed of for a value in excess of that ruling at the date of acquisition of the asset, or on April 6, 1974. The main exceptions are gains on principal private residence (assuming no change in current use), the first IR£2,000 (IR£4,000 for a married couple) of net gain, and certain gains in a business, farm or shares in a family firm. Since 1978, the tax has been applied to *real* gains only, that is to the proceeds from sale of the asset less its original cost adjusted in line with movements in the Consumer Price Index. The top rate of tax is 60 per cent, applying to gains realized within a year of acquisition, and this falls to 30 per cent on gains realized more than six years after acquisition. (A more stringent rate system is applied to gains from the disposal of development land.)

Capital gains pose some problems that do not arise with 'ordinary' income and this may be one of the reasons why they are taxed separately. First, strictly speaking, capital gains should be taxed as they accrue, not just when they are realized. However, this would require the *annual* valuation of all assets subject to CGT—an extremely costly exercise. Second, if capital gains were liable to the progressive income tax, then more tax is payable on a realization than on an accruals basis. This is because the whole of the gain is taxed in one year—the year of realization—and no taxable gain arises in any other year. Third, capital gains may be negative, even in nominal terms, and if there is a progressive tax, such as income tax, on capital gains the tax relief for a loss may be less than the tax payable on a gain of equal size. The system of taxation of capital gains in Ireland in general copes quite adequately with these problems, but it does so at the expense of treating capital gains differently, and on a much more favourable basis, than the rest of income.

A capital acquisition occurs when an asset changes hands for two reasons—when it is a gift between two living persons (an *inter vivos* gift) or when it is an inheritance. Capital Acquisitions Tax in Ireland is implemented under the Capital Acquisitions Tax Act of 1976 and applies to gifts received after February 28, 1976, and inheritances received after April 1, 1975. It has two features that distinguish it from the old death duties. First, unlike estate duty, it covers all gifts as well as inheritances, although the former are still taxed at a somewhat lower rate. Second, under CAT an inheritance is taxable in the hands of each heir, any one of whom may have inherited only part of the estate. Since each bequest is taxed separately, the total size of the estate is not, unlike with the old estate duty, the determinant of tax liability. As such, given that CAT is progressive, the total tax payable on any given estate is smaller, the larger the number of heirs.

There are many exemptions from CAT. The main one is that when the beneficiary is a spouse no CAT is payable. In the case of a child of the benefactor, or minor child of a deceased child, the first IR£150,000 is exempt. In the case of all other beneficiaries, the exemption limit falls to IR£30,000 or less. The marginal rates rise in six steps to a maximum of 55 per cent.

As a device for redistributing wealth (its main purpose) CAT's effectiveness is almost completely destroyed by the high value of the exemptions. Moreover, there is a very strong incentive to keep one's wealth in the immediate family. The scale of the exemption for immediate family may be explained by the desire to ease the intergenerational transfer of family businesses and farms. However, this does not justify the enormous difference in the exemption for assets passed to one kind of relative rather than another. In fact, such a difference could act against the interests of business, as there is clearly a marked tax advantage in passing one's firm or farm to a spouse or child rather than to a vigorous other relative or non-relative.

An Annual Wealth Tax was in force in Ireland for the period 1975-1977 inclusive, under the Wealth Tax Act of 1975. The tax did not cover all wealth, the main exemptions having been owner-occupied residences and the first IR£100,000 (for married couples). After that, tax was levied at a flat rate of one per cent per annum. 'It was introduced primarily as part of the cement in an interparty coalition coming to power in 1973 and was abandoned after the electoral success in 1977 of a party which had no political need to make gestures to the Left'.[27]

Although there were 'scare stories' circulating in the mid-1970s concerning the amount of capital leaving Ireland to avoid the AWT, this is not the main difficulty (if it even exists) with an AWT. The overriding concern with any AWT is that it founders on the problem of valuation. An AWT involves the valuation of all assets every year. However, for some items valuation is contentious, and collection and compliance costs can be enormous. There are also two major classes of asset where accurate valuation is not just expensive, but is unattainable.

First, there is 'human capital'. A person with higher-than-average intelligence and education will, *ceteris paribus,* have a higher-than-average future earning capacity, i.e. he/she represents an asset of higher-than-average value. 'What is more, human capital may well be an important way in which wealth is inherited: intelligence may be genetically transmitted, ambition and attitudes to education may be determined by the environment in which one is brought up and the opportunities for education may be influenced by parental wealth or income. In every sense, therefore, human capital is in principle similar to financial or physical capital'.[28] However, there is no acceptable method available to enable a precise monetary value to be put on the stock of human capital.

The second area where satisfactory valuation is impossible relates to pension rights. These rights quite clearly add to an individual's wealth (try removing them from someone to find this out!), and it has been estimated for the UK that the total value of occupational and state pension rights may be of the same order of magnitude as *all* other forms of personal wealth put together. Clearly, then, they are of enormous significance when considering the taxation of wealth, making the reasonable assumption that a similar situation applies in Ireland. However, their valuation involves making forecasts over a considerable time-period ahead—forecasts which are sensitive to the assumptions made about future earnings prospects, the future rate of inflation, and to whether or not pensions are indexed. 'It would be impossible to include pension rights in an individual's taxable wealth without provoking bitter dispute about the assumptions made in valuing this right'.[29]

3   TAXATION AND DISTRIBUTION

The concern in this section is an examination of the ways in which the taxation system affects the distribution of income and wealth between individuals in Ireland. In this regard it is useful to distinguish between *vertical* and *horizontal* equity in taxation. The former is concerned with how tax liabilities are arranged among people whose circumstances are acknowledged to be different, usually people with different income and/or wealth levels. Horizontal equity is based on the axiom that similar individuals should be treated similarly.

In practice, the principle of horizontal equity is most frequently violated when administrative arrangements are unsatisfactory. Examples of this, some of which were mentioned earlier, are: when tax impinges heavily on some transactions but can be avoided on others; when tax is paid principally by the honest, or those without effective tax consultants; and when border lines between taxable and untaxable goods or services cannot be satisfactorily defined. Most complaints about the tax system in Ireland emanate from inequities of this kind, i.e. the population at large appear to be concerned more with horizontal than with vertical equity.

Apart from the problems in practice, a major difficulty of principle in applying horizontal equity arises—the identification of 'similar circumstances'. This raises very awkward problems of fact and of values. The most urgent problem of horizontal equity in Ireland in recent years has been deciding how the tax system should take account of household composition; this problem is looked at in some detail in the section below on horizontal equity. The next section examines the evidence, and issues, surrounding the vertical distribution of income, and the effects of taxation thereon. The final section looks at the question of the distribution and taxation of wealth.

Horizontal Equity
In the discussion on income tax, a number of examples that have led to horizontal inequity were examined. These arose from the difficulty of applying a comprehensive definition of income for tax purposes. Most forms of non-monetary income are exempt from tax and thus the higher the proportion of remuneration in this form the less tax is paid. This clearly conflicts with the principle of horizontal equity: that all income should be treated similarly. The main examples of non-monetary income, as mentioned, are fringe benefits, such as a company car, and the benefits enjoyed as a result of owning physical assets, particularly housing. Another example of horizontal inequity is the more favourable tax treatment of a person who receives income in the form of wages. The recent protests from the PAYE sector about the taxation of farmers in Ireland were also largely invoking the principle of horizontal equity. Likewise, as seen earlier, the concern over excise duties arises from the fact that they can very seriously conflict with the principle of horizontal equity.

The issue that has aroused most controversy in Ireland in recent years, though, as mentioned, is that of deciding how households should be taxed relative to individuals. This problem arises for all direct personal taxes, but it shall be discussed here with reference only to income tax.

The simplest treatment of the tax unit is to adopt an *individual basis*: tax everyone as a separate individual. The difficulty is that households do exist, and to ignore the fact that the needs and financial affairs of households differ from those of single individuals would be considered by many a serious flaw in any tax system. The alternative is a *unit basis,* of which there are two principal variants —the quotient system and the dependency principle.

The argument for the individual basis rests on the view that the tax position of each person should only depend on the earnings and circumstances of that person, and not of others, even those others with whom one chooses to live. This would imply, for example, that IR£2,000 earned by the wife of a millionaire should be treated exactly the same, for tax purposes, as IR£2,000 earned by a cleaning lady with six children whose husband is out of work. Most people would consider it desirable to discriminate between these two situations, although on paper their personal financial circumstances may appear to be identical. It is also very easy to reduce tax liabilities with this system by transferring income from one spouse to the other, i.e. by income splitting. The IR£2,000 received by the millionaire's wife in the example above could simply be the investment income of her husband that was transferred into her name.

The Irish system rests on a combination of the dependency principle and the quotient system. Until 1980 it was based solely on the dependency principle. With this system the wife's income, if she has any, is simply treated as if it were the husband's, and in recognition of the 'burden' she imposes on him he receives a specially enhanced personal allowance. Likewise there were, until 1986, allowances for child dependents. A fundamental question here is: why should a single person be taxed more heavily than a married person (with the same money income) whose wife *voluntarily* does not work outside the home and who *voluntarily* chose to have children? Surely, it could be argued, there are substantial non-pecuniary benefits associated with having a wife and children— 'income' which is not taxable. In this sense there is discrimination in favour of married people. On the other hand, because the incomes of married couples are aggregated under the dependency principle, it follows that, with a progressive income tax, a married couple, with each partner having an income, would pay *more* tax than an unmarried couple with similar incomes. In this sense there is discrimination *against* married couples—this was the verdict of the Supreme Court in 1980 which led to the introduction of the quotient system, with respect to a spouse, that now operates in Ireland.

'The quotient system aggregates the whole income of the household and then subjects it to a rate schedule which differs from the schedule for single people in that every point on the scale has been multiplied by some figure, known as the quotient'.[30] In the Irish situation a quotient of 2 applies to spouses, i.e. all allowances and income bands are doubled for a married couple. A quotient of 1 would clearly imply that the combined income of a married couple would be treated identically to that of a single person. Strictly speaking, the system should also allow for children: in France, for example, the quotient for a married couple is 2 and is increased by 0.5 for each child in the family.

'The basis of the quotient system is the belief that the living standard of a couple is determined by their joint income, and the quotient is a means of relating that to the level attainable to a single individual. But a major difficulty is that the underlying premise is not really valid'.[31] For example, a couple in which the husband (or wife) earns IR£10,000 per annum and the wife (or husband) stays at home (thereby giving them an average of IR£5,000 per annum) is better off than two spouses each earning IR£5,000 per annum or a single person earning IR£5,000 per annum. Yet with a quotient of 2 they all receive the same post-tax income. The married people with one of the spouses working at home are better off in that the spouse that stays at home has more leisure time and/or may provide substantial non-pecuniary benefits for both of them in terms of gourmet meals, a spotless house and garden and so on. Besides, *vis-à-vis* an unmarried couple with the same income, one of whom stays at home, they receive far more favourable tax treatment, i.e. there now is discrimination in favour of marriage. For example, in 1980 a person with an adult dependent to whom he/she is not married or otherwise related and an income of IR£7,000 would have paid IR£1,868·25 in tax, whereas a person in similar circumstances, except that the dependent was his/her spouse, pays only IR£1,329·50.

The discussion above highlights the difficulty in applying the principle of horizontal equity to taxation. There is always room for debate and controversy as to what is meant by 'similar circumstances' or 'similar treatment'. As a result, issues concerning horizontal equity are likely to remain the dominant points of controversy in any future discussion of taxation in Ireland.

Vertical Equity
In an earlier section the *nominal* progressivity of income tax was alluded to when the rate structure was being examined. Table 5.7 below highlights this progressivity (defined as existing when the *proportion* of income which is taken in tax increases with income) for 1984/85. Thus, in principle, income tax in Ireland should effect substantial vertical redistribution. However, the concept of nominal progressivity is of limited interest because it takes account only of the basic allowances which all taxpayers receive in equal measure, and thereby ignores the scope for tax avoidance (through mortgage interest, payments in kind, etc.) and tax evasion that exists. Thus, a married person with a pre-tax income of IR£20,000 in 1984/85 almost certainly would not have paid an average rate of income tax of 33.7 per cent, as implied in Table 5.7. A further factor is that a tax schedule may be only markedly progressive beyond an income level that is so high that few, in fact, would be affected. Thus, the nominal progressivity may convey little about the *actual* progressivity of income tax. None the less, nominal progressivity is a *necessary* condition for the latter to hold.

Table 5.7
Nominal Average Percentage Rate of Income Tax on Specimen Incomes, 1984/85

Income (IR£)	Single person	Married couple without children[1]	Married couple with three children[1]
7,000	23.0	13.6	12.1
12,500	37.0	23.5	22.6
20,000	47.8	33.7	32.8
35,000	55.6	46.8	46.3
75,000	61.1	57.0	56.8

Sources: Sixty-Second Annual Report of the Revenue Commissioners, Stationery Office, Dublin 1986, Table 89.
[1]One spouse working.

To examine the actual progressivity of income tax (i.e. its effect on vertical distribution) both knowledge of, and a way of measuring the degree of inequality in, the distribution of incomes is needed. Only very recently were estimates made of the distribution of income for the country as a whole.[32]

A summary overall measure of inequality that is often used is the Gini coefficient. Its value lies between 1 and 0, with a low value indicating more equality than a high value. Using this measure, the available data suggest that Australia, Norway, Sweden and the UK have more equal distributions of pre-tax incomes than Ireland. Data on decile shares support this, with all of these countries having higher shares for the bottom two deciles, and lower shares for the top two deciles, than in Ireland. Despite having the highest share for the top decile, Japan has a relatively low Gini coefficient. This is mainly due to the high share of the bottom decile. Only France has a Gini coefficient that is significantly higher than Ireland's.

International comparisons of Gini coefficients are fraught with difficulties, however, and they should only be accepted as very crude indicators of differences in the degree of inequality between countries. International comparisons, though, certainly do not suggest that the distribution of incomes in Ireland is in any sense remarkably equal or unequal *relative* to the industrialized countries. However, in an *absolute* sense there is a very marked inequality in the distribution of incomes in Ireland—the bottom 10 per cent of households receiving only 1.5 per cent of total income, as opposed to a figure of 26.8 per cent for the top decile. It is this type of inequality that the income tax system was designed to reduce.

Pre-tax income is direct income (mainly earned income, retirement pensions and investment and property income) *plus* state money transfers (old-age pensions, unemployment and sickness benefits etc.). The Gini coefficient when only *direct* income was considered was as high as 0.45—thus state money transfers have a marked impact on income distribution, reducing the Gini coefficient from 0.45 to 0.38. Disposable income is defined as pre-tax income less income tax and social insurance contributions. Using this measure, income is more equally distributed, but not markedly so—the Gini coefficient is only reduced to 0.37. The implication is that direct tax has a minimal influence on the structure of distribution in Ireland: i.e. the amount of vertical redistribution brought about by income tax and social insurance contributions is minimal.

In moving from direct income to disposable income the effect of government *money* transfers and *direct* taxes have been ascertained. However, indirect government benefits (benefits in kind) and indirect taxes also affect the distribution of income.

In the case of Ireland, it was found that the combined effect of benefits in kind and indirect taxes in 1973 was regressive, with the Gini coefficient increasing to 0.38. Thus, the overall level of inequality remained virtually unchanged when direct taxes, indirect taxes and payments in kind are taken into account. It is, then, only when the effects of cash payments, such as unemployment benefit and old age pensions, are taken into account that state involvement in Ireland is seen to be redistributive. Moreover, it appears that

171

redistribution resulting from government intervention is considerably more marked in the UK than in Ireland: in the UK, the Gini coefficient for direct income was 0.43 (very similar to that for Ireland), 0.35 for pre-tax income, 0.33 for disposable income and 0.32 for final income (when indirect taxes and benefits in kind are taken into account).

Looking more closely at the redistributive impact of various measures, it appears that income tax made a modest contribution to redistribution but social insurance contributions appear to have had a regressive effect. Medical benefits were the most progressive of benefits in kind, but educational benefits were regressive. All indirect taxes were regressive, and excise duties were the most regressive of these. Thus, all broad categories of tax looked at, with the exception of income tax, were regressive, rendering the overall tax system regressive.[33]

The fact that direct taxation effects so little vertical redistribution may be a cause for concern among many people. As was seen, pre-tax incomes are very unequally distributed and the nominal progressivity of income tax is quite marked, yet little redistribution is taking place. Why is this? One factor is the generous system of allowances that makes tax avoidance for the higher income groups relatively easy. Life assurance premiums and mortgage interest payments, as mentioned, are tax deductible, and there is substantial evidence that these deductible expenses rise steadily with income, and so form a higher proportion of the incomes of the rich than of the poor. Another factor, undoubtedly, is the fact that a substantial proportion of the remuneration of some of the higher income groups is payable in kind and therefore not taxable.

Apart from the fact that direct taxation effects very little vertical redistribution, there is also increasing concern about the relationship between the system of direct taxation and the social security system. By 1977 the annual value of social benefit payments for unemployed single or married persons *exceeded* the level of tax-free allowances for these categories. There is clearly an element of paradox here, with the taxman collecting revenue from groups whose earnings are *below* the level of basic social support that is provided for those who have no resources of their own. This, plus a number of other anomalies in the system, has also led to a situation where some unemployed persons are financially better off remaining unemployed, at least for part of the year. The difficulty arises simply because the additional earnings of someone whose taxable income is sufficient to exhaust his tax-free allowances are taxed in full, while social security benefits are not taxed at all. A further problem is the sheer administrative complexity of the present taxation and social security systems, with many people unable to grapple with the plethora of forms and regulations necessary to benefit fully from these schemes.

In response to these problems a number of fundamental reforms have been suggested. One such proposal is to scrap *all* social security payments and replace them by a *single* payment (a 'social dividend') to households, the amount of which would depend on the size and composition of the household. This would be paid *automatically* to *all* households, and would be tax-free, thereby guaranteeing a minimum income for each household. *All* tax allowances would disappear and income tax would be imposed on all income other than the social dividend, probably at one single flat rate. A 'negative income tax' would have the exact same effects as a 'social dividend', and at least one major Irish political party has declared a commitment to the introduction of such a tax. However, the massive cost of a negative income tax system means that it is unlikely to be seriously considered for the foreseeable future.

Whatever system of direct taxation is introduced in the future, one problem that will probably always remain is the conflict between vertical equity and efficiency. Any attempt to increase the amount of vertical redistribution effected by the income tax system will have to be weighted against the increased work disincentive effects and/or tax evasion efforts that would almost certainly follow.

Taxation and the Distribution of Wealth
Probably the most resented form of inequality is that of wealth. The main reason for this is that the proportion of the wealthy who become rich as a result of personal savings from their *own* earnings is very small—the main sources of wealth are inheritance and capital gains, and most fortunes are the product of some combination of the two. In the UK it was found that 80 per cent of those who died wealthy had fathers who were wealthy.

Measuring the personal distribution of wealth is extremely difficult, and in most countries at present no adequate information is collected on a person's wealth except at the time of death. For the purposes of Capital Acquisitions Tax (formerly estate duties) a person's inheritance (i.e. wealth at the time of death) must be declared, these declarations providing a sample upon which the wealth of the population as a whole can be estimated. There are, however, a number of serious problems with this method. The sample may not be random, estates below a certain value are not liable for tax and certain assets may be undervalued. The most serious problem, mentioned earlier in relation to wealth tax, is that some major sources of wealth, such as pension rights, are excluded using this method.

Data for Ireland derived from estate duty returns suggest that 62 per cent of the adult population owned no wealth at all in 1966. Conversely, 65 per cent of total wealth was estimated to be owned by the top 5 per cent. The corresponding figures for Great Britain in 1966 were 56 per cent (owned by the top 5 per cent), with this figure having dropped to around 45 per cent by 1979. When pension rights are included as part of personal wealth the 1979 figure drops further to 27 per cent. If the data were further adjusted to include small estates, the figure for the percentage of personal wealth owned by the top 5 per cent of the adult population would probably be nearer 24 per cent. If similar adjustments are assumed in the case of the Irish data, it may be taken that the top 5 per cent of the adult population now own around 30 per cent of total personal wealth. It is this type of inequality that Wealth Tax and Capital Acquisitions Tax were designed to overcome.

As mentioned earlier, the Annual Wealth Tax was only operative in Ireland between 1975 and 1977. Besides, when in operation the revenue from AWT amounted to only about IR£6m—probably not much more than the administrative and compliance costs associated with the payment of the tax. For reasons mentioned earlier, CAT has also failed to effect any significant redistribution of wealth in Ireland. Indeed, the yield from this tax in 1983 was IR£14.5m, or IR£4.0m at 1974 prices: the yield from estate duty in 1973/74 was IR£13m.

Capital Acquisitions Tax offers the best realistic possibility of substantially altering the distribution of wealth in Ireland. However, its scope will have to be widened, and it will have to be much less generous in its allowances if it is to have this effect.

4   CONCLUSION

The Irish tax system was inherited from the UK on the foundation of the state in 1922, a system that had developed in a piecemeal fashion over a number of centuries. Since Independence, there have been three major inquiries into the Irish tax system. The first, undertaken by the Committee of Inquiry into Taxation on Industry, produced its report in 1956. A Commission on Income Taxation was appointed on February 18, 1957, and it made seven separate reports to the Minister for Finance, the formal report being submitted on March 28, 1962. It was not until eighteen years later (to the day), however, that a comprehensive review of the taxation system was initiated, when the Commission on Taxation was appointed. Its first report, on direct taxation, was published in July 1982, with four further reports published by 1986. The reports contain a comprehensive and far-reaching assessment of the Irish tax system and a wide range of policy recommendations are made.

The key elements in the reports are — the endorsement of the idea of a *comprehensive* income tax, to be levied at a *single* rate, with the unit of taxation being the family; the abolition of all allowances, deductions and exemptions, tax credits being substituted instead; the replacement of social insurance contributions by a social security tax levied at a single rate on *all* income; the income tax and social security tax to be supplemented by a progressive expenditure tax, to apply only to people with relatively high expenditure and the systematic adjustment of the tax system to deal with the distortions arising from inflation. These indeed, are radical proposals and they raise two queries. First, there seems to be general agreement that one should either opt for a comprehensive income tax or an expenditure tax, but not for a combination of both, as the Commission has done. Second, and perhaps much more seriously, in relation to the adoption of a comprehensive income tax and all that that implies, one wonders 'whether a reform of these proportions could ever go through the parliamentary process unscathed and whether one might end up with removing a few obstacles in the way of comprehensive income taxation initially but facing a worsening position later as new alleviations and new exemptions are introduced over the course of time'.

The Commission was well aware of this danger and stressed that, as many of their recommendations were interlinked, their proposals had to be viewed as a 'package'. It is pointed out by NESC, however, that evaluating the recommendations of the Commission 'is not an exercise the purpose of which is to accept or reject their reports *in toto*'.[35] Rather, the purpose should be to identify the extent to which the tax system can be reformed by implementing a subset, and not necessarily the totality, of the Commission's proposals. There are, however, enormous administrative and political difficulties in overhauling any taxation system. Indeed, even if such an overhaul were undertaken, it is inevitable that the resulting taxation system would have its own numerous defects. In reality, the search is not for some ideal system of taxation, but for that system which is less flawed than any other system. Identifying which that is, is rather more difficult than is commonly imagined.

175

Footnotes

1 J. A. Kay and M. A. King, *The British Tax System,* Oxford University Press, Oxford 1980 (second edition) and Oxford 1983 (third edition). Some other useful background reading can be found in *First Report of the Commission on Taxation — Direct Taxation,* Stationery Office, Dublin 1982.

2 In the case of income subject to the deposit interest retention tax, introduced in 1986, and the retention tax on certain fees paid by government departments, introduced in 1987, this would not be so.

3 NESC, *A Strategy for Development 1986-1990* (Report no. 83), Stationery Office, Dublin 1986, p. 79.

4 *Ibid.* pp. 232-233.

5 See Commission on Taxation Reports and NESC, *op. cit.*

6 NESC *op. cit.*, p. 79. The top marginal rate of 58 per cent (it was 77 per cent prior to 1977) is not high, though, by international standards. The rest of the section draws extensively on the NESC report.

7 Kay and King, 1980, *op. cit.,* p. 47.

8 This example is taken from *First Report . . . , op. cit.*

9 Kay and King, 1980, *op. cit.,* p. 12.

10 *Ibid.,* p. 56.

11 See *First Report . . . , op. cit.,* and Kay and King, 1983, *op. cit.,* for lengthy discussions on this topic.

12 The Foundation for Fiscal Studies in Dublin commissioned a study on this issue in 1986 and a report is due in late 1987.

13 See C.V. Brown, *Taxation and the Incentive to Work,* Oxford University Press, Oxford 1980, for full references and details of the various studies in this area.

14 See G.C. Fiegehen, *Companies, Incentives and Senior Managers,* Oxford University Press, Oxford 1980.

15 *First Report . . . , op. cit.,* p. 119.

16 See Kay and King, 1980, *op. cit.,* p. 136.

17 This is less true now than it used to be. For example, in relation to alcohol taxes, tax avoidance (e.g. duty-free purchasing, home-brewing of beer) and tax evasion (e.g. cross-border smuggling) may exist on a large scale. Besides, cross-border purchasing will always place a limit on the extent to which the government in Dublin can raise these duties — and, indeed, rates of VAT.

18 Kay and King, 1980, *op. cit.,* p. 136.

19 *Ibid.,* p. 127.

20 See J. W. O'Hagan, 'The Rationale for Special Taxes on Alcohol: A Critique', *British Tax Review,* no. 6, 1983, for a discussion of these arguments in relation to excise duties on alcohol.

21 Commission of the European Communities, *The Approximation of European Tax Systems, European File,* Luxembourg 1986, p. 3.

22 See Foundation for Fiscal Studies, *Harmonization of VAT and Excise Rates in the European Community: Impact on Ireland,* Dublin 1986, for a discussion of these.

23 See J. C. Stewart, 'Company Tax-Effective Tax Rates on Profits', *Journal of the Statistical and Social Inquiry Society of Ireland,* 1980/81, p. 122.

24 This section draws extensively on J. A. Bristow, 'Capital Taxes' (unpublished paper, Department of Economics, Trinity College Dublin), 1980.

25 Kay and King, 1980, *op. cit.,* p. 152.

26 A further tax that may be classified as a capital tax is the annual tax chargeable on the market value of residential property in Ireland. Tax is charged at the rate of 1.5 per cent on the *excess* of the amount of the market values of all residential properties of a person over an exemption limit (IR£65,000 at 1983 prices) and is payable provided the household income does not exceed a gross amount (IR£20,000 at 1983 prices).

27 *Ibid.* See Cedric Sandford and Oliver Morrissey, *The Irish Wealth Tax: A Case Study in Economics and Politics* (Economic and Social Research Institute General Research Series, paper 123), Dublin 1985, for a comprehensive discussion of the Irish experience with a wealth tax.

28 *Ibid.*

29 Kay and King, 1980, *op. cit.,* p. 162.

30 *Ibid.,* p. 205.

31 *Ibid.,* p. 207.

32 See B. Nolan, 'The Personal Distribution of Income in the Republic of Ireland', *Journal of the Statistical and Social Inquiry Society of Ireland,* 1977/78; B. Nolan, 'Redistribution of Household Income in Ireland by Taxes and Benefits', *Economic and Social Review,* October 1981; and P. J. O'Connell, 'The Distribution and Redistribution of Income in the Republic of Ireland', *Economic and Social Review,* July 1982.

33 Some important qualifications to this statement are necessary. See 'Discussion' following on Nolan, 1977/78, *op.cit.,* and Nolan, 1981, *op.cit.,* for details.

34 A. R. Prest, 'Taxation in Ireland', *British Tax Review,* no. 6, 1983, p. 355.

35 NESC, *op. cit.,* p. 239.

6 Fiscal, Monetary and Exchange Rate Policy

Brendan Walsh, Jim O'Leary and Anthony Leddin

1 INTRODUCTION

GOVERNMENTS WOULD like to stabilize output around its trend growth path. Demand management consists of using monetary and fiscal policy for this purpose. Fiscal policy alters the level of aggregate demand through decisions about the levels of government revenue and expenditure. The influence of monetary policy on demand is through control of the money supply, the availability of credit and the rate of interest.

There is no general agreement about how unstable the economy would be if left to its own devices. The 'Classical' view is that unregulated, market economies tend to operate in the region of full employment, apart from relatively short periods when, as the result of an exogenous shock, there may be some transitory unemployment. According to this school of thought, if the monetary authorities provide a suitable environment, and in particular if they ensure a steady expansion of the money supply in line with the growth of GNP, inflation will be avoided. The 'Keynesian' view, on the other hand, is that advanced economies are inherently unstable and have no tendency to maintain full employment in the face of shocks. Keynes attributed the malfunctioning of the economy to rigidities in the money and labour markets. He believed that private sector demand was unstable and in affluent societies maybe even had an inherent tendency to fall short of the level needed to maintain full employment. These problems could be mitigated by appropriate management of the government's contribution to aggregate demand.

The Keynesian view gained ground in academic and government circles during the 1940s and 1950s. The success of the Western economies in the post-war period in combining full employment with moderate rates of inflation was attributed to an enhanced role of government in the economy and a willingness to use fiscal policy to maintain a high and stable level of aggregate demand. If aggregate demand was excessive, the rate of inflation would tend to accelerate, but this could be corrected by a reduction in demand.

The apparently stable inverse relationship between inflation and unemployment observed by Phillips in his 1958 article fitted in very well with this line of thinking. The 'Phillips Curve' became a standard part of Keynesian theory and students were taught that there was 'a menu of policy options' between high inflation/low unemployment and low inflation/high unemployment.[1]

The Keynesian view was never accepted by economists such as Milton Friedman who continued to adhere to the Classical tradition of macroeconomics. In the 1970s his critique of Keynesianism gained ground. The ultimate development of this tradition is in the Rational Expectations school of macroeconomics, in which many of the pre-Keynesian or Classical propositions are reestablished. According to some proponents of this theory, stabilization policy is completely ineffective. There is nothing the authorities can do to move an economy closer to full employment than it would be in the absence of an active demand management policy. In fact, according to the *New* Classical school, misguided attempts by the authorities to 'fine tune' the economy have done much more harm than good throughout economic history.

The experience of most Western economies in adjusting to the oil shocks of the 1970s was difficult to understand within the Keynesian framework. Economists trained to think in terms of the Phillips Curve did not anticipate the simultaneous rise in inflation and unemployment that occurred. The emphasis on aggregate demand was based on the implicit assumption that aggregate supply would adjust more or less automatically. However, the oil price increase had to be analyzed in terms of an adverse supply shock. The resultant inflation was accompanied by a rapid growth in the money supply and this rekindled interest in the quantity theory of money.

This is not to suggest that Classical economics has been restored to its former pre-eminence as the accepted orthodoxy. The persistence of very high rates of unemployment throughout Western Europe in the 1980s is not easy to reconcile with the way Classical economists believe economies adjust to shocks. The vogue enjoyed by the simpler versions of monetarism was short-lived and ended when it became clear from the British experience in the 1980s that the assumption of a stable demand for money clearly did not hold.

Thus, neither the Keynesian nor Neoclassical orthodoxy seem to be wholly consistent with the facts. Macroeconomists are still very divided in their interpretation of recent economic history. Introductory textbooks now expose students to alternative schools of thought about unemployment and inflation, instead of presenting them with the 'Neoclassical synthesis' that gained widespread acceptance in the 1950s. There is now a more balanced emphasis on the importance of both aggregate demand and aggregate supply and a renewed interest in the distinction between 'cost constrained' and 'demand constrained' economies.[2]

Keynesian policies were directed at alleviating the unemployment that arises from a deficiency of aggregate demand. In a small open economy, with free access to world markets, the belief that unemployment is primarily due to a deficiency of aggregate demand is difficult to maintain. A relatively small increase in Ireland's share of world trade would absorb a dramatic increase in domestic output. The reason this increase does not materialize is that firms are unable to capture increased market share given the cost structure they face in Ireland. There may also be socio-economic factors at work, such as a lack of responsiveness to profit opportunities, but the importance of cost competitiveness for a small economy is clear. The exchange rate is a key factor in short-run movements in competitiveness. For this reason, and because of the intimate links with monetary policy, this chapter contains a brief discussion of Ireland's exchange rate policy.

This chapter is concerned only with reviewing the policies that affect the level of aggregate *demand*. Policies that are designed to raise the economy's long-run growth rate by increasing the productive potential of the economy and its responsiveness to aggregate demand are discussed in other chapters of this book.

2   FISCAL POLICY

Definitional Issues
The first issue to be resolved concerns the data sources to be used. Tax and public expenditure data are available in both budgetary and national income accounts format. The budgetary data are the most familiar and readily available and they dominate current discussions of fiscal policy. These data are, however, deficient on several scores. They relate to the tax revenue and expenditure of the central government only. Social insurance contributions (PRSI) and local authority taxes (rates) are not included on the revenue side, while spending from social insurance and other 'extra-budgetary' funds is excluded. The distinction between current and capital spending is not satisfactory. International comparisons based on budgetary data are likely to be misleading.

The national income accounts data published annually in *National Income and Expenditure* (*NIE*) are more comprehensive. Data for both central government (including extra-budgetary funds) and local authorities are provided, and consolidated in the 'public authorities' account, which corresponds closely to the 'general government' classification used in OECD publications. In econometric work involving long time-series and in international comparisons it is desirable to use national accounts data.

Starting with the public authorities' *current* income and expenditure, the standard textbook variables are related to the Irish *NIE* data:

G = public authorities' spending on *current* goods and services, also referred to as government consumption. This is item 102 in Table A.9 of the 1985 edition of *NIE*.

T = tax revenue and trading income of public authorities (i.e. the sum of items 95, 96 and 97 in Table A.9 of *NIE*). Direct, indirect and local taxes and PRSI contributions are included. (Before 1984 the trading income of the Post Office came under this heading.)

R = current transfer payments (i.e. the sum of items 100 and 101 in Table A.9 of *NIE*). This includes national debt interest, pensions, unemployment benefits and other social insurance and assistance payments.

The difference between tax receipts and transfer payments, T − R, is the net amount paid by the private to the public sector. This is referred to as Net Taxes, NT. The difference between NT and government current consumption, NT − G, is the national income measure of the current budget surplus/deficit. This is referred to as 'public authorities' savings/dissavings' in *NIE*.

NT − G is an important component of the public sector's impact on aggregate demand but it is not a comprehensive measure. This is because it refers to current spending and revenue only. Spending by the public authorities on roads, schools, hospitals and so on is classified in the Irish national income accounts as investment (I) rather than as G. The current budget deficit, as defined above, is therefore not comparable with the measures of the government deficit used in other countries, where this type of expenditure is included in G. A more comparable measure is obtained when the excess of government spending for capital purposes over its receipts of a capital nature is added to NT − G. The sum of these two magnitudes can be derived from Table A.19 of *NIE* and corresponds closely to the OECD concept of the 'surplus/deficit of general government'. The corresponding budgetary concept is known as the Exchequer Borrowing Requirement (EBR).

To obtain the broadest measure of the public sector's impact on aggregate demand it is necessary to add net borrowing by state-sponsored bodies and local authorities to the EBR. Large amounts have been borrowed under this heading in recent years to finance major projects undertaken by state-sponsored bodies and to cover the operating losses that many of them have recorded. The details are set out in the *Public Capital Programme*. (*NIE* does not contain separate information on state-sponsored bodies.) The sum of the current budget deficit, exchequer borrowing for capital purposes, and borrowing by state-sponsored bodies constitutes the Public Sector Borrowing Requirement (PSBR).

In discussions of fiscal policy in Ireland, the emphasis used to be on the current budget deficit, $(NT - G)$, rather than on broader measures such as the EBR or PSBR. However, in recent years there has been a tendency to focus on the more comprehensive measures. Economists believe that, while there are important differences between borrowing for current and capital purposes, these are not relevant for measuring the stance of fiscal policy, so that the PSBR provides the best indication of the impact of the public sector on the level of aggregate demand. Throughout the rest of this chapter when the public sector 'deficit' is referred to, the PSBR is implied.

Measuring the Stance of Policy.
This section considers whether and to what degree fiscal policy is expansionary or contractionary. In this context there can be some confusion as to whether the *level* or the *change* in the level of the deficit is what matters. It shall be seen that throughout the period reviewed in this chapter, the Irish public sector deficit has been very large. In one sense, therefore, it could be said that fiscal policy has been expansionary for all of this period. But it is more relevant to look at the *change* in the deficit and to characterize policy as contractionary during periods when the deficit is falling, expansionary when it is increasing and neutral when it is static.

An important issue arises in the interpretation of the actual budgetary data, which are *ex post*. A change in the recorded budgetary figures may arise from two sources: (i) a conscious decision by the government to change expenditure and/or taxation; or (ii) a change in the level of economic activity that results in a change in government revenue and/or expenditure.

The first is called a *discretionary* change, the second reflects the impact of *automatic stabilizers* on the government's revenue and expenditure. Clearly, when measuring the stance of fiscal policy it is important to try to distinguish between these two sources of change in the actual budgetary balance.

The most important automatic stabilizers are spending on unemployment compensation and other forms of income maintenance, and income and expenditure taxes. When economic activity is slack, the numbers unemployed rise and the government has to disburse more money in transfer payments. At the same time, revenue from taxation falls off. Hence the deficit increases even if there has been no conscious change in fiscal policy. When economic activity picks up again, these mechanisms go into reverse and the deficit shrinks. In this sense, the effect of automatic stabilizers tends to be self-cancelling over the business cycle.

The measure of the deficit obtained when the effects of automatic changes in revenue and expenditure have been removed is known as the 'cyclically-adjusted' or 'structural' deficit. Several ways of estimating the structural deficit have been developed. Basically, they all involve trying to calculate government revenue and expenditure at a constant ('full employment') level of economic activity. One set of estimates for Ireland is presented later in this chapter.

A further complication, and a further possible refinement, arises because of inflation. Anticipated inflation tends to be built into nominal interest rates.[3] For example, in Ireland in the early 1980s the interest rate on government debt approached 20 per cent. Most of this high nominal return was simply compensation for anticipated inflation. Paying for the anticipated decline in the capital value of the debt through high nominal interest rates is in fact equivalent to early repayment of some of the borrowed funds. An 'inflation-adjustment' can be made by removing the amount of government expenditure that is due to the inflation component of nominal interest rates. Furthermore, inflation reduces the real value of the government's outstanding debt. From a balance sheet point of view, it could be argued that the capital loss suffered by the public who hold government debt should be offset against the public sector's borrowing each year. Various approaches to inflation-adjustment incorporating either or both of these considerations have been used in the literature. Their use is quite controversial and there is no consensus as to the appropriate way to handle the effect of inflation on the measurement of the stance of fiscal policy, but there is agreement that it cannot be ignored.

It is clear from this dicussion that, in addition to the actual, *ex post*, deficit a number of more refined measures should be used to gauge the stance of policy. However, cyclically- and/or inflation-adjusted deficits have to be used with caution because of the unresolved issues involved in their estimation. From a practical point of view it is important not to loose sight of the fact that the actual deficit is the one that has to be financed!

Keynes recommended that fiscal policy should be counter-cyclical, that is, expansionary measures should be taken during periods when private sector aggregate demand (consumption, investment and exports) is weak, followed by retrenchment during periods when the economy recovers. This was the strategy expressed in the Irish White Paper *National Development 1977-80*:

In the initial stages of implementing the strategy, a significant increase in government expenditure and substantial tax cuts are required. However, in the subsequent stages stability will be restored to the government's finances . . . [para. 1.4]

Implementing such a strategy is fraught with difficulties. It is necessary to forecast the course of the economy accurately and to take corrective action so that measures begin to take effect at the right time. In practice, there are lags in diagnozing the need for corrective action, in changing policy and in waiting for the new policy to take effect. Because of these lags some economists believe that attempts to 'fine tune' the economy are doomed to failure. The feasibility of following the Keynesian prescription for counter-cyclical budgetary policy is also called into question by the asymmetry between the political ease of implementing expansionary measures, such as tax cuts or expenditure increases, during a downturn in economic conditions and the difficulty of reversing them during a recovery phase. This imparts a bias towards permanent deficits that was not envisaged by the earlier proponents of an active fiscal policy. With these general points in mind, the record of Irish fiscal policy since the mid-1970s, will now be examined. As background for our discussion Figure 6.1 shows the rate of change in real GNP since 1960.

Irish Fiscal Policy 1977-87
It is clear from Table 6.1 that fiscal policy, as measured by the change in the PSBR, went through two distinct phases between 1977 and 1987. The expansionary phase ended in 1981, and the contractionary phase is not yet (1987) over. Between 1977 and 1981 the PSBR rose from 12.5 per cent to 20.3 per cent of GNP. After 1981 it declined and is targetted to fall back to 12.5 per cent in 1987. While the growth of the PSBR was to a significant degree due to the increase in the current budget deficit, there has been no significant reduction in this component of total borrowing in recent years. On the other hand, borrowing for capital purposes and state-sponsored bodies' borrowing has declined from 12.9 per cent of GNP in 1981 to 5.6 per cent in 1987.

Figure 6.1
Annual Percentage Change in Real GNP, 1960-86.

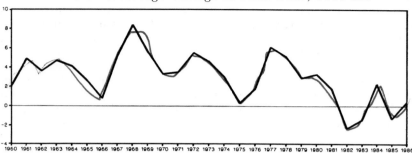

Sources: Central Bank of Ireland Quarterly Bulletin, various issues.

Table 6.1
Public Sector Borrowing Requirement (PSBR) and its Components as a Percentage of GNP, 1977-87

	Current budget deficit (a)	Exchequer borrowing for capital purposes (b)	Borrowing by state-sponsored bodies and local authorities (c)	PSBR (d) = (a) + (b) + (c)
1977	3.6	6.1	2.8	12.5
1978	6.1	6.3	2.5	14.9
1979	6.8	6.4	2.9	16.1
1980	6.1	7.4	3.8	17.3
1981	7.4	8.5	4.4	20.3
1982	8.0	7.7	4.2	19.9
1983[1]	8.1	5.7	3.2	17.0
1984	7.2	5.4	3.8	16.4
1985	8.4	4.8	2.8	16.0
1986	8.5	4.6	2.2	15.2
1987[2]	6.9	3.8	1.8	12.5

Sources: Department of Finance, *Economic Statistics,* Stationery Office, Dublin, November 1986; and *Budget Booklet,* 1987.

[1] Because of the setting up of An Bord Telecom and An Post there is a discontinuity in the series in 1983.

[2] Post-Budget estimates.

No consistent philosophy has guided Irish fiscal policy over the years.[4] The increase in borrowing for investment projects in the late 1970s was justified by the view that, in addition to the

185

infrastructure projects that are undertaken in the public sector in most countries, there are in Ireland opportunities of a more commercial nature that would not be financed by private capital markets. These should be undertaken by state-sponsored bodies or by grant-aided private firms. As a consequence of encouraging such projects and increasing the level of spending on infrastructure, public sector borrowing for capital purposes reached 13 per cent of GNP in 1981. Many of the investments financed by this borrowing have not yielded an adequate return to the economy. However, the decline in the level of borrowing for capital purposes since 1981 has been mainly due to the termination of several major projects (DART, the Dublin-Cork gas pipeline, the power station at Moneypoint and the refurbishing of the telephone system) rather than to any marked change of philosophy regarding the appropriate role for the public sector.

Borrowing to finance the current budget deficit first became a feature of Irish budgets in the early 1970s. It assumed major importance in the aftermath of the first oil crisis in the mid-1970s and, although this policy was in part rationalized in terms of offsetting the perceived deflationary effects of the rise in energy prices, in fact the current deficit was used primarily to cushion the fall in living standards caused by the deterioration in Ireland's terms of trade. In 1978 the borrowing requirement was increased as part of a deliberate attempt to attain the goal of 'full employment'. When the second oil shock hit the economy in 1979-80, the structural deficit was increased again for much the same reasons as applied in the mid-1970s. The reversal of fiscal policy in 1982 was motivated by the realization that it was essential to halt the drift towards bankruptcy implied by the trend in the public finances in the early 1980s.

In view of the rapid growth of the Irish economy at the end of the 1970s and its dismal performance since then, these unadjusted measures of fiscal policy clearly suggest that it has been perversely pro-cyclical, tending to reinforce, rather than offset, changes in the other components of aggregate demand.[5] Thus, during the years 1977-79 the economy would have recovered due to rapid growth of world trade. There was no need to reinforce the stimulus from this source by increasing the PSBR by one-third. The result was to boost the growth rate of the economy to an unsustainable level, resulting in distortions in the labour market and sowing the seeds of the financial predicament of the 1980s. Conversely, during the difficult years after 1981, the public sector should have helped to lift the economy out of recession by increasing the structural deficit, but by then the overriding concern with restoring order to the public finances necessitated a sharp reduction in the deficit.

The figures in Table 6.1 are unadjusted for the effect of cyclical factors or inflation. The OECD has published estimates of the adjusted deficit for some member countries.[6] Table 6.2 contains the estimates for Ireland. It may be seen that the cyclical adjustment alters the figures for the years 1977-81 relatively little but shows that the stance of fiscal policy has been more contractionary in recent years than is apparent from the unadjusted figures. This is because the rise in unemployment increased the level of income maintenance payments and depressed the level of tax receipts during the 1980s.

By international standards, Irish fiscal policy has been extremely volatile. The swings in the structural deficit have been far larger, relative to GNP, than those recorded in other OECD countries. For example, the Irish structural deficit increased by 7.8 per cent of GNP between 1977 and 1982 and declined by almost as much since then. In contrast, the 1982-84 US fiscal expansion involved increasing the structural deficit by only 2 per cent of GNP.

Table 6.2

General Government Budget Balance as a Percentage of GNP, 1977-83

	Actual	Structural	Structural, inflation-adjusted
1977	− 6.9	− 6.5	− 2.6
1978	− 8.8	− 9.2	− 6.5
1979	− 10.7	− 10.7	− 5.3
1980	− 11.6	− 11.7	− 3.8
1981	− 13.9	− 13.3	− 5.2
1982	− 16.1	− 14.3	− 7.2
1983	− 13.6	− 10.6	− 5.6

Sources: OECD, *Economic Studies,* no. 3, Paris, Autumn 1984.

In the early 1980s there was still a substantial body of opinion in Ireland that favoured further fiscal expansion as a counter-cyclical measure. However, by the elections of 1982 all the main political parties were agreed on the need to reduce the level of borrowing. The rapid growth of the public debt, and in particular of indebtedness to the rest of the world, created an awareness of the need for 'fiscal rectitude' in order to avert national bankruptcy. In popular discussion, the emphasis was placed on the need to phase out borrowing for day to day expenses, which was viewed as profligate. However, it quickly became apparent that eliminating the current deficit was a far more difficult task than had been anticipated. Moreover, economists queried the appropriateness of a current budget deficit target for two reasons. First, the distinction between government current and capital expenditure is not very clear cut. Some current expenditure in the areas of health and education might legitimately be deemed as productive as physical capital formation, while the quality of much public sector capital expenditure has been very poor in recent years. Second, stabilizing the ratio of the national debt to GNP has come to be used as the minimum criterion for the sustainability of fiscal policy and the size of the PSBR, rather than the current budget deficit, is the relevant consideration from this point of view.[7] To see why this is so, the relationship between borrowing and the national debt needs to be explored more formally. This is done in the next section.

The Effects of Budget Deficits

Deficits and the National Debt. The deterioration in the Irish public finances has created an awareness of the way in which interest on past borrowing mounts up and tends to make the current deficit self-perpetuating. Table 6.3 shows how the national debt [8] and national debt interest payments have risen relative to GNP, while Table 6.4

Table 6.3

The National Debt and the Cost of Debt Servicing, 1977-87

	National debt		Interest payments	
	IR£m	as % of GNP	IR£m	as % of GNP
1977	4,229	75.6	279	5.0
1978	5,167	79.1	361	5.5
1979	6,540	85.7	450	5.9
1980	7,896	87.7	582	6.5
1981	10,195	93.9	795	7.3
1982	12,817	103.4	1,143	9.2
1983	15,770	118.1	1,330	10.0
1984	18,492	128.0	1,566	10.8
1985	20,417	133.8	1,827	12.0
1986	24,350	148.0	1,817	11.0
1987[1]	26,208	151.5	1,965	11.4

Sources: Department of Finance, *Economic Statistics,* Stationery Office, Dublin, November 1986.

[1] It is assumed that GNP will be IR£17,300m. It is also assumed that the bilateral exchange rates of the Irish pound and the foreign currency composition of the external portion of the national debt will be the same at end-1987 as at end-1986.

shows how interest payments have grown as a percentage of government current spending. This table also shows that exclusive of interest payments there has been a current budget *surplus* in every year since 1982. Even more striking is the fact that exchequer borrowing other than for interest payments declined from 8.6 per cent of GNP in 1981 to 1.2 per cent in 1985. If the 1987 target is achieved, there will be a small surplus on the exchequer non-interest account.

Table 6.4
Interest Payments, Government Spending and Fiscal Imbalance, 1977-87

	Interest payments as a percentage of total current spending	Current budget deficit[1]	Exchequer borrowing
		(excluding interest payments and expressed as a percentage of GNP)	
1977	14.2	− 1.4	4.7
1978	14.9	0.6	6.9
1979	15.5	0.9	7.3
1980	15.7	− 0.4	7.0
1981	16.6	0.1	8.6
1982	19.4	− 1.2	6.5
1983	21.0	− 1.9	3.8
1984	22.4	− 3.6	1.8
1985	24.0	− 3.6	1.2
1986	22.5	− 2.5	2.1
1987[2]	23.4	− 3.3	− 0.6

Sources: as for Table 6.1.
[1]Minus sign denotes a surplus.
[2]Post-Budget estimates.

The deficit exclusive of interest payments is referred to as the primary deficit. (It is analogous to the trading income of a company.) This concept plays an important role in the dynamics of the debt/income ratio. The following framework helps to specify the conditions under which this ratio can be stabilized:[9] let d = the national debt/GNP ratio, b = the primary deficit as a percentage of GNP, i = the nominal interest rate, and r = the growth rate of nominal GNP. It may be shown that, in the simplest case,

$$\triangle d = b + (i - r)d$$

This says that the growth in debt/GNP ratio depends on the primary deficit as a percentage of GNP, the initial debt/GNP ratio and the gap between the nominal interest rate and the growth rate of nominal GNP. (This formula is simplified by ignoring the complications that arise from the distribution of the debt between domestic and foreign currencies.)

It is of interest to ask under what conditions the debt/GNP ratio will stabilize. This criterion is a *minimum* requirement for a sustainable fiscal policy. To see why this is the case, recall that there is a direct link between the debt/GNP ratio and the ratio of debt service (interest) payments to GNP. These interest payments have to be met out of taxation, so that if the debt/GNP ratio is rising, the burden of taxation necessary to pay the interest on the debt will also tend to rise.[10] Without attempting to pronounce on the optimal debt/income ratio, it can be safely stated that it is not optimal to allow the tax burden arising from the debt to increase indefinitely.

For the debt/income ratio to stabilize,

$$\triangle d \ = \ 0 \ \text{and} \ d \ = \ b/(r \ - \ i)$$

or, in words, either the growth rate of GNP must exceed the nominal interest rate *or* there must be a primary surplus. If there is a primary deficit *and* the nominal interest rate exceeds the growth rate of GNP, the debt/income ratio will grow without an upper bound. If this happens, the burden of taxation necessary to pay the interest on the debt will also grow without limit. Clearly, no economy could live with the long-run consequences of such a trend.

This simple algebra can be applied to the Irish situation. At the time of writing (mid-1987) the average nominal interest rate applicable to the Irish national debt is about 8.5 per cent. This rate is influenced by the trend in Irish interest rates, interest rates in the rest of the world and (a complication not allowed for in the simple formula) exchange rates between the Irish pound and the currencies in which the Irish foreign debt is denominated. On the basis of the available information about all these factors, it is expected that the relevant interest rate should decline rather than rise over the medium term. Interest rates in the range of 6.5 per cent to 8.5 per cent are therefore used to illustrate the application of the above formula. The growth rate of nominal GNP depends on (i) the rate of real GNP growth and (ii) the rate of inflation. At present, an inflation rate of 3 per cent seems a reasonable assumption, while real GNP should grow in the 2 per cent to 3 per cent range. A nominal GNP growth rate in the range 5 per cent to 6.25 per cent is therefore assumed.

Table 6.5
Surplus on Non-Interest ('Primary') Account as a Percentage of
GNP Required to Stabilize National Debt/GNP Ratio

Nominal GNP growth	Nominal interest rate		
	8.5%	7.5%	6.5%
6.25%	3.3	1.9	0.4
5.5%	4.4	3.0	1.5
5.0%	5.2	3.7	2.2

Sources: Adapted from NESC, *A Strategy for Development 1986-1990* (Report no. 83), Stationery Office, Dublin 1986.

Combining these assumptions allows the calculation from the above formula of the value of the primary deficit, b, required to stabilize the debt/GNP ratio. The results are shown in Table 6.5. It may be seen that taking the middle-of-the-road values of interest and growth rates yields a required primary *surplus* of 3 per cent of GNP. This compares with an actual primary *deficit* of 2 per cent in 1986 and a forecast surplus of 0.6 per cent in 1987. Thus, even if the fiscal targets set for 1987 are realized, they are not stringent enough to prevent the debt/income and interest/income ratios from continuing to increase. This modest goal requires a further fiscal deflation amounting to about 2.5 per cent of GNP.

The discussion brings out the extent to which the difficulty of restoring balance to the public finances is due to the fact that nominal interest rates are high relative to the growth rate of nominal GNP. The nominal interest rate, i, is the sum [11] of the real interest rate i^* and the rate of inflation, p; $i = i^* + p$, while the growth rate of nominal GNP, r, is the sum of the real growth rate, r^*, and the rate of inflation: $r = r^* + p$. It can be seen, then, that the underlying problem is that the real interest rate, i^*, is higher than the real growth rate of GNP, r^*. While the normal situation is for real interest rates to be positive rather than negative, they rose to historically high levels with the sudden reduction in inflation in the mid-1980s. It is to be hoped that real interest rates will decline and real growth rates will increase. If this occurs it will ease considerably the task of restoring balance to the public finances. If not, the problem of the public finances will remain intractable.

Deficits and the Level of Output. The effect on the economy of the major changes in fiscal policy that have occurred in Ireland over the past ten years depends on how responsive the economy is to fluctuations in aggregate demand. The simple Keynesian model, still found in introductory textbooks, answers this question in terms of the 'multiplier'. It is assumed that the economy is constrained by a deficiency of aggregate demand, rather than by cost or supply-side factors, so that an autonomous increase in investment or consumption spending increases the equilibrium level of output by a multiple of the initial increase in aggregate demand.

In the simplest model, the Keynesian multiplier is equal to (1/MPS), where MPS = the marginal propensity to save. The larger the savings leakage from each 'round' of spending, the smaller the multiplier. In reality, the multiplier is reduced by any leakage from domestic spending, which includes taxation and spending on imports as well as savings. Textbooks dealing with the American economy, where the marginal propensities to save and import, and the marginal tax rate, are low, contain discussions of the multiplier with illustrative values in the range 2.5 to 4.0. For the Irish economy, however, with its high marginal propensity to import, and high marginal tax rates, the simple Keynesian multiplier is unlikely to be higher than 1.[12] While a 'multplier' of 1 should not be confused with a 'multiplier' of 0, it is somewhat of a misnomer: an injection of public sector spending raises output by no more than the amount of that additional spending.

The effect of an increase in the deficit on the economy is also dependent on how it is financed. It shall be seen below that under Irish conditions there is a distinct possibility that increased public sector borrowing 'crowds out' private sector spending. To the extent that this occurs, the impact of fiscal policy on the economy is further reduced.

It is relevant to consider briefly the effect on equilibrium income of increased government spending that is financed by higher tax revenue rather than by an increase in the deficit. The 'balanced budget multiplier' (BBM) measures this. The simple BBM is $(1 - b)/(1 - b) = 1$ in a closed economy. In an open economy, the crucial parameter is the public sector's import propensity. Only if there are no direct imports in government spending will the BBM be unity. It is interesting to note, however, that in an economy where the private sector's marginal propensity to import was very high, the BBM, though less than unity, could be larger than the multiplier associated with deficit financed expenditure. This could arise because higher taxation curbs private sector imports and replaces them with domestic expenditure.

If the multiplier is as small as is suggested by all available estimates for Ireland, an expansionary fiscal policy has an inherent tendency to increase the share of public sector spending, and hence taxation, in GNP.[13] Taxes involve deadweight losses due to the way in which they distort the responses of economic agents. These longer-run adverse supply-side implications of fiscal policy were ignored by early proponents of Keynesianism, but they may have assumed major proportions in Ireland today.[14]

There have been two recent studies of the impact of fiscal policy on the Irish economy. Bradley *et al.* use an econometric model to evaluate the impact of discretionary fiscal policy over the years 1967-80. Their conclusions are summarized in the following quotations:

> The major failure of expansionary fiscal policies over the 1970s has not been their inability to increase GDP over the short run but rather their ineffectiveness over the long run...This turnabout in the effects of fiscal policy [is] due to the links between demand expansion and inflation....Rather than create an environment in which growth could flourish, fiscal policy during the 'seventies has imposed a financial constraint in the form of a massive public debt, which will hinder growth for further generations. [15]

Using a simpler model, Walsh assessed the impact of fiscal policy on unemployment over the period 1973-84. He concludes that there is some evidence that an expansionary policy tended to reduce Irish unemployment relative to that which it would otherwise have been, but that the effect was very small. In common with Bradley *et al.*, he finds that only by maintaining the deficit at a level that would have the gravest implications for the country's solvency would an expansionary fiscal policy reduce Irish unemployment significantly.[16]

Thus, not much support can be found either in economic theory or in the historical record for pursuing an active fiscal policy under Irish conditions. The increased output and employment that result from expanding aggregate demand through increased spending or tax cuts are likely to be short-lived and the longer-run financial implications of deficit spending could be disastrous.

Deficits and Financial Markets. Textbook discussions of how governments fund their deficits list the two fundamental options of issuing bonds or printing money. In Ireland virtually the entire deficit is financed by bond (government security) issue. The important distinction is between 'monetary' and 'non-monetary' borrowing. Government monetary financing (GMF) refers to purchases of government securities by Irish banks, including the Central Bank, and other forms of bank lending to the government,

(BLG), and all external financing of government debt, (GFB), which includes direct foreign borrowing by the government and purchases of government securities by non-residents. Therefore, GMF = BLG + GFB. These sources of funds increase the purchasing power at the disposal of the government without reducing that at the disposal of the private sector of the Irish economy. They increase the reserves of the banking system and may lead to an expansion of the money stock. (By how much the stock of money in circulation increases depends on the rate at which the demand for money is growing.) Non-monetary financing comprises lending by the Irish non-bank public to the government, through small savings schemes such as the Post Office Savings Bank and through purchases of government securities. This involves a transfer of savings from the private to the public sector of the Irish economy and has no effect on bank liquidity.

In the early 1980s, the greater part of the government's deficit was financed monetarily (Table 6.6). In 1981, for example, 84 per cent of the EBR was financed from monetary sources, with direct foreign borrowing by the government accounting for 75 per cent. Dependence on foreign borrowing has decreased in recent years and this has decreased the proportion of the deficit that is monetized. In 1986 only 44 per cent of the debt was financed by monetary means and only 38 per cent by direct foreign borrowing.

The manner in which the deficit is financed has important implications for its effect on the real economy. To see this, it is

Table 6.6
Financing the Exchequer Borrowing Requirement (IR£million), 1978-86

	Non-monetary sources	Monetary sources		Total EBR
		Bank lending to government	Government foreign borrowing	
1978	252	235	323	810
1979	283	267	459	1,009
1980	344	290	583	1,217
1981	285	187	1,250	1,722
1982	587	228	1,130	1,945
1983	733	194	829	1,756
1984	536	519	770	1,825
1985	1,051	75	889	2,015
1986	1,184	− 30	991	2,145

Sources: Central Bank of Ireland Quarterly Bulletin, various issues.
[1]These figures do not include borrowing by state-sponsored bodies.

helpful to explore the *flow of funds* between different sectors of the economy and between the domestic economy and the rest of the world. In some countries, Japan is a notable example, the private sector of the economy has a very high savings rate. Ample funds are available for acquiring the debt issued by the public sector and/or foreign assets. In the United States, on the other hand, private sector savings are low, and the public sector deficits of the 1980s have been financed by inflows from abroad (including Japan) through the capital account of the balance of payments. There is therefore an important link between the financial balances of the domestic private and public sectors and the country's current account balance of payments.

These relationships can be clarified using basic national income accounting identities. Starting from a closed economy with no public sector, *ex post*

$$S = I$$

where S = savings, I = investment. With a public sector, this has to be expanded to

$$S + NT = I + G, \text{ or } (S - I) = (G - NT)$$

that is, the private sector's surplus of savings over investment equals the public sector's deficit or dissavings. (At this point the complications arising from the classification of part of government spending as I is ignored.) Finally, in an open economy, the identity has to be enlarged to

$$S + NT + M = I + G + X$$

where M = imports and X = exports. Rearranging, this becomes

$$(S - I) + (NT - G) = (X - M)$$

which says that the sum of the domestic economy's private and public sectors' balances must equal the country's balance of payments on current account.

No direct estimates of the private sector's surplus, $S - I$, are available from the Irish national accounts data.[17] It can, however, be calculated as a residual, that is, as the difference between the PSBR and the current account of the balance of payments. A difficulty with this approach, however, lies in the uncertainty regarding the appropriate measure of the current account to use in the light of the large and growing residual that has emerged in the capital account of the Irish balance of payments in recent years.

Table 6.7
Sectoral Financial Balances as a Percentage of GNP, 1977-86

	Private sector financial surplus[1]	PSBR	Balance of payments	
			Current account	Net residual
	(a)	(b)	(c) = (a) − (b)	
1977	7.1	12.5	− 5.4	− 4.8
1978	8.1	14.9	− 6.8	− 1.4
1979	2.7	16.1	− 13.4	− 1.0
1980	5.8	17.3	− 11.5	+ 0.7
1981	5.6	20.3	− 14.7	+ 1.1
1982	9.3	19.9	− 10.6	− 1.9
1983	10.1	17.0	− 6.9	− 1.9
1984	10.4	16.6	− 6.2	− 2.3
1985	12.4	16.0	− 3.6	− 4.1
1986	13.2	15.2	− 2.0	− 9.5

Sources: Adapted from CSO, National Income and Expenditure, various issues.
[1] The private sector financial surplus has been estimated residually as the difference between the current account balance-of-payments deficit and the PSBR. From the National Income and Expenditure (NIE) booklet it is possible to derive a measure of this surplus by subtracting T-R-G-Ig from the current account deficit, where Ig equals gross physical capital formation by the public authorities (item 155 plus item 184 in NIE). This yields a much lower figure for the private sector financial surplus than that given in the table above since it treats such items as the capital spending of state-sponsored bodies and capital grants to enterprises as private sector investment.

Table 6.7 shows the estimates of the three sectoral balances obtained when (S − I) is calculated as a residual. The striking feature of these results is the rapid increase in (S − I) since 1981 from 5.6 per cent of GNP to 13.2 per cent. There is room for doubt about the accuracy of these estimates. The private sector may indeed be saving more in response to high real interest rates and in order to restore the level of financial assets that existed before the prolonged inflation of the 1970s. At the same time the level of private sector investment has certainly declined. Undoubtedly these forces have raised (S − I) from the very low level that was recorded in 1979, but whether it has reached over 13 per cent of GNP may be doubted.

The reasons for this scepticism are as follows. It may be seen from Table 6.7 that the net residual outflow on the capital account of the balance of payments has increased markedly since 1981 and rose very sharply in 1985 and 1986. This outflow may contain unrecorded debit items from the current account and private capital flows. These should be brought 'above the line' and included in the measure of the current account deficit which is relevant for policy analysis. This measure, which might be called the 'basic balance', would give a truer picture of the private sector surplus. Calculated in this manner, the private sector surplus would show a much less dramatic increase in recent years than does the unadjusted estimate.

It is regrettable that such uncertainty should surround the measurement of the sectoral balances, because their relative magnitudes have important implications for the effects of government deficits on the growth of real GNP. If the domestic private economy is generating a large volume of savings relative to the level of private capital formation, then government deficits are not likely to 'crowd out' private sector spending by competing for funds and raising interest rates. For example, in Japan private savings are very large relative to the demand for funds to finance private investment and the government deficit. There is a surplus of funds in the domestic economy and domestic interest rates are low by international standards. This encourages an outflow of savings to the rest of the world, which can only occur if there is a balance-of-payments surplus on current account. From this perspective, the Japanese balance-of-payments surplus is a necessary concomitant of the surplus of domestic savings. The situation in the United States is a mirror image of this. Taking the public and private sectors together, there is a deficiency of savings, which has raised interest rates and encouraged a capital inflow whose concomitant is a current account balance-of-payments deficit. In this case, the fiscal deficit has as its counterpart a trade deficit, and public sector spending crowds out export- and import-competing sectors.

It is difficult to locate Ireland on this continuum between Japan and the United States. The sharp increase in the private sector surplus recorded when it is estimated using the unadjusted balance-of-payments data suggests that there should now be relatively little difficulty in funding the PSBR from domestic sources. But it has been seen that this estimate may be misleading because a significant proportion of these funds are flowing out of the country. Thus, despite the apparent growth of the private sector financial surplus, 46 per cent of the exchequer borrowing requirement was financed through foreign borrowing in 1986.

Much larger inflows occurred in earlier years. These have had the effect of providing savings to the Irish economy and averting the upward pressure on interest rates that would have occurred if the deficit had been financed exclusively from domestic sources. An inflow of foreign savings, however, requires as its counterpart a balance-of-payments deficit on current account. This in turn implies a crowding out of domestic exporting and import-competing sectors. At the height of Ireland's dependence on foreign borrowing, in 1981 and 1982, the current account balance-of-payments deficit rose to a record 15 per cent of GNP.

On the other hand, when the exchequer has tried to fund most of its borrowing requirement on domestic money markets the effects on the availability of funds has been marked. In 1986, instead of funding a substantial proportion of the PSBR from foreign sources early in the year, the exchequer relied heavily on domestic sources of funds and encountered resistance in the last quarter. The differential between Irish and EMS interest rates widened by over three percentage points between June and October. While other factors, notably uncertainty concerning the exchange rate, contributed to this development, it could be viewed as an example of interest rate crowding-out.

Thus, whether the Irish PSBR is financed mainly from domestic funds or includes a significant proportion of foreign borrowing, it is likely that borrowing of this magnitude has an important effect on the availability of funds for private sector spending and/or on the competitiveness of the traded sector of the economy. To the extent that crowding-out occurs, it further reduces the impact of fiscal policy because, as public sector demand increases, private sector demand is reduced. Clearly, the substitution of public for private spending has no net expansionary effect. To the extent that it entails a substitution of consumption for investment, however, it lowers the long-run growth rate.

Another possible effect of deficits on private sector behaviour has been called the Ricardian Equivalence Theorem. This refers to the hypothesis that the private sector anticipates the burden of future taxation implicit in increased government borrowing and increases its saving in order to provide for this. If this were true then it would not matter whether the public sector finances its spending by raising extra tax revenue or by borrowing. In both cases the level of private sector spending would be reduced by the amount of the increase in public spending. Only 'balanced budget multipliers' would be relevant.

The realism of the Ricardian theory has been questioned, but some empirical support for the proposition is reported in the American literature. In Ireland, it is striking that the very large public sector deficits of the 1980s have been accompanied by increased private sector surpluses. While the nature of the causal relationship, if one exists, between the two magnitudes is far from clear, some support for the Ricardian theory is reported by Moore.[18]

3   MONETARY POLICY

Introduction
In a small open economy the scope for an independent monetary policy is limited. This is especially true when, as in Ireland before 1979, the exchange rate is fixed and the financial system totally integrated with that of a dominant neighbour. Since Ireland's participation in the European Monetary System (EMS) in 1979, monetary policy has assumed greater importance. There are, however, major constraints on the Irish authorities in this area. Ireland's exchange rate is more or less fixed to a basket of currencies in the EMS. The Irish interest rate still moves up and down in close sympathy with the UK rate. The quantity of money in circulation is influenced more by the demand for money within Ireland than by the decisions of the Irish authorities.

With these reservations in mind, the role of monetary (including exchange rate) policy as part of overall stabilization policy is examined.

Interest Rate Policy
Prior to 1979, Irish interest rates were determined by UK rates. The fixed exchange rate and the absence of exchange controls between the two countries ensured that this would be the case. There was no scope for any form of interest rate policy in Ireland. However, following Ireland's decision to enter the EMS in 1979, and the UK's decision not to participate, the degree of financial integration between the two countries was reduced by (i) exchange rate uncertainty and (ii) the introduction of exchange controls. This gave rise to the possibility that Irish interest rates could differ from foreign rates for some period of time without provoking capital inflows or outflows on a scale that would restore equality.

Figure 6.2 supports this view. Prior to EMS entry and for two years afterwards, Irish and UK interest rates moved closely in line. Between 1981 and 1985, however, a significant difference emerged between the two rates. In early 1982, Irish interest rates were six percentage points higher than UK rates. To see why there was such a radical change in the 1980s it is necessary to consider the factors that influence interest rates in a small open economy.

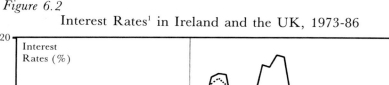

Figure 6.2

Interest Rates[1] in Ireland and the UK, 1973-86

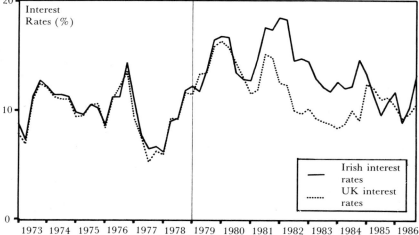

Sources: OECD, *Main Economic Indicators,* various issues.
[1] Treasury Bills (3 months).

An investor or borrower comparing these interest rates would also consider exchange rate movements. Fluctuations in exchange rates affect the return/cost of investing/borrowing abroad. *Interest Rate Parity Theory* (IRPT) states that the differential in interest rates will equal the difference between forward and spot exchange rates, which in turn reflects the expected change in the spot rate. Thus:

$$\frac{1 + R_f}{1 + R_d} = \frac{e^*_{t+1}}{e_t}$$

where: $R_{d,f}$ = domestic, foreign interest rate; e_t = spot exchange rate (defined according to UK convention as the foreign cost of a unit of domestic currency, \$/IR£) and e^*_{t+1} = expected exchange rate in time $t + 1$.

In particular, if the domestic currency is expected to depreciate then interest rates will rise relative to those in the rest of the world. Since 1979 Irish interest rates have been higher than UK rates during periods when it was expected that the Irish pound was 'overvalued' relative to sterling.

The background against which Irish interest rate policy now operates is a continuing high degree of financial integration with

UK financial markets and, since 1979, growing linkages with European (especially German) markets. Expectations about exchange rates are now formed in a complex manner by looking at the relationship between the Irish pound and both sterling and the deutschemark (DM).

Generally, countries that pursue an interest rate policy do so to influence the exchange rate or aggregate demand. This is not the case in Ireland. In this country, the objective is simply to *stabilize* Irish interest rates without affecting the long-run trend.[19] Without such a policy, there would be considerable variation in interest rates and this volatility would adversely affect economic growth.

To explain how a policy of stabilizing interest rates might be implemented, it is useful to refer to the Central Bank's balance sheet. The important point to note is that the Licensed Banks are required to maintain a level of reserves (RE) through the primary reserve ratio and that a surplus/deficiency in reserves will tend to be placed/borrowed on the interbank market. The supply and demand forces on the interbank market then determine the interbank interest rate which in turn affects all other rates in the system. Typically, changes in interbank rates will be quickly followed by changes in both the Associated and non-Associated Banks' interest rates and, after a lag, in Building Society rates.

Table 6.8

Central Bank Balance Sheet

Assets		Liabilities	
External reserves	(R)	Currency	(CU)
Central Bank credit to:		Licensed banks' reserves	(RE)
—banks[1]	(CCB)	Government deposits	(GD)
—government	(CCG)		
Other		Other	

[1] Central Bank credit to the Licensed Banks (CCB) is defined as the sum of rediscounted Exchequer bills, secured advances, the short term credit facility and, since May 1983, sale and repurchase agreements. For a discussion on these instruments, see Barry.[20] One important instrument, foreign currency swaps, is not included due to the non-availability of data.

One of the principal variables affecting RE is changes in the external reserves, R, on the asset side of the balance sheet. Changes in R reflect flows through the balance of payments which are influenced by factors such as relative rates of inflation and growth and relative interest rates, as well as exchange rate speculation. If, as a result of these factors, R decreases, RE will also fall and interbank interest rates will increase as banks borrow funds in order to maintain their liquidity ratios.

Thus the flow of funds into and out of the country through the balance of payments could lead to considerable short-term volatility in interest rates. To avoid this, the Central Bank could 'sterilize' the effect of a fall in R on interest rates by providing funds to the banks via the CCB variable or by lowering the reserve requirements. Similarly an increase in Licensed Bank Reserves (RE) due to a rise in R could be sterilized by increasing the primary and secondary reserve ratios or by reducing the amount of credit available to the Licensed Banks.

Two questions relating to this policy are examined in this section. (i) What has been the degree of sterilization since 1979 and how does it compare to the pre-EMS period? (ii) How effective is this policy in stabilizing interest rates?

To answer these questions it is necessary to calculate 'sterilization' and 'offset' coefficients. The first coefficient shows how the Central Bank *reacts* to changes in R by injecting or withdrawing funds from the money market. The second coefficient, in contrast, indicates what proportion of this injection/withdrawal is offset through a subsequent change in the external reserves. Sterilization and offset coefficients equal to -1 and 0 respectively would indicate complete sterilization and no offset. Interest rate policy would be both very active and very effective in this case.

There are two studies to date that deal directly with the above questions. Leddin estimated, using quarterly data, for the pre-EMS period (1972-79), sterilization and offset coefficients equal to -0.01 and -1.0 respectively.[21] This suggests that the Central Bank did not engage in sterilization prior to EMS entry, but if it had the policy would have been entirely ineffective due to complete offset through changes in the external reserves. Thus, pre-EMS, there was no significant interest rate policy in Ireland and no scope for an effective policy.

In contrast, the results for the post-EMS period (1979-84) indicate sterilization and offset coefficients of -0.75 and -0.79 respectively. This suggests that the Central Bank has pursued a sterilization policy and that the degree of offset was not as high as before 1979. The coefficients suggest that the Central Bank reacts to a IR£1m reduction in the external reserves by injecting IR£0.75m into the market. Of this, IR£0.58m (IR£0.75 × 0.79) is offset immediately through changes in the external reserves. The reduction in the absolute value of the offset coefficient relative to the pre-EMS period indicates imperfect capital mobility and is probably a consequence of exchange controls and exchange rate uncertainty. Both of these factors are a direct consequence of Ireland's participation in the EMS.

Similarly, Browne using monthly data, estimated a 'monetary model' of the Irish economy over the period January 1980 to April 1985.[22] He found that the Central Bank sterilized, in the same month, 60 per cent of any change in the external reserves. His results also indicated that any injection or withdrawal of funds would be *completely* offset through changes in the external reserves within a period of five months.

Although more empirical evidence is necessary before any definite conclusions can be drawn, the results of these two studies suggest that there is scope for only a very short-run sterilization policy in Ireland. There is still a high degree of integration between Irish and foreign financial markets. Attempts to sterilize changes in reserves arising from fluctuations in the balance of payments would prove costly and ineffective. As far as interest rates are concerned, Ireland is very much a 'price taker', unable to influence the overall level. An interest rate policy that attempted to do more than slightly reduce day-to-day fluctuations would prove ineffective and costly. If the Central Bank were to abandon its attempts to stabilize interest rates, it is likely that the banks would maintain excess reserves to avoid the costs associated with volatile interest rates.

Table 6.9
Consolidated Balance Sheet of the Banking System

Assets		Liabilities	
External reserves	(R)	Domestic money supply	(Ms)
Central and licensed bank lending:			
—To government	(BLG)		
—To non-government	(NGL)		

Credit Policy
Normally, macroeconomic textbooks that concentrate on large, closed economies, discuss 'controlling the money supply' as an instrument of monetary policy. In Ireland, the approach is to control *credit* rather than the *money* stock. To see why this should be, consider the consolidated balance sheet of the Irish banking system (Table 6.9), greatly simplified for expositional purposes (for more details, see Central Bank Reports). Hence $\Delta R \equiv \Delta Ms - \Delta(NGL + BLG)$, or $\Delta R \equiv \Delta Ms - DCE$, where DCE = domestic credit

expansion = increase in bank lending to government and to the private sector.

This identity can be extended to a theory of the balance of payments (known as the monetary approach to the balance of payments (MAB)). The basic assumption is that the money supply is determined by the demand for money (Md) which in turn is a function of a few variables. From this, the policy recommendation is to estimate the growth in Md and BLG and then set a guideline on NGL so as to achieve a desired R target. Suppose, for example, Md is estimated to increase by 20 per cent over the period. By assumption, Ms must also rise by 20 per cent. If BLG is expected to increase by 7 per cent and the objective is to have no change in R, the guideline for the period will be 13 per cent. The difference between a small open economy and a large closed one as far as monetary control is concerned lies in the crucial importance of maintaining an adequate level of R in the former.

The overall credit guidelines are referred to as the 'quantitative' guideline. (The 'personal lending' guidelines, discussed below, relate to the *composition* of the total increase in credit.) The Central Bank's targets and outcomes, for the period 1978 to 1981, are summarized briefly in Table 6.10.

Table 6.10
External Reserves: Targets and Outcomes[1]

Period	Stated external reserves objective	Outcome ΔR (IR£m)
1978[2]	– IR£200m	+ 51.2
1979	'. .little change. .'	– 262.5
1980	guideline should '. .induce some recourse by the private sector to external financing'.	+ 331.5
1981	'. .adequate level. .'	– 50.7

Sources: Central Bank of Ireland Quarterly Bulletin, various issues.
[1] From 1982 onwards, bank lending fell short of the guideline and as a result the guidelines could not have contributed to an external reserves target. No other policy was introduced in their place.
[2] 1978 was the only year a specific target was published.

An analysis of the underlying data suggests that the guidelines did not achieve the intended R target in 1978 and 1979 and, not surprisingly, this was due to inaccuracies in predicting BLG and Md. The policy in 1980 was to issue a restrictive guideline to encourage the banks to borrow abroad (foreign-currency-based lending was exempt from the guideline) and this approach proved successful.

One criticism of this policy[23] is that the level of external reserves is an inappropriate measure of the Central Bank's ability to maintain the exchange rate as it does not take account of government (and state-sponsored) foreign borrowing (GFB). As seen in the earlier section on fiscal policy, GFB has risen dramatically in recent years. If GFB is subtracted from the earlier identity then $\Delta R - \Delta GFB \equiv \Delta Ms - \Delta(NGL + BLG + GFB)$, or $\Delta NR \equiv \Delta Ms - \Delta(NGL + GMF)$ where NR = net external reserves = R − GFB; and GMF = government monetary financing (i.e. the Exchequer Borrowing Requirement less sales of government debt to the Irish non-bank public) = BLG + GFB.

Because NR takes account of net foreign liabilities, whereas R does not, it is a more appropriate policy target. It can be shown that even if the change in NGL had been zero over the period 1978 to 1983, the increase in GMF, *ceteribus paribus,* would have resulted in a decrease in NR. Hence it would have been impossible for the Central Bank to implement a policy of stabilizing NR.

In addition to the quantitative guideline, the Central Bank has tried to influence the *composition* of the total credit that is made available. A personal lending guideline (which applies to personal loans other than housing) has been issued to ensure that a significant proportion of total credit is reserved for 'productive' purposes.

It is important to note that the guidelines are not some costless control designed to achieve a worthwhile objective. There are very definite costs involved as they tend to stifle competition between the banks and cause a misallocation of resources in the economy. In order to illustrate this resource misallocation consider the growth in personal loans during the operation of the first two guidelines.

On a cumulative basis, personal loans *decreased* by 10.9 per cent between November 1978 and February 1980, but instalment credit *increased* by 25.9 per cent over the same period. Instalment credit was exempt from the guidelines but interest rates on this type of credit are roughly double those charged on personal loans. How can these trends be explained?

One possibility is that the banks discriminated against personal borrowers in order to maximize profits. If the banks decreased personal loans and increased 'productive' lending so as to maximize lending subject to the quantitative guideline, rationed personal borrowers could be expected to have recourse to instalment credit. Since the Associated Banks have important subsidiaries in the instalment credit market the net effect would be to increase the banks' group profits.

Imperfect substitution between the two forms of credit could result in reduced real expenditures in the economy and lower profits in the retail sector. Perfect substitution, on the other hand, would increase bank profitability. In both cases, the imposition of credit guidelines clearly involved some resource misallocation.

As a second illustration of the resource misallocation credit guidelines entail, relate the following statements (emphasis added) published in various issues of the *Central Bank of Ireland Quarterly Bulletin*, to the growth in personal loans, given in Table 6.11, over the period 1980 I to 1982 IV.

'. . . . the increase (in personal lending) for the nine months to November was somewhat in excess of the 6 per cent guideline . . . . . *The Central Bank has been in communication with banks* in breach of the 6 per cent guideline, with a view to taking appropriate action in the light of subsequent developments'. [1980 IV, p. 24]

'. . . . the increase in (personal) lending . . . . was not consistent with the objectives of monetary policy. Accordingly, *the banks concerned have been contacted* with a view to securing compliance with the intent of monetary policy'. [1981 II, p. 16]

'. . . . in view of this rapid increase (in personal credit), *the Central Bank informed* a number of banks that the intent of monetary policy was not being complied with *and advised these banks* . . . .'. [1981 IV, p. 25]

'. . . . growth in lending to the personal sector was relatively rapid and *banks have been contacted with a view to securing compliance* with the sectoral guideline of 7 per cent . . . .'. [1982 II, p. 15]

The communications apply to quarters 1980 III, 1981 I, 1981 III and 1982 I respectively. It will be observed from Table 6.11 that in the following quarters there was a fall in personal lending (the exception being 1981 IV when the growth rate moderated significantly). The decrease in lending indicates that the banks did not lend repayments on previous loans. This suggests that as a result of the guidelines, credit was made available on a 'stop/go' basis. Moreover, the Associated Banks engaged in non-price credit rationing. In terms of successfully obtaining a loan, it clearly made a difference in which month or quarter the borrower applied for the loan.

Table 6.11
Associated Bank Lending[1] Subject to the Personal Lending Guidelines,[2] 1980-82 (Cumulative Percentage Change from the Introduction of each New Guideline)

Quarter	1980	1981[3]	1982
I	3.1	14.2	6.5
II	3.6	3.8	1.5
III	11.9	11.1	9.5
IV	5.7	13.5	10.6

Sources: as for Table 6.10.

[1] Data are exclusive of house loans.

[2] The guidelines are enforced by 'special deposits'. Banks which breach the guidelines must place a deposit equivalent to the 'excess' lending with the Central Bank. The objective is to remove profits earned by the banks on excess lending.

[3] The directive in 1981 suggested that the growth in personal loans should be appreciably less than the quantitative guideline of 15 per cent.

It may, therefore, be concluded that credit policy was very limited with regard to its objective, which is to stabilize the level of external reserves. These reserves do not take into account the level of external indebtedness due to government foreign borrowing. None the less, credit policy through its selective effects on personal credit and its 'stop/go' nature may have entailed resource costs.

It could also be argued that the attempt to use credit policy to achieve an external reserve target is based on a rather strong interpretation of MAB theory. This is a long-run theory which reasonably predicts that the external reserves will increase if the growth in domestic credit is consistently held below the growth in the money supply. This does not necessarily imply that a desired level of reserves can be attained by introducing different credit policies each year. The available evidence not only supports the view that it is not possible to use credit policy in this way but also points to the possibility that guidelines have costly side effects.

4   EXCHANGE RATE POLICY

Introduction
The reason Ireland joined the EMS, while the UK declined to participate, centres largely on differences in anti-inflation policy. In the UK, the Labour Government's preferred approach to curbing inflation was monetary base control which required a flexible exchange rate.[24] The Irish authorities, in contrast, were influenced

by the fact that Germany had consistently lower inflation than the UK. They viewed a flexible exchange rate policy as inappropriate for a small open economy like Ireland. Instead, the preferred policy was to fix the exchange rate to a low inflation currency bloc, such as the EMS, in the belief that Irish inflation would converge to the rate of inflation prevailing in this bloc.

There was, however, an important implicit assumption in this argument, namely that Purchasing Power Parity (PPP) would hold under fixed exchange rates in the EMS, despite a significantly lower degree of trade integration between Ireland and Germany than Ireland and the UK. In fact, part of the logic of Ireland's decision to join the EMS lay in the belief that pegging the Irish pound to the DM would dramatically increase the degree of integration begween Ireland and Germany. As the degree of integration increased, conditions would have become more favourable for PPP.

The decision to join the EMS involved of course other important considerations such as the desire to contribute to an important new Community initiative and it was recognized that there would be significant costs involved. These costs were, however, reduced by a transfer of resources in the form of grants and low interest loans which formed part of Ireland's negotiations on EMS membership.

While joining the EMS was seen at the time to be a commitment to a fixed exchange rate with Germany, the 13 realignments that occurred between 1979 and 1987 have allowed very significant changes in bilateral rates to take place. The DM/IR£ rate, for example, has fallen from 3.80 to 2.68 or by 29 per cent. Thus it is clear that EMS membership involves an adjustable peg, rather than a fixed exchange rate.

Purchasing Power Parity

PPP basically states that purchasing powers of different currencies should remain relatively equal. The relationship may be interpreted as a simple equilibrium condition or as a theory of exchange rate determination and is normally written: $P_d.e = P_f$, or $e = P_f/P_d$, where P_d and P_f are respectively domestic and foreign prices and e is the foreign cost of a unit of domestic currency. A weaker version deals in rates of change, and states that percentage changes in exchange rates are primarily due to differences in rates of inflation: $\%\Delta e = \%\Delta P_f - \%\Delta P_d$. As a theory of floating exchange rates, PPP predicts that e will adjust so as to offset inflation differentials. That is, relative inflation rates explain exchange rate movements.

This theory can be turned around and used to explain inflation rates (see Chapter 9), especially for a SOE that pegs its exchange rate to a larger country. Under a fixed exchange rate regime, inflation rates should adjust to maintain PPP. Hence a convergence of inflation rates should be observed. In the case of a small open economy like Ireland, the inflation rate is assumed to be exogenously determined by the inflation rate in the country to which the currency is pegged. Up to 1979, there was little divergence between Irish and UK rates of inflation and this provided strong support for the theory.

PPP and Ireland's Experience in EMS

Following Walsh,[25] one way of examining PPP is to graph the variables e and P_d/P_f. This is done in Figures 6.3 and 6.4, for the case of Ireland and the UK and Ireland and Germany over the period 1979 to 1986. If the equation holds perfectly, the two curves in each graph will coincide. If, on the other hand, exchange rate movements do not fully offset inflation differentials, they will diverge. If the exchange rate falls by more than the ratio of inflation rates, the domestic economy enjoys a competitive gain, and *vice versa*.

Figure 6.3 shows that following EMS entry the two series diverged, with Ireland gaining a competitive edge relative to the

Figure 6.3

Index of the PPP Relationship Between the UK and Ireland, 1979 = 100

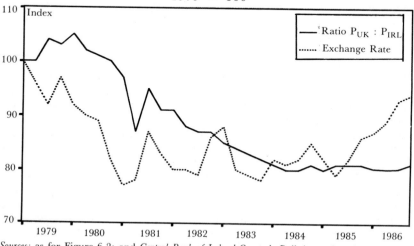

Sources: as for Figure 6.2; and *Central Bank of Ireland Quarterly Bulletin*, various issues.

UK. The oil crisis in 1979 unexpectedly caused sterling to appreciate against the dollar and the EMS currencies. However, between 1982 and 1985 the series periodically converged with each country at times having had the competitive advantage and no clear trend emerging. In 1986 the relationship again broke down. Factors such as rapid growth in UK money supply, associated with the final abandoning of monetary base control and the reintroduction of interest and exchange rate targets, and falling oil prices led to the depreciation of sterling. Irish inflation did not fall to offset the depreciation of sterling and the UK enjoyed a significant competitive gain. Allowing for EMS realignments, the evidence suggests that Irish prices do respond to sterling exchange rate movements, but, as the 1986 experience indicates, the response is not automatic or immediate.

The German case in contrast does not support PPP in either the short or long run. Figure 6.4 shows that even after seven years the two series continued to diverge, with the Irish economy continually losing competitiveness. This situation has arisen because of the weak influence of German financial markets on Ireland and the relatively low degree of trade interdependence between the two countries.

Figure 6.4
Index of the PPP Relationship Between Germany and Ireland,
1979 = 100

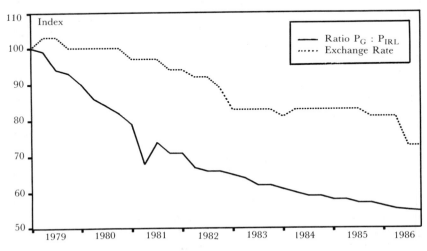

Sources: as for Figure 6.2.

An alternative method of examining Ireland's exchange rate is to calculate real exchange rates. Bacon,[26] for example, emphasizes the real trade-weighted exchange rate index. This index shows an 18 per cent loss in competitiveness relative to Ireland's main trading partners over the period 1979 to 1985. This has arisen principally because of a significant loss in competitiveness against the EMS countries. There was little change relative to the UK and a gain in competitiveness relative to the US over the period.

The depreciation of sterling motivated the Irish authorities to devalue in 1986. This illustrates a contradiction in Irish exchange rate policy. While the currency is pegged in the EMS band, there appears also to be an Irish pound/sterling target. This creates uncertainty and encourages speculation during periods when sterling is weak relative to the EMS currencies. It would be optimal from the Irish point of view if the UK joined the EMS exchange rate mechanism. With the Irish exchange rate fixed relative to an enlarged EMS, it would be very much back in the pre-1979 situation. The scope for an independent monetary policy would be greatly reduced. Ireland's exchange rate commitment would be the main source of discipline on the economy and interest rates and credit expansion would reflect this.

In summary, the evidence suggests that, against its main trading partners, Ireland has lost competitiveness due to exchange rate movements and relative inflation rates since 1979. This is particularly evident in the case of the EMS countries. However, there is also evidence that PPP theory does hold between Ireland and the UK. The relationship did break down following EMS entry, but after a period of approximately four years, it was reestablished. This situation continued until 1986 when a further significant divergence occurred. Hence, despite the change in exchange rate regime in both countries, Irish inflation continues to be strongly affected by UK inflation in the medium term. The influence of the EMS inflation rate on Ireland remains hard to discern.

This outcome obviously raises a question mark about the decision to enter EMS. It also raises doubts about the recourse to devaluation in 1983 and 1986. If PPP with the UK holds, the loss of competitiveness due to the depreciation of sterling would have been short lived. Devaluation simply increases the Irish rate of inflation in return for a short-term gain in competitiveness (or relief from what would have been a short-term loss of competitiveness). Above all it generates uncertainty about Irish exchange rate policy and this is reflected in a widening of the Irish/foreign interest rate differential.

The options for exchange rate policy in the future include a return to the sterling link or irrevocably fixing the currency to a standard such as the ECU or a trade weighted index.[27] Either of these options would reduce exchange rate uncertainty and promote a reduction in Irish interest rates.

5   CONCLUSION

Fiscal policy seeks to stabilize the economy by using changes in taxation and government expenditure to offset fluctuations in private spending. The effectiveness of this approach is reduced in a small open economy with high marginal tax rates. Over the years, government deficits have led to the accumulation of a very large national debt and the goal of stabilizing the ratio of debt to income now takes precedence over any use of public spending or taxation to regulate the behaviour of output and employment. The high rate of interest relative to inflation is the main reason why further reductions in the government deficit will be necessary if the economy is to escape the spiral of increasing debt and the high level of taxation associated with servicing this debt.

Credit policy in Ireland is designed to influence the external reserves. Interest rate policy attempts to *stabilize* interest rates and thereby facilitate economic growth. The exchange rate has been devalued on two occasions within the EMS in order to maintain competitiveness relative to the UK. Hence, monetary policy in Ireland does not consist of one single integrated policy but rather three separate policy instruments. At times there has been a lack of cohesion in the way these instruments have been used.

Moreover, there is little coordination between fiscal and monetary policy. Although the Central Bank has consistently preached fiscal rectitude it is forced to take the government's borrowing requirement as given. Since 1979, the Central Bank has balanced its growth and external reserves objectives by encouraging the banks and insisting that the government borrows substantial amounts abroad. If monetary policy has succeeded in its objectives, it has been due to substantial recourse to foreign borrowing.

Since 1979, Ireland has not been noticeably more successful within the EMS in moderating the rate of inflation than has the UK outside the EMS. At the same time, the difference between Irish and UK interest rates has widened. Looking to the future, the prospect of the UK joining the EMS seems to offer the best hope of reconciling the various goals that are pursued by the Irish authorities through exchange rate and monetary policy. However, if this occurs, the scope for independence in these areas will be greatly diminished.

Footnotes

1 These phrases were used in Paul A. Samuelson and Robert M. Solow, 'Analytical Aspects of Anti-Inflationary Policy', in M.G. Mueller (editor), *Readings in Macroeconomics,* Holt, Reinhart and Winston, New York 1966, p. 384.

2 See, for example, David Begg, Stanley Fischer and Rudiger Dornbusch, *Economics* (UK edition), McGraw-Hill, London 1985. A taxonomy of unemployment is provided in Edmond Malinvaud, *The Theory of Unemployment Reconsidered,* Basil Blackwell, Oxford 1977.

3 The hypothesis that increases in the rate of inflation lead to increases in the nominal interest rate is known as the Fisher hypothesis after the Yale economist Irving Fisher.

4 For an account of the background to the budgets of the period under review, see T.K. Whitaker, 'Financial Turning Points', in T.K. Whitaker, *Interests,* Institute of Public Administration, Dublin 1984.

5 To assess whether fiscal policy has been pro- or counter-cyclical the changes in the structural deficit should be correlated with the hypothetical value of GNP in the absence of changes in discretionary fiscal policy. These values are unknown, but can be modelled using the behaviour of the non-government components of aggregate demand.

6 See Patrick Muller and Robert W.R. Price, 'Structural Budget Indicators and the Interpretation of Fiscal Stance in OECD Countries', *OECD Economic Studies,* Autumn 1984.

7 This criterion was first applied in Ireland in *Building on Reality 1985-87,* the government's economic plan published in October 1984. It was discussed at more length in Patrick Honohan, 'The Public Debt and Borrowing: Issues of Interpretation', *Irish Banking Review,* March 1985.

8 The data on the national debt used in the table are from the *Finance Accounts* issued by the Department of Finance. These are reproduced in the *Central Bank of Ireland Quarterly Bulletin.*

9 The dynamics of the debt are discussed in E.V. Domar, 'The Burden of the Debt and the National Income', *American Economic Review,* vol. 33 (1944). The formulation used in the text is contained in Stephen M. Sheffrin, 'Long-run Effects of Budget Deficits', *Portfolio: International Economic Perspectives,* vol. 11, issue 4.

10 The relationship between the burden of taxation and stock of debt depends also on whether or not interest payments are liable to tax. In Ireland very little income tax is paid on the interest on government securities: interest received by non-residents and by pension funds is not taxable.

11 This is approximate only. With high inflation rates the product of the price index and the index of the real interest rate should be used.

12 See, for the American case, Robert J. Gordon, *Macroeconomics* (third edition), Little, Brown and Company, Boston 1984, Chapter 3, and for the Irish case D.A.G. Norton, *Economic Analysis for an Open Economy: Ireland,* Irish Management Institute, Dublin 1980, Chapter 11.

13 The multiplier is a marginal concept, dY/dG. If this is less than the inverse of the share of government spending in national income, Y/G, an increase in G will lead to an increase in G/Y. In Irish circumstances, a multiplier greater than 2 would be required to prevent G/Y rising as G is increased.

14 See Ian Irvine and Patrick Honohan, 'The Marginal Social Cost of Taxation in Ireland' (paper read to the Irish Economics Association annual conference, Kilkenny), May 1987.

15 John Bradley, Connell Fanning, Canice Prendergast and Mark Wynne, *Medium-term Analysis of Fiscal Policy in Ireland: A Macroeconometric Study of the Period 1967-1980,* Economic and Social Research Institute, Dublin 1985, pp. 153-156.

16 Brendan M. Walsh, 'Why is Unemployment so High in Ireland Today?' (Centre for Economic Research, University College, Dublin, Working Paper 48), 1987.

17 A figure for gross physical capital formation by the public authorities is provided in *NIE* (item 155 plus item 184) but it is difficult to allocate public sector grants for private sector investment and capital formation by state-sponsored bodies.

18 Michael J. Moore, 'The Irish Consumption Function and Ricardian Equivalence', (Central Bank of Ireland, Technical Paper), 1987.

19 See Tomás F. Ó Cofaigh, 'Observations on Interest Rates', in *Central Bank of Ireland Annual Report,* 1983, p. 102.

20 Kevin Barry, 'The Central Bank's Management of the Aggregate Liquidity of Licensed Banks', *Central Bank of Ireland Annual Report,* 1983.

21 Anthony Leddin, 'Portfolio Equilibrium and Monetary Policy in Ireland', *Economic and Social Review,* January 1986.

22 Frank X. Browne, 'A Monthly Money Market Model for Ireland in the EMS', *Central Bank of Ireland Annual Report,* 1986.

23 Robert Kelleher 'Recent Trends in Monetary Policy', ESRI, *Quarterly Economic Commentary,* Dublin, January 1980; and National Planning Board, *Proposals for a Plan: 1984-1987,* Dublin 1984.

24 HMSO, *The European Monetary System* (Cmd. 7405), London 1978.

25 Brendan M. Walsh, 'Ireland in the European Monetary System: The Effect of a Change in the Exchange Rate Regime', in M. De Crecco (editor), *International Economic Adjustment,* Basil Blackwell, London 1983.

26 Peter Bacon, 'Exchange Rate Policy' (paper presented to the Dublin Economics Workshop, Ninth Annual Conference, Kenmare), October 1986.

27 See Brendan M. Walsh, 'Irish Exchange Rate Policy', and Brendan R. Dowling, 'Irish Exchange Rate Policy' (papers presented to the Dublin Economics Workshop, Ninth Annual Conference, Kenmare), October 1986.

214

Part III

PERFORMANCE AND POLICY ISSUES AT A NATIONAL LEVEL

7 Economic Growth: Theory and Analysis

Sean Nolan

1   INTRODUCTION

THE DEFINITION, measurement, and evaluation of economic growth as a policy objective have already been examined in Chapter 2. This chapter has two purposes: to outline a theory of the growth process in the small open economy, noting the implications which the theory has regarding the forms which government intervention to promote economic growth should take, and to describe and analyze the actual growth experience of the Irish economy in the period since 1960. The structure of the chapter reflects these distinct foci, with the first half of the chapter containing a theoretical framework for analyzing the growth process in an economy such as Ireland, and the second half applying this framework in analyzing the main features of Ireland's growth experience.

The discussion of the growth process in a small open economy (SOE) is developed in two stages. The first stage (Section 2) consists of an examination of the determinants of the pace of economic growth in a closed economy, followed by an analysis of the determinants of growth performance in an SOE. This discussion highlights a number of important aspects of the growth process in an SOE — most notably the close linkage between the growth experience of the SOE and that of the larger economic system of which it is a part — and shows that growth policy in an SOE should be thought of as competitiveness policy, in the sense that it should be focussed on improving the competitive position of the SOE within the international division of labour. The second stage (Section 3) contains a formal analysis of the determinants of national output in an SOE, the purpose of which is to identify the major factors influencing the magnitude and sectoral composition of national output. A simple three-sector model of an SOE is developed, and is used to illustrate both the central role of the traded goods sector in determining the sustainable level of national output in an SOE, and the particular importance of the manufacturing sector in a non-resource-abundant SOE such as Ireland. Detailed discussion of the determinants of economic performance in the

216

traded goods sector of the economy — and the appropriate role for state policy in influencing that performance — is left until Chapters 10 and 11.

The discussion of the growth experience of the Irish economy since 1960 is developed in three stages. The first stage (Section 4) examines the extent of Ireland's integration into the European and international economies, and examines the applicability of the label 'small open economy' to the Irish economy. In the second stage of the discussion (Section 5), the main statistical features of the Irish growth experience in the post-1960 period are reviewed, and Ireland's experiences are related to the growth experience of the international economy during this time period. The final section of the chapter (Section 6) contains a discussion of the two most striking features of Ireland's recent growth experience — the rapid industrial expansion during the 1960s and 1970s, and the ongoing recession of the 1980s.

Before proceeding further, it is appropriate to give some precision to the meaning attached to the label 'small open economy'. In this chapter, the label is used to refer to an economy in which: (i) a significant fraction of the goods and services produced in the economy are traded goods, in the sense that they are goods which are directly exposed to international competition; (ii) the traded goods sector of the economy is integrated within a larger economic system, in the sense that the domestic market is merely a sub-component of a larger international market; (iii) domestic markets for traded goods are a sufficiently small component of the larger international market that changes in supply and demand conditions in the domestic market do not affect prices in either the SOE or the international market; (iv) financial linkages between the domestic economy and international financial markets are sufficiently close and the domestic economy is sufficiently small that domestic real interest rates are equal to, and completely determined by, real interest rates abroad. Underlying the discussion in this chapter is the implicit assumption that Ireland can be classified as an SOE; the legitimacy of employing this assumption in analyzing longer term growth issues is evaluated in Section 4 below.

2 COMPARISON OF GROWTH IN THE CLOSED ECONOMY AND THE SMALL OPEN ECONOMY

It is useful to commence the discussion of economic growth[1] by considering first the growth process in the closed economy, and addressing the question as to what determines the pace of economic expansion in such a situation. A comprehensive answer to this question would require an extensive tour through the history of economic thought; the brief discussion here is intended to provide a somewhat simplified synthesis of the answers provided by the major theories of the growth process in a closed capitalist economy.[2] The organization of the discussion below relies on modern Neoclassical theory, but elements of the discussion reflect Classical and Marxian themes.

Put in the most direct form possible, economic growth is a consequence of resource accumulation, where 'resource' is used in the broad sense to refer to physical capital, the 'human capital' embodied in trained workers, and the stock of technological knowledge. This can be most easily seen by means of an aggregate production function relating output of goods and services per worker, Q/L, to the inputs of physical capital goods per worker, K/L, and the average level of skills per worker, H/L; thus, $Q/L = F(K/L, H/L)$. Growth in output per worker is therefore associated with: increases in the stock of physical capital per worker available; increases in the average level of labour skills (i.e. the stock of human capital per worker); and an expansion in the stock of technological knowledge (i.e. shifts in the F relationship). An additional, but less significant factor influencing growth in output per worker relates to changes in the quality of the natural resource base of the economy. The key feature of natural resources (whether renewable or non-renewable) of relevance to economic welfare is not so much the available stock as the average and marginal costs (in terms of capital and labour) associated with resource production (as with oil or minerals) or resource utilization (as with agricultural land). Decline in these costs is therefore a fourth factor leading to expansion in output per worker. While any of these four factors will, *ceteris paribus,* generate economic growth, the four factors are closely interrelated in the actual growth process. For example, the effects of the new information processing technology on output per worker involves the expansion of the stock of knowledge, the acquisition of a new set of skills by many workers, and the augmentation of the stock of physical capital goods which *embody* the new technology. To isolate the underlying determinants of the pace of growth, however, consider the determinants of each of these four factors separately.

First, the physical capital stock of an economy increases provided that the level of gross investment in physical capital exceeds the magnitude of depreciation of the existing capital stock during the relevant time period. The capital stock *per worker* increases provided that gross investment exceeds depreciation plus the level of investment required to equip the net expansion of the labour force with the existing average level of capital per worker. The rate of growth of the capital stock per worker is therefore positively related to the level of gross investment and negatively related to the rate of depreciation and the rate of growth of the labour force. Since the depreciation rate and the rate of growth of the labour force are influenced by longer term factors and are exogenously given in the medium term, the key potentially variable determinant of the rate of growth of the capital stock per worker is the level of gross investment.

Second, in considering the determinants of increases in average skill levels in the labour force, it is useful to make a distinction between experience-based skills and skills acquired by education/training. Experience-based skills are a by-product of production activities; an individual's skill level increases with increases in his/her cumulative experience, while the societal stock of experience-based skills also increases over time for similar reasons. Education-based skills are acquired outside the production process, and require the usage of resources both directly in the form of teachers, libraries etc. and indirectly in the form of output foregone due to the student's absence from the labour force. The 'output' of education-based skills is thus dependent on the level of resources committed to education, i.e. on the level of resources invested in the production of human capital. The total stock of such skills in a society increases provided that the level of 'production' of human capital is sufficient to compensate for the depreciation of the stock of skills resulting from retirement and mortality. The average skill level increases provided that the level of investment in human capital is sufficient to compensate for the effects of depreciation and to equip the net increase in the labour force with the existing average level of skills. Since the rate of depreciation of the stock of skills and the rate of growth of the labour force are demographic factors largely exogenous to the growth process in the medium term, the primary variable factor influencing the expansion of average skill levels is the level of investment in human capital.

Third, the expansion of the stock of technological knowledge of a society over a period of time is attributable to a variety of factors, including the piecemeal innovation occurring as a by-product of the production process, and the partly fortuitous breakthroughs in basic scientific research which occur. The primary determinant of the magnitude of the improvement of the knowledge base of the economy, however, is undoubtedly the level of resources committed to research and development (R and D) activities in corporations, research laboratories and universities.

Fourth, as noted above, economic welfare is affected by the level of costs associated with the exploitation of natural resources, whether it be extraction costs as with oil or minerals or the complementary costs associated with using natural resources to produce output as with agricultural land. Trends in these costs over time depend on a number of factors, including: (i) the expansion of demand for products using natural resources as inputs, which ensures that less productive land and higher cost mines and oil wells are brought into use, generating higher average and marginal costs associated with resource exploitation and thereby lowering aggregate output per worker in the economy; (ii) the physical endowment of natural resources which affects the pace at which diminishing returns sets in; and (iii) the level of resources devoted to improving the existing resource base (e.g. land improvement) and expanding the known stock of resources (e.g. oil exploration).

To summarize the above discussion, growth in output per worker depends on a number of factors effectively outside policy influence in the medium term, including demographic factors (the rate of growth of the labour force and its age structure), technical factors (the rate of depreciation), and purely fortuitous factors (fundamental scientific breakthroughs, the physical characteristics of the natural resource base). The other key determinants are: the level of resources committed to skill acquisition; the level of resources committed to R and D, and the level of resources committed to improving or expanding the stock of natural resources. It should be noted that each of these forms of resource commitment are *investment* activities, viewed from the perspectives both of society and the individual making the commitment. From a societal perspective, each of the activities involves the diversion of resources away from present consumption to the production of an input (whether physical capital, skill, technical knowledge, or improved resource) which will generate extra output in the future. From an individual perspective, anyone carrying out any of these activities is incurring a set of costs today in the hope of generating an adequate return on this outlay in the future. It is appropriate, therefore, to define investment in the broad sense (henceforth aggregate investment) to include not merely investment in physical capital goods (the national income accounts definition) but also the resources committed to skill acquisition, R and D and resource exploration/improvement. Concluding, then, the key determinants of growth in output per worker open to alteration in the medium term are the level of aggregate investment and the allocation of aggregate investment between alternative investment possibilities. The other factors influencing the growth process are demographic, the rate of depreciation, and luck.

We now address the major economic question concerning the growth process; what determines the level of investment and its allocation between investment opportunities? Considering the allocation issue first, given adequately working financial markets, one would expect projects with higher rates of return to be undertaken in place of low return projects, and that investment in capital goods, R and D etc., would be allocated in such a way that rates of return, adjusted for differences in risk, on marginal projects in each of the investment categories would tend to be equalized. With regard to the determinants of aggregate investment, most theories of the growth process treat investment as being determined by the society's level of savings. Since saving is that portion of income not consumed, savings levels — and by extension investment — reflect the aggregate outcome of individuals' intertemporal choice (i.e. their choice between present consumption and future consumption). Savings levels thus depend on the rate of return on savings, intertemporal preferences (consumers' attitudes to present vis-à-vis future consumption), and the distribution of income between high-savings-oriented individuals and low-savings-oriented individuals. Some have argued that savings levels are therefore strongly influenced by the society's distribution of income, with savings and investment being higher the less equal is the distribution of income. The two points underlying this argument are that high returns on investment — as manifested in high profit rates and high rates of return on human capital investment (i.e. large wage differentials between skilled and unskilled workers) — encourage high savings levels and that an unequal income distribution concentrates income in the hands of those with high savings propensities (the affluent). The validity of this argument — a key component in the so-called 'trickle-down' theory associated with the Reagan Administration's supply-side economics — is theoretically uncertain, given the ambiguous relationship between the level of savings and the rate of return on savings. Were the argument correct, however, it would indicate that the closed economy faces two trade-offs in relation to the rate of growth — a fundamental trade-off[3] between the growth rate and the level of current living standards, and a secondary trade-off between the growth rate and the 'fairness' of the current distribution of income.

Having discussed the determinants of the rate of growth in a closed economy, the question arises as to the appropriate role, if any, for state policy in influencing the growth process (see also Chapter 2). Three general points about appropriate policy can be made. First, since the promotion of faster growth implies the allocation of more resources to investment and hence requires an increased sacrifice of current consumption, it is clear that the most desirable growth policy is not a policy designed to promote the fastest possible rate of growth — halving current living standards would undoubtedly dramatically increase the rate of growth, but it seems a high price to pay today for prosperity in the somewhat distant future. Second, since the promotion of economic growth will affect both the current distribution of income and the distribution of income between generations, any attempt to identify the optimal rate of growth seems futile, since the label 'optimal' immediately raises the question 'optimal for whom?' Third, even if one could abstract from the distributional issues, the so-called 'theory of the second-best' (see Chapter 2) suggests that, given the many imperfections associated with the market economy in a real-world context, it would be impossible to derive rigorous conclusions concerning the appropriate forms for state intervention. While noting these problems with designing policy, theoretical welfare economics does provide us with one key principle to be applied in identifying the role for the state in the growth process — the desirability of, and appropriate forms of, state intervention depend on the efficiency with which markets operate (see also Chapters 2 and 4). Where markets work well — i.e. where participants are numerous and well-informed, transactions costs are low and externalities are limited — state policy should be designed to minimize the impact on incentives of the state's general revenue-raising and income-redistribution policies; where markets work poorly, policy should be explicitly interventionist and directed at rectifying the consequences of the 'market failure'.

Applying this principle to the discussion of the growth process above, let us briefly consider the efficacy of markets in mobilizing savings and in allocating society's savings between the different forms of investment. First, it is generally held that, given a reasonably sophisticated and competitive financial system, financial markets would, in the absence of state intervention, work effectively in generating an appropriate level of savings, i.e. a level which reflected individuals' preferences for present vis-à-vis future consumption. In fact, state taxation policies (such as income and corporate taxation) do intervene in financial markets by lowering after-tax rates of return on savings and thereby altering incentives. Since financial markets work 'well', the policy implication is that the state should attempt to minimize the effects of the tax system on savings incentives, a policy conclusion which may conflict with the state's income distribution policies. Second, it is generally held that, with the exception of public goods (see Chapter 4), financial markets work well in allocating savings between different physical capital investment projects. A partial exception to this generalization, as mentioned in Chapter 4, might be highly risky, large minimum scale and long-lived investments. State policy with regard to investment in physical capital should therefore be focussed on the carrying out of investment in public goods (such as infrastructure) and on improving incentives for risky long-lived projects. Third, there is a general consensus that human capital investment is an area where the market mechanism works poorly, for reasons associated with the limited information of 'investors', the presence of significant externalities, and the inadequacy of the financial system in enabling individuals to finance such investment (e.g. the almost complete absence of student loans). State policy should therefore be explicitly interventionist in the area of the education system, and be designed to compensate for informational inadequacies and the problems of access to finance of would-be investors. Fourth, there are strong reasons for believing that market mechanisms will generate an inadequate level of investment in R and D, primarily because the inability of inventors/innovators to appropriate the full benefits of their investments means that the private rates of return on investment in R and D (which is what motivates investors) are markedly less than social rates of return (which is what governments should be concerned with). The state should therefore intervene by providing stronger incentives for R and D investment, via the tax system and direct government expenditures. Finally, with regard to the expansion of the natural resource base of the economy, state policy which maintains competitive pressures in the relevant industries and provides favourable treatment for long-run risky investment projects should be sufficient to ensure that markets work adequately in generating the appropriate level and composition of investment in natural resource improvement/discovery.

The discussion of growth in the closed economy can now be concluded. Growth in such an economy is determined by the magnitude of savings, and the allocation of savings between alternative forms of investment. Savings levels are determined by intertemporal preferences, rates of return and the personal distribution of income. State policy in relation to the growth process focusses on the adequacy of the market system in mobilizing and allocating savings; the stylized facts on the efficiency of various markets suggest that the appropriate policy package involves the minimization of the effects of the tax system on savings decisions, state incentives for R and D investment and, perhaps, long-run risky investments, and significant state intervention in the education system to ensure the ability of individuals to finance skill acquisition and to ensure the responsiveness of the output of the education system to changing skill demand patterns.

223

The analysis of the closed economy developed above provides a useful framework for understanding the growth process in the international economy, and in a large semi-closed economy such as the US economy. It also provides the basis for much of the *a priori* thinking which economists, 'practical men who believe themselves exempt from any intellectual influences' and 'madmen in authority' all avail of in discussing the growth process in other economies.[4] The applicability of the analysis and the associated policy implications in the case of a small open economy is, however, questionable. Its limited relevance in an SOE context can most easily be seen by considering the defining characteristics of the SOE — 'smallness' and integration of its financial markets and markets for goods and services into a larger economic system (henceforth labelled 'An Domhan', or 'The World') — and by noting that the position of the SOE in the larger system is analogous to the position of a small region in a large national economy.

Consider briefly the implications of these features of the SOE with regard to the nature of the growth process. First, the integration of the SOE's financial markets into the financial system of An Domhan ensures that there is no relationship between the level of domestic savings and domestic investment in an SOE. Should planned investment at the exogenously determined rate of interest exceed (be less than) planned savings at that interest rate, the excess demand for (supply of) investment funds leads to an inflow (outflow) of funds from abroad. Therefore, while domestic savings levels (and the determinants of savings levels) play the central role in the expansion process in the closed economy, they play no role whatsoever in influencing the expansion of output in the SOE. Second, the integration of the SOE's markets for (tradable) goods and services into An Domhan's markets implies that the magnitude and composition of output in the SOE depends on the attractiveness of the SOE as a location for production *relative* to other locations in An Domhan. Since an investment project is undertaken in the SOE (in the traded goods sector at least) only if the SOE is a more attractive location for the project, the level of investment in the SOE reflects the outcome of a competitive process in which the spatial allocation of investment in An Domhan is determined.[5] Capital investment in the SOE is therefore dependent on the exogenously-determined level of capital investment in An Domhan, and on the SOE's share of the aggregate level of investment. Given that investment, and hence output growth, in the SOE depends on its 'market share' of total investment, a key determinant of output growth in the SOE is the extent to which its attractiveness as a production location is changing relative to locations abroad, a factor which, of course, is completely omitted in the closed economy analysis. Third, the integration of the SOE's markets for goods and services into An Domhan's markets ensures that (i) there is no relationship between the level of domestic expenditures on R and D and the expansion of the stock of knowledge in use in the SOE, and (ii) there is no relationship between the level of domestic expenditures on resource exploitation/improvement and the cost and availability of tradable resources and resource-using goods in the SOE. The smallness of the SOE implies that any domestic expenditures on R and D are insignificant relative to total expenditures on R and D in An Domhan, while its integration within the larger economic system means that the services of new technology can be purchased from outside without domestic development.[6] For similar reasons, developments in the SOE's resource base have an insignificant effect on the costs and availability of produced resources (e.g. oil, lead, zinc) or resource-using products (e.g. wheat) in An Domhan or, as a consequence of market integration, in the SOE itself. As a consequence, two key variables in the growth process — the rate of technological improvement and trends in the costs of production of natural resources and resource-using goods — which are endogenous in the closed economy situation are exogenous in the case of the SOE.

The inapplicability of the closed economy analysis to the SOE situation should now be apparent. That which is of central importance in the growth process in the closed economy — the mobilization of domestic savings — is irrelevant in the SOE, while that which is of central importance in the SOE — its *relative* attractiveness as a production location — is, by definition, irrelevant in the closed economy case. Variables which are endogenously determined in the closed economy — interest rates, the rate of technical progress, and trends in resource costs — are exogenously given in the analysis of the SOE. The discussion of the limitations of the closed economy analysis in the SOE case has, however, indicated two key features to the growth process in the SOE — the importance of external trends in the large economic system of which the SOE is a component, and the importance of the changing locational attractiveness of the SOE within the large system.

We are now in a position to examine briefly the determinants of growth in the SOE, and the implications this has for policy formulation. Consider the case of an SOE integrated within a large closed economic system, An Domhan. First, consider the situation where the growth process in An Domhan is spatially unbiased, in the sense that growth does not affect the allocation of production *between* the regions which comprise An Domhan. Economic expansion in An Domhan is spatially unbiased, therefore, if and only if all the component regions of An Domhan are expanding at the same rate (as would occur, for example, if all regions had exactly the same economic characteristics). In such a situation, the rate of growth of the SOE is not merely equal to, but is also determined by the rate of growth of An Domhan, which in turn is determined by savings propensities, rates of return on investments and income distribution in An Domhan as an aggregate — factors which are effectively outside the control of policy-makers in the SOE. Second, note that deviations between the rates of growth in the SOE and An Domhan occur only if the aggregate growth process in An Domhan is spatially biased, in the sense that the interregional distribution of output is shifting. Such shifts occur provided there are either changes in aggregate characteristics of An Domhan which affect the spatial distribution of activity (e.g. the pattern of demand, transport and communications costs), or changes in the economic characteristics of the regions themselves which affect the spatial distribution of activity between regions (e.g. infrastructural development, changes in economic policies in the regions). Changes of the first type are clearly outside the control of domestic policy-makers in the SOE (e.g. Irish policy-makers and changing world oil prices), indicating that domestic policy can affect the SOE's growth rate only by affecting those characteristics of the SOE which affect its position in the spatial distribution of activity in An Domhan. The pace of growth in the SOE, therefore, is determined by the pace of expansion in An Domhan, and shifts in the position of the SOE in the interregional distribution of economic activity within An Domhan. Shifts in the competitive position of the SOE in the interregional distribution of economic activity can, in turn, be attributed either to systemic changes in An Domhan or to changes in the locational characteristics of the SOE itself or of competing regions.

Given this perspective on the determinants of growth in the SOE, what insights can be derived concerning the appropriate role, if any, for state policies in influencing the growth performance of the SOE? While detailed policy insights could be developed only by considering in some depth the determinants of the spatial allocation of economic activity among competing economies, some general points can be made at this juncture. First, the preceding discussion emphasizes the fact that much of what affects the growth performance of the SOE is outside the control or influence of domestic policy — a recurrent theme in discussions of most types of economic policy in an SOE. Second, domestic policy must naturally be designed to influence those determinants of domestic growth which can be affected by domestic policies; the appropriate focus for growth policy in an SOE should therefore be the competitive position of the SOE within the larger economic system. This provides a sharp contrast with the closed economy situation, where the focus of growth policy is on the mobilization and allocation of savings; in the SOE, growth policy is essentially competitiveness policy. Third, it should be emphasized that state policies designed to improve the competitive position of certain sectors of the economy in an SOE will necessarily weaken the competitive position of other sectors, indicating that the desirability of state intervention in influencing the competitive position of the economy is not obvious. For example, subsidies to the manufacturing sector weaken the competitive position of the agricultural sector, because the expansion of the manufacturing sector increases the demand for factors of production, which results in increases in the prices of less-than-perfectly mobile factors of production, thereby increasing costs in the agricultural sector. Fourth, while detailed policy conclusions require detailed analysis and models, one general theoretical principle concerning the appropriate role for state policy in influencing the SOE's competitive position can be stated — the principle that where markets work well, state policy should aim to minimize the effects of unavoidable state intervention, while where markets work poorly, state policy should be explicity interventionist and should be geared to correcting for the failure of markets.

Some specific policy implications of the above analysis can also be stated. One important, if negative, implication is that policies aimed at domestic savings levels in the SOE — such as more favourable tax treatment of income from savings — have no effect on the pace of growth in the SOE, a conclusion which contrasts markedly with the closed economy case. While such policies might be desirable on grounds other than the promotion of growth, the independence of savings and investment in the SOE means that savings policy changes are neutral in their effect on economic expansion. Indeed, 'trickle-down'-motivated policies in an SOE — i.e. concentration of income in the hands of the rich to generate higher savings and investment, thereby promoting higher incomes for the poor in the future — would have adverse effects. Since investment is not affected by higher savings levels, implying no effects of the concentration of income today on future trends in factor returns, the poor are made worse-off today and worse-off tomorrow (since their lower incomes today imply lower savings and hence lower income from savings in the future). A second negative policy insight is that incentives for R and D in an SOE cannot be rationalized on the basis of the encouragement of faster technical progress, since the rate of technical progress is effectively exogenously given. This is not to suggest that there are no 'competitiveness' arguments for encouraging domestic R and D under certain circumstances (e.g. where there are significant linkages between R and D and other economic activities), but it should be noted that some sophisticated arguments need to be developed in support of any such incentives.[7]

Two principles concerning growth policy in the SOE mentioned above — that policy must affect the SOE's competitive position if it is to have an impact on economic expansion, and that policy intervention is desirable only where markets work poorly — together provide a growth-motivated rationale for state intervention in the area of human capital investment. The SOE's competitive position is affected by the domestic availability of factors of production only where factors are less than perfectly mobile; thus the domestic availability of financial capital or of certain labour skills that are highly mobile does not affect domestic competitiveness, because the high degree of mobility ensures that the returns to such factors are equalized between the SOE and its competitors. For those labour skills that are only partly mobile, however, the local availability of skills and the responsiveness of the supply of such skills to changing demand patterns will significantly affect the competitive position of the SOE. For reasons discussed earlier, there is a general presumption that human capital investment — i.e. the production of labour skills — is an area where the market mechanism works poorly, indicating that state policy in the area of education and skill production should be deliberately interventionist. Indeed, in an SOE such as Ireland's, where the domestic linkages of industry are low and the key domestic contribution to production costs is labour, state intervention to improve the efficiency of the education system is a crucial strategic weapon in improving the competitive position, and hence the growth performance, of the economy.

Space limitations preclude the continuance of this somewhat eclectic discussion of the components of growth policy in the SOE. However, two general principles concerning appropriate growth policy merit repetition; first, for policy to affect the expansion of the SOE, it must be geared towards improving the competitive position of the SOE in the international economy, and second, for policy intervention to be desirable, it must be occasioned by some failure in the working of the market system, and be designed to rectify the failing of the market in question. These principles can be used to test the appropriateness of any state policies which have a growth-motivated rationale.

Given the relatively abstract nature of the discussion to date, it seems desirable to conclude the discussion of growth in the closed and small open economies with a concrete example to illustrate the main points made. The US, by general professional consensus, provides a good example of a large semi-closed economy, while the state of Connecticut is chosen as an example of an SOE integrated into a larger economic system. Connecticut is a state of approximately 3.2 million people, accounting for 1.3 per cent of the US population. Its financial and labour markets are closely integrated into the financial and labour markets of the US as a whole, while its major traded-goods-sector products are financial services (chiefly insurance) and defence goods (most notably Trident submarines).

Consider first the case of the US as a whole. The long-term growth in output per worker in the US is determined by the magnitude of the resources committed to investment in physical capital, education, R and D and resource exploration and improvement. As a competitive capitalist economy with a sophisticated financial system, investment in these activities reflects the rates of return to the different forms of investment; investment projects are undertaken provided the private rate of return (adjusted for risk levels) exceeds the prevailing rate of interest, while interest rates (over the longer term) move to equalize the demand for and supply of investment funds. The growth process in the US in the absence of government intervention would be characterized by a number of inefficiencies; because private rates of return on R and D are markedly less than social rates of return, there would be underinvestment in R and D, while the weaknesses of the market mechanism in the area of human capital investment would result in serious inefficiencies — e.g. with able students unable to obtain access to capital markets to finance their investment in their education. The actual policies adopted in the areas of R and D, investment and education at least partly succeed in addressing these failures in the market system, although the motivation underlying the policies adopted may bear little relation to the economic efficiency arguments discussed above (e.g. the role of national security concerns underlying much of the massive government funding of R and D expenditures).

Consider now the determinants of the pace of growth in Connecticut. Clearly, the primary determinant of the rate of growth in Connecticut is the rate of growth in the US economy as a whole; it is also obvious that, given the size of the state, there is nothing that policy-makers in Connecticut can do to influence the rate of growth in the US economy. Connecticut's growth experience is also affected by shifts in the spatial allocation of production in the US — shifts which can result from systemic changes in the US economy, or from changes in the locational attractions of Connecticut (or competing states). Examples of the former in recent years have included the shift in US demand patterns towards defence goods which boosted the relative position of Connecticut (Trident-based economic development!) and innovations in firm organization which, in conjunction with reductions in transport costs and communications costs, increased the mobility of firms and led to the movement of 'runaway shops' out of Connecticut (and the north-east of the US as a whole) to the lower wage non-unionized southern states of the US and affected detrimentally the Connecticut economy. Examples of the types of changes in the locational attractions of Connecticut or its competitors include changes in the tax incentives offered by the states, shifts in the infrastructural characteristics of the competing states, and development of 'agglomerations' of activities in specific locations which attract further activities (the most oft-cited example of which is Massachussetts' Route 128, where many 'high tech' computer firms carry out R and D and other high skill activities).

What about the role of policy in influencing the growth of the Connecticut economy? As an SOE, it is clear that most of what matters as regards the rate of growth of the Connecticut economy is beyond the influence of Connecticut's policy-makers — i.e. the rate of growth of the US economy, the pattern of demand in the US economy, the attractions, both 'natural' and policy-induced, of competing states. The state's policies can affect the growth of the Connecticut economy only if they affect the competitiveness of the state as a location for economic activity. The integration of Connecticut's financial and labour markets into the US economy as a whole implies that the availability of domestic supplies of labour and investment funds will not affect the state's competitive position, since wages and rates of return are equalized between the state and its competitors. As a consequence, policies directed at increasing domestic savings or the native supply of labour skills will not affect the competitive position or the volume or composition of the state's output. Identifying what policies would affect the state's competitive position requires a detailed discussion of the determinants of the competitive position of an SOE, which lies beyond the scope of this chapter. The actual policies used, however, include tax policy (the absence of a state income tax is a key attraction for corporate headquarters) and tours of Europe and Japan by the state's governor to encourage European and Japanese firms investing in the US to locate in Connecticut.

The example of Connecticut as an SOE hopefully illustrates a number of the points made above regarding the growth process in the SOE and the potential role for state policy. Anticipating the discussion in Section 4 below, it can be noted here that there are important similarities between the position of Connecticut vis-à-vis the US economy and the position of Ireland vis-à-vis the UK and European economies, and that much of what has been said regarding the growth process in Connecticut can also be said about the growth process in Ireland. The one important qualification to the comparison is that the degree of labour mobility between Ireland and its trading partners is significantly less than the very high degree of labour mobility between Connecticut and neighbouring US states. As a result, the quality and efficiency of Ireland's education and labour training system play an important role in influencing Ireland's competitive position — in contrast to the situation of Connecticut (or, more generally, regions of nation states), where labour mobility ensures that any inadequacies in the domestic supply of labour skills leads to migration into the state, rather than a weakening of the state's competitive position.

3 NATIONAL OUTPUT DETERMINATION IN THE SMALL OPEN ECONOMY: A MEDIUM TERM ANALYSIS

Introduction

The discussion of the growth process in the preceding section made much use of the concept of 'competitive position' — a catch-all expression used to refer to the set of factors which influence the relative attractiveness of the SOE as a location for economic activity, and hence determine the volume and composition of output in the SOE. A comprehensive examination of the determinants of an economy's competitive position in the international economy lies beyond the scope of this chapter; the more modest goal of this section is to develop a model of output determination in the SOE which identifies the major factors influencing both the magnitude and the sectoral composition of national output. The model is described as a medium term analysis because it abstracts from the short-run effective demand problems associated with the workings of the business cycle. Like all models, it represents a simplified — but hopefully not simplistic — view of reality, for it is only through simplification that the roles of such factors as industrial sector competitiveness, emigration opportunities, and foreign borrowing levels in influencing the level of national output can be clearly delineated.

Underlying the analysis is a classification of goods and services into three distinct categories. First, the domestic production structure can be decomposed into the *traded goods sector* — containing all those production activities in which domestic producers compete directly with foreign producers — and the *non-traded goods sector,* containing all those production activities not included in the traded goods sector. Examples of traded sector production activities include the production of shoes, cars, and zinc, while activities contained in the non-traded goods sector include building and construction, public administration, and health services. Second, the traded goods sector can be further broken down into a natural resource-based sector and a footloose sector, with natural resource-based goods being goods whose production involves the use of immobile natural resources as key inputs in the production process, and footloose goods being a catch-all expression for other traded goods. Examples of resource-based traded goods include oil and zinc, while shoes, cars, and semi-conductors provide examples of 'footloose' traded goods. The importance of distinguishing resource-based traded goods from other traded goods lies in the fact that the location of production of resource-based goods is determined in large part by the geographical location of natural resources (e.g. crude oil production); as a result, the scale of output of resource-based goods in a country is fundamentally limited by the domestic natural resource base — a limitation which does not restrict a country's output of footloose goods.

Determining how an individual economic activity should be classified is relatively straightforward, but at the aggregate level there is no exact correspondence between the theoretical categories and any of the published statistical classifications of economic activity (e.g. the agriculture-industry-services category). Conventional practice treats (i) the non-traded goods sector as consisting of the services sector, the public utilities (i.e. electricity, gas and water), and the construction industry, with (ii) the resource-based goods sector consisting of agriculture, forestry and fishing, along with mining and some resource-processing activities (e.g. creameries), and (iii) the footloose goods sector containing the manufacturing sector less those resource-processing activities included in the resource-based goods sector. Applying this classification scheme to 1981 data on the Irish labour force reveals that 61 per cent of the labour force was employed in the non-traded sector, with 21.5 per cent employed in the production of resource-based goods and 17.5 per cent employed in the 'pure' manufacturing sector.

The Model

Let Banba be a small open economy freely trading with the outside world. Banba's economy has the following characteristics:[8]

(i) *Production Structure*: Banba produces three types of goods — Food (f), Manufactures (m), and Services (s). Food is a resource-based traded good; it is produced using natural resources (R) and labour (L), with the relationship between inputs and output being represented by a production function of the form $Q_f = F_f(R, L_f)$. Manufactures are also traded internationally; the production of manufactures involves the use of know-how/experience (K) and labour (L), with the input-output relationship being represented by a production function of the form $Q_m = F_m(K, L_m)$.[9] Services are not traded internationally; the production of services involves the use of labour alone, with A_s workers being required to produce one unit of services sector output.

(ii) *Factor Supplies*: Banba possesses three factors of production: natural resources, know-how/experience, and labour. The stocks of natural resources and know-how/experience available in Banba are fixed in supply. Given the possibility of emigration/immigration, the size of the labour force in Banba is influenced by labour market conditions at home and abroad; the determinants of the size of Banba's labour force are discussed below.

(iii) *Market Structure*: Banba's goods and factor markets are organized competitively, in the sense that firms and workers take market prices as given *and* market prices adjust to equate supply and demand in the relevant markets. While the prices of food (P_f) and manufactures (P_m) are determined in international markets, factor prices and the price of services (P_s) are determined in domestic markets and must adjust to equate domestic supply with domestic demand in these markets.

(iv) *Demand Patterns*: Aggregate expenditure on goods and services in Banba is, by definition, equal to the value of national output *plus* the trade deficit (D); by assumption, Banba's trade with the outside world is balanced (i.e. $D = 0$).[10] Consumers in aggregate spend a constant fraction of total expenditure on each of the three goods — i.e. they spend a fraction β_f of total expenditure on food, a fraction β_m on manufactures, and a fraction β_s ($= 1 - \beta_f - \beta_m$) on services.[11]

A number of comments on the structure of the model are in order at this juncture. Note first that the variable K is a catch-all variable used to represent the set of factors (other than P_m) which influence

233

the demand for labour in the manufacturing sector; hence, it is a proxy for such factors as the competitive strengths of domestic firms, the accumulation of know-how and experience by workers, the non-price attractions of Banba as a production location for multinational enterprises (MNEs), etc. Note also that intermediate inputs and capital goods have been omitted from the model — a feature which, on first glance, may seem strange. The omission can be justified on the grounds that, when intermediate inputs and capital goods are traded goods, the costs associated with using these inputs (including financing costs) will be the same at home and abroad — implying that the costs of such goods will have no effect on the competitive position of Banba vis-à-vis the rest of the world. The complications that result when intermediate inputs are non-traded goods — whose prices may differ between Banba and the rest of the world — are ignored here.

Output Determination

Given the structure of the model, the prices of the three goods in Banba can be quickly ascertained: P_f and P_m are determined by the prices of food and manufactures in the world market, while competition in the services sector will ensure that P_s equals the cost of producing a unit of services, $W \times A_s$. To determine the level of national output in Banba — and the distribution of income between workers and the owners of natural resources and know-how — it is useful to focus attention on the labour market, and to develop a piece-by-piece analysis of the determination of the domestic wage level. The discussion proceeds by first examining the determinants of the aggregate demand for labour in Banba, and then considering the determinants of the aggregate supply of labour.

Let us begin with a discussion of the demand for labour in the traded goods sector of the economy — i.e. the food and manufacturing sectors combined. In the food sector, producers hire workers up to the point where the marginal revenue product of the last worker hired equals the wage rate (i.e. $W = P_f \times$ marginal physical product of labour in food production); as a corollary, the food sector's demand for labour schedule is given by the marginal revenue product of labour schedule (ff^1 in Figure 7.1). This demand curve is downward-sloping because of the law of diminishing returns.[12] The position of the curve depends on both the price of food (P_f) and the size of the stock of natural resources (R); increases (decreases) in either of these variables would shift the curve outward (inward). A similar argument can be invoked to show that the manufacturing sector's demand for labour schedule is given by the marginal revenue product of labour schedule in the manufacturing sector; again, this demand curve is downward-sloping, and its position depends on the price of manufactures, P_m, and on the size of the stock of know-how/experience, K. To avoid cluttering, the manufacturing sector demand for labour schedule is not shown directly on Figure 7.1; TT^1 shows the demand for labour schedule in the traded goods sector as an aggregate, and is thus the horizontal sum of the food sector demand schedule and the manufacturing sector demand schedule. (Hence, labour demand in the manufacturing sector at any given wage is equal to the horizontal distance between ff^1 and TT^1 at that wage level.)

Figure 7.1

Demand for Labour

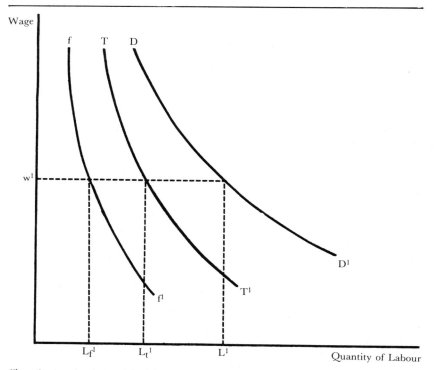

ff^1 = food sector demand for labour curve
TT^1 = traded goods sector demand for labour curve
DD^1 = aggregate demand for labour curve

To determine the level of demand for labour in the non-traded goods sector of the economy (i.e. the services sector), we must proceed somewhat differently. The need to adopt an alternative approach reflects the different influences on output in the traded and non-traded goods sectors of the economy; while output in the traded goods sector is determined by competitiveness considerations and is independent of the level of domestic demand for traded goods, output in the non-traded goods sector is independent of competitiveness considerations and must equal domestic demand for such products. The discussion proceeds, therefore, by identifying the determinants of the level of domestic demand for non-traded goods at any given wage level, then by identifying the associated level of employment in the non-traded goods sector, and then by examining how this employment level changes as the wage level changes — thereby deriving a non-traded sector demand for labour schedule.

We begin by manipulating some identities. Since the value of national expenditure (NE) equals the value of national output (NO), and the value of national output equals the value of output of traded goods (V_t) plus the value of output of non-traded goods (V_{nt}), it follows that

$$NE \equiv NO \equiv V_t + V_{nt} \tag{1}$$

Given that consumers spend a fixed fraction, β_s, of their total expenditures on non-traded goods (i.e. services), the value of total expenditure on such goods is $\beta_s \times NE$; since non-traded goods, by definition, cannot be imported/exported, total expenditure on non-traded goods must equal the value of output of non-traded goods (V_{nt}), implying that

$$V_{nt} = \beta_s \times NE = \beta_s \times (V_t + V_{nt}) \tag{2}$$

which implies in turn that

$$V_{nt} = V_t \times (\beta_s/(1 - \beta_s)) \tag{3}$$

and, as a corollary, that

$$NO \equiv V_t + V_{nt} = V_t \times (1/(1 - \beta_s)) \tag{4}$$

Equation 3 can be used to identify the value of total expenditures on non-traded goods that would prevail at any given wage level. Let W^1 be the economy-wide wage level. Under such circumstances, there would be L_f^1 workers employed in the food sector and L_t^1 - L_f^1 workers employed in the manufacturing sector (see Figure 7.1); associated with these sectoral employment levels are sectoral output levels (Q_f^1 and Q_m^1) which can be obtained from the sectoral production functions. Hence, associated with the wage level W^1 is a specific value of traded sector output, V_t^1, where $V_t^1 = P_f \times Q_f^1 + P_m \times Q_m^1$. Inserting this value of V_t into Equation 3 yields the value of non-traded sector output, V_{nt}^1, that would prevail at the wage level W^1.

To identify the associated level of employment in the non- traded goods sector, note that the value of non-traded sector output equals $P_s^1 \times Q_s^1$ and that the price of non-traded goods is $W^1 \times A_s$; hence, the quantity of services produced at the wage level W^1 is

$$Q_s^1 = V_{nt}^1/P_s^1 = V_{nt}^1/(W^1 \times A_s) \tag{5}.$$

Since the number of workers required to produce one unit of output of services is A_s workers, it follows that the level of employment in the non-traded goods sector at the economy-wide wage level of W^1 is

$$L_{nt} = A_s \times Q_s^1 = A_s \times (V_{nt}^1/(W^1 \times A_s)) = V_{nt}^1/W^1 \tag{6}$$

Adding L_{nt}^1 to L_t^1 yields the aggregate demand for labour at the wage level W^1 - an amount represented by the point L^1 in Figure 7.1.

To see how the level of employment in the non-traded goods sector varies as the wage level in the economy varies, consider the effect of a decline in the economy-wide wage level from W^1. The wage reduction has two distinct effects on the level of employment in the non-traded goods sector. First, the wage decline results in an expansion in the level of output of traded goods, V_t, which produces a 'multiplier' expansion in the value of non-traded goods (see Equation 3). Second, while the *value* of non-traded sector output increases, the fall in the price of non-traded goods resulting from the wage decline ensures that there is an even larger increase in the *quantity* of such goods produced (Equation 5) — and hence in the level of employment in the sector (Equation 6). Hence, the demand for labour schedule in the non-traded goods sector has the standard shape, with labour demand increasing as the wage falls. Again, to avoid clutter, this demand schedule is not shown directly on Figure 7.1; DD^1 shows the aggregate demand for labour schedule in Banba, and is thus the horizontal sum of the traded sector demand schedule (TT^1) and the non-traded sector demand schedule. (Labour demand in the non-traded (services) sector at any given wage is equal to the horizontal distance between DD^1 and TT^1 at that wage level.)

Before proceeding further, it is useful to recall the set of factors that influence the position of the various sectoral demand curves — and hence the position of the aggregate demand schedule. The position of ff^1 is dependent on the values of P_f and R; the position of TT^1 depends on the position of ff^1 and on the values of P_m and K; and the position of DD^1 depends on the position of TT^1 and on the values of T and β_s. Hence, the position of DD^1 — the aggregate demand for labour schedule in Banba — is dependent on the values of five key variables; the prices of food and manufactures, the stocks of natural resources and know-how/experience, and the distribution of consumer spending between traded and non-traded goods.[13]

Consider now the determinants of the aggregate supply of labour in Banba. By assumption, workers can choose to reside in Banba or abroad; since this choice is at least partially conditional on the economic attractions of working in Banba compared to working abroad, it follows that the size of the domestic labour force is sensitive to labour market conditions both at home and abroad. *Ceteris paribus*, the size of Banba's labour force is positively related to the level of wages in Banba — a relationship represented graphically by the labour supply schedule SS^1 in Figure 7.2.[14] The position of this aggregate supply schedule depends on labour market conditions abroad (i.e. wage levels, unemployment rates, etc.), on the extent of restrictions on migration between Banba and other countries, and on the size, age structure, and work preferences of Banba's population. *Ceteris paribus*, an improvement in labour market conditions abroad (e.g. rising wage levels) would shift Banba's labour supply schedule to the left, while a deterioration in labour markets abroad would shift the supply schedule to the right. Similarly, an easing in the extent of foreign countries' restrictions on immigration from Banba (or less intensive enforcement of existing restrictions) would shift Banba's supply schedule to the left, while tighter restrictions abroad on immigration from Banba would shift the supply schedule to the right. Finally, changes in the age structure of the population and in adults' preferences for participating in vis-à-vis remaining outside the labour force also shift the labour supply schedule in a predictable manner. To conclude, the aggregate supply of labour schedule has the conventional positively-sloped shape, and its position is influenced by (i) foreign labour market conditions, (ii) restrictions on inter-country migration, and (iii) the work preferences and age structure of the population.

Figure 7.2

Supply and Demand for Labour

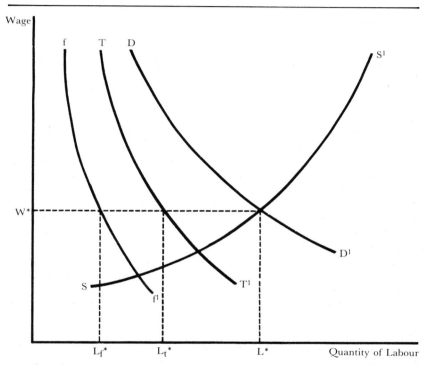

ff[1], TT[1] and DD[1] are defined in Figure 7.1
SS[1] = aggregate supply of labour curve

Having identified the positions of the aggregate supply and demand curves for labour, we are now in a position to determine national output, aggregate employment, and the distribution of income in Banba. In Figure 7.2, SS[1] represents the aggregate supply of labour schedule, while DD[1] is the aggregate demand for labour schedule taken directly from Figure 7.1. Given that, in the medium run, wages adjust to equate supply and demand for labour, the equilibrium level of employment is given by the point of intersection of the supply and demand curves; hence, W^* is the equilibrium wage level in Banba, with L^* being the associated equilibrium employment level. The sectoral distribution of the L^* workers can be obtained with the aid of the sectoral demand curves: L_f^* workers are employed in the food sector; $L_m^* = L_t^* - L_f^*$ workers are employed in the manufacturing sector; and $L_s^* = L^* - L_t^*$ workers are employed in the services sector. The associated sectoral output levels are $F_f(R, L_f^*)$ units of food, $F_m(K, L_m^*)$ units of manufactures, and L_s^*/A_s units of services.[15]

As always in supply/demand analysis, changes in any of the factors that influence the positions of the supply and demand curves result in changes in the equilibrium levels of national output and employment. In particular, changes in P_f, P_m, R, K, or β_s give rise to a shift in the aggregate labour demand curve, thereby moving the equilibrium outcome up/down the labour supply curve; while changes in foreign labour market conditions, immigration restrictions, etc. give rise to a shift in the supply curve, thereby moving the equilibrium outcome up/down the aggregate demand curve.

Properties of the Model
The model described above can be used to illustrate a number of general points concerning the determinants of a country's competitive position in the international economy. First, the model highlights the importance of the economic performance of the traded goods sector in determining the level of national output and employment in an SOE. Equation 4 above revealed that, given consumer preferences for traded vis-à-vis non-traded goods, the level of national output in Banba sustainable at any given wage level is dependent only on the value of traded sector output forthcoming at that wage level; as a corollary, increases in the value of national output over time are driven by the expansion of the traded goods sector, with the non-traded goods sector playing an essentially passive role in the growth process.[16]

Second, the model can be used to identify the circumstances under which equilibrium wage and income levels in Banba will be high by international standards. Given labour supply conditions, wage levels in Banba are dependent on the position of the aggregate demand for labour schedule, whose position in turn is dependent on the magnitude of Banba's stock of natural resources (R) and on the strength of its competitive position in the production of manufactures (as measured by the magnitude of K). Hence, high wage levels are sustainable only if either (i) Banba possesses an abundance of natural resources relative to the size of the labour force, or (ii) the country has a strong competitive position in the production of manufactures. Real world examples of countries which fall into the first category are Kuwait and Saudi Arabia: although neither country possesses a strong industrial base, oil reserves in both countries are sufficiently large relative to the size of these economies that per capita incomes and wage levels are extremely high by international standards. Examples of countries which fall into the second category are Switzerland and Sweden, where the high per capita income levels are sustained by a manufacturing sector which remains competitive internationally despite high domestic wage levels.

Third, the model can be used to identify the various ways in which a country's competitive position in the international economy can improve over time. From the preceding discussion, it is obvious that wages, incomes and total employment in Banba would increase if there were a sudden expansion in the stock of natural resources available domestically (e.g. oil discoveries) or if Banba's competitive position in the production of manufactures were to improve (e.g. the Japanese experience over the past twenty years). Domestic wage levels would also increase in both absolute and relative terms if Banba were to experience a favourable terms-of-trade shock — as exemplified by the experience of oil-exporting countries during the 1970s. Since natural resource discoveries and terms-of-trade shocks cannot be engineered by domestic policy-makers (although poorly-designed incentive packages can reduce the likelihood of the former), the policy implication of this discussion is that the main policy tool for influencing a country's competitive position in the international economy is *industrial policy* — loosely defined to be the set of policies that affect the competitive position of the manufacturing sector.

Finally, the model can be used to examine the effects of changes in the exogenous variables in the model (e.g. traded goods prices, foreign labour market conditions, etc.) on the levels of wages, incomes, and employment in Banba, and on the sectoral composition of output and employment. Consider, for example, the effects of an increase in the value of K — the stock of know-how/experience available in Banba — on the characteristics of the equilibrium outcome in Banba. *Ceteris paribus,* an increase in the stock of know-how/experience available in Banba results in an outward shift in the demand for labour schedule in the manufacturing sector *and* in an associated outward shift in the demand for labour schedule in the services sector (i.e. an increase in the distance between TT^1 and DD^1) — the latter shift occurring because the value of traded sector output produced at any given wage level increases. These movements in the sectoral demand curves produce an outward shift in the aggregate demand curve, which gives rise to an increase in the value of national output and in the equilibrium wage level. The new equilibrium is characterized by (i) a higher aggregate level of employment (since the outcome is 'further up' the labour supply curve); (ii) lower output and employment in the food sector (because the increase in the economy-wide wage level detrimentally affected the profitability of food production); and (iii) an increase in the share of the manufacturing sector in the value of total output (because the service sector share remains unchanged at β_s and the food sector contracts). Given space constraints, the analysis of the effects of changes in other exogenous variables on the domestic economy is left to the interested reader.

An Extension: Foreign Borrowing
One important assumption made in the development of the model above was the assumption that trade between Banba and the outside world was balanced, and hence that the value of national expenditure equalled the value of national output. Given that Ireland's economic experiences since the mid-1970s have been heavily influenced by the effects of external borrowing, it seems desirable to extend the basic model described above to examine the effects of such borrowings on the macroeconomy.[17]

We begin by extending the basic model to allow for the situation where Banba's trade is not balanced. Let Banba be experiencing a trade deficit of D units, with national expenditure exceeding national output by this amount (since $NE \equiv NO + D$). The existence of a disparity between NE and NO does not affect the position of the labour demand curves in the traded goods sectors of the economy; the position of these demand curves depends only on world prices and the stocks of natural resources and know-how/experience. As a corollary, the relationship between the value of traded sector output and the economy-wide wage level is not affected by the inflow of funds; at any given wage level, the value of traded sector output will be the same regardless of the magnitude of the trade deficit. The relationship between the wage level and the demand for non-traded sector goods is, however, sensitive to the magnitude of D: repeating the analysis employed in deriving Equations 2 to 6 above for the case where $NE \equiv NO + D$, it can be shown that the value of non-traded sector output associated with the wage level W^1 is $(V_t^1 + D) \times (\beta_s/(1 - \beta_s))$, with the associated level of employment in the non-traded sector employment level being $(1/W^1)$ times that amount. Hence, the *position* of the non-traded sector demand for labour curve — and by extension, the position of the aggregate demand for labour curve — is directly affected by the magnitude of D, with increases in D shifting both schedules outward.

Figure 7.3

Macroeconomic Effects of Foreign Borrowings

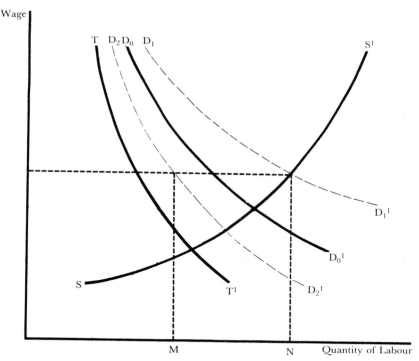

TT^1 and SS^1 are defined in Figures 7.1 and 7.2
$D_0D_0^1$, $D_1D_1^1$ and $D_2D_2^1$ are defined in the text

We now examine the effects of an infusion of externally-borrowed funds on the Banba economy. Let the initial situation (in period 0) be such that Banba's trade is initially balanced, with the equilibrium outcome being represented by the point of intersection of SS^1 and $D_0D_0^1$ in Figure 7.3. Assume that Banba experiences an infusion of B units of externally-borrowed funds in period 1 — an inflow which enables Banba to run a trade deficit of B units in that period. Given the argument outlined in the preceding paragraph, the infusion of funds shifts the aggregate demand for labour schedule outward (to $D_1D_1^1$) while leaving the traded sector demand for labour schedule unchanged at TT^1. This outward movement in the aggregate demand curve results in an increase in the equilibrium levels of national output, employment, and wages. The sectoral distribution of the aggregate output expansion is uneven, however, because the rising wage levels produce output and employment *declines* in the traded goods sectors of the economy; the 'leading' sector in this (temporary) economic expansion is the non-traded goods sector, where employment increases by more than enough to offset the job losses in the traded goods sectors.

Consider now the position of the Banban economy in period 2 — i.e. the period following the injection of borrowed funds. If there are no new borrowings made in period 2, Banba's exports must exceed its imports by an amount equal to the magnitude of the required debt service payments — i.e. the value of D must be negative in period 2. Under such circumstances, the aggregate demand for labour schedule shifts leftward until it lies to the left of $D_0D_0^1$ in Figure 7.3 — a shift which produces a contraction in the levels of national output, employment and wages. Even if borrowing levels in period 2 remain unchanged from the level recorded during period 1, the aggregate demand curve must shift leftward over time, because the magnitude of the trade deficit must decline to equal the value of new borrowings *less* debt service payments. The only way in which Banba can avoid a decline in national output during period 2 is if national expenditure continues to exceed the value of national output by the amount B — an outcome which is possible only if second period borrowings equal B plus the payments required to service the debt incurred in period 1. Hence, the (temporary) equilibrium attained in period 1 can be sustained in period 2 only if second period borrowings exceed first period borrowings, and can be sustained through period 3 only if third period borrowings exceed second period borrowings, etc.

In conclusion, analysis of the macroeconomic effects of foreign borrowings reveals that the initial effect of such borrowings is to produce a boom in the non-traded goods sector which results in increases in the value of national output and total employment.

Unless such borrowings are continually increased, however, the burden of debt service soon results in a contraction in output and employment demand (concentrated in the non-traded goods sector), with the timing and the depth of the associated recession being dependent on the timing of debt repayments and the scale of further borrowings (if any). The process of adjustment is also sensitive to the responsiveness of wage levels to reductions in the demand for labour: if wages are 'sticky' downwards, the inward shift in the aggregate demand for labour curve (say from $D_1D_1{}^1$ to $D_2D_2{}^1$ in Figure 7.3) will initially produce large scale involuntary unemployment (of magnitude MN), with this unemployment being eliminated over time through declines in wages (which increase the demand for labour) and through emigration (which reduces the supply of labour).

Conclusion

The goal of this section was to develop a model of output determination in a small open economy which identified the major factors influencing both the magnitude and the sectoral composition of national output. The model described above is clearly a very simple representation of reality, which leaves unanswered the crucial question as to what determines the size of Banba's manufacturing sector at given factor prices — an issue evaded by using the catch-all variable 'K' to determine the position of the manufacturing sector labour demand curve. Despite this omission, the analysis developed here is useful because it provides a consistent theoretical framework with which to analyze changes in domestic output and employment levels in an SOE which cannot be easily explained by reference to trends in the international economy. The analysis developed here also has important policy implications. In discussing the growth process in a small open economy in Section 1, the conclusion was drawn that government policy should focus on influencing the competitive position of the SOE in the larger economic system of which it is a part.

The analysis of this section has indicated that a country's position in the larger economic system is dependent on the economic performance of the traded goods sector of the economy, which provides the 'axis' around which the domestic economy turns. Recalling the general welfare proposition that government intervention is desirable if and only if markets work 'poorly', we can provide the following definition of the general features of an appropriate growth policy: *growth policy should focus on identifying and rectifying those weaknesses in the operation of market forces which detrimentally affect the performance of the traded goods sector of the economy.*

4   IRELAND'S INTEGRATION WITH THE INTERNATIONAL ECONOMY

This section of the chapter examines the nature and extent of the linkages between the Irish economy and the international economy, and assesses the applicability of the small-open-economy assumptions to Irish circumstances. Two methodological points should be noted at the outset. First, the assumptions employed in the construction of economic theories are almost always false in the narrow sense of being an exact representation of reality. Hence, the question to be asked in assessing the applicability of a specific theory to real world circumstances is whether or not the assumptions are a 'reasonable' — as distinct from an exact — representation of reality. Second, what constitutes a reasonable approximation to reality depends on the specific problem being analyzed: what is reasonable in the context of an analysis of medium term growth issues may well be unreasonable when analyzing, say, the short-run impact of changes in monetary policy. In the discussion below, the judgements made regarding what is 'reasonable' reflect the concern of the chapter with analyzing the growth process in the Irish economy over the longer term.

Product Market Linkages

The concept of 'small open economy' contains two distinct ideas concerning the nature of product markets in the SOE and their linkages with the external world; the share of traded goods (and services) in the total output of goods and services in the SOE is large, and markets for traded goods in the SOE and abroad are integrated *and* the SOE is small in such markets. A comprehensive examination of the extent to which these characteristics are features of the Irish economy lies beyond the scope of this chapter; we confine ourselves here to an examination of the trade orientation of the domestic economy, supplemented with some additional indicators on the degree of market integration, and a brief discussion of the 'smallness' issue.

The conventional measures used to assess the extent of both the relative size of a country's traded goods sector *and* the degree of integration of traded goods sector markets into external markets are the ratios of exports (X) and imports (M) of goods and services to GDP. These measures have a number of significant limitations, but are used here because of the ease with which they can be calculated.[18] Examination of the X/GDP and M/GDP measures for the Irish economy in the mid-1980s reveals two distinct features.

First, compari⌇
estimates for o
indicates that
unusually hig
which the rele
level of trade
one (Belgiu⌇
industrialize⌇
level of *entre*
can conclud
relations ar
comparison
the corresp
that the sig
traded-goo
twenty-fiv⌇
average o⌇
per cent i
a similar
attributed⌇

economy, to a degree probably unus⌇
First, external markets are of key
goods for domestic consumptio⌇
output. Comparison of manufa⌇
for 1980 reveals that 51 per c⌇
57 per cent of the domestic
by imports. Second, int⌇
between manufacturi⌇
activities in Ireland
sector) are of little
links between
industry.[20] A⌇
sector as an
individua⌇
integra⌇
most
ma⌇

manufacturing industry,
activities being replaced by export mark⌇⌇
activities using imported intermediate inputs.

More detailed insights into the significance of external linkages in the Irish economy can be obtained by examining a number of features of the two sectors of the economy where trade linkages are likely to be most significant — agriculture and manufacturing. Considering first the agricultural sector; external markets have long been of crucial importance to this sector. Such was the importance of exports that the protection of Irish farmers' access to such markets was the primary rationale underlying Ireland's application to join the European Community. Since joining the EC in 1973, the fraction of agricultural output being exported has increased further, with 60 per cent of the total value of output being sold abroad by the end of the 1970s. This export orientation is, of course, a strong indication that Ireland's agricultural sector is closely integrated with external markets. Institutional considerations provide further support for such a conclusion because the EC's Common Agricultural Policy is explicitly designed to organize and integrate agricultural markets in the Community and to equalize prices across markets.

A number of features of Ireland's manufacturing sector indicate that the sector is extremely closely integrated with the international

al in nation-state economies.
importance as both a source of
and a destination for domestic
cturing sector trade and output data
ent of total output was exported, while
demand for manufactured goods was met
a-industry and interindustry sales linkages
g sector activities and other production
(both inside and outside the manufacturing
or no significance, with the sole exception of the
he agricultural sector and the food processing
a consequence, not merely is the manufacturing
aggregate oriented towards external markets, but most
production activities at the micro level are effectively
ed with external markets because much of the output and
of the inputs are sent to/obtained from abroad; the
ufacturing sector is thus particularly exposed to external
mpetitive pressures.

A third indicator of the extent of the integration of the Irish
manufacturing sector with the European and international
economies is the extent of foreign ownership and control of Irish
manufacturing establishments (see Chapter 11). By the early 1980s,
foreign-controlled firms accounted for almost two-fifths of
manufacturing sector employment and for three-quarters of non-
food manufactured exports in the early 1980s. Thus, a sizable
fraction of the manufacturing sector is linked to the external world
by both direct control relationships and by sales linkages.
Comparison of the role of foreign-owned firms in Ireland with the
role of foreign-owned firms in other countries suggests that the
foreign firm share of employment in Ireland is high by international
standards, although not remarkably high, while the foreign firm
share of manufactured exports is very high in comparative terms,
with Singapore being the only other significant exporter of
manufactures where the foreign firm share of exports is comparable
to that of Ireland.[21]

Having discussed the 'openness' of the Irish economy and
examined the linkages between domestic and external markets for
traded goods, we now consider the extent to which the Irish
economy is 'small' within international markets for traded goods. In
the everyday sense of the term 'small country', it is almost self-
evident that Ireland is a small country. The population of the
Republic of Ireland accounts for a mere three-quarters of one-tenth
of one per cent of the world's population; or, put differently, only

1 out of every 1300 people in the world is a resident of Ireland. Even allowing for the fact that the world economy is far from being an integrated system, and that a more appropriate estimate of relative size is to compare Ireland's size to the size of the free trade area of which it is a component, Ireland is still very small, accounting for only 1.27 per cent of the population and 0.68 per cent of the total GDP of the ten-member European Community in 1981.[22]

For a country to be small in the theoretical sense of the term 'small country', however, it is not sufficient that the country be small in terms of population share or GDP share: theoretical 'smallness' implies that shifts in supply and demand conditions in the domestic economy should have no spillover effects on international markets, that domestic producers of traded goods should face no demand constraints, and that the country should be unable to influence the price it pays for internationally traded products. While, at first glance, it may appear obvious that countries which are small in the everyday sense must be small in the theoretical sense, there are two important reasons why this intuition can be incorrect. First, a general characteristic of small countries integrated into the international economy is that they become specialized in the production of a relatively small range of goods in which the country has a comparative advantage; as a consequence, countries which are small in an everyday sense may not be small in the markets for goods in which they are specialized (e.g. Saudi Arabia in world oil markets). Second, when the products of different firms within an industry are perceived as being different by consumers, firms in small countries may account for only a small share of total market output and yet still face downward-sloping demand curves (e.g. Irish Distillers in world liquor markets); while small countries may account for a small share of total consumption and yet still possess significant buyer power in international markets (e.g. an integrated national health service purchasing pharmaceuticals).

While detailed analysis would be required to identify the fraction of total traded sector activities where Ireland is truly 'small' in international markets, casual empiricism suggests that there are many traded products in which Ireland is small in the theoretical sense of the term (e.g. world oil markets), and that there are few (if any) industries in which the 'spillover' effects of shifts in supply and demand conditions in Ireland on international markets would be significant. However, it is also difficult to think of many Irish manufacturing firms which do *not* face demand constraints in export markets — at least in the short run. Thus, the Irish economy would appear to be 'small' in the sense that the external economic environment is exogenously given, but not necessarily 'small' in the sense that export demand is perfectly elastic at any given point in time. Given the concern with longer term growth issues, it is 'smallness' in the first sense of the term that is of most significance — suggesting that the 'smallness' assumption is not an unreasonable representation of Irish realities.

The examination of the extent to which the nature of Ireland's product market linkages with the external world match the features of the theoretical construct of an SOE can now be concluded. First, it has been shown that the significance of trade relationships in the Irish economy is substantial compared to other nation-states, suggesting that the traded goods sector is relatively large in the Irish economy and that the degree of integration between domestic markets and external markets is high. Second, a more detailed examination of the agricultural and manufacturing sectors provides stronger support for the conclusion that Ireland's traded goods sectors are heavily dependent on and closely integrated within external markets. Third, while it is clear that Ireland is, in a number of senses, a very small economy and a very small component region of a large free trade area, there are at least some sectors of Irish manufacturing industry where significant specialization and/or product differentiation have resulted in a situation where Ireland is not theoretically 'small', and where domestic suppliers, both individually and in the aggregate, face downward sloping demand curves or where Irish consumers, at least in the aggregate, have some buyer power. The fact that Ireland's goods markets do not exactly fit the SOE assumptions does not significantly affect the applicability to Irish circumstances of the theoretical analysis outlined in earlier sections of the chapter — but it does indicate that a detailed analysis of the determinants of the size and output structure of the manufacturing sector would have to address the analytical complexities associated with the presence of demand constraints on domestic producers.

Factor Market Linkages

In discussing the linkages between factor markets in Ireland and such markets abroad, attention is focussed on two distinct questions: (i) can real interest rates in Ireland differ significantly from real interest rates abroad over the longer term and (ii) can real wages in Ireland differ significantly from wages abroad over the longer term?

For obvious historical reasons, Ireland's financial markets have long been closely linked to UK financial markets, with Irish financial institutions having significant operational ties to the UK banking system. Prior to the founding of the European Monetary System and the breaking of the one-for-one parity link between the Irish pound and sterling in 1979, these linkages — accompanied as they were by the absence of impediments to capital movements between the two countries — ensured that Irish nominal interest rates did not differ significantly from UK interest rates. Since the fixed exchange rate with Ireland's dominant trading partner ensured that Ireland's inflation rate did not differ significantly from that of the UK, the equality of nominal interest rates between the two countries was accompanied by the approximate equality of real interest rates over the longer term. Since Ireland was obviously 'small' (in the economic sense of the term) relative to the UK, it followed that the real interest rate was exogenously given to the Irish economy.

In the post-EMS era — characterized by 'fixed-but-adjustable' exchange rates vis-à-vis the other EMS currencies and a flexible exchange rate vis-à-vis sterling — the relationship between Irish interest rates and interest rates abroad is significantly more complex than was the case in the pre-1979 period (see Chapter 6). None the less, a reasonably strong argument can be made that, over the longer term, the real interest rate is exogenously given to the Irish economy. Were it the case that investors were risk-neutral and that there were no constraints on intercountry capital movements, profit-seeking behaviour by wealth-holders would ensure that the interest rate differential between Ireland and the UK reflected (and equalled) the expected rate of appreciation of sterling vis-à-vis the Irish pound — thus $r^{ir} = r^{uk} + X_s$ where X_s is the expected rate of increase of the Irish pound price of sterling over the relevant time period. Under such circumstances, nominal interest rates in Ireland would be exogenously given (because X_s largely reflects the expected movements of the value of sterling relative to the main EMS currencies), and real interest rates in Ireland would be exogenously given over the longer term (because, over the longer term, X_s should equal the actual rate of appreciation of sterling, which in turn should reflect the inflation differential between the UK and the EMS countries).

In reality, of course, wealth-holders are not risk-neutral and the movement of capital between Ireland and the outside world is subject to capital controls; as a result, the *uncovered interest parity condition* above need not hold, implying that Irish financial markets are partially insulated from trends in UK (and other countries') financial markets. While this degree of insulation ensures that Irish interest rates are sensitive to supply and demand conditions in domestic financial markets (and, by extension, to changes in domestic monetary policy), it would be easy to overestimate the degree to which Irish real interest rates can differ from UK real interest rates over the longer term. For one thing, the efficacy of capital controls as a device to permit sustained deviations from interest parity conditions is quite limited, if only because the scope for illegal movements of capital (e.g. via over- and under-invoicing) in a highly open economy such as the Irish economy is such that sustained real interest rate differentials would be reflected in large scale illegal capital movements and an induced narrowing of the interest rate differential.[23] In addition, it is difficult to believe that the degree of aversion to risk on the part of Irish wealth-holders and borrowers (both public and private) can be such as to sustain significant real interest rate differentials between economies linked so closely over the longer term. Consequently, we conclude that the assumption that Irish real interest rates are exogenously given over the longer term — and, as a result, are not affected by domestic savings and investment levels — is not an unreasonable representation of Irish realities.[24]

When discussing the determinants of the aggregate supply of labour in the mythical economy of Banba in Section 3 above, it was assumed that the quantity of labour supplied in Banba was dependent on (i) domestic wage levels, (ii) foreign labour market conditions, and (iii) restrictions on intercountry labour migration, and that the *ceteris paribus* relationship between labour supply and domestic wage levels took the form of an upward-sloping supply schedule (as in Figure 7.2). At first glance, these assumptions seem to be a reasonable representation of Irish economic circumstances, for few would argue with the proposition that the size of the Irish labour force is sensitive to labour market conditions abroad, or with the proposition that the Irish labour force would be significantly smaller if certain foreign countries (Australia, Canada, the US) did not have quantitative restrictions on immigration levels in place. It should be noted, however, that the assumption that the conventionally-defined labour supply curve is upward-sloping reflects an underlying assumption that Irish wage levels can differ significantly from wage levels abroad — i.e. that the degree of international mobility of labour between Ireland and abroad is significantly less than perfect.[25] In the light of the arguments made above that real interest rates in Ireland cannot differ significantly from real interest rates in the UK, it seems appropriate to ask why real wage rates in Ireland *can* differ significantly from real wage rates in the UK.

The existence of a supply-side linkage between wage levels in Ireland and in the UK is attributable to the fact that workers can move freely between the two countries: if UK wages for a specific type of labour exceed the corresponding Irish wage level by 'too large' a margin, workers will move from Ireland to the UK, reducing the supply of this type of labour in Ireland, and thereby pushing up the Irish wage level until the differential is no longer 'too large'. The magnitude of the sustainable wage differential is dependent on the costs of migrating — where 'costs' is taken to include the disutility associated with relocation, the disutility involved in residing abroad instead of at home, and the search costs involved in acquiring sufficient information on labour markets abroad. Were it the case that these costs were trivial in magnitude, the magnitude of the sustainable wage differential between Ireland and the UK would be correspondingly small — implying that the Irish wage level would approximate to the UK wage level, and (given Ireland's 'smallness') would be determined by the UK wage level. In practice, while these costs may be small for certain categories of workers (e.g. students graduating from college with generic skills), they are likely to be quite significant for many other types of workers (e.g. workers with dependents, with Irish-specific know-how, with firm-specific skills). As a result, declines in Irish wage levels below the corresponding UK levels do not result in large scale emigration and the restoration of wage parity, but instead result in limited emigration (as those for whom the costs of migrating are lowest get out) and a corresponding contraction in the Irish labour supply, with the extent of the reduction in the domestic labour force increasing as the magnitude of the wage differential increases. In geometric terms, this process gives rise to an upward-sloping supply curve of the type drawn in Figures 7.2 and 7.3.

In conclusion, while the intercountry mobility of labour between Ireland and the UK is sufficient to ensure that wage levels in Ireland are quite closely linked to (the exogenously given) wage levels in the UK, the costs associated with migrating are sufficiently large for many workers that Irish wage levels can differ significantly from UK wage levels even over the medium term/long term. As a corollary, domestic labour market conditions play an important role in the determination of domestic wage levels, while the quality of the domestic education/training system (which affects the cost of purchasing skilled labour in Ireland) can be a potent influence on the competitive position of the domestic economy in the international economic system.

Technology Linkages

Although technology is essentially a produced commodity, it is treated separately from other goods and services here because: (i) technology has public good properties, in the sense that, once produced, its services can be made available to one individual or firm without preventing the use of its services by another individual or firm (in contrast to, say, the services of a house); and (ii) in part as a consequence of its public good features, the routes through which technology is diffused are many and varied. One implication of the public good feature of technology can be noted immediately: since technology, once it is produced in some location, need not be produced again elsewhere, one would expect that very small countries would be almost completely dependent on technology developed elsewhere. This is clearly the case in Ireland (see Chapter 11), as can be seen by a cursory glance at the origins of technologies in use in the various sectors of the Irish economy (e.g. manufacturing, health services, telecommunications). What is important from a normative perspective, however, is not the degree of reliance on imported technology, but whether or not the technology linkages between the domestic economy and the outside world are sufficiently developed to ensure that the domestic economy can obtain the services of externally-produced technology on competitive terms. If such linkages are sufficiently close (e.g. Connecticut and the rest of the US), then the absence of domestic development of technology is not an issue of policy concern; if this is not the case, then a case can be made for incentives for domestic R and D to encourage domestic technological progress. This subsection contains a brief discussion of the major channels through which technology is transferred to an economy, with the purpose of assessing the extent of such linkages in the case of Ireland.

It is useful to distinguish two distinct forms in which the technology associated with a new product or production process can be 'stored': new technology can be embodied in new capital goods (e.g. word processors, knitting machinery) or it can be disembodied knowledge (whether a book of blueprints or know-how) in the possession of an individual or firm. In the case of disembodied knowledge, it is useful to distinguish further between situations where the nature of the technology is such that the owner chooses to sell the services of the technology (i.e. licensing other producers) and those cases where the owner chooses to exploit the technology through exclusive intra-firm usage (e.g. IBM's exploitation of its computer technology and know-how).

Considering first the case where new technology is equipment-combined, it is clear that the services of the new technology can be obtained from abroad directly via goods markets; provided that there are no impediments to the importation of such products, domestic producers wishing to avail of the new technology are not placed at a competitive disadvantage by the absence of domestic R and D. Given the absence of impediments to trade between Ireland and the other EC countries, it is clear that this condition is satisfied in an Irish context. In the case where technology is exploited via licensing, domestic producers wishing to avail of the services of the technology can acquire these services at a cost which should not differ from the cost which producers abroad must pay to license the technology, *provided* that there are no impediments to domestic firms purchasing technology services. Under such circumstances, it is again the case that domestic producers are not placed at a competitive disadvantage vis-à-vis producers abroad by the absence of domestic development of the technology. While it would appear that the role of licensing in the process of technology transfer to Ireland is limited, there is no reason to believe that domestic impediments play any role in explaining the limited scale of licensing.

Finally, in the situation where the owner of technology chooses to exploit the technology through intra-firm usage alone, it is clear that domestic producers are placed at a fundamental competitive disadvantage (although it is not domestic development of the new technology which would make these producers competitive but intra-firm development). However, the domestic economy is not necessarily placed at a competitve disadvantage as a location of production by the external development of the technology, because the firm possessing the technology will choose to locate the production activities associated with the exploitation of the technology on the basis of a consideration of the relative attractions of competing production locations, not on the basis of where the technology is developed. Therefore, provided that the costs to firms becoming multinational are limited and the domestic economy maintains a non-discriminatory policy vis-à-vis direct foreign investment, the domesic economy is able to obtain the services of the new technology through direct foreign investment, and its competitiveness as a location is not affected by external development of the technology. The significance of diffusion of technology to Ireland via this route is obvious, as is illustrated by the very high foreign-firm shares of employment in industries where proprietal technology is a significant competitive factor (e.g. electronics, pharmaceuticals).

To conclude, examination of the distinct routes through which technology can be transferred (capital goods, licensing, direct foreign investment), reveals that the impediments to efficient technology transfer of externally-developed technology to Ireland are of little significance, and that as a consequence, the reliance on imported technology does not give grounds for policy concern. While precise policy conclusions would require a more detailed analysis of the transfer of technology, one implication that seems clear is that preoccupation with the development of domestic R and D in Ireland would be a fundamental mistake. The general weaknesses of the market mechanism in relation to the production of technology suggests that there may be circumstances where domestic incentives for R and D development are desirable (e.g. in relation to uniquely Irish problems); but, in general, any incentives for domestic technology production should be justified and evaluated in the same manner as incentives to any production activity.

Conclusion

The preceding discussion has examined the external linkages of the Irish economy in three stages, and has demonstrated that the assumptions explicit and implicit in the concept of an SOE — traded goods sector integration, financial market integration, (implicitly) technology 'market' integration, and 'smallness' — do not significantly violate the realities of the Irish economy. As a consequence, the policy insights generated in the discussion of the growth process in an SOE are applicable to policy formulation in Ireland. The positive discussion of the growth process in the SOE indicated that one can classify the determinants of growth in the SOE into two general categories — those factors which influence the rate of growth of the aggregate system of which the SOE is a part, and those factors which influence the changing position of the SOE within the spatial allocation of production in the aggregate system. In the discussion of the recent growth experience of the Irish economy in the remainder of this chapter, advantage is taken of this distinction. The next section discusses the major statistical features of the growth experience, and relates these features to the general experience of the international and European economies, while the final section attempts to explain the residual element in the growth experience — i.e. that element of the growth experience which cannot be explained solely by reference to the aggregate growth performance of the international economy.

5   IRELAND'S GROWTH EXPERIENCE SINCE 1960 — THE STATISTICAL RECORD

Given the central role of external economic factors in determining the pace of economic expansion in an SOE such as Ireland, it is appropriate to commence our discussion with a brief review of growth trends in the international economy. In examining the global growth experience since the end of the Second World War, two distinct time periods can be identified, with markedly different experiences being recorded during each. The two decades from the end of the post-war recovery to the first oil crisis of 1973-74 marked a period of sustained economic expansion during which both incomes and per capita incomes expanded at historically unprecedented rates. While there were substantial differences in the growth rates recorded by the various industrialized countries — even allowing for the effects of 'catching-up' by those economies ravaged by the war — such was the pace of global expansion that even in the more slowly growing economies (e.g. the UK) the rate of growth of income per capita was still higher than ever previously recorded. Among the numerous factors contributing to global economic expansion were the high savings levels sustained during the period, the absence of the macroeconomic instability which prevailed in both the 1930s and the late 1970s, the high levels of expenditures on R and D during the period, and the occurrence of a number of scientific breakthroughs both during and after the war.

Since the onset of the first oil crisis in 1973-74, the pace of global expansion has declined substantially. The GDP of the industrialized countries expanded at an annual average rate of 2.4 per cent between 1973 and 1986, compared with the 5.0 per cent rate recorded in the 1960-73 period; the corresponding decline in the case of the developing countries was from 6.0 per cent to 3.7 per cent.[26] The fall-off in the annual rate of growth of GDP in the EC mirrored the declining growth rate of the industrialized countries, with the EC growth rate averaging 4.5 per cent between 1961 and 1973, and 1.9 per cent in the 1973-86 period. There were, however, significant differences between the experiences of the three major regions of the industrialized world — Japan, the EC and the US. In the US, the growth slowdown manifested itself in a dramatic decline in the annual rate of growth of labour productivity — from 2.9 per cent (1961-73) to 0.7 per cent (1973-82) — with employment continuing to grow quite rapidly; in the EC, in contrast, employment barely expanded in the corresponding period, while productivity growth was substantially faster than in the US. The ongoing improvement of Japan's position in the international economy was reflected in output and labour productivity growth rates that were higher than those recorded in the rest of the industrialized world. The primary cause of the global growth slowdown was the macroeconomic instability that characterized the international economy in the post-1973 period, instability which in turn was attributable in part to the difficult adjustments in production structures, price levels and global income distribution associated with the oil price shocks of 1973-74 and 1979-80, and in part to the anti-inflationary policies adopted by the industrial economies in the wave of the second oil price shock.

In discussing Ireland's growth experience since 1960, it is useful to divide the relevant two-and-a-half decades into three distinct sub-periods: the period from 1961 until the first oil price shock of 1973, the period from 1973 until 1981, and the period from 1981 until 1986. While the post-1960 period provides the focus of attention, data on Ireland's growth experience during the 1950s are included where available to provide a comparative perspective.

Output Growth

The standard measure of the value of goods and services produced in an economy is Gross Domestic Product (GDP). Although subject to a number of limitations both as a welfare measure and as an output growth measure, the rate of growth of GDP is the best available measure of the pace of economic expansion. Table 7.1 presents data on GDP growth in Ireland since 1949, along with data on the rates of growth of employment and output per worker (i.e. labour productivity). As is clear from the table, the pace of economic

Table 7.1

Growth in Real Output and Output per Person, 1949-86[1]

	1949-61	1961-73	1973-81	1981-86
Gross Domestic Product[2]	2.0	4.1	3.6	1.9
Employment[3]	− 1.3	0.0	0.9	− 1.6
GDP per worker	3.3	4.1	2.6	3.5

Sources: CSO, *National Income* and *Expenditure* and *Trend of Employment and Unemployment,* various issues; *ESRI Quarterly Economic Commentary,* December 1986; and NESC, *A Strategy for Development 1986-1990* (Report no. 83), November 1986.

[1] Growth rates are compound average annual growth rates.

[2] GDP is measured at constant factor prices.

[3] Employment estimates for 1973 were derived by interpolation using annual average growth rate for the period 1971-75.

expansion in Ireland since the return to a peacetime economy has been quite uneven. During the 1950s, output grew at an unimpressive 2.0 per per annum, while employment declined by 1.3 per cent per annum. The 1960s saw a marked increase in the rate of economic growth, which averaged 4.1 per cent per annum during this period; this doubling of the growth rate was sufficient to eliminate (but not reverse) the decline in aggregate employment. Following the first oil price shock in 1973-74, the pace of economic growth eased somewhat; since the 0.5 percentage point decline in the growth rate was accompanied by a 1.5 percentage point decline in the rate of growth of labour productivity, total employment increased by almost one per cent per annum, with most of the employment gain being accounted for by expansion in services sector employment. Since 1981, the annual growth rate has returned to the level attained during the 1950s, with total employment declining at a somewhat faster rate than that recorded during the 1950s.

Some features of this uneven record of economic expansion can be explained by reference to trends in the international economy; thus the decline in the Irish growth rate from 4.1 per cent per annum in the period 1961-73 to 2.9 per cent per annum in the period 1973-86 can be attributed to the general slowdown in the pace of global economic expansion following the first oil price shock noted above. Other features of domestic economic performance, however, cannot easily be explained in terms of international trends. First, the rate of growth of the international economy during the 1960s did not differ significantly from that recorded during the 1950s, implying that the doubling of the Irish growth rate between 1949-61 and 1961-73 can only be explained by reference to changes in the competitive position of the Irish economy within the international economy. Second, the rate of growth of the industrial economies did not differ significantly between the late 1970s and the early 1980s — e.g. European Community GDP grew by 1.9 per cent per annum between 1973 and 1981, and by 1.8 per cent per annum between 1981 and 1986 — implying that the sharp decline in the pace of economic expansion in Ireland during the 1980s must also be explained by reference to changes in the determinants of Ireland's share of global output. These issues are examined in detail in the next section of the chapter.

The pattern of growth at the sectoral level is set out in Table 7.2.[27] Recognizing that services sector output consists almost exclusively of non-traded goods, and hence that output growth in the services sector is dependent on output growth in the traded

goods sectors of the economy, the data indicate that Irish economic
expansion has been industry-led, with the industrial sector recording
the highest rate of output growth in each of the three periods — a
record which provides a sharp contrast with the relatively low output
growth rates recorded in the agricultural sector. Given that the
industrial sector consists of building and construction (non-traded),
public utilities (non-traded), mining and quarrying (of little
significance), and manufacturing, it follows that the manufacturing
sector has been the leading sector in the growth process in Ireland.
It is noteworthy, however, that the primary source of employment
expansion since 1973 has been the services sector, where low labour
productivity growth rates have ensured that relatively slow growth
in sectoral output has been accompanied by significant increases in
service sector employment.

Table 7.2

Sectoral Growth Experience, 1949-86[1]

	1949-61	1961-73	1973-86[2]
Output			
Agriculture	0.9	1.7	1.5
Industry	3.6	6.2	3.2
Services	1.6	3.7	2.7
GDP	2.0	4.1	2.9
Employment[3]			
Agriculture	-2.7	-3.1	-3.5
Industry	-0.2	1.9	-0.8
Services	-0.4	1.1	1.8
Total	-1.3	+ 0.0	-0.0

Sources: as for Table 7.1.

[1] Compound annual growth rates.

[2] Output estimates for 1986 are derived from ESRI, *op. cit.*

[3] Employment estimates for 1973 were derived by interpolation using the annual average
growth rate for the period 1971-75.

The contrasting experiences of the three sectors in the growth
process have been reflected in the changing relative importance of
the sectors in the composition of national output and total
employment. Agriculture's share of GDP declined from 29.5 per
cent in 1949 to 17.3 per cent in 1978, with the unfavourable
experience of the sector in the post-1978 period being reflected in a
further decline of its share of GDP to 10.7 per cent by 1985. The
decline in agricultural employment produced an even sharper

decline in the sector's share of total employment, from 42.9 per cent in 1949 to 20.4 per cent in 1978, with a further decline to 15.7 per cent by 1985. The declining relative importance of agriculture has been accompanied by an increase in the relative size of both the industrial and services sectors, with the former accounting for one-third of total output and two-sevenths of total employment in 1985, and the latter accounting for more than one-half of both output and employment in the same year.

Real Income Growth
Although GDP is the most appropriate measure of the value of goods and services produced in a country, the most appropriate measure of incomes accruing to the residents of a country is Gross National Disposable Income (GNDI). The relationship between these two measures is given by the national accounts identity:

GNDI ≡ GDP + Net Factor Payments from Abroad (NFI)
        + Net Transfer Payments from Abroad (NTP)

GDP is, of course, the primary influence on GNDI, but NFI and NTP are both items of importance in Ireland's national accounts. In the past, NFI (mainly returns from Irish-owned capital invested abroad) and NTP (mainly emigrants' remittances) were both positive entries in the national accounts: in 1961, each amounted to 2.5 per cent of GNDI, with GDP accounting for 95 per cent of GNDI. Since the 1960s, Ireland's dependence on inward direct foreign investment as the source of manufacturing sector expansion and on foreign capital markets as a source of funding for public sector deficits has given rise to continued annual increases in the magnitude of gross factor payments to foreigners; by 1984-85, repatriated profits and interest payments on foreign borrowings had reached such levels that NFI amounted to *minus* 11.6 per cent of GNDI. While transfer payments from abroad have increased in relative importance — largely as a result of the net transfer of funds to Ireland from the European Community — the increase has been small relative to the rapid expansion in factor payments to foreigners; as a result, GDP is now significantly larger than GNDI, averaging 106.5 per cent of GNDI during 1984-85.

Table 7.3 provides a summary statement of the trends in the growth of real incomes in Ireland since the late 1940s. The general pattern of income growth, not surprisingly, reflects the trends in output growth; thus the rate of growth of GNDI more than doubled between the 1950s and the 1960s, declined by a full percentage point between the 1960s and the late 1970s, and then declined further during the 1980s. In recent years, however, the continuing increase in factor payments to foreigners has produced a widening discrepancy between the GDP growth rate and the GNDI growth rate: while GDP measured at constant market prices increased by 4.0 per cent per annum during the 1973-81 period and by 1.2 per cent per annum between 1981 and 1986, GNDI measured in a similar fashion grew by only 3.4 per cent per annum in the former period and by less than 0.1 per cent per annum during the latter period! The minimal growth of GNDI during the 1980s, in combination with the ongoing growth in the size of the population, resulted in a decline in GNDI per capita during the period 1981-86 — a decline which is in sharp contrast to the 2.4 per cent per annum *increase* in income per capita recorded during the much-maligned 1950s.

Table 7.3
Growth in Real Income and Income per Person, 1949-86[1]

	1949-61	1961-73	1973-81	1981-86
Gross National Disposable Income (GNDI)[2]	1.9[3]	4.4	3.4	0.1
Population	-0.5	0.7	1.4	0.8
Employment	-1.3	0.0	0.9	-1.6
GNDI per person	2.4	3.6	1.9	-0.7
GNDI per worker	3.2	4.3	2.4	1.7

Sources: as for Table 7.1; and OECD, *Main Economic Indicators,* March 1987.
[1] Growth rates are compound average annual growth rates.
[2] GNDI is measured at constant market prices.
[3] GNP growth rate.

In Section 2 above, it was argued that small open economies such as Ireland do not face a trade-off between between the level of investment and the level of current consumption because access to international capital markets ensures that changes in the level of investment can be accomplished through changes in external borrowing levels rather than through offsetting changes in consumption levels. Ireland's experience during the late 1970s provides a striking illustration of this point, for investment increased from 26.9 per cent of GNDI in 1977 to 28.0 per cent of GNDI in 1981 while consumption expenditures (public and private) increased from 78.3 per cent of GNDI in 1977 to 86.9 per cent of GNDI in 1981 — expansion made possible by an increase in net foreign borrowings (public and private) from 3.2 per cent of GNDI in 1977 to 14.9 per cent of GNDI in 1981. It should be noted, however, that the absence of an immediate trade-off between consumption and investment levels does *not* mean that there is no trade-off between current consumption levels and the future income levels of domestic residents in an SOE. The SOE is in a position similar to that of an individual with a friendly bank manager: investment is not constrained by current savings levels (e.g. the individual buying a house) but the lower is the level of savings today (given investment expenditure), the lower is the future level of disposable (i.e. post-debt repayment) income — a point clearly highlighted by the disparity between the rates of growth of GDP and GNDI in Ireland during the years 1981-86.

International Comparisons
This brief examination of the main features of Ireland's growth experience in the post-1960 period concludes by comparing Irish income levels and growth rates to those of other countries. Intercountry comparisons of income levels are subject to a number of statistical limitations, with comparisons of income growth rates being even more problematic. As always, the justification for use of the statistics is that they are the best available measures, rather than the best imaginable measures.

Table 7.4 provides comparable estimates of both levels and rates of growth of GNP per capita for selected countries and for groupings of countries combined on the basis of GNP per capita.[28] Considering, first, GNP per capita levels, the data reveal that Ireland is an affluent country by the standards of the middle and lower income countries which account for three-quarters of the world's population, but is less than affluent by the standards of the industrialized countries. Countries with comparable income levels include Spain, Israel, Singapore and Greece. While income per capita levels as conventionally measured tend to overestimate the differences in real economic welfare levels between affluent and poor countries, the comparison of Ireland's income per capita level with the income levels of the poorest half of the world's population in the lower income countries is quite striking; Irish GNP per capita is approximately 19 times the magnitude of GNP per capita in the low income countries.

Examination of the income per capita growth rates recorded by the countries represented in Table 7.4 reveals that Ireland's GNP per capita is growing somewhat more slowly than income levels in the developed and middle income economies. While the differences in the growth rates are small, and should be treated with some

263

caution given the statistical limitations of such calculations, it is none the less a clear indicator that Ireland is not 'catching up' with the developed countries and is 'falling behind' relative to the most successful of the industrializing countries, e.g. Singapore, Taiwan, South Korea and Brazil. Comparison of Ireland's growth rate with those of other EC countries reveals that, over the period 1960-85, Irish income levels have been increasing at a somewhat slower pace than the income levels of the Continental member countries, with Irish income per capita being approximately half the GNP per capita of the ten-member EC in the early 1980s. However, Irish GNP per capita has increased significantly faster than UK GNP per capita over the same time period, with a corresponding narrowing of productivity and wage differentials between Ireland and its major trading partner in both commodities and labour power.

Table 7.4

Economic Welfare and Economic Growth —
International Comparison

	GNP per Capita 1981 (US$)	Average Annual Percentage Growth in GNP per Capita 1960-81
Developed Market Economies	11,120	3.4
Upper Middle Income Countries	2,490	4.2
Lower Middle Income Countries	850	3.4
Lower Income Countries	270	2.9
Selected Individual Countries:		
US	12,820	2.3
UK	9,110	2.1
Spain	5,640	4.2
Singapore	5,240	7.4
Ireland	5,230	3.1
Israel	5,160	3.6
Greece	4,420	2.4
Portugal	2,520	4.8
Brazil	2,220	5.1
Korea	1,700	6.9
China	300	5.0
India	260	1.4

Sources: World Bank, *World Development Report 1983,* Oxford University Press, New York 1983.

6   IRELAND'S GROWTH EXPERIENCE SINCE 1960: AN ANALYSIS

This section of the chapter concerns itself with explaining two features of Ireland's post-1960 growth experience which cannot be easily explained by reference to trends in the international economy: (i) the sharp contrast between the pace of economic expansion during the 1950s and the rates of growth recorded during the 1960s and early 1970s, and (ii) the marked disparity between the growth rates recorded during the late 1970s and the corresponding figures for the first half of the 1980s.

'Boom and Bloom'
In developing an explanation for the acceleration in the pace of economic growth during the 1960s, it is useful to begin with a discussion of the growth experience of the Irish economy in previous decades. Prior to the 1960s, the position of the Irish economy in the international division of labour had not altered substantially since the 1860s, when Marx described Ireland as 'only an agricultural district of England, marked off by a wide channel from the country to which it yields corn, wool, cattle, industrial and military recruits'.[29] Although the relative size of the agricultural sector had declined continually, the sector still accounted for two-fifths of employment during the 1950s, and provided three-quarters of total merchandise exports — with live animals alone accounting for one-third of total exports. While the industrial sector had increased in both absolute and relative terms during the post-1932 period, the sector consisted predominantly of production activities which were either naturally non-tradeable (e.g. construction) or effectively non-traded because of the protectionist trade policies in place at the time (e.g. car assembly). Viewed in terms of the model outlined in Section 3 above, Ireland during the pre-1960 period was a natural-resource-based economy: the agricultural sector provided the traded sector base of the domestic economy, the traded subcomponent of the industrial sector was miniscule in size, and the remainder of the labour force was employed in the production of non-traded goods and services.

The key dynamic factor affecting domestic output and wage levels during this period was the ongoing upward shift in the labour supply schedule, resulting from the increasing wages and employment opportunities in external labour markets (the US, Britain and the 'Colonies'). Upward movements in wage levels combined with technical progress in agriculture led to declining agricultural employment while output levels remained broadly unchanged. Declining agricultural employment was accompanied by declining employment in the non-traded goods sector, in part because the ongoing reductions in transport costs led to a reduction in the range of goods and services which were naturally protected from external competition (and hence a reduction in the size of the non-traded goods sector associated with any given level of output in the traded goods sector). The 'engine of growth' in this period was therefore the shifting labour supply schedule; this migration-driven process resulted in increasing domestic wage and income levels, but an ongoing decline in employment and population. These trends were temporarily halted by the protectionist trade policies adopted during the 1930s, which effectively expanded the size of the non-traded goods sector by eliminating the exposure to external competition of many manufacturing sector activities; the result was an increase in domestic employment (due to the expansion of the size of the non-traded goods sector associated with a given level of traded sector output). After this once-off expansion in the size of domestic employment was complete, the traditional dynamic patterns of the economy continued to operate, and mass emigration resumed with the post-war restoration of 'normal' labour market conditions in the UK and the US; thus total employment declined by 1.3 per cent annually during the period 1949-61, while, on average, 1.3 per cent of the population emigrated each year.

Ireland's growth experience during the 1960s provided a sharp break with these long-established patterns: the annual rate of growth of GDP during the years 1961-73 was more than double the growth rate recorded in the 1950s, total employment stabilized around its 1961 level, and the population actually expanded after more than a century of persistent decline. While agricultural output continued to grow relatively slowly, the industrial sector expanded at the unprecedented rate of 6.2 per cent per annum despite significant reductions in the magnitude of tariff barriers. More importantly, the traded subcomponent of the industrial sector expanded rapidly, with manufactured exports growing at an annual rate of 14.5 per cent in volume terms over the period; the rapid growth of manufactured exports was reflected in the increasing export orientation of the manufacturing sector, with the fraction of manufacturing sector output destined for export markets increasing from 13.4 per cent in 1961 to 30.3 per cent in 1973.[30] By the mid-1970s, the 'width' of the traded sector base of the Irish economy had expanded to include both the bulk of the agricultural sector and a significant fraction of the manufacturing sector (along with tourism); the non-traded goods sector had expanded in a derivative fashion.

In attempting to explain the rapid growth of the 1960s (which was rapid by historical standards but not remarkable by the standards of the international economy), the question to be asked is 'why did the subcomponent of the Irish manufacturing sector producing internationally-traded goods grow so rapidly?' From the discussion in Section 3 above, answers to this question could take one of two forms: (i) Irish wages declined relative to wage levels abroad, resulting in a movement *along* the manufacturing sector labour demand curve, *or* (ii) changes in domestic and/or international economic circumstances resulted in an outward *shift* in the manufacturing sector labour demand curve. In fact, there is little reason to believe that improved wage competitiveness (i.e. declining relative wage levels) was the driving force in manufacturing sector expansion: the uninspiring performance of the agricultural sector (which presumably would also have benefitted from declining wage levels) and the increase in the ratio of Irish GDP per capita to UK GDP per capita (see Section 5 above) both suggest that industrial expansion was driven by 'labour-demand-pull' rather than 'labour-supply-push' considerations. Hence, the question to be answered in explaining the rapid growth of the manufacturing sector — and by extension, the growth of the economy as a whole — is 'why did the demand curve shift?', i.e. what changes in domestic and international circumstances provided Ireland with a competitive niche in the production of manufactures for export?

Before providing an answer to *this* question, it is useful to note certain features of the development of the manufacturing sector during the 1960s and early 1970s. First, foreign-owned firms played a central role in the growth of the manufacturing sector after 1960, with increases in employment in subsidiaries of foreign firms accounting for approximately three- quarters of the increase in total manufacturing sector employment between 1960 and 1973. By 1973, 'newly arrived' foreign firms — defined to be firms which had received IDA new industry grants — accounted for more than half of manufactured exports, and had contributed an even larger fraction of the increase in the volume of exports during the preceding twelve years. In contrast, employment in domestically-owned firms grew quite slowly during the period — at an annual rate of 0.7 per cent per annum — with a significant fraction of these employment gains being recorded in sectors at least partially insulated from international competition (e.g. cement production).[31] Second, the type of direct foreign investment (DFI) attracted to Ireland during the 1960s and early 1970s was quite different from the 'tariff-hopping' domestic market-oriented DFI that had occurred in previous decades; the 'typical' foreign subsidiary set up during this period was a wholly-owned subsidiary which exported close to 90 per cent of its output, imported about four-fifths of its material inputs, and relied on the local economy only for labour and non-traded goods and services.[32]

Given these particular features of the industrialization experience, it seems clear that the rapid growth of an internationally competitive manufacturing sector in Ireland during the 1961-73 period was largely attributable to the sustained inflow of export-oriented DFI into Ireland during these years — which of course raises the question as to why Ireland was the recipient of significant inflows of DFI of this type. The answer to *this* question comes in two parts — one involving changes in the external environment which Ireland confronted, the other involving changes in the domestic policy framework.

Prior to the 1960s, multinational firms' involvement in the manufacturing sectors of traditionally less industrialized economies took the form of tariff-protected production for the domestic market of the host country (e.g. the car assembly industry in Ireland pre-1973); at the end of the 1950s, local sales accounted for more than 95 per cent of the total sales of US subsidiaries operating in developing countries.[33] Export production by multinational firms expanded extremely rapidly during the 1960s and 1970s, with the result that, by 1977, it accounted for one-fifth of total affiliate production in the developing countries, and for one-fifth of total developing country manufactured exports. Export production by multinational firms in the industrializing countries has typically involved wholly-owned subsidiaries carrying out one or more of the standardized production activities of the parent firm, importing the bulk of the material inputs into the production process, and exporting most, if not all, of the output — a pattern very similar to that observed in Ireland. The emergence and rapid growth of this type of direct foreign investment in the international economy can be explained by a number of factors, including sharp declines in transport and communications costs, organizational innovations which have facilitated the development of multinational firms, and policy changes in both home and host countries.

It is clear that the development of the new form of DFI as a feature of the international economy was of key importance in explaining the observed trends in the pattern of direct foreign investment in Ireland. However, Ireland would have attracted relatively little export-oriented DFI were it not for the major changes in trade and industrial policies implemented during the

1950s and 1960s. (See Chapters 1 and 11 for detailed discussion of the major policy reforms.) Studies of the role of countries' incentive packages in attracting foreign investment suggest that, while incremental changes in the incentive package have a limited effect on the volume of DFI attracted to a particular country, a country must provide a favourable environment for foreign firms — including, *inter alia,* non-discriminatory treatment of foreign firms, access to inputs at world prices, and reasonable freedom to repatriate profits and/or capital — if it is to attract export-oriented DFI on a significant scale.[34] Hence, the movement towards freer trade, the introduction of tax incentives and capital grants, and the removal of various restrictions on DFI all played a role in ensuring that Ireland had the locational attractions necessary to attract a significant share of the expanding pool of 'footloose' DFI.

To conclude, the argument offered here is that the acceleration of the pace of economic growth during the 1960s was attributable to the development of an internationally competitive subcomponent of the manufacturing sector, that the development of this subcomponent of the manufacturing sector was attributable to large scale inflows of export-oriented direct foreign investment, and that the occurrence of this inflow of direct foreign investment resulted from changes in the global economic environment which Ireland confronted occurring in conjunction with the liberalization of trade and foreign investment policies in Ireland. In the post-1960 period, direct foreign investment provided Ireland with a new 'engine of growth' which shifted outwards the aggregate demand for labour schedule (via its effect on the manufacturing sector and trade sector demand curves) sufficiently fast to keep pace with, and later outstrip, the upward movement in the labour supply schedule; as a result, the downward trend in the level of total employment was halted, and later reversed.

'Doom and Gloom'

The 1960s marked the highpoint of Irish economic expansion, with GDP growing by some 4 per cent per annum between 1961 and 1973. The global economic slowdown following the first oil price shock was initially reflected in a mild slowdown in the pace of economic expansion in Ireland, with the rate of growth of GDP during the 1973-81 period being about one-half of a percentage point below the growth rate recorded during the preceding twelve years. After 1981, however, the slowdown in the rate of growth became much more marked, with GDP growing at less than two per cent per annum — a 1950s style growth rate, with the new twist that GNDI was not growing at all.

Viewed from a European perspective, the decline in the Irish growth rate after 1973 is not surprising: the performance of the European economy since 1973 has been distinctly unimpressive, with unemployment increasing substantially in most countries. What is interesting, however, is the timing of the growth slowdown: while EC GDP measured at market prices grew by 1.9 per cent per annum between 1973 and 1981 and by 1.8 per cent per annum between 1981 and 1986, the corresponding figures for Ireland were 3.8 per cent and 1.2 per cent respectively.[35] Thus, by European standards, Ireland experienced a relatively limited slowdown in the rate of growth during the late 1970s, and a dramatic decline in the growth rate during the 1980s. How can this 'timing' phenomenon be explained?

Before providing an answer to this question, it is useful to examine the post-1973 trends in the level of direct foreign investment in Ireland and in the size of Ireland's trade deficit. During the late 1970s, the foreign firm component of the manufacturing sector continued to grow rapidly, with employment in such firms expanding at the remarkable rate of 4.7 per cent per annum between 1973 and 1980; while employment in domestic firms grew much more slowly — at about 0.5 per cent per annum over the same period — the expansion in the foreign firm subsector was sufficiently rapid to ensure an impressive rate of growth of output, exports, and employment for the manufacturing sector as a whole. Since 1980-81, however, there has been a sharp slowdown in inward direct foreign investment — whether measured by IDA new 'job approvals', actual IDA grant expenditures, or the profit repatriation behaviour of existing firms. One explanation for the timing of the slowdown in direct foreign investment is that the inflow of new US-owned firms during the late 1970s — which accounted for the bulk of the expansion of the foreign firm sector during these years — reflected a once-off adjustment to Ireland's membership of the Community, and that, once this adjustment was complete, further expansion of the foreign firm sector was directly related to the growth of the European economy as a whole. While this explanation seems reasonable and fits the 'big picture' quite nicely, solid verification of the hypothesis is lacking — suggesting that the argument should be treated as tentative rather than confirmed.

Before discussing the behaviour of the broadly-defined trade deficit (i.e. the deficit on trade in goods and services) since 1973, it is useful to recall the analysis of the macroeconomic effects of external borrowing provided in Section 3 above, where it was shown that changes in the scale of the deficit on trade in goods and services had significant effects on the macroeconomy, and that the burden of debt servicing gave rise to important dynamic adjustment effects in the case where such deficits were funded by external borrowings. Table 7.5 provides evidence on the evolution of the deficit on trade in goods and services over the period from 1973 to 1985; also shown in the table are estimates of the annual level of new external borrowings by the consolidated public sector (defined to be the Exchequer, the Central Bank, and the semi-state bodies), and estimates of the annual level of such borrowings less interest, paid to foreigners, on the national debt.[36] The last of these measures provides an estimate of the net transfer of funds from abroad by the consolidated public sector; or alternatively can be viewed as the net 'contribution' of the consolidated public sector to the funding of the trade deficit.

Table 7.5
Public Sector Borrowings and Trade Deficits, 1977-85[1]

	A	B	C	D
1977	9.0	749	226	85
1978	11.8	1081	465	326
1979	13.3	1235	591	407
1980	14.7	1391	907	702
1981	11.7	1094	964	685
1982	8.1	738	859	518
1983	3.5	318	677	271
1984	0.1	14	521	83
1985	-2.3	-233	505	34

A = deficit on trade in goods and services as a per cent of GDP
B = deficit on trade in goods and services (IR£million, 1980 prices)
C = external borrowings by the consolidated public sector (IR£million, 1980 prices)
D = external borrowings by the consolidated public sector *less* national debt interest paid to foreigners (IR£ million, 1980 prices)

Sources: CSO, *National Income and Expenditure,* various issues.
[1] Estimates for all years except 1985 are three-year moving averages; estimates for 1985 are annual figures. Nominal estimates were converted into 1980 prices using the GDP implicit price deflator.

The data in Columns A and B of the table provide striking evidence on the expansionary stimulus provided to the Irish economy by the sharp increase in the trade deficit between 1977 and 1980, and the strongly contractionary stimulus provided by the dramatic decline in the magnitude of the trade deficit between 1980 and 1985 — culminating in a trade surplus in the latter year.[37] The data in Column D provide equally striking evidence on the role of the public sector in providing the net transfer of funds from abroad that financed the trade deficit: thus, the net infusion of funds by the consolidated public sector increased dramatically between 1977 and 1980-81, and declined in equally dramatic fashion over the ensuing four years. The data in Column C indicate that the sharp decline in the net infusion of external funds by the public sector was only partly due to a reduction in the level of external borrowings, with the remainder of the decline being attributable to the rising burden of interest payments on prior external borrowings.

We are now in a position to offer an explanation for the timing of the slowdown in the pace of economic expansion in Ireland since 1973. During the late 1970s, the Irish economy grew at a significantly faster rate than the European economy as a whole for two distinct reasons: (i) US firms interested in servicing the enlarged Community market provided a continuous inflow of new investment projects, which resulted in ongoing expansion of manufacturing sector output, exports, and employment, and (ii) large scale external borrowings by the public sector from 1977 onward provided a strong expansionary stimulus to the domestic economy, which resulted in output growth in the non-traded goods sector of the economy and a sharp deterioration in the trade deficit. The construction industry provides an interesting example of the latter effect at work; real expenditures on building and construction increased by 9.7 per cent per annum during the period 1977-81.

As discussed in Section 3 above, the rising burden of interest payments on the external debts accumulated during the 1970s would have had a contractionary effect on the pace of growth during the 1980s even if the export-oriented foreign firm component of the manufacturing sector had continued to grow at the rates of the late 1970s *and* new public sector external borrowing levels had remained at the inflated levels of 1981. In fact, the foreign firm subsector did not grow at rates anywhere near the rates recorded during the 1970s, while the level of new external borrowings by the public sector declined by almost 50 per cent in real terms between 1981 and 1985. The slowing down of the traditional 'engine of growth' — inward direct foreign investment — resulted in slower output growth in the traded sector component of the manufacturing sector, while the dramatic decline in the net infusion of external funds by the public sector resulted in a marked slowdown in the growth of output and employment in the non-traded goods sector of the economy. Again, the construction industry provides an illuminating example of the second of these effects; real expenditures on building and construction declined by an average of 8.8 per cent per annum during the years 1981-86.

In conclusion, the timing of the growth slowdown in Ireland can be explained by reference to changes in the pattern of direct foreign investment between the 1970s and the 1980s and to the effects of the rapid increase in public external debt during the late 1970s — a debt 'binge' whose effects broadly mirror the set of effects identified in the discussion of the macroeconomic effects of external borrowing in Section 3.

Footnotes

1 Economic growth is taken to mean the expansion of Gross Domestic Product per worker; statements below concerning resource accumulation should therefore be interpreted as statements concerning increases in resources per worker.

2 For further reading on the major theories of the growth process under capitalism, consult Mark Blaug, *Economic Theory in Retrospect*, Cambridge University Press, Cambridge 1978, on the Classical school; M.C. Howard and J.E. King, *The Political Economy of Marx*, Longman, London 1975, on Marx's analysis; and Graham Hacche, *The Theory of Economic Growth: An Introduction*, Macmillan, London 1975, on the Neoclassical and neoKeynesian schools.

3 The first of these trade-offs is labelled fundamental in that it is merely the statement of an identity, and hence is automatically true. The second trade-off is labelled secondary in that it reflects assumptions about specific economic parameters (which may or may not be correct), and also because it could be partially offset by appropriately-designed state policy.

4 The quotations are from Keynes' famous concluding passage in *The General Theory of Employment, Interest and Money*, Macmillan, London 1936, p.383.

5 The reader will see immediately that this process descriptively captures the determination of the level of *foreign* direct investment in the international economy; it also is *in effect* the process by which domestically-controlled investment is determined. While domestic firms do not actually scan the world for an optimal location, competition in the goods markets ensures that the global outcome is as though such a process were occurring, since domestic capitalists will survive competitive pressures only if the SOE is the optimal location.

6 Two partial qualifications to this statement may be noted. First, the effective utilization of technology purchases from abroad often requires some domestic R and D to adapt the technology to the specific situation of the purchasing firm and the local environment. Second, under certain circumstances, technology cannot be purchased in open markets, because the owning firm prefers to exploit technology through intra-firm use only; if, however, other considerations make the SOE an attractive location for production, then the technology will be exploited in the SOE via direct foreign investment.

7 This point needs to be remembered in the light of the 'glorification' of R and D activities in NESC, *A Review of Industrial Policy* (Report no.64, referred to as the Telesis Report), Stationery Office, Dublin 1982.

8 The technical details of the model are left in the background to make the analysis accessible to the lay reader. The model presented here can be thought of as a special case of the dependent economy model described in W.M. Corden and J.P. Neary, 'Booming Sector and De-Industrialization in a Small Open Economy', *Economic Journal*, December 1982, pp. 825-848.

9 F_f and F_m are assumed to be well-behaved production functions characterized by constant returns to scale.

10 Formally, the deficit on international trade in goods and services is identically equal to the difference between domestic expenditure (C + I + G in the national accounts) and gross domestic product (C + I + G + X — M).

11 Formally, it is assumed that all consumers have identical tastes which can be represented by a Cobb-Douglas utility function.

12 Note that the stock of natural resources is, by assumption, fixed, implying that the law of diminishing returns can be applied.

13 In addition, any changes in the production functions in either the food or manufacturing sectors would affect the positions of TT^1 and DD^1 through the impact of such changes on the marginal physical productivity of labour in the relevant sector.

14 It is assumed that labour is less than perfectly mobile between Banba and abroad; were labour to be perfectly mobile, the wage level in Banba would be determined exclusively by labour market conditions abroad, and would be unaffected by any changes in the demand for labour in Banba.

15 Other variables of interest — such as the equilibrium value of national output, the associated distribution of income between workers and resource-owners, and the associated pattern and volume of trade between Banba and the rest of world — can also be obtained from the information provided. These calculations are left as an exercise for the interested reader!

16 Technical improvement in the non-traded goods sector (i.e. declines in A_s) will result in an increase in national welfare; while the value of national output will remain unchanged, the price of non-traded goods will decline, leaving all residents of Banba better off.

17 Since foreign borrowing in this model cannot affect the production potential of the domestic economy, the analysis developed here is best thought of as an analysis of the effects of external borrowing which is used to finance increased consumption levels.

18 The most significant of these limitations is that exports and imports are gross value measures, whereas GDP is a value-added measure, implying that comparisons of X and M with GDP are not comparisons of like with like.

19 World Bank, *World Development Report 1986*, Washington DC, Annex Table 5.

20 A number of studies have shown that the non-food manufacturing sector imports at least four-fifths of its material input requirements, while national accounts data indicate that less than one-third of the value of expenditures on new capital goods in 1984-85 was spent on domestically-produced capital goods.

21 Data sources are documented in Sean Nolan, 'Transnational Enterprises and Manufactured Exports from Industrializing Countries: Theoretical and Empirical Significance' (mimeo), 1983.

22 Indeed, Ireland's economic size is not large when compared with a significant number of the world's largest corporations; a comparison of the magnitude of total sales and employment in the Irish manufacturing sector with the sales and employment of the world's largest manufacturing firms indicates that, in 1980, twenty-eight of these firms had sales larger than the entire Irish manufacturing sector, while ten firms employed more workers.

23 The ever-increasing 'errors and omissions' term in Ireland's balance-of-payments statistics suggests that there is significant scope for unrecorded transactions between Irish residents and non-residents.

24 Patrick Honohan's conclusion on the significance of international capital mobility in influencing Irish interest rates is worth noting here: 'it would be foolish to underestimate the importance of foreign interest rates in influencing Irish interest rates, and no practitioner is likely to take such an analysis seriously', *Administration,* vol. 29, no. 4, pp. 371-372.

274

25 With perfect labour mobility, the aggregate supply of labour schedule confronting the Irish economy would be flat — i.e. the wage level would be exogenously given by wage levels abroad.

26 Sources for the statistics quoted in the text include: International Monetary Fund, *World Economic Outlook*, various issues; World Bank, *World Development Report*, various years; OECD, *Economic Outlook*, various issues; and OECD, *Main Economic Indicators*, various issues.

27 Table 7.2 does not contain a breakdown of the sectoral growth experience of the 1973-86 period into two subperiods because the unusually sharp year-to-year fluctuations in the value of agricultural sector output at the beginning of the 1980s make estimates of the growth rates for subperiods highly sensitive to the choice of a 'break' year.

28 More recent data — for the years up to 1984 — can be found in *World Development Report 1986*. This data is not used here because the marked overvaluation of the US dollar in 1983-85 results in significant overestimation of both real income and real income growth rates for those countries whose currencies were linked to the dollar during these years.

29 *Capital, Volume 1,* International Publishers Co., New York 1967, pp. 702-703.

30 Estimates calculated from raw data in *Review of 1972 and Outlook for 1973*, Stationery Office, Dublin 1973. The term 'manufacturing sector' here refers to the conventionally-defined manufacturing sector excluding food processing.

31 Details of the sources and methods employed in constructing the estimates used in this paragraph are available from the author upon request.

32 This description of the 'typical' foreign-owned firm is based on the data provided in Dermot McAleese, *Profile of Grant-Aided Industry*, Industrial Development Authority, Dublin 1977.

33 For data sources, see Nolan, *op. cit.*

34 The fact that a favourable policy environment is required if a country is to attract export-oriented DFI is attributable to the specific characteristics of such investment: since production is directed at external markets and requires only labour from the domestic economy, the bargaining position of the domestic economy is extremely weak.

35 These figures do not match the GDP growth rates in Table 7.1; the EC and Irish figures reported in the text are for GDP measured at constant market prices, while the Irish figures contained in Table 7.1 are for GDP measured at constant factor cost. The 'market prices' measure for Ireland is used here to ensure that we are comparing like with like.

36 Lack of data on interest payments *by* foreigners to the Central Bank and *to* foreigners by the semi-state companies precludes the estimation of new borrowings less interest payments for the integrated public sector; since the inflow of payments to the Central Bank is at least partially offset by the outflow of payments by the semi-state companies. The measure used in Table 7.5 should be a good proxy for the integrated public sector 'contribution' to the funding of the trade deficit.

37 To economists accustomed to working with effective-demand-driven models of output determination, the notion that an increase in the trade deficit has expansionary effects undoubtedly seems strange; it may be more intuitive to label (M - X) as 'net infusions of funds from abroad'.

8 Employment

Kieran A. Kennedy and Thomas Giblin

FOR MORE than a century after the Great Famine, employment in Ireland fell almost without intermission. It is scarcely a matter of surprise then that unemployment was always relatively high in Ireland. What might seem more surprising, however, is that even though employment rose substantially in the decade 1971-81, unemployment rose also to reach a higher level in 1981 than had been recorded since the 1930s. The 1981 figure itself, of course, now looks moderate by reference to the 1986 unemployment level, which is twice as high.

To understand the relation between employment and unemployment, it is necessary first to consider the major demographic factors affecting the size of the labour force and these factors are examined in Section 1. Section 2 discusses changes in the level and structure of employment and unemployment over the past twenty years, and the outlook for the future. Section 3 outlines the framework in which employment policy must operate, with particular reference to the economic forces influencing the supply of, and demand for, labour in the Irish setting. The final section then sketches the range of policy options that could be considered in order to effect an improvement in labour market prospects.

The chapter also seeks to place the Irish experience in an international context by making appropriate comparisons with the other member states of the EC and with the US. This is important not only in bringing the distinctive features of the Irish employment situation into sharper relief, but also to underline the fact that Irish labour market conditions are profoundly influenced by developments abroad.

1   DEMOGRAPHIC BACKGROUND

Changes in the size of the labour force are dependent on changes in three main factors: the size of the population, its age structure and the rate of labour force participation among the active age groups.

Size of Population

The period since 1961 has been one of exceptional demographic change in Ireland. After more than a century of decline, the population began to increase as emigration fell in the 1960s and was transformed into a net inflow in the 1970s. Over the twenty years, 1961-81, the population rose by 625,000 (22 per cent), in contrast with a *fall* of 278,000 (9 per cent) in the previous forty years of independence. This transformation was all the more remarkable in that it coincided with decelerating population growth in Europe, and to a lesser extent in the US. Population growth in Ireland slowed markedly in the 1980s, and in 1986 there was a slight fall, the first after 25 years of unbroken expansion.

Changes in the size of a country's population are dependent on its birth and death rates (which together determine its rate of natural increase), and on the level of net migration. In Ireland the birth rate (i.e. live births per 1,000 inhabitants) has two distinct features. First, it has been exceptionally high among developed countries over the last 25 years; in 1980 the Irish rate of 21.8 compared with the EC average of 12.6 and a US figure of 15.9. Second, the stability of the Irish birth rate has been in marked contrast to the major falls in the European and American ratios since the mid-1960s (Table 8.1). Since 1980, however, the Irish birth rate has fallen to 17.6 in 1985 and, as explained later, is expected to decline further.

Table 8.1

Birth Rates per 1,000 Population, EC and US,
Selected Years, 1960-85

Year	Bel.	Den.	Fr.	Ger.	Gr.	Irl.	It.	Lux.	Neth.	Port.	Spn.	UK	EC12	US
1960	17.0	16.6	17.9	17.4	18.9	21.5	17.9	15.9	20.8	23.9	21.7	17.5	18.0	23.7
1970	14.8	14.4	16.8	13.4	16.5	21.8	16.5	13.0	18.3	20.0	19.6	16.3	16.4	18.4
1980	12.6	11.2	14.9	10.1	15.4	21.8	11.3	11.4	12.8	16.2	15.2	13.4	12.6	15.9
1985	11.6	10.5	13.9	9.6	11.8	17.6	10.1	11.2	12.3	12.8	12.5[1]	13.3	11.9[2]	15.7[2]

Sources: Eurostat, *Demographic Statistics*, Luxembourg 1986; and *Statistical Abstract of the US, 1986*, US Bureau of the Census, Washington DC.
[1]1983
[2]1984

The stability of the Irish birth rate was the product of two opposing forces: a rising marriage rate and a declining fertility rate.

Table 8.2 gives marriage rates (i.e. total marriages per 1,000 population) for the EC countries and for the US, for various years between 1960 and 1985. Since the figures include remarriages, cross-country comparisons are affected by differences in divorce and remarriage rates. This factor partly accounts for the high marriage rate in the US, where in the period 1980-82, for instance, 612,000 out of the total of 2,426,000 marriages involved remarriage of the bride.

The Irish marriage figures are unusual in two respects. First, they start from a relatively low level, even allowing for the absence of divorce in Ireland. Second, the Irish rate rose substantially up to the early 1970s at a time when it was falling in several European countries, and converged towards the European average. This change involved an end to the traditional Irish pattern of marrying

Table 8.2

Marriage Rates (Including Remarriages) per 1,000 Population, EC and US, Selected Years, 1960-85

Year	Bel.	Den.	Fr.	Ger.	Gr.	Irl.	It.	Lux.	Neth.	Port.	Spn.	UK	EC12	US
1960	7.2	7.8	7.0	9.4	7.0	5.5	7.6	7.1	7.8	7.8	7.7	7.5	7.9	8.5
1970	7.6	7.4	7.8	7.3	7.7	7.1	7.3	6.3	9.5	9.0	7.3	8.5	7.8	10.6
1980	6.7	5.2	6.2	5.9	6.5	6.4	5.7	5.9	6.4	7.4	5.7	7.4	6.2	10.6
1985	5.8	5.7	4.9	6.0	6.3	5.2	5.2	5.4	5.7	6.7	4.8[1]	6.9	5.7[2]	10.5[2]

Sources: as for Table 8.1.
[1]1983.
[2]1984.

late or not marrying at all. Between 1960 and 1977 the average age at marriage fell from 27.2 to 24.0 for brides, and from 30.9 to 26.2 for grooms, but since then the average has risen by over one year for both brides and grooms. Though the marriage rate in Ireland had fallen back somewhat by 1980, the decline was much less than in Europe. From 1980 to 1985, however, the Irish marriage rate fell more than in Europe, and was somewhat below the European average in the latter year.

The traditional low marriage rate in Ireland was offset by a high fertility rate. It may be seen from Table 8.3 that the total fertility rate (i.e. the average number of births per woman during the child-bearing span) was very much higher in Ireland in 1961 than in

Europe, and that since then it has not fallen as much as in Europe or the US. Indeed in all of the other EC countries (except Portugal

Table 8.3
Total Fertility Rates,[1] EC and US, Selected Years, 1961-84

Year	Bel.	Den.	Fr.	Ger.	Gr.	Irl.	It.	Lux.	Neth.	Port.	Spn.	UK	US
1961	2.64	2.55	2.81	2.46	2.19	3.79	2.41	n.a.	3.21	3.01	2.86	2.78	3.62
1971	2.21	2.04	2.54	1.92	2.30	3.98	2.41	1.92	2.38	2.76	2.84	2.41	2.28
1984[2]	1.61	1.40	1.81	1.33	1.82	2.58	1.53	1.43	1.49	2.20	2.34	1.77	1.82

Sources: as for Table 8.1.
[1]Per woman during the child-bearing span.
[2] For the following countries, the data relate to the year in parenthesis: Belgium (1982), Germany (1983), Portugal (1980), Spain (1979), US (1981).

and Spain) and in the US, the fertility rate is now well below the replacement level of about 2.1 which is needed to maintain a constant population. The trend in the Irish total fertility rate, however, conceals the fact that there has been a much bigger decline in the *marital* fertility rate, which was offset by the rising share of young married women among the total of all women of child-bearing age. In recent years, the rate of decline in marital fertility in Ireland has accelerated sharply, and if this trend continues, then the birth rate is likely to fall further.[1]

Table 8.4
Rates of Natural Increase per 1,000 Population, EC and US, Selected Years, 1960-85

Year	Bel.	Den.	Fr.	Ger.	Gr.	Irl.	It.	Lux.	Neth.	Port.	Spn.	UK	EC12	US
1960	4.7	7.1	6.5	5.9	11.6	9.9	8.8	4.1	13.2	13.3	13.1	6.0	7.2	14.2
1970	2.3	4.6	6.1	1.3	8.1	10.4	7.3	0.8	9.9	9.7	11.3	4.5	5.0	8.9
1980	1.1	-0.3	4.7	-1.5	6.3	11.9	1.7	0.2	4.7	6.4	7.4	1.6	2.7	7.1
1985	0.4	-0.9	3.9	-1.9	2.5	8.2	0.6	0.2	3.8	3.2	4.7[1]	1.5	1.9[2]	7.0[2]

Sources: as for Table 8.1.
[1]1983.
[2]1984.

The death rate (i.e. deaths per 1,000 inhabitants) in Ireland has remained close to the European average in recent decades, and has fallen from 11.5 in 1960 to 9.4 in 1985. The combination of a high and relatively stable birth rate and a declining death rate has resulted in a higher rate of natural increase in Ireland than in Europe or the US (Table 8.4).

Historically the natural increase in Ireland was more than offset by exceptionally high levels of emigration and Figure 1 shows the sensitivity of population changes to changes in net external migration. Net emigration averaged 40,000 per annum (1.4 per cent of the population) in the decade 1950-59, but fell to 18,000 per annum (0.6 per cent) in 1960-69. In the 1970s the flow of external migration was reversed and a substantial net inflow of 10,000 per annum on average (0.3 per cent) was recorded in the ten years 1970-79. Coming on top of the high rate of natural increase, this resulted in population growth at an average annual rate of 1.5 per cent in the 1970s, far higher than in any other EC country or the US. In the 1980s, net emigration has resumed at an accelerating rate, resulting in a progressive slowing down in population growth and an actual fall in 1986.

Figure 8.1

Components of Population Change, 1930-86

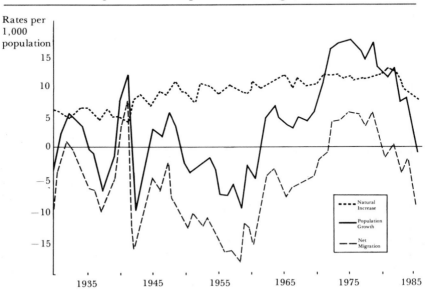

In no other Western country is population affected so substantially by external migration flows. The bulk of Irish external migration flows since the Second World War have been to and from the UK, and are sensitive to economic conditions in that area as well as at home.[2] This creates an important link between the labour markets in the two countries, which means that increases in the demand for labour in Ireland are likely to evoke an increased supply of labour through a reduction in the outflow of emigrants, or the return of former emigrants. There are indications that a significant part of the large rise in emigration in recent years has been to the US — much of it illegal — due to the favourable labour market conditions there relative to Ireland, Britain and much of the rest of Europe.

As to the economic implications of population growth, the majority of economists has tended to adopt the Malthusian perspective that rapid population growth is adverse to living standards. Indeed, it was this gloomy prognosis that first earned for economics the title of the 'Dismal Science'. A minority, however, has challenged this view, arguing that the model fails to give due weight to the potential advantages of a growing population (e.g. economies of scale, increased division of labour) and underestimates the extent to which technological progress can keep the 'Malthusian Devil' at bay.[3] What can be concluded with certainty, however, is that the economic implications of population growth will vary considerably depending on the underlying economic and social conditions: clearly the impact on an economy already on the margin of subsistence will be more severe, in the short run at least, than in a rich economy with a high savings rate.

An important condition is the density and distribution of population. Despite the growth in the last 25 years, the absolute size of the Irish population remains small (3,537,000, April 1986), and population density is well below the European average. In 1986, the number of inhabitants per square kilometre was only 49 compared with an EC average of 175. Low population density gives rise to several economic costs. For example, it tends to increase the cost per head of infrastructural requirements (e.g. roads, railways, telecommunications, electricity network), which have high fixed costs and where running expenses are pushed up because of low utilization in sparsely populated areas. At the other extreme, however, very high population densities can bring their own problems in the form of increased pollution, congestion, etc. It is therefore possible for a country with a low population density, but which is unevenly spread, to experience at the same time the costs of low density in some areas and of congestion in other areas. In Ireland population change has long been accompanied by a shift from the west to the east of the country, especially Dublin and surrounding counties. This is due not only to higher external migration from the west, but also to the impact of internal migration and the smaller rate of natural increase in the west because of the lower proportion of its population in the reproductive age groups.

Age Structure and Participation
A further important factor in assessing the economic implications of population change is the share of the population that is economically active. The age structure of the population will determine the proportion in the working age groups, known as the active age population. Those under 15 years and those aged 65 and over are conventionally treated as constituting the inactive (or dependent) age groups — even though some of the latter group are, in practice, engaged in economic activity. Table 8.5 shows the percentages in these two dependent age groups for Ireland in comparison with other EC countries and the US. An exceptionally high proportion of the Irish population is concentrated in the young dependent age group. The Irish figure of 29.7 per cent in 1984 compares with 21.9 per cent in the US, 20.4 per cent in the EC and only 15.6 per cent in Germany. To some extent this is offset by a lower percentage in the 65 + category. Nevertheless, Ireland has a lower share of its total population in the active age groups than any other EC country or the US.

Table 8.5

Percentage of Population in Dependent Age Groups,
EC and US, 1984

Age	Bel.	Den.	Fr.	Ger.	Gr.	Irl.	It.	Lux.	Neth.	Port.	Spn.	UK	EC12[1]	US
0-14	19.3	18.8	21.6	15.6	21.5	29.7	19.9	17.6	19.7	24.2	23.9	19.5	20.4	21.9
65 +	13.7	14.9	12.9	14.7	13.3	10.6	12.8	13.2	12.0	11.8	11.8	14.8	13.5	11.8

Sources: Eurostat, *Demographic Statistics,* Luxembourg 1986; and OECD. *Labour Force Statistics 1964-1984,* Paris 1986.
[1]1983.

Of course, not all of those in the active age groups are economically active in the sense of being members of the labour force, i.e. engaged in, or seeking, gainful employment. The proportion of the total population in any age group that is in the labour force is known as the participation rate. Table 8.6 gives a breakdown of labour force participation rates by age and sex for the EC countries and the US in 1981. Three categories call for special comment — females, the young (under 25 years of age) and the old (60 years and over).

Female labour force participation in Ireland is low by international standards. In particular, the participation rate for the age group 30-59 is only about half the EC average. This, of course,

Table 8.6

Labour Force Percentage Participation Rates by Sex and Age, EC and US, 1981

Age group	Bel.	Den.	Fr.	Ger.	Gr.	Irl.	It.	Neth.	UK	EC[1]	US
Male											
14-24	47.0	55.2	51.9	53.5	42.1	61.5	43.8	42.6	59.6	51.5	71.5[2]
25-59	90.7	93.9	93.6	93.7	93.3	94.8	88.9	91.4	94.3	92.6	92.3
60 +	11.9	24.7	12.8	14.4	32.8	41.4	15.2	16.1	25.4	17.9	30.2
Total	65.7	70.9	70.0	69.9	70.9	75.7	64.7	66.9	71.8	69.0	77.0
Females											
14-24	43.1	49.0	44.7	48.6	27.8	47.8	33.1	40.8	46.6	42.9	61.7[2]
25-59	47.0	76.0	59.8	50.5	37.5	27.9	34.3	33.5	57.5	48.8	63.3
60 +	2.5	9.4	6.0	3.8	9.0	7.7	3.1	2.0	7.3	5.1	14.0
Total	35.0	53.3	43.5	37.2	29.0	29.0	26.9	26.8	41.4	36.4	52.1

Sources: Eurostat, *Labour Force Sample Survey 1981*, Luxembourg 1983; and International Labour Organization, *Yearbook of Labour Statistics 1982*, Geneva 1982.
[1] The figures do not include Luxembourg, Portugal and Spain.
[2] 16-24 years.

is due to the low participation rate among married women which, even though it rose from almost 8 per cent in 1971 to 17 per cent in 1981 and 24 per cent in 1984, is still much below that of most other Western countries. Moreover, despite the rise in the participation rate of married women, the female share of the labour force has risen only slightly in the past two decades — from 26.3 per cent in 1961 to 29.4 per cent in 1984 — because of the rising marriage rate. With the levelling off in the marriage rate and the decline' in marital fertility, it seems likely that there will be a more rapid 'feminization' of the Irish labour force in the coming years.

Irish participation rates in the youth age group have always been high due to the tendency to leave education earlier than on the Continent. Since the early 1950s, however, there has been a substantial increase in educational participation in Ireland particularly following the introduction of free secondary education in 1967. The number of persons aged 15-24 in full-time education went up from 78,000 in 1961 to nearly 230,000 in 1985. Allowing for the increase in the population aged 15-24 years, this represented a rise in educational participation from 20 to 37 per cent.

Among the older age group (60 +), labour force participation in Ireland has also been higher than in other countries, largely due to the structure of the economy — in particular, the high proportion engaged in farming who are self-employed. Historically, reluctance to retire may also have been linked to the relatively underdeveloped social welfare system. In recent years, however, the trend has been towards earlier retirement, helped by improvements in pension schemes and by the declining share of the agricultural sector.

Labour Force

The net outcome of the changes already described in population, age structure and participation was to arrest the secular decline in the Irish labour force in the decade 1961-71, and to produce in the following decade 1971-81 a very high rate of growth. In the former decade the average annual rise was 3,000 per annum, and in the latter, 16,000 per annum. The age structure of the labour force also changed considerably over this twenty-year period. The numbers aged 45 and over actually fell, while there was a rise of almost 40 per cent in those aged 25-44, and of 33.5 per cent in those aged under 25. With the resumption of substantial net emigration in the 1980s, the growth rate of the labour force from 1981-86 averaged only 3,000 per annum.

Table 8.7

Average Annual Percentage Growth Rates of the Total Labour Force, EC and US, Various Subperiods, 1970-85

Period	Bel.	Den.	Fr.	Ger.	Gr.	Irl.	It.	Lux.	Neth.	Port.	Spn.	UK	EC12	US
1970-75	0.9	0.9	0.7	0.0	0.0	1.3	0.4	2.3	0.4	0.2	0.7	0.4	0.4	2.2
1975-80	0.7	1.4	0.8	0.2	1.1	1.6	1.3	0.5	1.4	1.6	-0.2	0.6	0.8	2.6
1980-85	0.2	1.3	0.4	0.5	2.3	0.8	0.9	-0.5	1.6	-0.2	1.1	0.6	0.7	1.5

Sources: Eurostat, *Employment and Unemployment 1986,* Luxembourg 1986; and OECD, *Labour Force Statistics 1964-84,* Paris 1986. Figures for Ireland taken from D. Conniffe and K.A. Kennedy (editors), *Employment and Unemployment Policy for Ireland,* ESRI, Dublin 1984; NESC, *Manpower Policy in Ireland* (Report no. 82), Stationery Office, Dublin 1985; and *ESRI Quarterly Economic Commentary.*

Table 8.7 compares the growth rates of the Irish labour force with those of the EC and US for various subperiods since 1970. Only in the US, where the impact of relatively rapid population growth was augmented by an enormous rise in female participation, was the growth rate of the labour force in the 1970s higher than in Ireland. But in the early 1980s, labour force growth in Ireland dropped considerably due to the discouraging employment situation and consequent emigration.

2   EMPLOYMENT AND UNEMPLOYMENT: TREND AND STRUCTURE

After a protracted long-term decline with only brief intermissions, the level of total employment in Ireland stabilized in the 1960s and increased rapidly in the 1970s (Table 8.8). The overall change has been accompanied by changes in the sectoral structure of

Table 8.8

Level and Structure of Employment in Ireland, Selected Years, 1961-86

	1961	1971	1981	1986
	'000			
Agriculture	360	272	196	161
Industry	253	320	363	296
of which Manufacturing	175	211	236	n.a.
Building	58	84	101	n.a.
Mining and Utilities	20	24	27	n.a.
Services	405	457	587	600
of which Public	118	150	237	n.a.
Private	288	304	350	n.a.
Total Employment	1018	1049	1146	1057
	%			
Sector Shares				
Agriculture	34.5	25.9	17.1	15.2
Industry	24.9	30.5	31.7	28.0
Services	39.8	43.6	51.2	56.8
Total Sector Shares	100.0	100.0	100.0	100.0

Sources: as for Table 8.7

employment that are common to most countries in the course of development. Agricultural employment has fallen by 20,000 in the past twenty-five years and its share in total employment has more than halved. Industrial employment grew rapidly in the 1960s but was replaced by services in the 1970s as the main contributor to employment growth. Indeed in the 1980s, as the depression intensified, industrial employment declined in absolute terms and in 1986 was 20 per cent below the 1980 peak. Services employment also grew more slowly in the 1980s and total employment fell to an estimated 1,057,000 in 1986 compared with 1,156,000 in 1980.

While employment grew faster in Ireland in the 1970s than in Europe, this position was reversed in the 1980s. Taking the period 1973-85 as a whole (Table 8.9), Ireland's experience was very similar to the EC as a whole, with total employment at much the same level in both years. In virtually all EC countries the only sector experiencing employment growth in this period was services, and few of the EC countries experienced much overall employment increase. This contrasts sharply with the US situation where total employment rose by 2 per cent per annum on average.

It may be seen from Table 8.8 that of the total net increase in non-agricultural employment of 173,000 between 1971 and 1981, just over half occurred in public services. These include not only civil servants, the gardai and the army, but also teachers, nurses, doctors, etc. in the education and public health services, as well as employees in many non-commercial semi-state bodies, but excluding the commercial semi-state corporations. There has been a tendency to regard this expansion of Irish public sector employment as quite abnormal. In fact, however, one of the most pervasive features of the employment experience of developed countries in the 1960s and 1970s has been the relatively rapid rise in public sector employment — as may be seen from Table 8.10

Table 8.9

Average Annual Percentage Growth Rates of Total
Employment by Sector, EC and US, 1973-85

	Bel.	Den.	Fr.	Ger.	Gr.	Irl.	It.	Lux.	Neth.	UK	EC10	US
Agriculture	-2.5	-1.8	-3.1	-2.7	-1.0	-3.3	-3.4	-4.5	-0.8	-1.3	-2.6	-0.6
Industry	-3.0	-1.3	-1.7	-1.7	0.9	-0.8	-0.7	-1.8	-1.3	-2.5	-1.6	0.5
Services	1.2	1.8	1.7	0.9	2.6	1.9	2.7	2.7	2.0	1.2	1.6	2.7
Total	-0.4	0.6	0.0	-0.4	1.0	0.1	0.6	0.1	0.8	-0.2	0.0	2.0

Sources: Eurostat, *Employment and Unemployment*, Luxembourg 1986; Irish figures as for Table 8.7; US figures from OECD, *Labour Force Statistics 1964-84*, Paris 1986.

which gives average annual growth rates of public and private sector employment for OECD countries for various subperiods from 1960 to 1982. It may be noted that in virtually all countries in nearly all four subperiods, public sector employment grew rapidly and, with the major exception of the US in the 1970s, at a much higher rate than private sector employment. The growth of public sector employment in Ireland was relatively low in the 1960s by international standards, but relatively high in the 1970s. Nevertheless, the share of the public sector in total employment in Ireland is still relatively low.

Table 8.10
Average Annual Percentage Growth Rates of Public Sector and Private Sector Employment, OECD Countries, Various Subperiods, 1960-82

| | 1960-65 | | 1965-70 | | 1970-75 | | 1975-82 | |
	pub.	pri.	pub.	pri.	pub.	pri.	pub.	pri.
Australia	2.6	n.a.	3.5	2.8	3.7	0.8	1.2	1.2
Austria	2.0	-0.4	2.5	-1.2	4.6	0.2	2.5	-0.3
Belgium	2.5	0.7	1.7	0.5	3.0	0.0	2.7	-1.1
Canada	n.a.	n.a.	4.8	1.6	3.9	2.9	1.6	1.9
Denmark	n.a.	n.a.	6.7	-0.5	7.5	-1.2	4.4	-1.1
Finland	4.1	0.3	5.0	-0.4	5.0	-0.2	4.1	-0.8
France	-0.5	0.7	2.2	0.7	2.5	0.0	1.3	-0.1
Germany	4.6	0.1	2.5	-0.5	3.7	-1.2	1.6	-0.4
Greece	n.a.	n.a.	1.3	-0.8	2.7	0.3	3.7	0.5
Ireland	1.8	0.1	3.2	-0.6	5.3	-0.3	4.2	0.4
Italy	2.8	-1.3	2.4	-0.3	3.8	-0.3	1.9	0.3
Japan	2.9	n.a.	1.7	n.a.	3.0	0.4	1.3	1.1
Netherlands	1.0	1.5	1.9	0.7	2.1	-0.5	2.2	-0.5
New Zealand	2.5	2.5	2.4	1.9	2.8	1.9	1.2	0.9
Norway	3.5	0.7	4.2	0.3	4.0	0.1	3.5	0.4
Portugal	2.0	-2.7	7.6	0.1	3.0	-0.9	n.a.	n.a.
Spain	n.a.	n.a.	2.2	0.7	7.3	-0.5	1.6	-2.0
Sweden	4.5	0.2	6.9	-0.5	5.3	-0.4	3.7	-0.8
Switzerland	3.4	2.1	3.9	0.5	3.0	-1.0	1.5	-0.1
UK	-0.1	1.0	2.5	-0.9	3.2	-0.6	0.1	-1.1
US	2.9	1.5	4.0	2.0	1.1	1.2	0.9	2.2
Mean	2.7	0.5	3.3	0.3	3.7	0.1	2.2	0.1

Sources: OECD, *Employment in the Public Sector,* Paris 1982; and OECD, *Economic Studies,* no. 4, Spring 1985. The Irish figures relate to the periods 1961-66, 1966-71, 1971-75 and 1975-81 and are taken from Conniffe and Kennedy, *op. cit.*; and NESC, *Manpower Policy in Ireland, op. cit.* Public sector employment covers public administration and defence, health and education services, and non-commercial semi-state bodies. Private sector employment is measured as total employment less public sector employment.

287

Using a comparable definition of the public sector — somewhat less comprehensive than that used for Ireland in Table 8.8 — the share of public sector employment in total employment in Ireland in 1980 was 14.4 per cent compared with 21.3 per cent in the UK and 16.7 per cent in the US. Among OECD countries, only Greece (5 per cent) Japan (6.5 per cent), Portugal (8.8 per cent), Spain (11.9 per cent) and Switzerland (10.2 per cent) had markedly lower shares. It is true, however, that relative to its level of income per capita, the Irish share is on the high side. Moreover, there is widespread belief in most countries that the rapid rates of growth of public sector employment experienced since the Second World War are not sustainable in the future. Whether or not this belief is translated into practice is likely to depend considerably on the pace of economic growth: with slow growth, rising public sector employment could place a severe strain on taxation.

Unemployment

Despite our familiarity with the phenomenon of unemployment, there are very considerable difficulties both in defining the concept and in applying it to derive empirical measures. The problem essentially arises in trying to draw a clear-cut distinction between three groups in the adult population: the gainfully employed, the unemployed, and the economically inactive. While there are many complexities in defining gainful employment (is a relative assisting part time on a farm, for instance, in gainful employment?), they are much less formidable than those that arise in drawing the boundary between the unemployed and the economically inactive.

Conceptually there is wide international agreement that for purposes of *statistical enumeration* an unemployed person should be defined as one who is without a job, seeking work, and available for work. In economic terms, however, these criteria are far from clear cut, since the wage at which a person is seeking work would generally be relevant. Even for statistical purposes, the application of the criteria is by no means straightforward.[4] Moreover, one would like to add a fourth criterion of capability for work, but that would be open to even wider differences of interpretation. In practice, all measures of unemployment contain arbitrary elements, and the different sources — censuses of population, labour force surveys and the register of applicants for unemployment benefits — all yield somewhat different results, which therefore require to be handled with some caution, particularly in intercountry comparisons.

Notwithstanding these conceptual and measurement difficulties, the data undoubtedly do provide worthwhile indicators of levels and trends. They show that, traditionally, unemployment in Ireland has been high by international standards. As a result of the acceleration in economic growth in the 1960s the unemployment rate fell compared to the 1950s, but never went below about four per cent of the labour force; and despite the exceptionally rapid growth in employment in the 1970s, the unemployment rate rose considerably during that decade. Nevertheless, the more remarkable feature about the 1970s was the fact that, despite the very much higher growth in the labour force, the Irish unemployment rate rose less from 1970 to 1980 than in the EC as a whole (Table 8.11).

This undoubtedly owed much to the more expansionary fiscal policies followed in Ireland. But these policies led to an unsustainable public finance position, and the necessary measures to check government borrowing in conditions of prolonged world depression have contributed to a much more rapid rise in unemployment in Ireland than in Europe or the US since 1980. In the seven years from December 1979 to December 1986, the total registered unemployment has almost trebled from 89,000 to 250,000. The rise has been particularly marked among those aged under 25 years, with the numbers rising almost four-fold from 20,000 to 78,000.

Table 8.11

Percentage Unemployment Rates,[1] EC and US,
Selected Years, 1970-85

Year	Bel.	Den.	Fr.	Ger.	Gr.	Irl.	It.	Lux.	Neth.	Port.	Spn.	UK	EC[2]	US
1970	2.1	1.0	1.3	0.6	n.a.	5.3	4.4	0.0	1.3	n.a	n.a.	2.5	2.0	4.8
1980	9.1	6.7	6.4	3.4	1.1	8.2	7.2	0.7	6.2	6.7	9.9	6.0	6.1	7.0
1985	13.5	8.8	10.3	8.6	2.2	17.7	13.0	1.6	13.4	7.7	19.9	12.3	11.7	7.2

Sources: Eurostat, *Employment and Unemployment*, Luxembourg 1986; and OECD, *Labour Force Statistics 1964-84,* Paris 1986.
[1] Registered unemployed as a percentage of the civilian labour force.
[2] For 1970 the figure relates to EC10 and for 1980 and 1985 to EC12 (i.e. including Portugal and Spain). The 1980 figure for EC10 was 5.7.

Unemployment is not evenly spread across different groups but can vary considerably by age, sex, occupation, industry and region. Young persons tend to experience a higher-than-average rate of unemployment in all countries, due to age-related structural problems (lack of skills and experience) and frictional elements involved in settling into steady employment.[5] In 1979, the unemployment rate among those under 25 in Ireland was 3.5 percentage points higher than for adult workers. This gap, however, was less than in the EC as a whole, so that the youth unemployment rate in Ireland was below the European average. Since then, however, not only has total unemployment risen more in Ireland but the gap between youth unemployment and that of older workers has widened, so that the Irish youth unemployment rate of 25.5 per cent in 1985 was above the EC average of 21.0.

The registered unemployment rate among females has always been considerably lower than for males in Ireland. In this respect, Ireland resembles the UK, but both countries differ from the majority of EC countries where unemployment rates for females are now much higher than for males. Indeed in some European countries, such as Belgium and Denmark, there are, absolutely, more females unemployed than males.

Unemployment is always well above average for unskilled and semi-skilled labourers. Not surprisingly, therefore, the building industry, which has a relatively high concentration of such workers, has a very high unemployment rate. In 1985, for instance, the unemployment rate in the building industry was 25.7 per cent (measured on a labour force survey basis and excluding first job seekers) as against the overall figure of 15 per cent. Regionally in Ireland, the north-west has experienced an unemployment rate well above the average; in 1985 the unemployment rate in the north-west and Donegal was 22.6 per cent (including first job seekers) compared with a national average of 17.4 per cent. The Dublin rate in 1985, at 19.4 per cent, was also above the national average.

Finally, the duration of unemployment is a matter of considerable social concern. The number of persons on the Live Register for over a year rose from 17 per cent in 1971 to 35 per cent in 1980 and 45 per cent in 1986. The latter figure is even more disturbing in view of the fact that during a recession the proportion of long-term registrants normally tends to fall because of the large influx of new unemployed. The most plausible explanation is that in the deteriorating labour market the better educated and more adaptable workers are competing even for lower level jobs, thereby lengthening the duration of unemployment among the more vulnerable groups. There is a danger that this could result in the creation of growing numbers of older unskilled unemployed, who would be difficult to reemploy.

Dependency

Reference was made in Section 1 to the fact that in assessing the economic implications of population change, a key factor is the share of the population that is in some sense dependent. Perhaps the most comprehensive indicator of dependency is the share of the population (P) that is gainfully employed (E). Given that normally the population as a whole must be supported by those at work, the lower is this ratio, the greater is the overall burden of dependency. Table 8.12, which gives data on E/P for the EC countries and the US in 1984, shows that Ireland has an exceptionally low share (31.4 per cent) of its total population in employment. This means that for every person gainfully employed in Ireland in 1981, there were on average two dependents, whereas at the other extreme in Denmark, there was just over one dependent per worker on average. Putting the matter another way, even if average income per *worker* in Ireland were brought up to the Danish level, income per head of *population* would still have been 50 per cent greater in Denmark.

This measure in turn can be decomposed into three other partial measures of dependency that are familiar:

$$E/P = E/L \cdot L/P(A) \cdot P(A)/P$$

where L represents the labour force and P(A) the active age population (15-64). The proportion of the labour force in employment E/L is a measure (in reverse) of the unemployment rate. L/P(A) is a measure of the aggregate labour force participation rate. P(A)/P is an indicator of age dependency: the lower its value the greater the proportion of the population in the inactive age groups.

It may be seen from Table 8.12 that Ireland comes out badly on all three indicators compared with the EC average or the US. The most marked discrepancy in 1984 related to the low proportion of the population in the active age groups. A high degree of age dependency can impose heavy burdens on society — particularly in regard to education for the young and health care for the old.

It should also be noted that an improvement in one of the three component indicators of dependency does not necessarily guarantee that the overall degree of dependency will decline. For example, unless job opportunities increase, a rise in labour force participation among the active age population could simply be associated with a higher unemployment rate rather than an improvement in the employment/population ratio.

Table 8.12
Indicators[1] of Labour Force and Age Dependency, EC and US, 1984

	Bel.	Den.	Fr.	Ger.	Gr.	Irl.	It.	Neth.	UK	EC10	US
E/P	37.2	48.7	39.1	41.4	35.4	31.4	36.9	35.8	42.5	38.2	45.1
E/L	87.0	91.5	90.3	91.8	91.9	84.5	89.8	86.1	88.8	88.8	92.9
L/P(A)	63.5	80.3	66.0	64.7	58.8	62.2	60.0	60.1	72.8	64.5	73.4
P(A)/P	67.3	66.3	65.7	69.7	65.5	59.8	69.2	68.1	65.7	67.0	66.3

Sources: OECD, *Historical Statistics 1960-1984*, Paris 1986.
[1] See text for explanation of the indicators.

Future Population and Labour Force

It has become conventional to make future population projections on the basis of plausible assumptions about the behaviour of the key demographic variables influencing population change. No matter how plausible the assumptions may appear, however, it must be emphasized that some of the variables are highly volatile, and sensitive to economic and social conditions at home and abroad. The particularly critical variables are fertility and external migration, and deviations from the levels assumed can be on such a scale as to cause even the most carefully prepared projections to fall far wide of the mark.

Labour force projections can be derived from the population projections by making assumptions about future participation rates. Here again it must be emphasized that participation rates can vary considerably depending on economic and social conditions. Three population groups are of key significance in this regard. Among the 15-24 year age group, increased educational participation has reduced the numbers in the labour force and this trend is likely to continue, but probably at a reduced rate. At the other end of the age spectrum, trends towards earlier retirement are likely to continue to reduce labour force participation among the older age categories, and may even receive greater impetus from formal schemes of early retirement, voluntary redundancies and extended pension arrangements. The dominant influence in determining future overall labour force participation, however, concerns the participation of women. This will undoubtedly increase, but the rate of increase is likely to be sensitive to labour market conditions.

An indication of the problematic nature of population and labour force projections may be seen by comparing the figures in a recent CSO projection with the actual outcome.[6] In April 1985 this projection, on the basis of differing assumptions about external migration and fertility, put the population increase from 1981 to 1986 in the range of 22,000-27,000 per annum. In the event, when the census figures became available a little over a year later, emigration turned out to be higher than the highest figure assumed, and the actual population increase was 19,000 per annum. The labour force projections were much further from the mark. The projected range was 12,000-16,000 per annum, whereas the actual outturn was 3,000 per annum. The greater divergence in the labour force projections is strongly influenced by the fact that emigration tends to be heavily concentrated in the active age groups. What can be said with assurance is that even with moderate emigration, a very considerable increase in employment would be required in coming years in order to secure a substantial reduction in unemployment. It is in the light of this formidable challenge that the range of policy initiatives that might bring about a reduction in unemployment must be explored in Section 4. Before doing so, however, it will be helpful to discuss in the next section the meaning of full employment as an objective, and the major economic forces that influence the levels of employment and unemployment in the Irish context.

3   OBJECTIVES AND CONSTRAINTS

The Objective of Full Employment
The idea that government intervention was neccessary to secure full employment, and that this should be a major objective of economic policy, gained ground in most Western countries after the Second World War. The intellectual roots of this idea are generally ascribed to Keynes' *General Theory*, published in 1936. Previously, the dominant economic theory denied the possibility of the economy settling at an unemployment equilibrium if market forces were allowed to operate freely. It was recognized, of course, that temporary or frictional unemployment would arise even in the most smoothly operating system due to seasonal variations, labour turnover, etc. It was also recognized that structural factors, such as the decline of major industries concentrated in particular regions, could involve more protracted unemployment. Nevertheless, it was held that high levels of unemployment could endure only because workers, or their unions, were unwilling to allow wages to fall to the market clearing rate. In this perspective unemployment was seen as voluntary, since the expansion of employment was cost constrained due to the attitudes of labour.

Keynes, however, insisted that even if workers were prepared to accept a cut in money wages, this would not necessarily ensure full employment because of a deficiency of aggregate demand. Such 'involuntary' unemployment could only be remedied by government action to redress the demand deficiency. Contemporary critics argued that such action would inevitably be price inflationary, but for long their forebodings were not realized. Most Western governments maintained high levels of demand in the post-war era and succeeded in preserving full employment without unacceptably high levels of price inflation.

New factors intervened in the 1970s, however. The oil price shocks presented a most unpleasant combination: they lowered real income, worsened the balance-of-payments position, and were both demand deflationary and price inflationary. Initially, precedence was given to maintaining employment by countering the demand-deflationary impact. But following the second major oil price increase towards the end of 1979, the governments of the major economies were determined to use fiscal and monetary policy to resist the price-inflationary consequences — even though such action intensified the demand-deflationary impact of the oil price increase. As unemployment continued to rise, the commitment of governments to a full employment objective has waned. This approach has been supported by the reemergence of a school of economic thought which argues, once again, that the economy is fundamentally self-regulating and that government action to secure full employment — apart from measures to free the market — is neither necessary nor particularly desirable.

If high unemployment persists, however, governments cannot indefinitely disclaim responsibility for the level of employment. For one thing, governments in all modern societies must ensure at least a minimum living standard for those in need, and this now constitutes a sizeable burden in respect of the unemployed. Moreover, if a non-interventionist approach to employment is seen to leave large numbers indefinitely unemployed, then it is very likely that an alternative government will come to power on the basis of an interventionist approach. A new feature which manifested itself in the 1970s, however, is the difficulty for even large countries to adopt a go-it-alone policy in regard to expansion of domestic demand. With the considerable freeing of trade in the post-war period, countries have now become much more interdependent. The abortive attempt by the French socialist government in 1981 to stimulate the economy foundered quickly in the face of import leakages and balance-of-payments difficulties (see Chapter 3). Of course, a concerted international reflation of demand would be an entirely different matter, but would require international agreement which has not been forthcoming so far.

There has always been a degree of arbitrariness in specifying what constituted full employment, since some minimal level of unemployment will exist in every labour market due to frictional factors (see Chapter 2). In Ireland a report by the NIEC (National Industrial Economic Council) in 1967 specified two per cent unemployment as constituting full employment.[7] By the mid-1970s this target was looking increasingly unrealistic and a 1975 NESC report adopted a new figure of four per cent unemployment.[8] Two years later, another NESC report suggested that five per cent unemployment would be an appropriate estimate of full employment for Ireland.[9] In recent years, there has been a notable reluctance by the authorities to talk at all of full employment. Instead policy objectives are stated in terms of unspecified reductions in the level of unemployment. While this pragmatic approach is realistic, it does not throw any light on whether full employment remains an ultimate objective of policy and, if so, what level is regarded as constituting full employment. It would appear that the intensity of any society's commitment to full employment depends crucially, if often implicitly, on a judgement about the costs of unemployment relative to the costs of trying to reduce it.

The Costs of Unemployment

Estimating the net cost of unemployment raises complex conceptual and measurement problems. It is usual to approach the problem from three different angles. First, there is the resource cost to the community arising from the loss of the output of the unemployed and from the adverse social effects (e.g. vandalism) that might arise due to unemployment. Second, there is the exchequer cost of paying unemployment compensation and the loss of tax revenue, which together amounted to an estimated IR£1,400 million in Ireland in 1985. This cost, of course, is not additional to the first category, since it involves a transfer from the employed to the unemployed — though some elements of resource cost arise in the collection and disbursement of funds. Third, there is the cost endured by the unemployed individual. Contrary to the view sometimes expressed, empirical studies have shown that the majority of the unemployed incur a severe reduction in disposable income vis-à-vis earnings from their previous employment. As well as financial deprivation, some of those out of work suffer social and psychological problems which are difficult to quantify in money terms.[10]

While estimates of the above costs are instructive, they must be regarded as overstating the costs in the economic usage of that term. They are valid estimates of economic cost only to the extent that unemployment could be eliminated without any cost. Otherwise they have to be qualified by taking account of the costs that would arise in bringing down unemployment. Such costs are extremely difficult to estimate, since they are likely to vary considerably depending on the precise causes of unemployment, an issue about which there is often wide disagreement.

Whatever the causes of unemployment, the remedies are rarely, if ever, entirely costless. Where unemployment is due to demand deficiency, the expansion of demand may give rise to inflationary pressures and/or balance-of-payments difficulties, while the main-tenance of a high level of demand can induce a sluggishness in responding to structural changes. Where unemployment is due to a labour cost constraint, then those at work must be prepared, in the short term at least, to accept pay restraint; and if they are not prepared to do so, there may be no way the authorities can enforce the necessary restraint without infringing democratic liberties. Where unemployment is due to resource constraints affecting the other factors of production (capital, enterprise, infrastructural facilities, etc.), there will inevitably be costs involved in remedying these deficiencies.

The foregoing discussion would point to three broad conclusions in regard to full employment as an objective. First, the inclusion of full employment among the major objectives of economic policy is ultimately a value judgement — though of course one to which many would subscribe, at least in principle. Second, even when full employment is treated as a major objective, it can scarcely be accorded an absolute priority without regard to the costs of achieving it, and the impact of these costs on other objectives of policy. Third, the difficulty or cost of achieving full employment depends not only on the scale, but also on the nature of unemployment, and both can vary over time.

Determinants of Labour Supply and Demand in Ireland
Before considering the range of policy options available for achieving an improvement in the employment outlook, it is essential to specify the major forces influencing the supply of, and demand for, labour in the Irish context. Little more needs to be said about the supply of labour, which is largely determined by the demographic and other forces discussed in Section 1. It is important, however, to reiterate that these forces — and especially external migration and labour force participation — are influenced by the

state of the labour market at home and abroad. The fact that the supply of labour in Ireland is sensitive to the demand for labour means that increases in employment will not be matched by equivalent reductions in unemployment due to the induced increase in labour supply. Thus, success in creating jobs enlarges the number of jobs that are needed, though fortunately not *pro rata*.

The demand for labour is crucially influenced by the volume of output. While increased output does not guarantee higher employment, without it sustained employment growth would necessarily be associated with a continuous contraction in average living standards. It can be argued that some contraction in living standards is essential, but few would argue that this would be acceptable as a continuing process. Consequently, most economists would take the view that increased economic growth is a necessary, though perhaps not a sufficient, condition for the expansion of employment (see Chapter 7).

As was pointed out clearly in Chapter 7, there would also be wide agreement that, because of the small scale of the Irish economy and its dependence on imports, the expansion of output depends in the first instance on the traded goods sectors — agriculture, natural resources, manufacturing and various services such as tourism. Export expansion in these sectors is necessary to pay for imports, whereas expansion in the non-traded sectors of the economy would, if unaccompanied by expansion in traded goods, give rise to balance-of-payments difficulties.

Increased output in the traded goods sector can have a number of beneficial consequences on employment. First, it may expand employment directly in the production of traded goods. Second, even where this is not so, as in agriculture, it can still induce increased employment indirectly by purchases of materials and services from other sectors and by increased consumption out of the higher incomes resulting from productivity growth. Third, it yields more tax revenue which can, if so desired, be used to increase output and employment either in the public sector itself, or in activities performed by the private sector but financed by the exchequer.

The expansion of output in the traded goods sector depends on the state of the world economy and on domestic supply conditions. It is sometimes argued that, since the Irish share of markets abroad is so small, even a depressed world economy need not constrain expansion of Irish sales if the latter were sufficiently competitive. The reality is, however, that when world markets are depressed, other countries do not stand still either, but strive to reduce their costs also. Thus for any given level of competitiveness in Ireland, the performance of exports will in practice be greater the more buoyant are world demand conditions. Moreover, depressed demand conditions abroad inhibit the flow of foreign enterprise investment on which Ireland has depended so heavily for increased exports.

Domestic supply conditions embrace the availability, quality and cost of productive resources and the efficiency with which they are combined — in other words, competitiveness in the widest sense. It is important to emphasize that since the traded goods sector purchases inputs from the non-traded market sector, and that since all sectors have to pay taxes to support the public sector, competitiveness is crucially affected by the efficiency and cost of non-traded, as well as traded, activities (see Chapters 7 and 12). Competitiveness is often spoken of only in the sense of prices and costs, and indeed sometimes only in terms of the price of labour. But while these factors are important, it would be wrong to ignore the non-price aspects (such as management, technology, marketing, etc.), where arguably Ireland may be at an even greater disadvantage.[11] Nor would it be wise to assume that free market forces alone can combat these deficiencies. The Telesis Report[12] took the view that there were substantial barriers facing indigenous industries in a relatively newly-industrializing country like Ireland in access to technology and markets; that foreign firms had not in general developed these functions in Ireland; and that considerable structural changes would need to be effected in indigenous industry to surmount the barriers involved.

The demand for labour is influenced not only by the level of output but also by the composition of output and by the techniques used in its production. The last two factors are in turn influenced by technology and by relative factor prices. Consequently the output-growth/employment-growth relationship is in principle quite variable, and in practice there has been a wide divergence between European and US experience, with the former experiencing much higher productivity growth and low employment growth relative to output growth. However, some doubts must exist about the scope for significantly influencing the relationship in the traded goods sector in Ireland by altering relative factor prices. Considerable potential remains for relatively rapid productivity growth in indigenous enterprises resulting from such factors as the improved allocation of resources, economies of scale and the reduction in the lag in the application of best-practice techniques; mobile foreign firms tend to use standardized technological processes rather than altering techniques in response to local factor price relativities; and Irish wage costs are already at an absolute level which rules out the more labour-intensive products. The scope for encouraging more labour-intensive activities and methods of production may be greater in some non-traded sectors.

Considerable attention has been focussed in recent years in all Western economies on the effect of increased taxation and social welfare benefits on labour supply and demand. Debate on the disincentive effects of unemployment compensation is not new and, rather suspiciously, tends to recur whenever there is high unemployment. The views in the economic literature range from those like Minford,[13] at one extreme, who maintains that the rate of benefit is a major determinant of unemployment, to those at the other extreme, like Atkinson *et al*,[14] whose research failed to identify any robust benefit effect. While obviously it is important to preserve a gap between unemployment benefits and after-tax wages, it should also be borne in mind that as long as buoyant demand for labour existed in Europe up to 1973, quite liberal unemployment compensation did not induce much unemployment.

The effect of taxation on work effort is also an unsettled issue (see also Chapters 2 and 5). On the one hand, a rise in the income tax rate tends to discourage work effort through the substitution effect, in that it makes leisure relatively more attractive. But on the other hand, the reduction in income encourages more work effort to compensate for the loss of income. At the theoretical level, there is no way of saying which effect will prevail. What can be said, however, is that for a given tax take, the higher the marginal rate relative to the average or effective rate, the greater the disincentive involved. The reason is that the income effect is broadly similar, but the substitution effect of the higher marginal rate is greater. At the empirical level, the most significant disincentive to work effort that has been identified relates to the participation of married women, while for other workers the net effect may even be to increase work effort slightly. A more substantial distortion produced by high marginal tax rates may be that they encourage switching of labour supply into the 'black economy' where the tax burden can be evaded.

The effects of taxation on the *demand* for labour may well be more significant. Particular concern has been expressed in recent years about the impact of tax rates on competitiveness — arising particularly from the effect on labour costs both of employers' PRSI (Pay-Related Social Insurance) and pressure for wage increases by workers to compensate for reductions in their real take-home pay due to increased direct and indirect taxes. This could affect the demand for labour in two ways: by reducing output and by encouraging substitution of labour for capital. The evidence suggests that the first of these effects is much the more important of the two.[15] Taxes may also influence the demand for labour by discouraging risk-taking and reducing both the incentive to invest and the resources to finance it. While no one could deny that these effects are important, there has been remarkably little quantification of their magnitude. A crucial aspect, but particularly difficult to measure, is the question of incidence, i.e. who ultimately bears the tax? It would be incorrect to assume, for instance, that all of the employers' PRSI is added to labour costs, since some of it is likely to be shifted back in the form of lower wages,[16] and to that extent it does not damage competitiveness.

4   POLICY OPTIONS

The policy options available for addressing the high, and still rising, level of unemployment in Ireland can now be reviewed. These policy options can be divided into five broad approaches, as follows: increasing the demand for labour; reducing the supply of labour; better matching of demand and supply; redistributing work; and living with unemployment. These approaches are not all mutually exclusive. Moreover, within each approach, there are choices about which particular policy measures might be used. Each approach is now discussed in turn.

Increasing the Demand for Labour

The most attractive means of solving the unemployment problem would be to ensure enough jobs for all. There is wide agreement that a necessary, if not sufficient, condition of achieving a substantial increase in employment is to secure a faster rate of output growth. There is also general agreement that the foundation of any such strategy must be in the traded goods sector. Fiscal expansion financed by borrowing is ruled out, not only because of the present state of the public finances, but also because it would founder in the face of balance-of-payments difficulties.

The chief policies for raising the output of traded goods are incomes policy; development policies for agriculture, industry and traded services to overcome the technological, marketing and other barriers; and measures to increase efficiency in the sheltered sectors, both public and private. Development strategies for the traded goods sectors and policies to raise efficiency in the sheltered sectors have been set out in considerable detail in separate studies by the

ESRI[17], the National Planning Board[18], and the National Economic and Social Council.[19] There is considerable overlap and broad agreement between the three sets of proposals in this regard.

Incomes policy represents an attempt to effect an agreed change in the distribution of factor incomes in a way that is favourable to the expansion of output and employment. Wage and salary rates in *all* sectors eventually affect the competitiveness of the traded sector. Reducing or restraining wage rates tends to enhance profitability, thereby stimulating output and encouraging investment in new or expanded capacity, with beneficial effects on employment. But if workers and their unions are to be persuaded to agree to lower pay increases, they must be offered a convincing trade-off. One possible trade-off would be a reduction in tax rates. This would be attractive to workers since it would obviate, or at least moderate, the need for reducing take-home pay. Given the state of the public finances, however, it could only be achieved to a significant degree in the years immediately ahead by public expenditure cuts additional to those already needed to reduce public borrowing. Insofar as these public expenditure cuts involved reduced public sector employment, the short-term effect would inevitably be a rise, rather than a fall, in unemployment. The reason is that even if it could be shown that the benevolent cycle from tax reductions to pay restraint to profitability to output to jobs, would ultimately generate more new jobs than those lost in the public sector, the cycle would take some time, whereas the public sector employment cuts would be immediate. An incomes policy designed to secure a net overall reduction in unemployment would therefore require a sacrifice not only in factor incomes but also in take-home pay. The trade-off for such pay restraint could be job creation itself. If this were to have any hope of acceptance the government would need to be able to convince workers and their unions that wage restraint would, in practice, translate into increased jobs — whether in the traded sector or elsewhere.

But would increased output of traded goods generate enough jobs to reduce unemployment without further government intervention? The answer to that question is not only important in itself but also in ensuring the acceptance of reasonable pay restraint, one of the pre-conditions of increased output of traded goods. The answer depends first on how rapid the growth of output in traded goods can be. Unfortunately, given the outlook for the world economy, it is difficult to be sanguine about the prospects of very high growth rates. Second, the answer depends on the direct relationship between output growth and employment growth. In

Irish manufacturing, this relationship is strongly affected by changes in the mix of industries. In recent years most of the growth in output has been concentrated in a small number of activities — notably electronics and pharmaceuticals — where direct labour forms only a small share of the value of output. As a result, even though the volume of total manufacturing output grew by over five per cent per annum from 1980 to 1986, employment fell by over three per cent per annum.

Third, the answer depends on how many new jobs would be induced in the other sectors through purchases of materials and services as inputs to traded goods, or through consumer purchases out of higher incomes. A major constraint in this regard is the high import leakage resulting from the small and very open nature of the Irish economy; in this connection, the relatively closed nature of the US and Japanese economies places them in quite a different situation as regards induced effects of output growth. There is the added constraint on induced employment expansion of a good deal of underutilized labour already in some services (e.g. transport), while in others (such as banking and telecommunications) substantial labour-saving technological developments are awaiting application. One way out of these constraints would be to widen the base of the traded goods sector by developing the direct export of services (e.g. education and training) that are not traded much at present.[20]

On the basis of the foregoing analysis, it is hard to be confident that any feasible development strategies would be able to bring about an increase in employment sufficient to match the natural increase in the labour force over the next few years, let alone begin to bring down the level of unemployment. Can the government intervene to create more jobs over and above the direct and induced employment resulting from expansion of the traded goods sector? The ESRI study, mentioned above, argued that not only could it do so, but that it must do so as a condition of maintaining support for the incomes and other policies needed to expand the traded goods sector. The idea would be to use the revenue buoyancy, which would be yielded by the expansion of productivity and incomes in the traded goods sector, to fund the creation of more jobs. The jobs could be in the public sector itself or they could be in building and service activities supplied either by domestic private firms or by local community groups. It was fully recognized, however, that such an approach could not be initiated until the public finances were corrected, and until the development strategies had begun to work.

In practice the public finance imbalances have not been corrected nor has there been any progress towards achieving further growth of output of traded goods. Not surprisingly, therefore, since 1982 efforts have been made to reduce public sector employment. The notion of funding extra employment out of exchequer resources has not been abandoned, however. On the contrary a plethora of state-supported training, work experience and other programmes have been introduced designed to mitigate the worst effects of unemployment.[21] The net effect has been to curb the more expensive forms of public sector employment while trying to provide at least temporary occupation for a greater number of persons at lower rates of pay.

Reducing the Supply of Labour

Increasing the demand for labour, however, is not the only way of reducing unemployment. A more negative approach would be to try to reduce the supply of labour. One option would be to adopt policies to accelerate the fall in the birth rate by, for example, facilitating more extensive and cheaper birth control services. Aside from the controversial moral and political issues involved, this would bring no reduction in the growth of the potential labour force for another 15 years or so. In the meantime, it could have the perverse effect of *increasing* the labour supply of females with fewer home duties.

A second option would be deliberately to encourage emigration. In fact emigration has resumed at an accelerating rate in the 1980s, but it is nevertheless unlikely that any Irish government would adopt emigration as an explicit policy instrument. Such an approach would be widely interpreted as an admission of failure in economic and social management.

A third option would be to attempt to reduce labour force participation. Some methods of doing so which were applied in the past would now be quite unacceptable socially — such as the ban on married women in many public sector occupations. Some other methods which might be socially acceptable (e.g. longer educational participation or early retirement) would be prohibitively costly if their only justification lay in bringing about a reduction in labour supply.

It may be concluded that, while the future labour supply will partially adjust itself to prevailing labour market and other economic and social conditions, the prospects for deliberate policy measures specifically to reduce labour supply are limited.

303

Better Matching of Demand and Supply

While the term 'manpower policy' has many meanings, it is most commonly applied to measures designed to equip workers to respond better to the present and prospective demand for labour. Such measures can help to reduce unemployment in a number of ways. Information and placement services can help to reduce frictional mismatches. Training programmes can alleviate skill bottlenecks. In principle manpower planning can help to direct educational and training policy so as to anticipate future skill requirements, though in practice detailed forecasting of the occupational and technical pattern of demand for labour is hazardous. Finally improvements generally in the quality of labour can raise efficiency and competitiveness, and help to increase the demand for labour.

These measures do not derive their main justification from the existence of high unemployment, since they can be important in improving the functioning of the labour market at any time — even when unemployment is low. Indeed, as long as the overall demand for labour is depressed — whether due to deficient aggregate demand, or cost and resource constraints aside from the quality of labour — they may have only limited effect in reducing unemployment.

In recent years, the concept of manpower policy has been extended to include measures designed to raise the demand for labour — even if only on a temporary basis — especially among groups thought to be particularly disadvantaged. Thus, along with other functions, the Youth Employment Agency finances wage payments to young persons employed in approved community projects. Like regular public sector employment, these and other special employment schemes almost invariably involve a net cost to the exchequer — even taking account of the saving of unemployment benefit and any tax yield from the incomes paid — and this must be financed, sooner or later, out of taxation.[22] The net cost depends crucially on the level of wages paid and the cost of administration. The utility of the facilities and services provided by such schemes is largely a function of how well they are organized and managed.

In general, it is easier to design special employment schemes for the public than for the private sector in such a way that they involve a genuine net increase in employment, rather than merely financing jobs that would have taken place anyway. This 'deadweight' effect can be large in the case of programmes like the Employment

Incentive Scheme, under which an employer who recruits an additional worker of a specified kind can claim a weekly subsidy for a given period. Any firm which would have increased its employment anyway will, therefore, receive a windfall gain; and even in depressed conditions some firms will still be increasing employment. An assessment of this scheme concluded that over 70 per cent of the extra jobs for which the subsidy was paid would have occurred even without the subsidy.[23] There is also the further possible hazard of 'displacement', namely that the extra subsidized job created by one employer may cause the loss of a job for a competing employer.

A proliferation of such schemes, and of special agencies to organize them, can lead to fragmentation of responsibility and interagency friction. Also, because the labour market is continually evolving, there is a danger that specialized agencies may become locked into dealing with one group when the problems have shifted to another group. Thus, for example, as the demographic structure changes over time the priority attached at one time to youth unemployment may need to shift later to older workers. Moreover, within any broad priority area it is important to respond to the most acute needs. For example, an ESRI survey of the transition from school to work showed that in 1982 over 25 per cent of those aged under 25 had left school without any formal qualification, and among those unemployment was 70 per cent higher than the overall average youth rate. Even more disturbing was the finding that the training services were not reaching this segment, since 80 per cent of them were also without training. A major reorganization of the Irish manpower services agencies is at present in train.[24]

Redistributing Work

In principle, unemployment could be eliminated without any increase in the total volume of gainful work, provided the latter were divided up among the total labour force. The idea has a certain intuitive appeal on grounds of equity: if enough employment for all cannot be provided, why not spread it fairly? In practice, matters are more complicated. Nevertheless, several options have been mooted with the objective of redistributing work so as to bring down unemployment.

A key point to note about such proposals as a reduction in the standard working week, or formal work sharing, is that they must generally involve income sharing also. Otherwise, unless the reduction of hours of work in itself raises productivity, the costs of production would rise, with damaging consequences for employment. Historically, rising productivity has accompanied the reduction in the standard week. But the process has been a gradual one and only a small fraction of the increased productivity could be attributed to reduced hours *per se.*

Income sharing is unlikely to prove attractive to the generality of employees, and especially not to heads of households. Those most likely to be interested in work sharing would be members of the secondary labour force, primarily married women and students seeking part-time work. The net outcome of work sharing could be to attract more of these into the labour force, so that the eventual net impact on unemployment could even be negative.

The compulsory reduction or banning of overtime would not necessarily result in a reduction in unemployment either. In fact a reduction in overtime generally takes place anyway in recessions, and helps to maintain the existing workforce in employment. Imposing by law an additional reduction in overtime could raise production costs. It could also generate pressures for higher wages for standard hours in cases where regular overtime has come to be regarded by employees as an integral part of their remuneration. The elimination of double-jobbing would be even more problematic. Apart from the practical difficulty of enforcing such a ban, especially when the job occurs in the 'black economy', the second job might not match the skills and location of the unemployed, so that many such jobs could simply disappear.

The overall conclusion must be that measures to redistribute a given level of employment are unlikely to secure much of a reduction in unemployment. While a number of them — such as a reduced standard week, more flexible access to part-time work, career sabbaticals, etc. — would be desirable in themselves, they are more suited to periods of increasing general prosperity, rather than as a panacea for dealing with an acute unemployment problem.

Living with Unemployment

If — despite the best efforts with the foregoing approaches — unemployment were to continue indefinitely at a very high level, then society would have to reconsider how its attitudes and institutions should change to cope better with a prospect of permanent unemployment. It is unlikely that measures will be taken to substantially improve the financial circumstances of the unemployed because of resource constraints. Efforts to ease the distress caused by unemployment must thus focus on the psychological and social costs involved. Many of the social and psychological problems relating to unemployment stem from the low regard in which those without a job are held, both by themselves and by others. These social costs are much increased by the tendency for unemployment to be highly concentrated by social class and district, with the danger of consolidating an alienated subculture in unemployment ghettos. Work-experience programmes and positive discrimination in job provision could be used to provide a vital link between areas of high unemployment and the 'working' economy.

The question would also arise whether the system of unemployment compensation, which was designed for a lower level and shorter duration of unemployment, would remain suitable for conditions of sustained unemployment. At present those in receipt of unemployment compensation are largely precluded from undertaking gainful employment, so that legally they can only fill in their day in voluntary work or leisure activities. One proposal to change this system radically would be for the state to replace unemployment benefits with the payment to *all* adults, whether at work or not, of a sum equal to, say, unemployment assistance, and leave them free to earn what they wished afterwards by way of taxable income. The idea would have much to recommend it in terms of increasing the flexibility of choice between full-time work, part-time work, voluntary activities, home duties and leisure activities. It would also go some way towards removing the stigma attached to joblessness. But attractive though the idea might be on these grounds, it has to be ruled out as prohibitively costly.

The same holds *a fortiori* for the analogous, but even more far-reaching, proposals of devotees of the leisure society. This perspective is that, because of accelerated technological progress, only a minority of the active age population will need to be engaged in the production of the goods and services that are required to satisfy the basic wants of all. There will therefore be enough resources, so it is argued, for the state to provide all with an adequate income, leaving the majority free to engage in creative leisure activities of their own choice. In effect this is a proposal for income sharing without work sharing! In discussing the work redistribution approach earlier, it was pointed out that the chief barrier to work sharing was resistance to income sharing. If that is correct, then it is certain that there would be even greater resistance to income sharing that did not involve work sharing.

5   CONCLUSION

The discussion of policy options has brought to the forefront a point of fundamental importance about employment, namely its central role in the broader issue of income distribution and redistribution. If the market system can provide enough jobs for all who are willing and able to work, then this will go a long way towards widely distributing the fruits of economic progress. In that case, the state's redistribution activities could be confined to measures for moderating disparities in after-tax incomes, helping those with many dependents and taking care of those who are unable to work.

If, however, the market system, even when given maximum feasible encouragement by the state, still leaves a large and growing minority unemployed, the state is now confronted with a more acute income redistribution problem. There are more people who require help, and less from whom the necessary resources can be drawn. In essence, the state can either go on paying unemployment compensation, or it can create or fund jobs in the provision of useful goods and services that would not otherwise be demanded and supplied — or at least not to the same extent. Either approach imposes a burden on the exchequer, but the burden of the second is likely to be greater — in the short run at any rate. It will therefore have a greater disincentive effect on the demand for labour in the market sector. But unless these disincentive effects are considerably greater than has been established to date, the approach will involve a net increase in employment and in the provision of useful services. This will certainly be the case if a reasonable growth of productivity can be maintained in the market sector, so that the extra jobs can be financed through revenue buoyancy rather than by raising tax rates. It can therefore be regarded as a method of income redistribution which provides a better living standard for those who would otherwise be unemployed, while at the same time enabling them to produce worthwhile services for the community. Whether the community will regard such services as a sufficient compensation for the taxes needed to finance them will depend not only on their view of the value of such services, but also on their commitment to the goal of full employment.

Footnotes

1 For more detailed discussion, see J.J. Sexton and M. Dillon 'Changes in Irish Fertility Patterns over the Period 1961-81', *ESRI Quarterly Economic Commentary*, May 1984.

2 See B.M. Walsh 'Expectations, Information and Human Migration: Specifying an Econometric Model of Irish Migration to Britain', *Journal of Regional Science*, no. 1, 1974 (ESRI Reprint no. 39); and P. Honohan, 'The Evolution of the Rate of Unemployment in Ireland 1962-1983', *ESRI Quarterly Economic Commentary*, May 1984.

3 See, for example, J.I. Simon, *The Economics of Population Growth*, Princeton University Press, Princeton, New Jersey 1977. Simon notes that, by the fifth edition (1817) of his

book, Malthus himself had come to acknowledge the importance of these factors and to adopt a more optimistic view.

4 For further discussion, see CSO, *Report of the Interdepartmental Study Group on Unemployment Statistics,* Stationery Office, Dublin 1979.

5 For further discussion, see K.A. Kennedy, 'Youth Unemployment in Europe', *Social Studies,* Spring/Summer 1986.

6 CSO, *Population and Labour Force Projections,* Stationery Office, Dublin 1985.

7 *Report on Full Employment,* Stationery Office, Dublin 1967.

8 NESC, *Population and Employment Projections 1971-86* (Report no. 5), Stationery Office, Dublin 1975.

9 NESC, *Population and Employment Projections 1986: A Reassessment* (Report no. 35), Stationery Office, Dublin 1977.

10 R. Breen, 'The Costs of Irish Unemployment' (paper delivered to Dublin College of Catering Conference, 'Unemployment: The Challenge to Society', Dublin), July 1986.

11 C. Carroll, *Building Ireland's Business: Perspectives from PIMS,* Irish Management Institute, Dublin 1985.

12 NESC, *A Review of Industrial Policy* (Report no. 64), Stationery Office, Dublin 1982.

13 P. Minford, 'Labour Market Equilibrium in an Open Economy', *Oxford Economic Papers,* November 1983 (supplement).

14 A.B. Atkinson, J. Gomulka, J. Mickleright and N. Rau, 'Unemployment Duration and Incentives: Evidence from the Family Expenditure Survey in the United Kingdom', *Annales de l'Insee,* October/December 1983.

15 J. Bradley and J. FitzGerald, 'Industrial Output and Factor Input Determination in an Econometric Model of a Small Open Economy', *European Economic Review,* 1987 (forthcoming).

16 J.G. Hughes, 'Pay-roll Tax Incidence and the Burden of Direct Taxation in Ireland' (unpublished seminar paper, Economic and Social Research Institute, Dublin), 1984.

17 D. Conniffe and K.A. Kennedy (editors), *Employment and Unemployment Policy for Ireland,* ESRI, Dublin 1984.

18 National Planning Board, *Proposals for Plan 1984-87,* Dublin 1984.

19 NESC, *A Strategy for Development 1986-90* (Report no. 83), Stationery Office, Dublin 1986.

20 K.A. Kennedy, *The Unemployment Crisis* (The 1985 Busteed Memorial Lecture), University Press, Cork 1985.

21 See NESC, *Manpower Policy in Ireland* (Report no. 82), Stationery Office, Dublin 1985, Chapter VIII.

22 The burden on the Irish taxpayer, however, may be relieved to the extent that the exchequer in turn receives a subsidy from the EC for such schemes.

23 See T. O'Mahony, 'An Evaluation of the Employment Incentive Scheme' (unpublished Department of Finance study, cited in NESC, *Manpower Policy in Ireland, op. cit.*).

24 See *White Paper on Manpower Policy,* Stationery Office, Dublin 1986.

9 International Trade, Balance of Payments and Inflation

Dermot McAleese

IN CHAPTER 3, the balance of payments and inflation were considered in a general context and the reasons for assigning them the status of secondary policy objectives were explained. This chapter looks at these matters in a specifically Irish context. How successful has the Irish economy been in maintaining balance-of-payments equilibrium and in restraining inflation? What policy instruments have been used? What policy instruments are available for use by an economy of Ireland's size? To what extent do events in the world economy and institutional commitments arising from European Community membership constrain the range of policy options for addressing economic problems? These and other questions are considered in this chapter.

The opening section deals with trade and balance of payments. The pattern of Irish trade is analyzed under four headings: the level of trade (trade dependence); the commodity compositon of trade; the geographical distribution of Irish exports and imports; and the terms of trade.

The Irish balance of payments is then discussed. The components of the balance-of-payments statements are described and the automatic adjustment mechanisms are sketched. Because of the high import content of domestic output and aggregate demand in a small open economy, these automatic mechanisms are more powerful in Ireland's case than in those of larger countries. In most circumstances, however, they will need to be supplemented by deliberate policy measures. Deflation, trade intervention (tariffs, non-tariff barriers, export subsidies), devaluation and competitiveness are the four main methods of rectifying a balance-of-payments deficit. The arguments for and against each approach are examined. The effects of European integration on the foreign trade and payments policy of the Irish economy is next assessed.

This involves discussion of the new trade regime implied by membership of the European Community and the economic consequences of participation in the European Monetary System (EMS). The Single European Act envisages even closer integration between Ireland and the Community between now and 1992.

The final section begins with an outline of three features of inflation in Ireland: the high inflation rate prevailing in the last decade, the close tie between Irish and British inflation rates up to 1980 and the sharp fall in inflation since 1985. Much of this experience can be explained by factors which are external to the economy, notably by Ireland's adherence to the sterling link and since 1979 to 'stability within the EMS'. But, without accounting for the reasons underlying the choice of a particular exchange rate regime and reluctance to change it, as occasion demands, the 'imported inflation' model could be accused of explaining away rather than explaining the causes of Irish inflation. Attention therefore is directed to the economic rationale of exchange rate policy. The role of domestic inflationary pressures and responses to inflation by government and the trade unions also receive consideration.

1   INTERNATIONAL TRADE

Like most small economies, the Irish economy is heavily dependent on foreign trade. In 1986, imports of goods and services amounted to 52 per cent of GDP, compared with an EC average of 27 per cent; the corresponding figures for exports of goods and services were 57 per cent and 30 per cent (Table 9.1). The trade ratios for Belgium and Luxembourg are higher, while the larger countries of the Community record considerably smaller ratios. Trade ratios in most EC countries have been increasing rapidly during the last two decades. The Irish economy also has become more open, reflecting an accentuated level of specialization in the industrial and agricultural sectors. This openness makes it possible to reap the gains from international exchange; it also means greater sensitivity to world economic fluctuations, less autonomy in the formulation of domestic economic policy and a growing interdependence with the outside world (see Chapter 7).

The world trade environment in the 1960s was particularly conducive to growth. Industrialized countries' trade in goods (merchandise trade) expanded by an annual average of 9.0 per cent,

Table 9.1

Comparative Figures of Trade Dependence

	Percentage ratio imports (goods and services) to GDP		Percentage ratio exports (goods and services) to GDP	
	1960	1986	1960	1986
Belgium	39	69	38	73
Denmark	33	32	32	34
France	13	22	15	23
Germany	16	26	19	30
Greece	17	29	9	20
Ireland	37	52	32	57
Italy	14	24	14	25
Luxembourg	74	83	87	89
Netherlands	46	53	48	58
Portugal	24	37	17	36
Spain	7	16	10	21
UK	22	26	21	27
EC12	19	27	20	30

Sources: Commission of the European Communities, *European Economy: Annual Review 1986-87,* Brussels 1986.

a rate just slightly above the figure for Irish trade. A marked slowing down of 'tempo' of expansion occurred during the 1970s as the industrial world struggled to contain inflation, cope with the oil price increases and address the problem of growing domestic unemployment. Ireland was one of the few industrialized countries which managed to maintain the growth of exports at the rate achieved in the 1960s. An annual growth rate of 8.2 per cent was recorded between 1961 and 1970 as compared with 8.0 per cent between 1971 and 1980.

The increase in merchandise trade volume owed much to the expansion of manufactured exports. Starting from a very small base in the early 1950s, they grew to absorb 18 per cent of total exports in 1961 and 65 per cent in 1986 (see Table 9.2). What is remarkable is the sustained pace of expansion over a long period of time. During these thirty years Ireland shed its historical dependence on primary products exports. Nowadays, live animals and food account for only one-quarter of total merchandise exports.

A similar but less pronounced pattern of change is observed in merchandise imports. Manufactured goods accounted for 72 per cent of total imports in 1986 compared with 54 per cent two decades

Table 9.2

Percentage Composition of Merchandise Trade by Commodity Group, 1961 and 1986

	Exports			Imports		
	1961	1986	Value 1986 £m	1961	1986	Value 1986 £m
Live animals and food	61	23	2,194.4	16	11	982.7
Beverages and tobacco	4	2	228.3	3	1	96.7
Raw materials, fuels and oil	9	6	491.1	19	12	1,025.4
Manufactured goods	18	65	6,105.0	54	72	6,252.4
Other	8	4	369.4	8	4	272.5
Total	100	100	9,388.2	100	100	8,629.7

Sources: CSO, *Trade Statistics of Ireland*, Stationery Office, Dublin, various issues.

ago. Primary product imports have declined in relative importance. The rapid growth of imports of manufactures is, of course, related to the growth of manufactured exports. To appreciate this, consider the type of firm which produces these exports — for example, IDA-sponsored overseas enterprises specializing in the final or intermediate processing of manufactured products. To produce their output, these firms require imported machinery, components and intermediate goods of all types. On average they import 36 per cent of the current value of their output. So more exports automatically draw in more imports (see Chapter 11).

An important implication of this higher import propensity is that the net balance-of-payments contribution of a given value of industrial exports is substantially below that of agricultural or services exports (see Chapter 7). For example, manufactured exports contributed 38 per cent of the total increase in exports which occurred between the years 1961 and 1973. Agricultural exports contributed 33 per cent and services (tourism, transport, etc.) 27 per cent. If allowance is made for the import content of these categories, manufactures' contribution falls to 30 per cent, while the corresponding figures for agriculture rises to 42 per cent.[1] The distinction between gross and net exports is worth making, if only to draw attention to the important role played by the less spectacular expansion of food exports and tourism in this critical period of Irish economic history.

Merchandise imports can be classified by main use as well as by commodity. In 1986, capital goods accounted for 14 per cent of total imports, materials for further production for 59 per cent, and consumer goods for the remaining 27 per cent. Some may be surprised at the small share of imported consumer goods — these are the goods most people have in mind when they think of imports. During the last decade, the proportion of consumer goods in the total import bill varied by no more than a few percentage points around its present level.

Table 9.3
Percentage Composition of Merchandise Trade by Geographical Area, 1960 and 1986

Area	Exports		Imports	
	1960	1986	1960	1986
UK	75	34	49	41
Rest of EC	7	38	15	26
Others	18	28	36	33
Total	100	100	100	100

Sources: as for Table 9.2.

At the time of Independence, most Irish merchandise trade was with the UK, making the economy heavily dependent on the fortunes of the British economy. The situation has now changed dramatically (Table 9.3). The UK is still the largest customer, but its share of Irish merchandise exports has fallen from 75 per cent in 1960 to 34 per cent in 1986. The movement away from the UK market has been replaced by a movement towards Continental European markets. Over one-third of Irish exports are sold on these markets and one-quarter of imports originate there. (The member states of the EC, excluding the UK, are the only group of countries with which Ireland runs a trade surplus.) In common with experience in most European countries, a substantial incursion into the Irish market has been made by Japanese goods. The Japan-EC trade imbalance is a matter of some concern to the European Community, although less so to Ireland since the Japanese import boom has largely been at the expense of other importers rather than Irish producers (motor cars, sound recording equipment, etc.).

The diversification of merchandise export markets can be attributed to four factors: the relatively slow growth of the UK economy during the last few decades; the influx of overseas manufacturing enterprises with worldwide and European-orientated market strategies (Irish-owned manufacturing firms still rely heavily on the British market); the opening of the Continental market for Irish agricultural produce as a result of EC membership; and the development of new export markets in the Middle East and in LDCs for food products and other goods. OPEC countries absorbed five per cent of total Irish exports in 1982. Nigeria, Libya, Mexico, Saudi Arabia, Iraq, and Egypt scarcely figured in the export statistics a few years ago but are now important customers for Irish products. The more diversified market structure for Irish merchandise trade is welcome from an economic viewpoint in that it protects the country from the effects of a recession in one particular market. However, since the economy is, more than ever, dependent on foreign markets, the diversification of trade has altered the form rather than the degree of economic dependence.

The commodity terms of trade is an important concept for a small trading economy (see Chapter 7). It represents the ratio of changes in export prices to changes in import prices. If import prices rise and export prices stay constant, the terms of trade will deteriorate; if export prices rise faster than import prices the terms of trade will improve. As Table 9.4 shows, Ireland's terms of trade have shifted markedly over time. In the period 1968-73 the terms of trade improved because of the boom in agricultural prices. A drastic 18 per cent deterioration was recorded in 1974 because of the oil price rise. As shown in Chapter 7, the decline in Ireland's terms of trade from its high point in 1973 offset much of the value of increased GNP during the 1970s.[2] That is, more was being produced, but the purchasing power of this output in terms of imports had diminished. Between 1981 and 1986, the terms of trade improved from 98.1 to 108.7 as a result of the fall in oil prices, weak world commodity prices and the decline in the value of the US dollar relative to the Irish pound. Over the last two decades as a whole, the terms of trade has not changed systematically from its level in the early 1960s.

Table 9.4
Terms of Trade (Goods and Services): 1968-86 (1980 = 100)

	1968	1973	1974	1978	1981	1986
Ireland	110.8	127.2	108.4	110.5	98.1	108.7

Sources: as for Table 9.1.

Trade in services was, until recently, a neglected aspect of international exchange. Yet services are an important component of world trade — amounting to 25 per cent according to some estimates — and parts of it are growing rapidly. Exports of Irish services are equivalent to approximately one-fifth of Irish merchandise exports. Unfortunately, trade in these 'invisibles' is much more difficult to identify than merchandise trade, which may explain the greater attention afforded to the latter. Tourism and travel is the largest services item recorded in the balance-of-payments statement, coming after trading and investment income. The latter includes interest paid on foreign debt and interest earned on official reserves as well as dividends and interest received on private capital held abroad by Irish residents and earned by foreign residents with capital in Ireland.

Over the years, a growing contribution to Irish export activity has been made by firms engaged in construction-related activities and by consultancy organizations in the public and private sectors. Estimates by Córas Tráchtála (CTT) suggest a value for these exports of IR£139m in 1983.[3] Irish building contractors have been working in African and Middle Eastern countries. Typical assignments in this sector have included a radar tracking station in Nigeria, office buildings in Zimbabwe and prefabricated housing for airline staff in Bahrain. A number of major Irish contractors have become so involved as to have achieved multinational status. Medical and other consultancy services have also contributed to trade in services. Public sector enterprises such as Aer Lingus, ESB, CTT and IDA have been active in this field. For example, approximately 800 Aer Lingus staff in Ireland are engaged in the maintenance of other countries' aircraft. Guinness Peat Aviation is an example of a private sector Irish success in the international aircraft business. The net foreign exchange flows arising from these types of export activity are as yet small in aggregate, but they are becoming increasingly important.

2   BALANCE OF PAYMENTS: POSITION AND POLICY

Ireland's balance of payments has been the subject of much change and controversy in recent years. The major change has been the emergence, for the first time in decades, of a significant surplus in merchandise trade. The extent of this change is evident from the figures of Table 9.5 which show the 1981 deficit of IR£1,698m being transformed into an estimated surplus of IR£617m by 1986. Equally remarkable has been the huge increase in the deficit on trading and investment income. The main reason for this is the large increase in interest payments due on the foreign debt (see Chapter 4). The other major factor is the large outflow of profits and interest payments from foreign manufacturing firms in Ireland. There is nothing inherently undesirable, of course, about such outflows — it is to be expected that overseas subsidiaries should earn profits and wish to repatriate them. The large surplus on international transfers is also of recent origin and primarily arises from Ireland's membership of the European Community (see Chapter 7 and later in this chapter).

Table 9.5
Balance of International Payments, (IR£m) 1979-86

	1979	1981	1986
Merchandise	-1,365	-1,698	617
Services	66	84	66
Trading and investment income	-283	-505	-1,968
International transfers	556	524	1,095
Balance on current account	-1,026	-1,595	-190
(as % of GNP)	(13.9)	(15.3)	(1.2)
Private capital	304	277	67
Official capital	374	1,197	1,147
Banking transactions	139	12	440
Official external reserves[1] (transactions)	286	-9	49
Net balance on capital account	1,102	1,478	1,703
Net residual[2]	-76	117	-1,513

Sources: CSO, *Revisions to the Balance of International Payments and National Accounts,* Stationery Office, Dublin, May 1984; and *Central Bank of Ireland Quarterly Bulletin,* Winter 1986.
[1] An increase (decrease) in reserves represents an outflow (inflow) in the balance of payments statement. Reserve changes include a transactions component and a valuation component.
[2] This is the balancing amount, credit or debit as appropriate, which must be included to ensure an accounting equivalence between the total of all credit entries and the total of all debit entries, i.e. this balance plus the balance on current account plus the balance on capital account must by definition sum to zero. A sum of IR£18m representing a valuation change in the reserves must be added to IR£1,513m to complete the balancing statement.

It is worth emphasizing, perhaps, that Table 9.5 looks only at *net* flows. In terms of *gross* flows, merchandise trade is still the largest component by far. For example, merchandise exports in 1986 were valued at IR£9,386m, well in excess of the gross value of tourism earnings or transfers.

That the balance of payments must always balance is a truism. The difficulty lies in identifying its separate components. The distinction between autonomous transactions, which occur independently of the overall condition of the balance of payments, and *accommodating transactions*, which react passively to it, has been made in Chapter 3. The strength of this approach is its recognition

317

of the organic link between capital and current transactions. For example, suppose Aer Lingus were to decide to purchase an aircraft for IR£100m, credit being supplied by the vendor. Imports would rise by IR£100m and the contra entry would be IR£100m capital inflow. It would be wrong to infer that a current account deficit 'forced' the country to borrow IR£100 abroad: causality could have gone the other way. The two variables are clearly interdependent. The main problem lies in classifying transactions into accomodating and autonomous categories. There is, for example, the difficulty of distinguishing a long-term loan from a short-term capital flow (the rule-of-thumb definition of long-term as investment in bonds of more than one year's maturity is clearly unsatisfactory). Suppose the government borrows long in order to bolster reserves and stave off balance-of-payments adjustment; should this be classified as accommodating or autonomous? Further examples of transactions which create problems of interpretation can easily be imagined.

The appearance of a huge residual item in the balance-of-payments statement has led to much controversy. The residual is the balance left over after all known items in the balance of payments have been quantified. By definition, it equals the amounts which the CSO has been unable to identify. When these amounts are small and likely to change sign from year to year nobody worries too much. However, when they grow in size, there is an understandable uneasiness and pressure builds up to improve statistical procedures. The famous 'black hole' controversy of 1984 led to a substantial revision of balance-of-payments statistics and to a more thorough identification of the outflow of repatriated profits and services payments of overseas subsidiaries. Despite these revisions, however, the residual still looms very large, reaching over IR£1,500m in 1986.

What caused this dramatic increase in the residual? We do not know for certain but three factors are likely to be important. First, *leads and lags*. If the Irish pound is expected to devalue, Irish exporters delay receipt of foreign currency payments and Irish importers try to speed up the process of payment. Given a total value of external trade of IR£18 billion, it is easy to see how quantitatively important these perfectly legal but difficult-to-identify delays can be. Second, *capital outflow outside the net of exchange controls* arising from lack of confidence in the Irish economy. Given the openness of the economy, there are an infinite number of leakages through which capital could leave the country. Third, *cross-border transactions*. Although the CSO makes allowances for these, they may not be making enough provision for the huge volume of transactions as shoppers from the Republic head North in search of bargains. Thus, the residual can arise because of incomplete coverage of current as well as capital transactions.

Whatever the precise cause of the residual, it is clear that not all is well with Ireland's balance-of-payments position. Certainly there has been an improvement in the current account deficit, represented by a fall in the deficit/GNP ratio from 15 per cent in 1981 to 1 per cent in 1986. This improvement has been brought about by the fall in import prices, the decline in investment (particularly large public sector projects such as Moneypoint, DART, Bord Telecom re-equipment etc.) and the sluggish demand for consumer durables such as motor cars. But the fall in the deficit may be exaggerated and some part of the residual may refer to underestimated current payments. An even more important aspect is the outflow of capital. 'Black hole' is rather a sensational way of describing this outflow. The capital is not lost to the country. It accrues in the accounts of Irish people abroad, earns money for them and, given the right circumstances, it could return and be put to productive use. For this to happen, however, the investment and general competitive climate in the Irish economy has to be favourable.

Consideration of the balance-of-payments statement naturally leads on to a discussion of balance-of-payments *adjustment mechanism.* This refers to the processes whereby *ex ante* imbalances between the supply and demand for external funds are brought into *ex post* equilibrium. Starting from a position of initial current account balance, consider the effects of, say, a fall in the value of manufactured exports caused by an exogenous shift in foreign demand. Two factors are immediately set into operation which tend to reduce the deficit thereby created. First, the import content of exports in small open economies like Ireland's tends to be very high (as much as 50 per cent of the value of manufactured goods sales). So the fall in demand for exports automatically creates a decrease in the demand for imports required as inputs for their production. Second, the fall in aggregate demand generated by the decline in export demand (i.e. exports minus imported inputs) percolates through the economy. The amount of income affected in this way hinges crucially on the value of the foreign trade multiplier, i.e. on the marginal propensity to import, the marginal savings propensity and the marginal tax rate. The higher the marginal propensity to import, the greater is the extent to which a fall in demand will be translated into a decrease in imports. In Ireland, the marginal propensity to import may be as high as 0.7. This explains the basic strength of the automatic adjustment process in small open economies in response to changes in aggregate expenditure. Note, however, that the adjustment mechanism is still only a partial one. The initial deficit is greatly reduced but not eliminated. Consequently, other mechanisms must come into play in order to restore equilibrium.

At this stage, capital account transactions can be introduced into the analysis. The net deficit will appear in the form of a decline in deposits held in domestic banks. The balance-of-payments deficit in other words reduces the domestic money supply and, at constant prices, the value of real balances. If it is accepted that households maintain a given relation between their cash balances and levels of expenditure, further changes in income and imports must occur in order to preserve monetary equilibrium.

There are a number of ways in which this adjustment could occur. Reduced cash balances could be viewed as causing a fall in consumption which directly reduces import demand. Alternatively, these balances may be replenished by sales of bonds, in which case bond prices tend to fall, interest rates rise and a fall in investment demand may occur, leading again to lower imports. Financial intermediaries can also be introduced into the analysis. The adjustment process might be viewed as leading from reduced reserves in the banking system, to increases in the interest rate on overdrafts, to reduced borrowing for investment and/or consumption. The decrease in aggregate demand, by whatever process it comes about, must continue until full equilibrium can be restored.

The automatic adjustment mechanism described above stresses the link between the net deficit on current account, the deterioration in liquidity position of individuals and/or domestic banks, and the translation of the latter into a reduced level of advances and, eventually, lower aggregate demand. While relatively simple in theory, in practice the process may take a long time to work through the system. If private capital is internationally mobile, it may be that a very small increase in domestic interest rates will attract net private capital inflows which offset the current account deficit and temporarily ease the liquidity constraint. However, it is unlikely that private capital will continue to flow into the country indefinitely unless corrective action is taken to deal with the underlying balance-of-payments problem. Official policy could also encroach upon the automatic adjustment mechanism by 'sterilizing' the monetary effects of balance-of-payments disequilibrium. For example, the Central Bank might offset the liquidity-reducing effects of the deficit by short-term measures designed to increase domestic liquidity.

Alternatively, the government might borrow abroad in order to restore the liquidity loss without detriment to the level of gross official reserves. But since reserves are not finite and a sustained deterioration in the *net* reserves position (gross official reserves less public foreign debt) would not be acceptable to the Central Bank, eventually some action would have to be taken to restore balance-of-payments equilibrium.

The argument so far can be summarized as follows. A strong automatic adjustment mechanism is at work in a small open economy. Changes in the demand for exports, for example, can quickly translate into changes in the demand for imports. In the short run the adjustment will tend to be incomplete and the process of adjustment may be delayed by *ad hoc* government interventions. In a *laissez-faire* world, eventually the automatic adjustment process would be complete. The way in which adjustment is effected, however, may be costly in terms of employment and growth. The basic aim of balance-of-payments policy is to ensure that the process of adjustment is carried through with the minimum loss in terms of output and efficiency. Rather than waiting for reserves to run out and for foreign borrowing capacity to be exhausted, the objective is to head off such difficulties by appropriately designed policies. This gives economic 'actors' an opportunity to make structural changes in good time before crisis point is reached.

The need for balance-of-payments policies can perhaps best be illustrated by considering what happens in their absence. Suppose, as has happened in some LDCs (Ghana, for example), a government permits the country to reach a stage where reserves and borrowing capacity are depleted. In such circumstances, the country does not go bankrupt — there is no mechanism by which a sovereign state can be wound up and its assets disposed of as would happen in the case of an individual firm. What happens is that the country will find it progressively more difficult to secure essential imports. Firms supplying imports will demand payment in advance — and where is the foreign exchange to come from? The result will be shortages of spare parts, factories unable to operate because of delays in obtaining raw materials and components, breakdown in transport due to shortage of petrol etc. Cumulatively, these effects are seriously damaging to growth. Corrective action taken earlier could have avoided many of these losses.

Balance-of-payments policy therefore aims at maintaining a current account deficit at a sustainable level or, what amounts to the same thing, a sustainable long-run *basic* balance of zero. What policy instruments are available to the government to achieve this objective? One method is through expenditure-reducing policy, another through expenditure-switching policy. The former policy amounts in effect to deflation. Reductions in the real level of economic activity (below the trend growth, not necessarily in absolute terms) bring about a decrease in the level of import demand. Because of Ireland's high propensity to import, it is argued that this policy could be highly effective in restoring balance-of-payments equilibrium. It would not, however, be the most efficient method. Balance-of-payments equilibrium is a secondary, not a primary policy objective, and, as was seen in an earlier chapter, the Irish economy has manpower and capital resources which are underemployed. In these circumstances what is needed is more output directed towards exports and import-competing activities, not less output. Expenditure-switching policy is appropriate, not expenditure reduction. This means finding ways of improving export performance and curbing imports through commercial policy, exchange rate changes and competitiveness.

Commercial policy comprises price and non-price measures designed to restrict imports and stimulate exports, e.g. tariffs, quotas, export subsidies. Since discrimination against trade with member countries is explicitly ruled out by the Treaty of Rome and extra-EC trade is governed by the Common Commercial Policy, the Irish government has little independent discretion in this matter. Even if it had, commercial restrictions would not be an appropriate policy for rectifying the balance of payments. True, it can and has been resorted to in extreme circumstances for this end by other countries (for example, the UK import deposit scheme in 1966 and the short-lived 10 per cent import surcharge imposed by the US in 1971). Such restrictions, however, run the risk of inviting retaliation, encourage inefficient industries, discriminate against exports and, whatever their short-run effectiveness, tend to have little effect on the long-run balance of payments. These various aspects of protection are well documented in the case of Ireland (see Chapter 1).

Devaluation, or a depreciation of the exchange rate, makes exports more attractive to purchase. Thus, when the Irish pound declined in value from parity with sterling to 75 pence sterling, UK imports became dearer in terms of Irish pounds, and Irish exports cheaper in terms of sterling. Devaluation is not discriminatory between different types of imports, nor does it create a bias against exports. For these reasons, economists consider it a superior policy to protection as a method of improving the balance of payments. Although sharp exchange rate fluctuations have been a feature of the world monetary system in the 1970s, reservations have been expressed about the effectiveness of devaluation in the Irish context. For one thing, a devaluation raises exporters' costs by raising the price of imported inputs, an effect which tends to be more pronounced in a small trade-dependent country. Devaluation tends to be inflationary both in terms of its strong initial impact-effect on prices and the consequential increase in nominal wages which might be sparked off through indexing clauses and cost-of-living adjustments. Ireland's low price elasticities of demand for imports and the uncertain price responsiveness of the export sector leads to the conclusion that a large percentage devaluation would be required in order to achieve a modest proportionate improvement in the balance of payments. In discussing price elasticity, care must be taken to distinguish short-run from long-run effects. In the short run, devaluation may worsen the deficit. This is attributable in part to the celebrated 'J-curve' effect which occurs because of a low short-run elasticity of demand for imports and in part to the initial gap between exports. Only in the medium to longer term do the favourable competitive effects (assuming no compensatory income claims) come into play. At the same time, experience shows that compensatory income claims often *are* exacted. The Central Bank model of the Irish economy, for example, indicates that any competitive advantage secured by devaluation has tended to be substantially eroded within a year.[4]

There is none the less no shortage of instances of small country devaluations. Sometimes, such devaluations are forced upon the country by capital speculation. In other instances, maintenance of institutional links implied a devaluation, such as the sterling link and the EMS in the case of the Irish pound. Devaluations can also occur in order to protect a country against competitive disadvantages arising as a result of devaluation in the currency of that country's trading partners. The action is prompted by the asymmetry which exists between the effects of devaluation and revaluation in a small economy. An Irish pound devaluation, for example, will feed back into the Irish domestic price level very quickly. But an Irish pound revaluation will have much slower feedback effects on domestic prices. Price expectations are sticky downwards. Although eventually price expectations would change and adjustment would occur, the loss in competitiveness in the traded sector in the intervening period may have done irreparable damage. Finally, some small countries have devalued in order to improve their competitive position, backing up their action with specific policies designed to suppress compensatory income claims and to stimulate maximum supply responsiveness in export- and import-competing industries. Exchange rate policy has, therefore, a significant role to play in balance-of-payments adjustment. It can play an effective positive role provided it is backed up by appropriate incomes and fiscal policies. Smooth and prompt adjustment of exchange rates is an essential element in the prevention of balance-of-payments disequilibrium.

Improved domestic competitiveness is a third major policy option.[5] Competitiveness must be defined in a broad sense to include price and non-price factors such as product quality, reliability of supply and back-up marketing services. Raising a nation's competitiveness must involve incomes restraint but it can take many other forms as well. Improvements in infrastructure, correcting bottlenecks in the supply of skilled labour, establishing an orderly industrial relations system, all have the effect of cutting down production costs and raising the competitiveness of export- and import-competing industries. A country's long-run competitive position can also be profoundly influenced by its policy towards research and development and its success in product innovation and technology, as Japanese success testifies. In the short run, however, incomes restraint is the vital factor, for it brings with it all the advantages of devaluation without any of its inflationary disadvantages. Competitiveness will be a vitally important objective for any Irish government in the next few years.

3   INTEGRATION WITH THE EUROPEAN ECONOMY[6]

Paralleling Ireland's move from home-market-oriented to export-oriented policies during the 1960s were a series of commitments to international institutions. Ireland joined the IMF and World Bank in 1957, applied for EC membership in 1961, became a member of GATT in 1967, and entered the EC in 1973. Of these steps, the last one was the most significant. The European Community brought with it more far-reaching obligations and opportunities than any previous economic arrangement since Independence.

Theoretical analyses of customs unions frequently proceed in terms of trade creation and trade diversion, the former referring to the creation of trade arising from substitution of Community for domestic sources of production and the latter representing the diversion of supplies from cheaper extra-Community sources to dearer member sources. Such analyses have little relevance to Irish membership of the EC. The pattern of trade precluded the possibility of much significant trade diversion and only a limited amount of trade creation was to be expected following free access to Continental European markets (the main impact of free trade had already been felt as a result of the Anglo-Irish Free Trade Area). Much more important were the dynamic gains from integration for industry (enhanced attractiveness of Ireland as a location for overseas manufacturing investors, further possibilities of specialization for existing firms) and the long-term price gains expected in agriculture (see Chapter 10).

An important consequence of EC membership is that intra-Community trade cannot be impeded without reference to the Commission in Brussels. The conduct of this trade is governed by the Community's policies, such as competition policy and the CAP, and it is in this context that allegations of dumping, implicit export subsidies or other unfair trading practices have to be investigated. The government's control over trade with countries outside the Community is similarly circumscribed. Extra-EC trade falls within the ambit of the Common Commercial Policy, the objective of which, in the words of the Rome Treaty, is 'to contribute to the harmonious development of world trade'. Since 1973, Ireland has, through the Community, participated in numerous multilateral and bilateral agreements: the GATT Tokyo Round, the Generalized System of Preferences, the Multifibre arrangement, the Lomé agreements and the trade arrangement with China. Negotiations for a new multilateral trade round are scheduled to begin in 1987 and the Community will be a major participant. The negotiations will cover trade in services and agricultural trade, as well as addressing problems posed by non-tariff barriers.

The trend towards world trade liberalization, confident in the 1960s, proceeded unsteadily in the 1970s, and hangs in the balance in the current decade. Although Irish trade with extra-EC is only one-third of total trade, and trade with LDCs is a much smaller proportion still (8 per cent), the tariff reductions arranged under the Common Commerical Policy have a significant bearing on Ireland's welfare, both indirectly, through displacement effects in export markets, and directly, through displacement on the Irish market. By way of illustration, it has been shown that a balanced expansion of IR£1m (1976 prices) in the value of manufactured trade with LDCs would create 58 jobs in export activities, but displace 97 in import-competing activities, implying a net employment loss of 39 jobs.[7] Comparison of similar employment coefficients for other EC countries indicates that the burden of adjustment to freer trade with the LDCs would fall disproportionately on the Irish economy. This does not imply that Ireland should oppose such liberalization. It suggests only that the evolution of the Community's trade policy is not a matter of indifference.

Formal integration into the European economy was strengthened by Ireland's participation in the European Monetary System (EMS).[8] The EMS came into existence in January 1979. Each member of the system has a fixed 'central exchange rate' against the new European Currency Unit (ECU). For each country there is a percentage divergence indicator which determines upper and lower intervention limits at which central banks must support the currency (2.25 per cent, but 6 per cent for the lira). Thus all member currencies are pegged to the ECU, which in turn is a weighted average of the member currencies. The logic of the system is that balance-of-payments adjustment should rely on internal measures — such as 'competitiveness' as described above and expenditure-reducing/expanding policies rather than exchange rate changes. The fact that this logic accords closely with the needs of the Community explains Ireland's participation in the system.

Britain alone of the EC countries refused to participate in the EMS exchange rate arrangements. In March 1979, the one-to-one parity with sterling was broken, for the first time since 1926, and the currency union between Britain and Ireland which dated back to 1826 came to an end (see Chapter 1). The Irish pound/sterling rate fluctuated in 1979, but began a steep decline in the second half of 1980 which lasted into the first quarter of 1981. The effective exchange rate of the Irish pound (the average exchange rate based on a trade-weighted average of individual currencies) declined by 11 per cent between December 1979 and December 1980. Thus, while the EMS has been partially successful in creating a zone of monetary stability for continental members of the Community, that has not been the case for Ireland. Moreover, the pattern of Ireland's competitive position has steadily deteriorated vis-à-vis EMS member states (see Chapter 6). This change in the pattern of competitiveness is not healthy. Besides, EMS has not insulated Ireland from large variations in the exchange rate between the ECU, sterling and the dollar. These variations have caused considerable trouble for Irish exporters. Unless a greater convergence in inflation rates is achieved, the EMS will fail in its objective of providing a stable exchange rate system in which changes in parity are infrequent, agreed mutually, and conditional on corrective measures being adopted by the divergent country.

A final aspect of EC membership is the transfers and capital flows associated with it. Ireland is a large net recipient of funds from the

Community. The largest single item is the transfer under the Common Agricultural Policy, representing subsidies on agricultural exports sold on the world market and other supports. Smaller transfers have been received from the Social Fund. In addition, Ireland has obtained substantial loans from the European Investment Bank to finance development projects, together with grants from the Regional Fund and current and capital contributions under the EMS agreement ('EMS money'). The public sector has also been active in securing loans from commercial banks, notably from Germany, where nominal interest rates have tended to be well below Irish levels. Trade integration has thus been accompanied to some extent by capital market integration. This ready access to the capital markets of Continental Europe helped to finance the large balance-of-payments deficits in the period 1978-83. To a certain extent, these deficits were matched by exceptionally high investment levels — at 30 per cent of GNP, Ireland's investment had then reached Japanese proportions — and the role of foreign capital in financing them is to be welcomed. To the extent that the deficits reflect an unwillingness to trim consumption to production capabilities and an inefficient use of capital, however, a less sanguine view of the 'open door' to European finance is justified.

While membership of the European Community was intended as a step towards greater integration in the European economy, certain disintegrative consequences have appeared as an unintended side-effect of this process. The Common Agricultural Policy, in its labyrinthine complexity, has failed in its aim of unifying the market for agricultural produce. While price variations between Northern Ireland and the Republic were in existence well before 1973, they continue to persist, reflecting initially the Irish government's preference for a speedier transition to European price levels than the British government would allow, and, latterly, the divergence between the depreciated value of the pound sterling and its 'green pound' rate (see Chapter 10). On another point, participation in the EMS worked towards the partial disintegration of the capital market between Dublin and London, with the imposition of exchange controls by the Irish government on capital transactions with the UK. Moreover, the break with sterling has made trade with Britain and Northern Ireland more difficult rather than less difficult. The Community is still a long way from the economic and monetary union envisaged in the Treaty of Rome. For all its shortcomings, however, most serious studies of Irish experience in the EC have concluded that Ireland is much better off inside the Community than it would have been outside. For this reason, the economic proposals of the Single European Act which envisage the dismantling of frontier controls on intra-Community trade by 1992 have been widely welcomed.

4   INFLATION AND EXCHANGE RATE

Three features of Irish inflation can be observed from Table 9.6. First, Ireland has been a high-inflation country by the standards of industrial European countries. Prices increased by around 14 per cent on average during the 1970s, almost three times the rate in Germany, and appreciably higher than the European Community (EC) average. Second, a close correspondence existed between Irish and UK inflation rates up to 1980: from 1955 to 1978 Ireland's Consumer Price Index (CPI) rose on average by 6.7 per cent per annum compared with a figure of 6.5 per cent for the UK.[9]

Table 9.6
Average Annual Percentage Rise in Consumer Prices,
1971-80 and 1984-86

	1971-80	1984-86
EC	10.6	5.5
Germany	5.2	1.4
Ireland	14.3	5.5
UK	13.3	4.8

Sources: as for Table 9.1.

There were of course differences in individual years, in part attributable to indirect tax and subsidy changes, but the overall conformity of the two price indices was remarkable. Third, by 1986 the inflation rate had fallen to its lowest level since the early 1960s. So inflation is not inevitable; it can be brought down. No explanation or understanding of inflation in Ireland can be complete without taking these three aspects into account.

Explaining Irish Inflation
Irish inflation has, at one time or another, been attributed to three types of influences: 'imported' price increases, government policy (fiscal and monetary), and 'wage-push' caused by trade unions. These will be analyzed in turn.

Given the small size of the Irish economy and its high ratio of exports and imports to GNP, a rise in the price of traded goods, whether caused by a 1972-style commodity price boom or an OPEC oil-price increase such as those of 1973-74 and 1979-80, must, in the absence of powerful countervailing policies, have a strong impact on the domestic price level. Exactly how strong an impact depends on the 'pass-on effect' from import prices to domestic prices, wages and salaries and profit margins. This subject stimulated some controversy in the early 1970s with input-output analysis pointing to a lower impact than that suggested by those who assumed compensating pay claims and factor price increases imported through an integrated market in factors of production. There was no disagreement, however, on the basic issue that the inflationary impetus of a rise in the price of traded goods would be substantial. Indeed, in the context of a fixed exchange rate with sterling, it was argued that the Irish inflation rate was 'imported' virtually in its entirety from the United Kingdom (see Chapter 3). The empirical evidence supporting this claim was unambiguous. Hence the explanation of pre-1979 inflation can, with confidence, be ascribed to the sterling link.

But this was not the whole story. As noted in Chapter 3, countries such as Austria, Switzerland and Germany suffered the same supply-price shocks yet managed to keep inflation down to single figures. The key to their success was currency appreciation which reduced the domestic price of their imports and exports. Moderation in domestic income demands ensured that the appreciation of their exchange rates, which tended to make their exports dearer in foreign currency, did not unduly damage their export competitiveness. In terms of Irish experience, therefore, an understanding of the inflationary process requires an understanding of the constraints which prevented the authorities from breaking the sterling link and not merely of the commodity and factor-market linkages

The main constraint on exchange-rate appreciation was the fear that incomes would not adjust to the new currency regime but would instead continue to follow the British trend. A failure to synchronize wage behaviour with stronger exchange rate policy would have led to a decline in industrial competitiveness and more unemployment, not dissimilar to the experience in the United Kingdom following the rise in its real exchange rate. Thus, those who saw unemployment as a major cause for concern tended to advise against the risks inherent in a break with sterling. At the same time, economists agreed that a stronger currency regime would tend to reduce inflation and that, in the long run, higher levels of unemployment would tend to bring real wages down to a level closer to equilibrium. But the long run extended into years rather than months. Wages respond slowly to increases in unemployment. Real per capita compensation of employees has continued rising in the UK in each year since 1979 — and so has average compensation per employee in the European Community — notwithstanding the unprecedented increase in the numbers unemployed.

At the time of the EMS negotiations, it was expected, both in Ireland and in the UK, that membersip would involve transference to a less inflationary exchange-rate regime. This expectation was based on the small open economy model of inflation, outlined in Chapter 3 and in the discussion on exchange rate policy in Chapter 6. Given that most of Ireland's trade is with the UK and EMS countries, the model in essence asserts that the Irish inflation rate (P) is determined in the following manner: $P_{IRL} = W_{UK}(P_{UK} + E_{UK}) + W_{EMS}(P_{EMS} + E_{EMS})$ where the Ws refer to trade weights and the Es to the rate of change in the Irish price of foreign currencies.

If Ireland chooses E_{UK} to be zero, as it did prior to 1979 (i.e. to have a fixed exchange rate with sterling), E_{EMS} is the rate of change in the sterling price of foreign currencies. An essential element of this argument, is that if, for example, P_{UK} = 20 per cent and P_{EMS} = 5 per cent, then E_{EMS} = 15 per cent, i.e. the exchange rate will respond to differentials in inflation rates between the UK and EMS countries. (This is the so-called purchasing power parity view of exchange rates.) Therefore, $P_{UK} = (P_{EMS} + E_{EMS})$ and, from the equation above, $P_{IRL} = P_{UK}$. The key feature is the assumption that causation runs from the exchange rate to the rate of inflation and not vice versa.

With EMS membership in 1979, E_{EMS} became zero (approximately), the model thus implying $P_{IRL} = P_{EMS}$. Now, given that P_{EMS} was considerably less than P_{UK} in the 1970s (see the UK and German figures in Table 9.6 for a rough indicator of this differential), the expectation was that P_{IRL} would fall substantially. As may be seen in Table 9.6, this was clearly not the case. What went wrong? First, purchasing power parity broke down, i.e. $(P_{UK} + E_{UK})$ greatly exceeded P_{EMS}. The significant real appreciation in sterling fed into Irish prices. Second, instead of this leading to a large shift in Irish purchasing from the UK to the Continent (i.e. to a dramatic change in trade weights), trade patterns remained broadly stable. The collapse of purchasing power parity combined with the overall stability of trade shares explains why Ireland's inflation was higher than the EMS rate and why pre-

EMS expectations in this regard turned out to be very wide of the mark.

There is little doubt, then, that a substantial part of Ireland's post-EMS inflation was 'imported'. Given the difficulties in quickly replacing imports whose prices were denominated in dollars or sterling by imports with prices denominated in EMS currencies, the combination of inflation in dollar and sterling prices and their stronger exchange rates gave a substantial fillip to Irish domestic prices. Domestic inflationary forces also helped this process along by pushing up the price of non-traded goods. Nevertheless, the basic insight of the small open economy model still applies. Having decided on an exchange rate target, the rate of inflation is externally determined.

Again, the question arises: why did the Irish authorities not counteract this imported inflation by a revaluation of the Irish pound within the EMS? Fear of the competitive consequences of such action because of slow downward adjustment of income claims must again be the main answer. Technical adjustment problems within the EMS were not likely to have been a major impediment. Policy has been 'to maintain stability of the Irish pound within the EMS', an objective which allows a certain degree of latitude in interpretation.

The exclusion of the pound sterling from the exchange rate mechanism of the EMS has been described by the European Commission as 'a substantial defect' in the system,[10] a view which would be endorsed by most Irish economists. The Irish authorities are at present riding two horses: on the one hand, EMS obligations must be adhered to which means infrequent realignments and then only after consultation with EMS partners; on the other hand, there is concern that the Irish pound/sterling rate should be consistent with other policy objectives. If sterling strengthens, the Irish authorities must seek a revaluation or else accept the consequences of higher inflation. If sterling weakens, the authorities can either do nothing in the expectation that the loss in competitiveness will be transitory or else seek a depreciation.

The nature of the dilemma was never more acutely evident than in the course of 1986. From mid-1985 onwards, both sterling and the dollar began to weaken relative to the ECU. This meant a sharp appreciation of the Irish pound relative to these two key currencies. The Irish pound rose from 79p sterling in the third quarter of 1985 to 95p at end-1986. From virtual parity with the dollar in summer 1985, the Irish pound rose to $1.38 by June 1986. Adjustment of internal prices to these new exchange rates was extremely slow, thus confirming the view of those who predicted severe competitive disadvantages if the Irish pound lost touch too quickly with a depreciating sterling. The Irish government reacted with a decision in August 1986 to seek a devaluation within the EMS to offset part of the unwarranted appreciation of the Irish pound. A depreciation of 8 per cent was agreed by the EMS which took the financial markets completely by surprise. While the surprise factor augured well for the devaluation — the best time to devalue is *before* such action is judged inevitable by the market — and the basic logic of the 'unwarranted appreciation' formula was eminently defensible, the realignment was only partially successful in its aims. The problem was that sterling and the dollar continued to weaken. By early 1987, the Irish pound exchange rate vis-à-vis these two currencies had exceeded the end-July level. Irish exporters were complaining and exchange rate uncertainty was deterring the return of capital outflows. In such circumstances, the government had to balance two conflicting considerations. The competitive argument states that a country in dire need of employment must not make that task more difficult by allowing an unjustified appreciation of its currency. Stability factors, however, suggested the contrary conclusion, that any unilateral seeking of a further realignment would destroy confidence in the Irish pound, delay further the re-inflow of capital and result in higher interest rates which would be every bit as damaging to Ireland's traded sector as the overvalued currency. There is no easy way out of this dilemma. Truly it has been said that exchange rate policy is an art rather than a science. It is also true that Irish exchange rate policy must have regard to the general competitive position of the economy in deciding on the response to sterling and dollar fluctuations and EMS realignments.

Inflation and Domestic Policies
The statement that, for a given exchange rate, inflation is largely externally determined needs careful interpretation. It does not mean that domestic inflationary pressures are unimportant. Domestic inflationary pressure in excess of 'imported' levels results in firms, hotels and individuals being driven out of business. It means uncompetitive domestic production and more imported goods in Irish shops. The effects of domestically-induced inflation are 'suppressed' through higher unemployment levels, more import penetration and worsening balance-of-payments deficits. Eventually, pressure is placed on the exchange rate thus undermining the basic premise of the imported inflation model.

This suggests that the small open economy approach is a useful starting point to an understanding of Irish inflation but an inadequate point on which to end.

An ironic feature of post-1979 experience is that either continued adherence to sterling parity or movement to an effective exchange rate target would have involved a much stronger exchange rate option than was provided by the EMS. Either of these alternatives would have involved less inflation but at the price of more unemployment and loss of competitiveness.

Where does the government stand in all this? Having decided on an exchange rate policy, its task is to ensure that fiscal and monetary policies (the latter determined in conjunction with the Central Bank) are consistent with maintaining the Irish pound's position in the EMS (see also Chapter 6). There is little evidence that this is being done. Government expenditure has continued to grow and borrowing has escalated. The increase in foreign borrowing has been a particular feature in recent years, leading to an outstanding official foreign debt at end-1986 of IR£12bn. The Central Bank has on a number of occasions expressed its concern about the size of the balance-of-payments deficit, the scale of foreign borrowing and the resultant deterioration in official net indebtedness (foreign debt less external reserves). It is, of course, possible to argue that the Central Bank should have adopted a more restrictive credit policy. Had it done so, however, and the policy been effective, the burden of adjustment would have fallen on the private sector. Since, in the last analysis, the Central Bank must take the government contribution as given, the private sector is the only sector amenable to influence. Yet it is the private sector which most economists feel needs to be encouraged and the public sector which needs to be restrained. Setting credit policy in terms of domestic credit expansion (DCE) presents the problem in an illuminating format; but it does not make the problem any easier to resolve. There is no doubt, however, that fiscal policy has compromised the overall stance of monetary policy and also the viability of a strong exchange rate policy (see Chapter 6).

The place of trade unions in the inflationary process is a contentious issue. The unions themselves claim that they respond to inflation but do not create it and that pay moderation could be readily secured if only prices were not rising so fast. There is an element of truth in this. Econometric studies reveal a consistently strong relationship between earnings, on the one hand, and prices and productivity on the other. (Unemployment plays an insignificant role in the short run in these equations, a finding which is consistent with recent experience in Western Europe.) It is equally true that trade unions, like everybody else, have a strong temptation to wait until inflation falls before agreeing to practice moderation. And even if all unions agreed that a cooperative solution based on low-pay norms was optimal, the incentive to individual unions to seek above-the-norm increases would remain strong.

In the small-open-economy framework, trade unions do not cause inflation but they can cause unemployment. Producers in the traded goods sector (which includes manufacturing, agriculture and exposed services such as tourism) are constrained in their pricing policy by international competition. Hence, wage claims in excess of productivity increases cannot be recouped through higher prices in the way they can be in the sheltered sector. If the trade unions succeed in forcing them through, the effect is to reduce profitability, lessen the inflow of foreign investment and deter domestic investors. Sooner or later, employment and output suffer. Trade unions and professional organizations can also impede the efficient operation of the labour market through restrictive practices and limitations on recruitment which have the effect of raising labour costs and undermining competitiveness. Strikes in vital sectors of the economy can also damage employment prospects by casting doubt over Ireland's reliability as a supplier to foreign markets.

Even if one accepts that the Irish rate of inflation is heavily influenced from abroad, trade unions and similar pressure groups can still influence inflation through actions which render a particular exchange rate policy unsustainable. One example of such action would be where they insist on wage and salary increases which cause unemployment in the traded goods sector and worsen the balance-of-payments deficit, thus bringing nearer the point of forced devaluation. Trade unions must also accept a large measure of responsibility for the state of government finances through their insistence on large non-pay concessions — ranging from enhanced social welfare payments to job creation targets in the public sector — as the price of their consent to national pay agreements. Trade unions have repeatedly resisted efforts to cut government expenditure (e.g. closure of loss-making state-sponsored ventures, raising the school-entry age, health sector economies) while at the same time protesting their opposition to tax increases. Whether this is a reflection of an excessively pliable government or overly 'successful' bargaining on the part of the unions is a moot point. The fact is that government responds to pressures and, if the trade unions have pushed the government towards a financial precipice which weakens its capacity to resist inflationary pressures, as they have done, they must share responsibility for the consequences.

334

5   CONCLUSION

In an economy such as Ireland's, inflation can best be understood by looking first at the exchange rate policy and analyzing its inflationary implications in terms of an 'imported' inflation model. The second step is to analyze the role of government, trade unions and other internal factors which play a decisive role in determining whether the exchange rate regime is sustainable.

Price stability was once described as 'a public good which all can enjoy but which is not in anyone's interest to supply'. All want less inflation — but less of somebody else's inflation. Everybody complains about rising prices but each person is slow to see the connection between the rise in his or her earnings and the increase in prices which higher earnings, if they are extended to others, must inevitably entail. This *public good* aspect of inflation goes a long way to explaining why most people dislike inflation and yet why governments encounter opposition in trying to curb it.

Inflation has been brought down steeply in the UK and Europe, at the cost perhaps of an increase in unemployment, and some popular discontent, and it is primarily for this reason that the rate of price increase has fallen in Ireland also. Were it not for the high tax increases forced upon the economy in recent years by the growth in public sector expenditure, the reduction in Irish inflation might have been even more marked than it was.

A lower rate of inflation, in Ireland and abroad, leaves room for a sustained attack on the balance-of-payments constraint. The growth of foreign official debt must be reduced and competitiveness must be preserved in order to ensure that, when recovery does come, it will not be brought to a premature halt from the faster growth of the British and Continental European economies. Imports have been growing at a much slower rate, largely because of the depressed state of consumer demand. When that depression lifts, it is essential that the competitiveness of Irish producers is such that they secure as large a share of the increased demand as possible.

It is clear that the balance of payments, inflation and the exchange rate are interlinked phenomena in an economy such as Ireland's. Inflation through its effects on competitiveness can have implications for the balance of payments. The balance-of-payments profile, by determining the sustainability of a given exchange rate, can have an important bearing on the rate of inflation. What the Irish economy needs is an exchange rate *regime* which exerts downward pressure on the level of inflation and, within that regime, an exchange *rate* which ensures a strong level of competitiveness relative to our major trading partners. In this way only can the dual objectives of price stability and balance-of-payments equilibrium be satisfactorily attained. In striving to attain them, Irish economic policy would be giving practical adherence to Article 104 of the Treaty of Rome which stipulated that 'each member state shall pursue the economic policy needed to ensure the equilibrium of its overall balance of payments and to maintain confidence in its currency, while taking care to ensure a high level of employment and a stable level of prices'.

Footnotes

1 D. McAleese, 'Outward-Looking Policies, Export Growth and Economic Performance: the Irish Experience', in A.A. Artis and J. Nobay (editors), *Contemporary Economic Analysis: Proceedings of the 1977 AUTE Conference,* Croom Helm, London 1978. See also D. McAleese, 'Ireland in the World Economy', in K.A. Kennedy (editor), *Ireland in Transition,* Mercier Press, Dublin 1986.

2 See also K.A. Kennedy, 'Employment and Unemployment Prospects for Ireland', *Irish Banking Review,* September 1980.

3 Cited in Sean Condon, 'New Horizons in Service Exports', *Export Review,* December 1983.

4 J. Flynn, 'A Simulation Model of the Effects of Exchange Rate Changes on Inflation and the Trade Balance', *Central Bank of Ireland Quarterly Bulletin,* Summer 1986.

5 Much has been written on Irish competitiveness in recent years. See B.M. Walsh, T. Baker and D. McAleese, *Report of the Committee on Costs and Competitiveness,* Stationery Office, Dublin 1981; D. McAleese, 'Competitiveness and Economic Performance: The Irish Experience', in J. Black and A. Winters (editors), *Policy and Performance in International Trade.* Macmillan, London 1983; and Denis Conniffe and Kieran A. Kennedy (editors), *Employment and Unemployment Policy for Ireland,* ESRI, Dublin 1984, Chapter 6.

6 An excellent overview of the economic consequences of European integration for the Irish economy is presented in Alan Matthews, 'The Economic Consequences of EEC Membership for Ireland', in David Coombes (editor), *Ireland and the European Communities,* Gill and Macmillan, Dublin 1983. Other useful references include J. Lee, *Reflections on Irish Membership of the European Community,* Irish Council of the European Movement, Dublin 1984; and P.J. Drudy and Dermot McAleese (editors), *Ireland and the European Community,* Cambridge University Press, Cambridge 1984.

7 The effects of the Common Commercial Policy are evaluated in Alan Matthews, *The European Community's External Trade Policy: Implications for Ireland,* Irish Council of the European Movement, Dublin 1980; D. McAleese and P. Carey, 'Employment Coefficients for Irish Trade with Extra-EEC Countries: Measurement and Implications', *Economic and Social Review,* January 1981; and D. McAleese, 'Ireland and the European Community: The Changing Pattern of Trade', in Drudy and McAleese (editors), *op. cit.*

8 See C.H. Murray, 'The European Monetary System, Implications for Ireland', *Central Bank of Ireland Annual Report, 1979;* C. McCarthy, 'EMS and the End of Ireland's Sterling Link', *Lloyds Bank Review,* April 1980; and B.M. Walsh, 'Ireland and the European Monetary System', in Drudy and McAleese (editors), *op. cit.*

9 Patrick Geary, 'How Much Inflation is Imported?', in D. McAleese and L. Ryan (editors). *Inflation in the Irish Economy: A Contemporary Perspective,* Helicon, Dublin 1982.

10 Commission of the European Communities, *European Economy,* Brussels, November 1983 p. 122.

Part IV

POLICY ISSUES AT
A SECTORAL LEVEL

10   The Traded Sector: Agriculture

Alan Matthews

1   INTRODUCTION

IN EARLIER chapters, the contribution of the agricultural sector to national economy aggregates such as GDP, employment and exports has been discussed. Though agriculture's share of these aggregates has declined over time, it remains an important sector of the economy and relatively more important in Ireland than in most other member countries of the European Community (EC). In 1985 the agricultural sector in Ireland accounted for 11 per cent of GNP and 16 per cent of total employment, compared with an average of 4 per cent and 8 per cent respectively for the EC-10 member states. Only in Greece does agriculture make a more important contribution to national output, although in Spain and Portugal as well as Greece the importance of agricultural employment is relatively greater. The purpose of this chapter is to examine the objectives and operation of government policies directed towards this sector.

There are two main reasons why government intervenes in the agricultural sector. One is to ensure that agriculture makes the fullest possible contribution to the primary and secondary objectives of national economic policy outlined in Chapters 2 and 3: full employment, growth, equity, price stability and balance in foreign payments. The other reason is to address the social and economic problems which arise in the sector itself. This intervention has led to significant regulation of, and public aid to, Irish agriculture.

Table 10.1 gives details of state and EC agricultural spending in recent years. EC expenditure in relation to agriculture is channelled through one of two arms of FEOGA, the EC Agricultural Fund. Expenditure under the Guidance Section of FEOGA is related to measures for the structural reform of agriculture, such as farm investment aids or assistance towards the cost of retirement pensions for farmers. It also provides aid to improve marketing and processing structures in agriculture and the food industry.

Expenditure under the Guarantee Section relates to the cost of the price support arrangements which underpin the minimum prices guaranteed to farmers. It is evident that the great bulk of EC

Table 10.1

State and EC Expenditure (IR£millions)[1]

	State expenditure in relation to agriculture	EC (FEOGA) expenditure in relation to Irish agriculture	
		Guidance	Guarantee
1976	129.4	2.5	102.0
1978	155.1	9.3	366.0
1980	199.3	26.4	380.4
1982	292.9	57.5	341.3
1983	305.8	76.5	436.7
1984	309.2	48.8	644.6
1985	295.2	57.2	836.6
1986[2]	320.0	46.0	884.0

Sources: Department of Finance, *Budget Booklet*, various years; and Commission of the European Communities, *Developments in the European Communities*, various issues.

[1] State expenditure in relation to agriculture does not include general administration and overhead costs.

[2] Estimates.

spending in relation to Irish agriculture concerns the price guarantees. National spending in relation to agriculture also remains important, and accounted for 34 per cent of total expenditure in relation to agriculture in 1986.

One measure of the significance of this expenditure is to compare it with the income earned by farmers and their families from agriculture. In 1972, the last year prior to joining the EC, total state expenditure in relation to agriculture (including price support and items such as agricultural research and education and disease eradication) amounted to 41 per cent of the income arising in agriculture. By 1982, this figure had risen to 73 per cent, and in 1986 it is likely to have exceeded this. It is fair to point out that not all spending in relation to agriculture reaches farmers; such expenditure includes fees to veterinary surgeons, salaries of agricultural advisors, the cost of intervention storage and other payments to persons outside of farming directly. On the other hand, the comparison ignores the support provided indirectly to farming through the higher prices which consumers must pay for their food. It can be concluded that there are few other sectors of the economy where public policy has such a profound impact on the prosperity and livelihoods of those working there.

Table 10.2
Structure of Agricultural Output 1972, 1981 and 1985
(per cent of total output by value)

	1972	1981	1985
Cattle	40.6	36.2	37.7
Milk	23.6	30.9	35.4
Pigs	10.3	7.5	5.6
Poultry and eggs	4.5	4.2	3.6
Sheep and wool	4.5	4.1	3.9
Horses	1.2	1.6	2.0
Total livestock and livestock products	84.7	84.5	88.2
Cereals	6.1	7.3	5.0
Other tillage and turf	9.2	8.2	6.8
Total crops and turf	15.3	15.5	11.8

Sources: CSO, *Irish Statistical Bulletin*, various issues.

Since 1973, agricultural policy has been formulated within, and largely determined by, the EC framework. Much of this chapter will be taken up with an examination of the operation of EC schemes and regulations. The importance of these EC factors should not conceal the scope which still exists for discretionary national action, as evidenced by the important role still played by national spending in relation to the sector. National agricultural policy measures, in addition to EC policies, are still very relevant to any overall assessment.

2   CHARACTERISTICS OF THE AGRICULTURAL SECTOR

The structure of Irish agriculture is indicated in Table 10.2, which describes the broad pattern of output in the three years 1972, 1981 and 1985. Climatically, Ireland is better suited to grassland than crop production, and of the total agricultural area (including rough grazing) of 5.7 million hectares in 1985, over 90 per cent was devoted to grass. Livestock and livestock products accounted for 88.2 per cent of total output in 1985 (84.7 per cent in 1972). Within this group, milk output increased its share significantly at the expense of all other livestock enterprises. The share of cereals in total output increased during the 1970s, due in particular to the increased acreage and yields of barley, but there was a significant drop in output in 1985 due to poor weather. Growth in total output was accompanied by an increase in the volume of purchased inputs; the share of purchased inputs in gross output increased from 41 per cent in 1960 to 61 per cent in 1985. Table 10.3 shows the importance of the increased use of fertilizer and lime and animal feedstuffs on farms, and also the extent to which mechanization has substituted for hired labour over the period.

One of the principal attractions of EC membership for Irish agriculture was the opportunity to end its dependence on the relatively low-price UK market and gain access to the EC market at much improved prices. Figures on the destination of agricultural exports show the marked change which has occurred between 1972

Table 10.3

Farm Production Expenses, 1960 and 1985
(per cent of total expenses)

	1960	1985
Animal feedstuffs	23.8	28.8
Fertilizers and lime	10.1	17.4
Seeds	5.5	2.4
Rates	10.2	-
Wages and salaries	18.9	6.2
Machinery and building expenses	18.1	31.5
Others	13.4	13.7

Sources: as for Table 10.2.

and 1985. During that period the proportion of agricultural exports going to the UK fell from 74 per cent to 30 per cent, the proportion going to other EC countries rose from 15 per cent to 23 per cent, and exports to third country markets showed a dramatic increase from 11 per cent to 47 per cent. Total agricultural exports amounted to 18 per cent of total export earnings in 1986 on a trade statistics basis; if export refunds received from the FEOGA Guarantee Section on agricultural exports to third countries are included this figure increases to 25 per cent.

In any discussion of agricultural policy the structural diversity of Irish farming must be recognized. Though the average size of holding was 22 hectares in 1983, 60 per cent of holdings were less than 20 hectares, 31 per cent were between 20 and 50 hectares and 9 per cent were larger than 50 hectares. Small farms are thus more numerous, but their share of the total land area is much less significant. In 1983, farms less than 20 hectares controlled 26 per cent of the total area, farms between 20 and 50 hectares controlled 41 per cent of the total area, and farms over 50 hectares controlled 33 per cent of the total area. The total number of holdings has fallen over time, but in contrast to other countries the decline is very gradual. There were 289,500 holdings over 0.4 hectares in 1960, and 264,000 such holdings in 1980. There has been a much more rapid drop in the farm labour force, which is reflected particularly in a decline in the number of employees and relatives assisting on farms. In total, the agricultural labour force (including a relatively small number of forestry and fishery workers) fell from 390,000 in 1960 to 169,000 in 1985.

Table 10.4 presents the development of certain indices in Irish agriculture during the 1970s and early 1980s. What emerges most clearly from the table is the instability with which agriculture has had to cope during this period. It was expected that EC membership would result in a substantial increase in farm output prices, and the table shows that farm output prices increased substantially faster than the general rate of inflation during the period 1970 to 1978. This was a unique development in modern times and contrasts, for example, with the earlier period from 1953 to 1970 during which real agricultural prices steadily declined. The increase in the agricultural price level during the 1970s was the result of three factors: the harmonization of the pre-entry Irish price level with the EC price level, subsequent increases in the level of EC common prices, and increases as a result of successive devaluations of the Irish 'green pound' (for an explanation of this last phenomonen, see below).

Table 10.4
Development in Certain Indices in Irish Agriculture, 1970 to 1986 (average, 1969-71 = 100)

	'71	'72	'73	'74	'75	'78	'80	'81	'82	'83	'84	'85	'86[1]
Real output prices	97	109	126	108	118	142	107	104	97	93	88	81	79
Real input costs	98	94	105	122	122	124	116	110	103	101	100	96	88
Output/input prices	99	116	121	88	97	115	92	96	94	92	88	85	90
Volume—gross output	105	111	111	113	120	134	133	133	141	146	158	155	150
Volume—net output	104	110	109	115	128	129	125	119	133	135	156	151	136
Real per capita income	104	140	163	126	157	205	129	132	144	152	173	161	148

Sources: NESC, *Farm Incomes: Analysis and Policy* (Report no. 65), Stationery Office, Dublin 1982; and Department of Agriculture, *Annual Review of the Situation in Agriculture*, 1986.
[1] Estimates.

Part of the expected benefits of the increase in output prices was offset by rapid increases in the price of inputs. Agriculture suffered severely from the first oil price increase in 1974 because of its dependence on oil-based inputs such as fertilizer and machines. Because the increase in oil prices coincided with a glut in the cattle market which depressed cattle prices, the ratio of output to input prices, which is the key determinant of farming profitability, was lower in 1974 and 1975 than before EC entry. There was a rapid recovery during the remaining years of the transition period to full EC membership, and by 1978 the output/input price ratio stood at its highest level since 1972. The consequence of this relative improvement in agricultural prices was a redistribution of income in favour of farmers in those years. Between 1971 and 1978, the average farm income per family worker in farming rose in real terms by 7.8 per cent per annum, compared to an increase of 4.9 per cent per annum in average real industrial earnings.[1]

Unfortunately, 1978 proved to be a high point in farming fortunes. Between 1978 and 1980, farm product prices rose by only a further 3 per cent, while the cost of farm inputs rose by 30 per cent. The adverse effects on both production and farm incomes are shown in Table 10.4. It was not until 1982 that the volume of gross and net output again reached their 1978 level. A further 'cost-price' squeeze was evident in the period 1983-85, when input prices rose by 9 per cent while output prices remained unchanged. Despite this unfavourable environment there was a substantial recovery in output during the first half of the 1980s; the volume of gross agricultural output increased at an annual average rate of 3 per cent (albeit from a low base in 1980). Output declined again in 1985 and 1986, partly because poor weather conditions had a major adverse effect on the crops sector and partly because of EC restrictions on milk production. There was also a recovery in real per capita farm incomes in the early 1980s, but incomes in the mid-1980s were still only 80 per cent of the level they had reached in 1978. It is worthy of note that the ratio of output to input prices in the early 1980s was actually lower than in the period prior to EC membership when there was such a volume of complaint about the unprofitable conditions in farming.

The reasons for this sudden turnaround in farming fortunes are complex. The fundamental problem is that since 1978 Irish farming has been unable to recoup (through higher prices) its higher input costs due to inflation. The harmonization of Irish and EC prices is now complete and no longer contributes to agricultural price increases. The only remaining sources of higher prices are increases in the common EC price levels or changes in the Irish 'green pound' rate. Because of the EC's financial problems, common price increases agreed in Brussels have been kept to low or zero figures, particularly in 1982 and subsequent years. The relative stability of the Irish pound within the European Monetary System (see Chapter 9), despite an Irish inflation rate which considerably exceeded the average for other participating countries, has meant few opportunities to benefit farmers by further devaluations of the 'green pound'. With the prospect of a continuing restrictive approach being adopted to the Common Agricultural policy generally, the outlook for Irish agriculture is more difficult than at any time since Ireland became a member of the EC.

3   OBJECTIVES OF AGRICULTURAL POLICY

The two main reasons suggested in the previous section for government intervention in the agricultural sector were economic and social problems arising in agriculture itself, and the state's attempt to ensure that the sector made the fullest contribution to various national policy goals. Four separate goals of state agricultural policy can be distinguished, namely, a production objective, an income distribution objective, a farm structure objective and a stabilization objective.

The production objective follows naturally from the belief that rapid growth in the economy as a whole is exceedingly difficult if agriculture and its dependent industries are growing only at a moderate pace. Increased agricultural output not only contributes directly to economic growth, it also makes a substantial contribution to the balance of payments and to employment prospects both on and off the farm. Successive governments have, therefore, pursued policies designed to stimulate and to accelerate the rate of growth of agricultural output. A subsidiary production objective has been to increase efficiency in the production, processing and marketing of farm products.

Two separate income distribution objectives should be distinguished. The overriding one has been the concern for equity between the farm population as a whole and the non-farm sector; in the words of the Third Programme, 'to ensure that farmers who work their land fully and efficiently share equitably in the growing national prosperity and that a reasonable relationship is maintained between farm incomes and incomes in other occupations'. In addition, the state has been concerned with income distribution questions within agriculture, and specifically with the need to aid the smaller and economically more vulnerable farms in securing an acceptable level of income.

The farm structure objective is closely related to the issue of income distribution within farming. The state has expressed a fundamental value, both in the Constitution and elsewhere, that increased farm production should be encouraged from the maximum number of family farms. The emphasis on the family farm as the desired unit of farm production has been supported by economic, social and political arguments. This policy goal has implications for such issues as land ownership and land tenure, the growth of part-time farming and the extent to which the state and business corporations should be encouraged to become involved in agricultural production.

Stability of prices and supplies is desired both by farmers and consumers. It has also been possible in the past to distinguish a fifth goal (a market objective): the attempt to improve conditions of access to external markets for agricultural exports. This goal may now be regarded as being met by membership of the European Community.

As noted earlier, agricultural policy must now be formulated within the framework of the EC. The question can be raised, are the policy objectives which the Irish Government would like to pursue consistent with those adopted by the Community? Article 39 of the Treaty of Rome sets out the objectives of the EC's Common Agricultural Policy (CAP) as being: to increase agricultural productivity; to ensure a fair standard of living for the agricultural population; to stabilize markets; to guarantee regular supplies; and to ensure reasonable prices to consumers.

In principle, these objectives coincide with those of the Irish government, though there are some important differences of emphasis. For example, the CAP objectives specifically recognize the consumer interest in the formulation of agricultural policy, although this has remained at the level of rhetoric and has not been very meaningful in practice. The role of agriculture in the maintenance of an attractive environment is also increasingly recognized in the CAP. The Irish government puts more emphasis on the growth objective, given the problems of lack of employment and the relatively lower living standards in this country. There is the potential for conflict here in the future as the EC moves further along the road of introducing explicit quantitative restrictions on the amount of agricultural produce it is prepared to underwrite with price guarantees. This EC policy (which is disussed in more detail later in this chapter) is seen most clearly in the case of sugar and milk, though supply control measures have also been introduced for other commodities (e.g. restrictions on new planting of vines, and the digging up of orchards). If other EC countries are required to restrict production, then Ireland cannot expect to secure a permanent exemption. The more extensive and the more strictly enforced such measures of supply control become, the more difficult it will be for Irish agriculture to pursue a strategy of maximum growth in the future.

The National Planning Board document, *Proposals for Plan 1984-87* (Dublin 1984), hints at the change in strategy which may be required. 'The most important objective of policy in the medium-term', it writes, 'should be to increase the value added of the agricultural sector'. Its decision to focus on value added rather than total output as the objective of policy reflects the view that a strategy for farmers of cost minimization rather than output maximization will become more important in the future.

Growth

The rate of growth in the agricultural sector can be measured either in terms of Gross Agricultural Output (GAO) or of Gross Agricultural Product (GAP). GAO measures total off-farm sales plus consumption of farm produce by the farm household plus changes in livestock inventory. GAP measures the contribution of agriculture to value added in the economy and is obtained by subtracting purchased inputs (excluding labour) from gross output. The growth in GAO overestimates agriculture's contribution to value added because it does not take account of the extent to which the increase in output has been due to an increase in the volume of purchased inputs. However, it tends to be the indicator most frequently used when measuring growth rates because it is more readily available and probably more accurate. A further measure, Net Agricultural Output (NAO), which is defined as GAO less purchases of the major farm materials of seeds, fertilizer and animal feeds, falls between the previous two. It is sometimes used as a proxy for GAP and the two series have moved closely together in the past.

How does the record stand with respect to the growth of agricultural output? An international comparison of growth rates is shown in Table 10.5. This comparison is a trifle unfair to Ireland's performance because output in 1973 was slightly above trend and output in 1985 slightly below. Measuring the growth in output between these two years thus underestimates the trend rate of growth over the period. Leaving aside Spain, the outlier (which was mainly due to the expansion of its irrigated agriculture producing high-value fruit and vegetable crops), the growth rate of gross output (GAO) in Ireland was higher over this period than for most other EC member states except the Netherlands and Denmark. When the growth rates for value added (GAP) are examined, however, a less favourable picture emerges. The reasonably high growth rate of total output was achieved by an even faster growth in the use of purchased inputs. In Denmark, the Netherlands and the UK the reverse was the case, so that in each of these countries the rate of increase in agricultural value added exceeded the rate of growth in total output, and exceeded the Irish rate as well.

Table 10.5

International Comparison of Agricultural Growth Rates (average annual percentage), 1973-85

	Gross agricultural output (GAO)	Gross agricultural product (GAP)
Belgium	0.7	1.1
Denmark	2.8	4.0
France	1.1	0.6
Germany	1.2	0.9
Greece	1.8	1.2
Ireland	2.5	2.3
Italy	1.4	1.0
Netherlands	3.5	3.9
Portugal	n.a	n.a
Spain	14.5	12.6
United Kingdom	1.5	3.5

Sources: Commission of the European Communities, *Agricultural Situation in the Community*, 1986.

A second problem is the very narrow base of farmers on which agricultural growth depends. The data in Table 10.6 show that on roughly half of farms, accounting for in excess of an estimated 40 per cent of the land area, the volume of production was stagnant or declined during the years 1973-77, a period of relatively favourable output-input price ratios. At the same time, the top 25 per cent of farms showed dramatic increases in output. In commenting on these figures, the National Planning Board suggests that the reasons for this disparity in growth performance lie in those personal characteristics which provide the motivation and capacity to seek out and use modern farm technology. Among the most important characteristics which are positively associated with growth at farm level are the age and educational attainment of the farm operator and the family composition of the farm household. Younger, better educated farmers who are married and have children are more likely to have a record of improving output at farm level than farm operators with the converse characteristics.

Table 10.6
Per Cent of Farms Classified by Growth Rates
of Agricultural Production Achieved Between 1973 and 1977[1]

Per cent change in nominal output	Per cent of farms	Per cent of land occupied
less than 50	21	18
50-100	29	28
100-150	26	28
150-200	14	16
over 200	10	11

Sources: G.E. Boyle, 'Some Agricultural Productivity Puzzles Re-examined' (An Foras Talúntais, Economics and Rural Welfare Research Centre's Sixth Annual Conference), November 1982.
[1] Between 1973 and 1977 the aggregate price index of agricultural products increased by just over 100 per cent. On farms where the increase in ouput in nominal terms was less than 100 per cent, it is implied that the volume of output was stagnant or contracting, and vice versa.

When selected social statistics for Irish farmers are examined, the prospects for future growth are not reassuring. About 75 per cent of farmers have had primary education; only about 25 per cent of farmers have had secondary or higher level education. Over half of all farm operators are over fifty years of age, and only about 10 per cent are under 30. Less than half of all farmers are married and with a family. The National Planning Board concluded after an examination of these figures that without a radical alteration of policy the proportion of farmers from whom significant development might be expected in the future may not exceed 20 per cent of the farm population, occupying only about one-quarter of the land area. The policies which might be used to improve this situation are discussed later in this chapter.

Farm Incomes
The historic tendency for farm incomes to lag behind the growth in non-farm incomes has provided a major justification for government

intervention in the agricultural sector in all industrialized countries. The ratio of average agricultural incomes to average earnings in the rest of the economy is shown for some recent years in Table 10.7.

Table 10.7

Index of Disparity between Per Capita Farm
and Non-Farm Incomes[1]

1970	1973	1974	1977	1978	1979	1980	1981	1982	1983	1984	1985
0.63	0.83	0.68	0.73	0.90	0.69	0.64	0.53	0.60	0.63	0.70	0.63

Sources: CSO, *National Income and Expenditure* and *Trend of Employment and Unemployment*, various issues; and Department of Finance, *Economic Review and Outlook*, various issues.

[1] The agricultural sector is defined to include forestry and fishing. Non-farm income is the sum of non-agricultural wages, salaries and pensions (including employers' contribution to social insurance) plus the income of the independent non-agricultural traders and professional earnings.

Values less than 1 indicate that average earnings of the farm labour force lagged behind other earnings in that year.

A number of reservations must be expressed about this comparison of farm and non-farm incomes. Farm income is underestimated by the valuation of farm produce consumed by farm households at agricultural rather than retail prices though this is not now very substantial. The concept of an average income in an industry which includes a wide range of farm sizes and farm types, part-time as well as full-time farmers, may be very misleading. Not all agricultural income accrues to farmers and not all farmers depend solely on their agricultural income for their livelihoods. The comparison is made in per capita terms and makes no allowance for differences in hours worked between the two sectors. Differences in taxation should be allowed for, while it should be noted that the farm income figure already incorporates an element of subsidy from existing price support programmes. Moreover, the income arising from agriculture is the reward not only to farm labour but also to management and capital inputs. In particular, interest payments on farm investment which have grown rapidly in recent years must be deducted to arrive at the disposable income of farmers.

On the presumption that, in spite of these qualifications, an income gap does exist, two questions need to be asked. What causes it, and what is its significance? The orthodox answer to the first question runs in terms of the nature of the aggregate demand for and supply of agricultural products. As people's income rises, they tend to spend a smaller proportion of it on agricultural products: the income elasticity of demand is low. But, because of technological advances, the supply curve for agricultural products is thought to be shifting rapidly and agricultural output will tend to rise by much the same rate as output of the non-agricultural sector. The consequence will be a downward pressure on the aggregate price level for agricultural products relative to other commodities, which leads to a slower growth in real farm income than in incomes elsewhere. With a sufficient degree of mobility of the farm labour force out of farming and into jobs in other sectors of the economy, equality in per capita income levels would be maintained. The reason why farm incomes tend to lag behind the growth in non-farm incomes is because the mobility of labour out of farming is too slow, due to imperfections in the labour market, time lags or social reasons.

There is an alternative, not necessarily conflicting, view that suggests that migration alone is unlikely to restore equality in per capita income levels between the farm and non-farm sectors. The income gap may represent not a difference in the level of remuneration of particular qualities or skills, but rather that the farming community has a poorer endowment of these qualities or skills on average than the rest of the community. If this is the case, it is likely that workers in farming do earn as much in their present occupation as they would in alternative jobs, given that because of their relatively poorer educational level and age structure alternative jobs would be relatively poorly paid. In support of this, Frawley has noted that in the majority of cases where farmers take off-farm employment, this employment is in poorly-paid manual occupations.[2] The fact that there was a considerable outflow from farming in the last two decades without any real improvement in the disparity index between the two sectors also suggests that an even faster rate of out-migration would not necessarily have effected any greater change.

Given that an income gap exists, what significance should be attached to it? Is it a matter for policy action, and, if so, what is the appropriate policy? It is by no means obvious that raising farm prices to increase farm incomes directly is the most appropriate action. If people are prepared to remain in farming, albeit at a lower level of income, in return for the psychic satisfaction of living in the country or of being their own employer, then it is difficult to see a case for subsidizing their particular preferences. If low incomes on farms are the result of poor management of farm resources, then measures to intensify production may be a more appropriate route to higher income levels than the subsidization of farm prices. National Farm Survey results published by the Agricultural

Institute show wide disparities in output per hectare on different farms, so that in the context of a managed market with guaranteed prices there does seem to be scope for higher incomes through better management. If differences in the endowment of education and skills are the cause of the income disparity, then the appropriate policy would be to invest in the further education of those working on farms and by means of structural policies (see below) to try to encourage a more balanced age distribution. Finally, it may be that the income differential persists because of imperfections in the labour market. Because of urban unemployment it may pay farmers to remain in a job with an assured income than to take the risk of a higher paid job but with a greater chance of becoming unemployed. Or because of lack of information, farmers may not be aware of alternative job opportunities. In either case programmes outside agriculture would be a better solution to the problem of low farm incomes than subsidizing them directly.

Whatever the reasons for the persistence of the income gap, there exists a large number of low income farmers. National Farm Survey figures for 1985 reveal that 48 per cent of all farm operators had a family farm income of less than IR£2,500 (excluding part-time farm operators, 12 per cent of full-time farmers fell into this category). Many of these farm operators, through no fault of their own, have a low level of schooling and for age or other reasons are not in a position to learn new skills. Nor in the face of inadequate demand for labour are their chances of off-farm employment good. There has, therefore, been public acceptance of the need to support farm incomes on grounds of social equity. There has also been concern about the social consequences of too-rapid migration from the land on the viability and cohesiveness of rural communities, particularly in the absence of non-farm employment in the immediate locality. Finally, the political influence of the farm organizations in lobbying for agricultural support should be acknowledged.

Incomes on farms, not surprisingly, are highly correlated with size of farm. In 1985 family farm income on full-time farms ranged from IR£7,058 on farms in the 10-20 hectare size group, IR£10,682 in the 30-50 hectare size group, to IR£18,241 in the 100-plus hectare size group. Income disparities are accentuated by the fact that there is a greater concentration on the low-yielding enterprises by the smaller farms. These figures indicate why the small, less-than-20-hectare farm is increasingly under pressure. Statistics on the change in the number of holdings in the various size groups reveal that it is farms in this size group which are disappearing at the fastest rate. In the past, special efforts were made to assist the development of

351

smaller farms, particularly in the western areas. However, the agricultural performance of smaller farms deteriorated relative to larger units. Conway showed that in the 1950s and 1960s growth in agricultural output was almost completely confined to farms over 50 acres in the east and south, and to farms over 100 acres in the north and west.[3] In the 1970s, output continued to grow faster on larger farms, although income gains were fairly uniformly distributed.[4] One would expect smaller farms to have a poorer output performance due to a concentration on part-time farming and a demographic structure among farm households less favourable to expansion. A NESC report, for example, has estimated that there are 28,000 small farms occupied by elderly single farmers.[5] The present options open to small farm operators are described later in this chapter.

A Desired Farm Structure
Support for a reasonably egalitarian distribution of land based on the family farm as the basic unit of agricultural production has been a consistent theme of agricultural policy. The Constitution includes as part of Article 45 the injunction that: 'The State shall, in particular, direct its policy towards securing ... that there may be established on the land in economic security as many families as in the circumstances shall be practicable'. The Land Commmission, which was established in 1881 primarily as a rent-fixing body, was given extensive powers to acquire, purchase and distribute land to relieve rural congestion and to create economically viable holdings (i.e. holdings capable of providing satisfactory incomes at prevailing levels of living). Since 1923, 62,000 uneconomic holdings were enlarged through its activities, though only about one-third were brought up to the standard of viability recommended at that time.[6] This standard has itself been changing. The minimum size fixed during the 1920s was 22 acres, 25 acres in the 1930s, 33 acres in the 1950s and in the 1960s the standard was 40-45 acres of good land. The Inter-departmental Committee on Land Structure Reform argued that this policy of wide distribution did serve the social function of enabling more families to remain in farming in improved circumstances, and contributed to the absence of serious agrarian disturbance in this century.

More recently, the preference for family farming has been given expression by granting more favourable tax treatment to full-time family farms. Concessions in the income tax code (e.g. the possibility between 1974 and 1980 to opt for a notional assessment of income) and in the provisions for capital taxation (e.g. the value of agricultural land can be reduced when assessing liability for capital transfer tax in the case of full-time farmers) have been designed to strengthen and facilitate the continued existence of the family farm. Another aspect has been the control of the purchase of land by non-nationals and, to a lesser extent, by non-resident farmers, which has been designed in part to prevent the growth of absentee farmers. Recent statements have reiterated official opposition to the growth of large-scale farming. There are some instances of corporate finance entering farming, though the size structure of Irish farms is not likely to encourage this on any large scale.

Price Stabilization

Price fluctuations are more likely to occur in agriculture than in other industries because of the inelastic nature of the demand for its products with regard to price, coupled with the influence of weather variability on production and the competitive nature of the industry in which the level of production is the result of the decisions of thousands of small producers. The effect of price fluctuations is compounded by the biological nature of production, which sets up a lagged response to price and creates cyclical production patterns. Cattle, pigs and potato production provide examples of this phenomenon in the absence of government measures to prevent it.

Price fluctuations can occur on a daily, weekly, seasonal or cyclical basis and may play a necessary part in evening out supply and demand patterns. In Ireland the predominance of grass-based production results in a very pronounced seasonal pattern in the output of milk and cattle. This seasonal variation in throughput creates difficulties for processors who are required to maintain sufficient capacity to meet demand at peak and who find that much of their plant, labour and equipment is underutilized throughout the year. Seasonal price variation in these circumstances, by taking account of the higher costs of production during the winter months, would help to even out the flow of milk or cattle throughout the year. Many creameries are now moving to a system of bonus payments for milk produced in the earlier months of the year, while the meat industry has been pressing for seasonal variation in the guarantee price of beef to reflect the higher costs of winter production.

Price stabilization is sought to even out cyclical price variations over a number of years. Unstable prices may have an adverse effect on the demand for agricultural products: for example, in periods of high potato prices, consumers may switch to substitutes such as rice or bread and it may be difficult to regain the market when prices subsequently fall. They also create uncertainty for farm planning, and may lead producers to make unwise production decisions. Price instability in the cattle sector, given the pattern of specialization into calf producers, store cattle rearers, and fatteners, causes large transfers of revenue among the producers of various types of cattle. The Review Body on Beef Intervention has shown that fluctuations in the price of fat cattle are magnified as one moves closer to the calf stage, and with many small farmers depending on suckling cow herds and store cattle production, the brunt of price instabilty is borne by them.[7] However, price stabilization can have its drawbacks. Where the fluctuation in price is due to a variation in supply, then price stabilization may aggravate income instability. This is because the inverse relationship which normally prevails between price and quantity tends to stabilize revenue. It has also been argued that price instability may encourage farm investment where it results in windfall profits and where the propensity to invest out of such profits is higher than out of expected income. In practice, there are few cases of pure price stabilization: measures to stabilize prices are usually also a means of farm income support.

4   POLICY MEASURES AND ISSUES

The policies available to the government to pursue the objectives set out for the agricultural sector can be classified under four headings: price policy, productivity policies, structural policies and programmes outside agriculture. While this classification is useful for purposes of exposition, these policies will overlap to a great extent. Price policy has clear implications for price stabilization and farm income support, but it may also encourage productivity growth by removing uncertainty. Productivity policies will be largely directed at encouraging efficiency and the growth of output, but they will also influence farm income levels and the viability of a particular size structure of holdings. Structural policies will influence not only farm structures but also the potential for output expansion and the level of farm incomes, and so on. The EC's Common Agricultural Policy lays most emphasis on price policy whereas policies under the other three headings are less developed. It will be found, therefore, that the degree of discretion open to an Irish government is much greater in the case of the other three types of policy than is the case with price policy.

Price Policy
Under the Common Agricultural Policy there are a number of ways

in which the markets for different commodities are organized. The most important group includes those products with a support price in addition to external protection. Included in this group are most cereals, sugar, milk, beef and veal, pigmeat, sheepmeat and certain fruits and vegetables. In the case of sugar, the guaranteed price is limited to a specified volume of production from each member state by means of quota arrangements. In the case of milk, production is limited to a specified quantity by means of a penal 'superlevy' on production over this level. The second group comprises those products with external protection only, and includes eggs, poultry, flowers and some fruits and vegetables. There is a small group of products (durum wheat, olive oil and tobacco) which receive additional product aid along the lines of deficiency payments. This system enables prices to the consumer to be kept comparatively low, while the difference ('deficiency') between the support price and the market price is made up directly by government aid. A variable premium scheme with the same effect operates in the UK for beef, and there are elements of a deficiency payments scheme in the support of sheepmeat prices in some member states. Finally, there is a small group of products, of which potatoes is the most important from an Irish viewpoint, for which no common market organization exists as yet and where national regulations are still valid.

For each product a *target price* is set each year by the Council of Agricultural Ministers at the price review in the spring. In order to try to ensure that producers receive this price, the Commission has at its disposal a number of policy instruments, including import controls, market intervention, export subsidies and direct aids. The most important form of import control is the *variable levy*. The size of this levy is fixed on a regular basis by the Commission and approximately equals the difference between the Community target price for a commodity and the lowest price at which an exporter is prepared to supply the Community. For commodities subject to the variable levy system it ensures that no produce can be imported into the Community at a price less than the Community target price and so undermine the market price received by EC producers. If third country exporters try to become more competitive and lower their offer price, the Commission simply increases the size of the variable levy so that the selling price within the EC remains the same. Some commodities receive protection, in addition, from a customs duty while for others a customs duty alone is the sole form of protection.

On the internal market, price support to producers of some commodities is further strengthened by a guarantee that the Community stands ready to purchase farm produce from producers at a price (called the *intervention price*) usually set some 10 per cent or so below the target price, though much lower in the case of fruit and vegetables. This arrangement establishes a floor under the market, although, for various reasons, market prices may at times fall below intervention levels. If market prices rise significantly above intervention levels, then a product may be released from store, tariffs and levies may be suspended and, in exceptional cases, export taxes may be imposed in order to keep internal EC prices down. These measures are designed to fulfil that part of the CAP's objectives which seeks to provide a secure supply of food at reasonable prices to consumers. As a final measure to guarantee prices to producers, provision is made for *export refunds* (subsidies) to enable farm produce to be exported outside the Community, despite internal market prices being at much higher levels than world prices in most years. Finally, as noted above, for some products the guaranteed price is implemented directly by the payment of government aid to producers.

The uniform operation of these mechanisms requires that common guaranteed prices are fixed each year for all member states. Because of the monetary fluctuations and exchange rate instability which the EC has experienced since 1969, it has proved difficult to maintain a common price regime for farmers in all countries. A 'green currency' system requiring complex operations with monetary compensatory amounts (MCAs) has grown up to insulate farm and food prices in member countries from the effects of changes in the value of their currencies. The rationale and effects of these MCAs can be briefly described as follows.

Under the CAP, farm prices are set in units of account (European Currency Units, or ECUs) and converted into national currencies at exchange rates referred to as representative or 'green' rates. Although there is a presumption that a country's green rate and market rate of exchange with the ECU will be the same, this is not necessarily the case. If the target price for wheat is set at 300 ECU/tonne, and if the Irish green rate is such that IR£1 = 1.5 ECU, then the target price for wheat in Irish pounds will be IR£200. If the Irish pound was now to revalue against the other currencies in the ECU, and its green rate followed, so that IR£1 now equalled 2 ECU, then the price of wheat in Irish currency would fall to IR£150. On the other hand, if the Irish pound was devalued with respect to the ECU, and the green rate followed, so that IR£1 was now worth only 1 ECU, then the price of wheat in Ireland would rise to IR£300. This result can be generalized. A revaluation of a country's green rate against the ECU will result in lower farm and food prices; a devaluation of a country's green rate against the ECU will result in higher farm and food prices.

For political reasons EC governments may be unwilling to alter their country's green rate when there is a change in the market value of their currency. When the German mark revalues, for example, the German government should also revalue its green rate so that prices to German farmers fall. Because of the strength of the farm lobby in Germany, however, that government has sometimes refused to change its green rate when the mark revalued so as to avoid the wrath of its farmers, and German farm prices denominated in marks remain the same.

The devaluation of the pound sterling during the period 1975-79 should have led the UK government to devalue also the sterling green rate, which would have meant that farm prices in the UK would have risen. Because the UK at that time had a Labour government, which was unwilling to see food prices rise as a result of the devaluation of sterling, it refused to change its green rate and farm prices in the UK denominated in sterling remained unchanged.

When a government refuses to alter its green rate when there is a change in the market rate of exchange of its currency, this leads to distortions in trade in the absence of compensating measures. Take the case of Ireland and assume that the Irish pound has devalued against other ECU currencies. Irish farmers expect to receive higher prices for their produce as a result. In the numerical example above, the price of wheat is expected to increase from IR£200 to IR£300 per tonne. If the Irish government is very conscious of the effect of the devaluation on food prices, however, it may refuse to devalue the green rate and the price of wheat in Ireland would remain at IR£200. Irish farmers know, however, that if they sell their wheat in the UK they will be paid in sterling, and if they bring this sterling to their bank they will receive the equivalent in Irish currency at the higher market rate of exchange. Although there has been no change in the UK sterling price, the Irish price will be higher at IR£300 when the sterling proceeds are exchanged at the bank. It will thus become much more profitable to sell wheat in the UK than in Ireland, where the government is trying to maintain the wheat price at its original level of IR£200.

To offset the advantage of selling in the UK or elsewhere outside Ireland, it will be necessary to levy a border tax on exports equal to IR£100, in order to equalize returns. If there were agricultural imports into Ireland before the devaluation, it will now be necessary to pay an MCA subsidy to these exporters to maintain the attractiveness of the Irish market. This is the rationale of MCAs. They prevent the distortions in trade which would result when governments wish to maintain a green rate of exchange different from the normal market rate of exchange. They allow quite different national farm price levels to exist within the Community, while at the same time ensuring that farmers of any one country always receive their 'national' price regardless of whether they sell at home or abroad.

As currency differences grew within the Community during the 1970s, so did the differences in farm prices. At one stage the differences between prices received by UK and German farmers increased to over 40 per cent. The paradox is that when MCAs rise to this level they create new distortions in the allocation of resources within the Community. Production is encouraged in countries with appreciated currencies, because their farmers now find they can purchase farm inputs — on which no MCAs are payable — at more favourable prices even though they have suffered no reduction in farm product prices. Production is discouraged in countries with depreciated currencies, because their farmers must pay higher prices for their fertilizers, oil and machinery after the devaluation, yet the MCAs prevent them from receiving any compensating advantage in terms of higher farm product prices. Ireland has often been disadvantaged in this way.

The Commission has proposed on various occasions a more automatic adjustment mechanism for green rate changes to try to reduce the significance of MCAs in agricultural trade. When the EMS was initiated in 1979, a 'gentleman's agreement' was introduced whereby all member states, except the UK, agreed that any new MCAs created after that date would be phased out over two years provided that this did not lead to a drop in support prices in national currency for countries which had revalued. The qualification was vital. Because of the restrictive price policy pursued in the 1980s, prices in ECUs have not been increased fast enough to permit countries whose currency has revalued (Germany and the Netherlands in particular) to revalue their green rates sufficiently to abolish their MCAs.

In 1984 the Commission hit on a new scheme. It recommended that, after a currency realignment, the value of the ECU for agricultural purposes would be increased by a 'correction factor' reflecting the amount by which the country with the largest revaluation had revalued. This strategy ensured that revaluing countries would never need to revalue their green rate of exchange and thus eliminated the need for MCAs in these countries.

However, it also meant that the value of the 'agricultural ECU' gradually increased over time, so providing all other member states with the opportunity for larger 'green currency' price increases. It was thus a very inflationary mechanism and permitted weaker currency countries to escape the full rigours of the EC's restrictive prices policy in the 1980s. In 1987 the Commission proposed yet further modifications which attempted to reconcile the interests of farmers in strong currency countries (where farm prices should be falling) with the budgetary requirements for a strict agricultural pricing policy.[8] These proposals met with strenuous opposition from Germany, in particular, and it now seems unlikely that the Commission's goal of eliminating the MCA mechanism by 1992 (the date for the completion of the internal market envisaged in the Single European Act) will be met.

Through the operation of the CAP, price policy has ensured a greater degree of internal price stability than in other countries and has meant higher per capita incomes for a greater number of farmers than would otherwise have been the case; the policy has come in for heavy criticism. Target prices usually exceed world prices and for a number of commodities, such as milk, cereals, olive oil and wine this has led to the growth of unsustainable surpluses for which no remunerative market exists. The policy has also been criticized for its high costs. Approximately three-quarters of the Community budget is devoted to agriculture, though this is due in part to the failure to develop Community policies in other areas. The Commission points out that market support expenditure is equivalent to no more than 0.4 per cent of the Community's Gross Domestic Product, 2.5 per cent of the Community's expenditure on food and 5.6 per cent of the gross value of the Community's agricultural output.[9] This calculation, however, only takes into account that part of the cost of the policy which is borne by the taxpayer. As the price support mechanisms under the CAP operate primarily by raising consumer prices through import controls and market intervention, the consumer cost of the policy is much greater than that part borne by taxpayers. Just how much greater depends on the price levels at which alternative supplies are available on the world market.

As a net agricultural exporter, Ireland is a prime beneficiary of the CAP price policy. It gains as a result of the transfer from European consumers on account of the price differential between what they presently pay for Irish produce and what they would pay if the CAP ceased to exist, and by net payments from the Guarantee Section of FEOGA, the fund which finances EC agricultural spending, as well. It follows that any reduction in the EC's commitment to guarantee high prices for agricultural products would have a detrimental effect on this country.

Yet change is being forced on the CAP by a combination of internal and external circumstances. In 1984 the EC reached the limit of its own resources permitted by the legislation which established its financing system. Unlike national governments the EC is unable to borrow, and thus depends on getting the agreement of all member states to raise the contributions they are prepared to make to the Community. Agreement was reached in 1984 to raise the ceiling on VAT revenue accruing to the Community from 1.0 to 1.4 per cent, although, as the price of this agreement, new rules to restrain the growth in agricultural expenditure were also introduced. In practice, these rules proved unenforceable and agricultural spending continues to drive the Community to the brink of bankruptcy.

These internal strains are compounded by external pressures. The EC's need to export its growing surpluses with the aid of export subsidies means that it is taking an ever-increasing share of a slow-growing world market at the expense of traditional agricultural exporters such as the US. These traditional exporters are naturally aggrieved, and have placed enormous pressure on the EC to limit the growth of its supplies. These internal and external pressures have led to a restrictive price policy within the CAP in recent years, designed to reduce the level of real farm prices, and to the setting of production thresholds and quotas on the amount of produce which the EC is prepared to finance. The surplus problem became so serious in dairying that the 'superlevy' system agreed in 1984 amounts to an absolute prohibition on increasing milk production above the base year level. Falling real prices and quantitative restrictions on the major products will continue to characterize EC agricultural policy for the remainder of the 1980s.

Attention was drawn earlier to the fact that farm profitability is not determined solely by the trend in output prices. What matters is the relative movement of output and input prices. It is unfortunate that the trend in Irish input prices, which is largely determined by the domestic inflation rate, has in recent years tended to exacerbate the problems of a falling output price level. Irish input prices have risen faster than the input prices facing farmers in other EC countries, and this has intensified the price-cost squeeze facing farmers here. This disparity should be less important in future now that the Irish inflation rate has begun to converge to the average rate experienced by the other participants in the EMS.

Productivity Policies

Policies directed towards existing farm managers whose purpose is to encourage a better utilization of resources on farms are called productivity policies. Policies in this category include: grant aid towards farm investment; input subsidies; animal health measures; research, education and advisory programmes; land reclamation and drainage; and taxation.

Subsidies and grants are intended to encourage productivity to the extent that they induce farmers to use more current inputs or to undertake more capital investment than they otherwise would; they also contribute directly to raising farm incomes. The value of these aids can be difficult to ascertain as they are paid on the entire consumption of a subsidized input or with respect to the total investment undertaken, and it is difficult to know how much would have been used or invested in the absence of aid. Input subsidies have played an important part in the past in government efforts to stimulate agricultural output. Subsidies for the use of fertilizer and lime were introduced in the First Programme for Economic Expansion to encourage the expansion of grassland production. The subsidy was criticized by the Committee on the Review of State Expenditure in Relation to Agriculture which felt that spending money to encourage fertilizer use without ensuring that farmers also made the necessary complementary changes in their methods of production was generally a waste of resources.[10] The fertilizer subsidies were finally abolished in 1978 as being incompatible with EC membership. Headage grants to encourage an increase in cattle numbers have also been widely used. An example is the scheme for expansion of the cattle breeding herd, introduced in 1982 for a three-year period, to encourage an increase in cow numbers by paying grants on additional calved heifers kept by herdowners above their normal cow herd replacements.

During the 1980s a variety of government initiatives designed to lower interest rates for particular groups of farmers were introduced. These programmes fell into two categories; direct interest subsidy schemes, and a state guarantee against adverse exchange rate movements on Eurocurrency borrowing at cheaper interest rates. These schemes had the twin objectives of encouraging farm development in an era of high interest rates and of providing assistance to farmers who were in financial difficulty because of adverse weather conditions or the high interest rate levels. Because the distribution of farm borrowings is highly skewed, these subsidies are highly regressive, and they have also been expensive to the state. They are defended on the grounds that they helped to retain a corps of experienced farmers in farming despite unforeseen financial difficulties, and that without them expansion at current interest rates, particularly of cattle production, would be virtually impossible.[11]

Throughout the 1970s aid for farm investment was channelled through the Farm Modernization Scheme. Its operation has been briefly summarized by NESC:

> The philosophy behind the Farm Modernization Scheme, introduced in Ireland in February 1974, is that aid to farmers for capital improvements and herd expansion should be given in the context of a development plan for the farm rather than for specific projects. The amount paid is graduated according to the initial income position of the farm and the level of income target of its development plan. Maximum levels of aid are given to farmers who can develop their farms over a period of six years to provide an income comparable to average non-agricultural earnings in the region (development farmers). Lower levels of aid are given to farmers who already earn at least the average industrial wage (commercial farmers), and to farmers whose resources are not sufficient to allow them to reach a comparable income within a specified time period (other farmers). This latter group will not, however, require a development plan to qualify for aid towards farm improvements.[12]

The scheme made a significant impact on farming during its period of operation. A total of 105,000 farmers were admitted to the scheme by the end of 1982. Of these farmers, approximately 5 per cent were judged to be commercial, 25 per cent were put in the development category and the remaining 70 per cent were placed in the other, or transitional, category. One of the reasons for the high proportion of 'other' farmers was that the labour income on the farm was calculated by deducting from gross income an allowance for capital employed, whether owned or borrowed. The level of farm incomes is generally low in this country, and to focus on the labour income element alone made it even more difficult for smaller farmers to achieve the comparable income target. The scheme was thus criticized for directing most assistance to medium-sized and larger farms at the expense of smaller ones, and some changes to make it easier for smaller farms to reach development status were introduced in later years.

During the period of operation of the Farm Modernization Scheme, a total of IR£217 million was paid out by way of capital grants, representing a total investment of around IR£1,000 million on farms. The vast bulk of this on-farm investment went into the provision of modern buildings. There is controversy over whether this investment yielded a commensurate rate of return, but Department of Agriculture figures suggest that on the basis of expected prices and costs when development plans were being drawn up a rate of return to the state of around 15 per cent was anticipated. The realized rate of return will have been less because of the deterioration in price and cost conditions which occurred since the end of the 1970s.

The Farm Modernization Scheme was terminated on September 30, 1985, following the expiry of the EC Directive 72/159. Under the revised EC agricultural structures policy, approved in March 1985, a new Farm Improvement Programme has been introduced. Under the new programme investment aid is provided to full-time farmers who have adequate training and farming experience, whose income per man work unit is below the reference income for the region and who undertake a farm improvement plan designed to improve the income per man work unit by at least five per cent. Additional investment aid is available for young farmers. The major differences with the earlier Farm Modernization Scheme are that the three categories of farmers no longer exist and that investment aids for certain enterprises, for example, dairying, where market conditions are unfavourable, are restricted.

Ireland has a good animal health status facilitated by the fact that it is an island and that livestock is exported rather than imported. However, there are a number of economically important diseases, particularly bovine tuberculosis and brucellosis, for which control and eradication programmes are in operation. The costs of animal disease arise from the lower productivity of animals which are ill, the loss in value as a result of being excluded from certain export markets, as well as the public health danger where the diseases are transmissible to humans. As most of these costs are borne by farmers themselves, it might be argued that it is in their own interests to cope with them without state aid. The Committee on State Expenditure in Relation to Agriculture pointed out, however, that major eradication schemes require a degree of regulation which is beyond the ability of farmers themselves to enforce and that without state aid by way of compensation, individual farmers could not afford to embark on eradication programmes. The programmes have been enormously costly, both to the state and to individual farmers. The cost to the state alone has varied between IR£15 and IR£20 million annually during the past five years, though farmers have been contributing an increasing proportion of these costs through disease levies since 1984. The country was declared free of brucellosis in 1984, but progress with respect to bovine TB remains disappointingly slow. A number of reasons have been suggested for its continued high incidence, including defective testing, tag switching, inadequate management of the scheme, the high volume of cattle movements in the country and stop-go funding policies. A consistent policy over at least a ten-year period will be required to bring the disease incidence down to acceptable levels.[13]

State support for the agricultural research and advisory services is similarly justified on the grounds of their collective nature. The economies of scale associated with research make it impractical for individual farmers to consider undertaking it, while the public good nature of research results means that private firms will underinvest in agricultural research because of the difficulty of ensuring that they can recoup their investment (see Chapter 7). Agricultural education and advisory work is the responsibility of An Chomhairle Oiliúna Talmhaíochta (ACOT). Particular attention is now being paid to the training of young people entering farming for the first time. ACOT have established a *Certificate in Farming* (the 'Green Cert') course to cater for this group. In the future it is likely that possession of this certificate will be a requirement for receipt of state development aid.

Farm development is also influenced by the system of farm taxation through its effect on incentives and on the availability of cash for reinvestment. Income taxation on farming profits was reintroduced for a limited number of farmers in the 1974 Budget. The number of farmers liable for tax was gradually extended until by 1983 all farmers were in principle fully within the income tax system. In practice, only around 44,000 farmers were required to make returns to the Revenue Commissioners, although most of the remainder would have had incomes below the threshold for tax liability. The tax yield has averaged around IR£30-35 million per annum in recent years.

In the planning document, *Building on Reality,* the government announced their intention to introduce a farm tax based on a flat-rate payment of IR£10 per adjusted acre, for farms over 20 adjusted acres, in order to double the yield from farmer taxation. Progress in classifying farms according to their adjusted acreage was much slower than envisaged, and in the first year of operation of the tax, 1986, a tax liability of only IR£5 million was assessed of which less than IR£1 million was paid in that year. The incoming government abolished the farm tax in 1987 and reverted to a system of taxing farm incomes based on farm accounts. In the calculation of liability to tax, farming profits are calculated in accordance with normal accounting practice, but extra allowances are available for capital expenditure and for increases in stock values.

In the past some farmers paid rates on their land, though not on domestic dwellings or farm buildings. The valuation of land for rating purposes was carried out in the middle of the last century, and had not been subsequently updated, with the result that there were many anomalies in the rates burden borne by different farmers. Farmers successfully brought a court action to have rates declared unconstitutional for this reason, and rates on land were abolished in 1983. There are arguments in favour of replacing rates on land by another, more equitable, form of land tax as a way of encouraging the more efficient utilization of land (indeed, the farm tax discussed above can be seen as a form of land tax) and these arguments are considered in the next section.

Structural Policies

Structural policy is designed to influence the pace and direction of land transfers over time. It has two principal objectives: to bring about improved land use by encouraging the transfer of management control of land to those more likely to make efficient use of it, and to secure the desired pattern of structure and ownership of farming. It has already been seen that structural policy as implemented by the Land Commission in the past was primarily concerned with the latter objective. It is only recently that there has been more emphasis on the role of structural policy in bringing about more efficient land use, by encouraging both the earlier transfer of land from present occupiers and greater land mobility.

The report of the Inter-departmental Committee on Land Structure Reform identified three characteristics of the Irish land tenure system which are obstacles to improved land use. These are: the predominance of owner-occupancy; the strong sense of attachment to the family holding which results in the bulk of land being exchanged through family transfers rather than through the land market; and the prevalence of short-term, eleven-month leasing. These three factors in combination give rise to a very inflexible tenure system.

The consequence of this tenure system is the relatively late age of inheritance and succession. A Macra na Feirme Farm Inheritance Survey reported that 68 per cent of those handing over the farm during their lifetime did so after they reached the age of 70 years, and that almost half of those receiving farms did not get title until after the age of 35.[14] A later survey for the NESC came up with an average age of succession of 31 years for the new generation of farm operators (i.e. excluding those cases where the farm passes to another member of the family of the same generation).[15] Apart from difficulties created for the individual heirs in that, for example, marriage may have to be postponed until after ownership is obtained, late succession may adversely affect agricultural performance on the assumption that there is a negative correlation between age and progressive farming. A second defect of the present land tenure structure is that smaller but efficient farmers are at a disadvantage in acquiring extra land. It is also very difficult for a young farmer to begin in farming other than by inheritance. The same NESC report estimated that only one out of every ten of the new generation of farm operators between 1971 and 1975 entered farming through the purchase of land.

The first step towards encouraging earlier transfer was the Farm Retirement Scheme introduced in 1967. The scheme failed to attract support, and only 38 farmers eventually participated. Following EC membership, a new Retirement Scheme was introduced. Under it, farmers over 55 years of age and with less that 50 acres of land could opt to dispose of their land by sale or lease to the Land Commission or to a development farmer in return for an annuity based on the sale value and a pension. Unfortunately, despite an encouraging start, this scheme met a similar fate to its predecessor. Reasons suggested for the falling-off in the scheme's popularity include the failure to maintain the value of the pension in line with inflation, and the fact that receipt of the pension affected a farmer's entitlement to the state pension and some associated non-cash benefits. Even a successful scheme would have had a limited national impact, however, as it did not apply in any case to transfers within the family, which account for the great majority of land transfers in the country.

Long-term leasing has been suggested as another way of encouraging greater land mobility, by separating the question of land ownership from the management control of land. The assumption is made that there would be fewer inhibitions about more frequent changes in management control than in ownership itself. There has been little discussion of the possible effects of such a change on agricultural structures or productivity. The Inter-departmental Committee Report on Land Structure Reform lists a number of factors which have inhibited the emergence of long-term leasing, including public attitudes which presume a right for persons in occupation of lands for a considerable length of time to retain possession when a letting contract expires, the difficulty for credit agencies in securing advances made to leaseholders, and a tendency in earlier years for the Land Commission to discourage leasing. In order to encourage medium-term leasing, a tax-break on lease income from land has been introduced.

A land tax could be another instrument to encourage greater land mobility and farm development. This would be because a flat-rate tax on land, taking account of soil quality, would be a heavier burden on less efficient farmers, and so would put pressure on them to release their land to more efficient farmers or to farm it more efficiently themselves. This latter effect would be strengthened if farmers following a development plan were exempted from the land tax.

The role of the Land Commission in the creation of viable holdings has been described earlier, but its operations became increasingly slow, expensive and of doubtful effectiveness. The Inter-departmental Report on Land Structure Reform recommended that the direct involvement of the state in the acquisition and allocation of land should be replaced by the indirect regulation of land transfers through the market. In its view, the purpose of regulation would be to improve the competitive position of the smaller landholder while trying to ensure that land coming on the market passes into the control of persons most likely to utilize it effectively. A government White Paper on Land Policy published in 1980 accepted the need for the monitoring and control of land market transactions. This control would be exercised positively, by providing incentives to those deemed to be priority applicants for additional land, and negatively, by imposing surcharges on purchases by less-favoured applicants (non-residential farmers, larger farmers) and by refusing consent to certain transactions. However, the White Paper did argue in addition for the retention of the Land Commission and its powers of compulsory acquisition. It saw a need for these powers as long as a substantial acreage of land remains underutilized in the hands of owners who are not interested in its development. Direct state involvement in land acquisition and division was also justified by the structural and demographic problems of western farming, where total reliance on the open market system might deprive many smallholders of what might well be their only prospect of increasing their holdings to a reasonable level of viability. However, in 1983 the further acquisition of land by the Land Commission was suspended pending the introduction of legislation to abolish it. Future land policy remains under discussion in the Department of Agriculture.

Non-Agricultural Programmes

There are many farmers with small acreages who benefit little from price policy, for whom programmes of agricultural development do little to help them achieve an acceptable standard of living, and who will not be affected by policies of structural reform. For these farmers, programmes outside agriculture may be the best way to alleviate rural poverty. Two such programmes, the provision of off-farm employment and direct income aids, are considered in this section.

The spread of rural industrialization in the past decade has given many small farmers the chance to improve their incomes by giving them the opportunity for off-farm employment. It may also contribute to structural reform if the availability of industrial employment persuaded the heir to a farm to relinquish his/her title, but there is little evidence that this is occurring on any scale. Currently, farmers with off-farm employment account for 25 per cent of the farming population. Part-time farmers are not concentrated in any one occupational group but are widely dispersed across occupations and professions. It can arise either when a farmer seeks off-farm employment or when a trader or business person invests in farming. Whichever the route, the statistics show that the phenomenon is concentrated in the smaller size groups: 75 per cent of part-time farms are holdings of less than 20 hectares, 45 per cent are less than 10 hectares in size.

There is great controversy about the desirability of this trend towards a greater incidence of part-time farming. There is no doubt that, other things being equal, total family income is higher on farms with off-farm employment than on farms without. The drawback is that part-time farming may result in a less intensive pattern of land use. Data from the National Farm Survey show that part-time farms have a lower level of productivity per hectare than full-time farms, and a slower rate of growth in the volume of output. This relatively poor aggregate performance is due to the fact that part-time farmers concentrate their farming in drystock production to a much greater extent than full-time farmers. These drystock systems (cattle and sheep production) suit multiple job holders because they have relatively low labour requirements per unit of output. When farming system is adjusted for, part-time farmers tend to perform similarly to full-time ones.

It is sometimes argued that part-time farmers should be discriminated against in the matter of state support, on the grounds that their off-farm job implies a weaker commitment to farming. This argument was considered by the National Planning Board and rejected for two reasons. First, the bulk of such farmers have very small holdings which even if farmed to the limits of existing technology might not provide an acceptable standard of living for the occupants. Second, they saw no case in equity for discriminating against an extensive drystock farmer, for example, who happens to have an off-farm job, and his neighbour who also operates an extensive drystock system but who does not have an off-farm job. The objective should be to bring about a more efficient use of land overall, perhaps through the introduction of a fiscal charge on land as suggested in the previous section.

Curry has suggested that certain selectivity factors operate in the recruitment of farmers to off-farm employment and that many low-income farmers will simply not be interested for age or other reasons in seeking an off-farm job. Direct income payments may be one way to help this latter group. Two principal schemes of this kind presently operating are social security and payments under the Disadvantaged Areas Scheme.[16]

Farmers are entitled to unemployment benefit and assistance provided they meet the eligibility criteria. Receipt of unemployment benefit is conditional on having a minimum number of insurance contributions paid or credited, and farmers who have off-farm jobs, as well as those who are unemployed following a period of more permanent work, may be entitled to claim. Unemployment assistance depends on the recipient satisfying a means test. For some years in the western counties means were assessed on a notional basis on a farmer's land valuation. It was felt that a factual means test was a disincentive to the farmer to increase his output, because the higher the income from his farm, the lower the assistance received.

Now that the old system of land valuation has been declared unconstitutional, the state has reverted to a factual assessment of means. Given that many of the recipients are elderly farmers, it is doubtful if this change in the administration of the scheme will have much effect on the level of farm output.

The Disadvantaged Areas Scheme is relatively recent, having been introduced in 1975. Its coverage is mostly limited to the western counties and to one or two areas of high altitude outside. Its purpose is to encourage farmers to remain in these areas in order to ensure the continuation of farming, the maintenance of a reasonable level of population and the preservation of the countryside. Income supplements are paid to farmers based on their number of livestock units, up to a maximum of 30 livestock units per farm. There is a further distinction in this country between seriously disadvantaged areas and less favoured areas, with the former being allowed to include dairy stock in the calculation of livestock units. The scheme has been heavily criticized as inappropriate in Irish circumstances, where there is little evidence of outright abandonment in the areas designated, and because the distribution of aid under the scheme is related neither to equity nor productivity objectives.[17]

The danger with schemes of direct income aid, where the aid is related to farm area or to farm activities, is that by encouraging farmers to retain their land they are in direct conflict with the objectives of other schemes, such as the Farm Retirement Scheme, whose purpose it is to facilitate agricultural restructuring by persuading farmers to release their land. It has been proposed instead that the aid provided under these schemes should be redirected either into development schemes where the assistance would be conditional on evidence of farm development or towards providing more generous inducements to farmers prepared to release their land.[18]

5   CONCLUSION

This chapter has described the extensive nature of state intervention in the agricultural sector. Four objectives of state policy have been looked at: growth in agricultural output, farm income support, a desired farm structure, and price stabilization. The policy instruments available to the government to achieve these objectives have been classified under the four headings of price policy, productivity policies, structural policy and programmes outside of agriculture.

This review of Irish agricultural policy raises a number of questions for discussion. Are the goals of this policy appropriate ones? Are they consistent? Is the right mix of policy instruments being used to achieve these goals? Are particular policies implemented in the most cost-effective fashion? What are the distributional consequences of government intervention? With respect to agricultural policy, many of the 'rules of the game' are now determined in Brussels. Should the Irish government be attempting to change these rules? In what direction?

The future environment in which agricultural policy will operate is also changing. At EC level, the need for modifications arises, in the first instance, from the development of surpluses of certain agricultural products which are at present disposed of outside the Community at substantial cost to its budget. The second argument for change is that the policy is too costly and pre-empts too high a proportion of Community funds, and that the present ceiling on budgetary expenditure by the EC will force adjustments to the CAP even where policy-makers themselves cannot agree. Third, there is the criticism that the CAP is ineffective in meeting certain of its objectives and, in particular, that regional disparities within the Community have continued to increase. Fourth, there is the fact that the operation of CAP results in resource transfers between contributory and beneficiary states which are difficult to justify on either economic or equity grounds. Finally, there is the prospect that the balance within the EC between producers, on the one hand, and consumers and foreign trade interests on the other, may be shifting in favour of the latter as the importance of agriculture in the Community economy declines.

Any change in the CAP has a significant impact on the farm policy environment in this country. The prospects for the CAP for the remainder of the 1980s are not encouraging from the point of view of farmers. For this reason, there should be an increased emphasis on the domestic policy objectives. A more rigorous structural policy to improve land use, and a more cost-effective choice of productivity policies to increase farm efficiency, are two possible responses by the state to the unfavourable external environment. The adjustments demanded of the agricultural sector over the next few years will not be easy ones. About the only certainty is that agricultural policy will continue to be a lively source of controversy in the years ahead.

Footnotes

1 Calculated from NESC, *Economic and Social Policy 1980-83: Aims and Recommendations* (Report no. 53), Stationery Office, Dublin 1980, Table 7.

2 J. Frawley, 'Rural Development in a Regional Context — A Sociological Approach' (unpublished paper, An Foras Talúntais), 1975.

3 A. Conway, 'Inter-Farm Differences in Growth of Output' (unpublished paper, An Foras Talúntais), 1974.

4 A. Matthews, 'The Changing Distribution of Income in Irish Agriculture', *Proceedings of the Agricultural Economics Society of Ireland,* 1981.

5 NESC, *Rural Areas: Social Planning Problems* (Report no. 19), Stationery Office, Dublin 1976.

6 *Report of the Inter-departmental Committee on Land Structure Reform*, Stationery Office, Dublin 1978.

7 *Report of the Review Body on Beef Intervention and Cattle Slaughter Premium Systems*, Stationery Office, Dublin 1976.

8 Commission of the European Communities, *Report on the Agrimonetary System* (COM (87) 64), Brussels 1977.

9 Commission of the European Communities, *The Common Agricultural Policy and its Reform* (European Documentation Periodical 1/1987), Brussels 1977.

10 *Report of the Committee on the Review of State Expenditure in Relation to Agriculture,* Stationery Office, Dublin 1970.

11 A. Matthews, 'Agricultural Credit and Public Policy', *Irish Journal of Agricultural Economics and Rural Sociology*, 11.

12 NESC (Report no. 19), *op.cit.*

13 R. O'Connor, *A Study of the Bovine Tuberculosis Eradication Scheme* (Research Paper 133), ESRI, Dublin 1986.

14 Macra na Feirme, *Farm Inheritance and Succession*, Dublin 1973.

15 NESC, *New Farm Operators, 1971 to 1975* (Report no. 27), Stationery Office, Dublin 1976.

16 NESC (Report no. 19), *op.cit.*

17 P. Cox, 'EEC Directive 268 and the Disadvantaged Areas' (paper read to Regional Studies Association (Irish Branch)), 1977.

18 NESC, *Policies to Accelerate Agricultural Growth* (Report no. 40), Stationery Office, Dublin 1978.

11   The Traded Sector: Manufacturing

Frances Ruane*

AS ALREADY discussed at some length in Chapter 7, to facilitate higher rates of domestic consumption in an open economy without undue pressures on the balance of payments or exchange rate, increased production of internationally-traded commodities is essential. Such commodities may either satisfy domestic consumption needs directly or be exported to finance the foreign exchange requirements of consumer imports. In the Irish context, the expansion of tradable industrial output, and manufactured output in particular, has been seen as an essential component in this process because of the limited potential for expanding the main resource-based industry, agriculture (see Chapter 10). Consequently, Irish industrial policy over the past thirty years has promoted the growth of tradable manufactured output. Substantial inflows of direct foreign investment, over that period, have facilitated the expansion of manufacturing, and have also given temporary relief to the balance-of-payments constraints on the expansion of domestic demand.

However, after a fifteen-year period in which there was rapid growth in output, exports and employment in manufacturing, the past fifteen years has witnessed a dramatic slowdown in growth rates and in the past five years manufacturing employment has declined significantly. In order to understand this recent change in the fortunes of the manufacturing sector and the role of policy in that change, this chapter examines the role of the manufacturing sector in the economy and its performance, focussing in particular on the rapid rate of turnover of projects and jobs. The major policies which have played a key role in the industrial strategy are examined and their impact on industrial expansion is evaluated.

* The author is very grateful to John FitzGerald, Economic and Social Research Institute, and Peter O'Brien and Paul Cronin, Industrial Development Authority, for providing the data used in Section 2, and to John FitzGerald, Paul Turpin and the editor for comments and suggestions on the chapter. Finally, research and production assistance from Dale Chua and Angela Street, Queen's University, Kingston, Ontario, is gratefully acknowledged.

1   ROLE OF THE MANUFACTURING SECTOR

The current approach to the development of the Irish manufacturing sector dates back to the 1950s, when it was gradually realized that the agricultural sector would not be a major source of income and employment growth in the latter half of the twentieth century. Since Ireland was thought to be a resource-scarce country, expansion of manufacturing output, with its high income and price elasticities and relatively labour-intensive production processes seemed to be the most likely growth and employment sector for the economy. Consequently, a growth strategy based on the promotion of manufacturing projects was proposed. A complication was the existence of an inefficent and stagnant import-substituting manufacturing sector which by the late 1950s was becoming rapidly uncompetitive despite high tariff protection. Thus the strategy became one of promoting manufacturing output for export only, as this would avoid competition with existing import-substituting firms. At the same time, as part of the industrial strategy, protection would be phased out as Ireland followed the Western European movement towards free trade, which culminated in Ireland joining the European Community in 1973.

A key assumption underlying the rationale for adopting this strategy was that while at least initially an exporting sector required government support to develop, in the long term there would be a strong manufacturing sector which would be self-sustaining and that its growth would stimulate growth elsewhere in the economy.[1] This strategy of promoting those exports which have high growth potential, so that the growth will spill over into the rest of the economy through production and consumption linkages, is referred to as *export-led growth*.[2] The likely success of such a strategy depends both on its appropriateness to the Irish context and on finding the correct policies which may be used to implement it. For export-led growth to be a viable economic strategy, two key elements are essential: first, that the promotion of these commodities does not crowd out growth elsewhere in the economy; and second, that the consumption and production linkages, which are crucial if the growth in exports is to be translated into a growth in national output, must be realized.

Even if these two elements are present, the strategy will only be effective if the choice of policies used to implement it is appropriate. For example, the selection of the commodities chosen for promotion must be those in which the country ultimately has a comparative advantage, so that even if these sectors are not competitive immediately, they will be sufficiently profitable in the future to justify support in the intitial period. Furthermore, the markets for the promoted commodities must continue to grow, and finally, the methods of promotion and the support of particular commodities must operate so as to ensure that the conditions required for export-led growth to be realized are met in practice. In the final section of this chapter, an attempt will be made to identify the extent to which the failure of the manufacturing sector in recent years to achieve the stated objectives of self-sustaining growth in the promoted sectors and induced growth elsewhere in the economy is the result of inappropriate policies, and the extent to which it arises from the limitations on any export-led-growth strategy operating in the Irish context.

Before discussing the choice of policies used to implement Ireland's export-led-growth strategy, the recent performance of the manufacturing sector is examined.

2   TRENDS IN MANUFACTURING

Over the period 1957 to 1985, the volume of manufactured output more than trebled, while employment in manufacturing grew from

Table 11.1

Average Annual Percentage Growth Rates in Manufacturing Output and Employment,[1] 1957-86

	Volume of ouput	Employment
1957-62	6.98	2.07
1962-67	5.61	1.63
1967-72	5.85	1.53
1972-77	5.43	1.32
1977-82	3.73	0.61
1983	7.65	− 6.01
1984	n.a.[2]	− 3.65
1985	2.68	− 3.32
1986	2.80	− 1.96

Sources: Department of Finance, 'Data Bank of Economic Time Series', February 1987.

[1] Volume of output in manufacturing is measured by Gross Domestic Product at factor cost at constant 1975 prices, and employment is average employment in manufacturing firms covered by the Census of Industrial Production.

[2] Because of a change in the deflator used for two major components of manufactured output, namely computers and chemicals in 1984, no accurate measure of the true volume change in manufactured output is available yet for 1984.

over 163,000 in 1957 to over 200,000 in 1986. However, the rates of growth have by no means been constant over this period as Table 11.1 indicates; this table shows the trend in output and employment growth for each five-year period from 1957 to 1982, and for the years 1982-86, taken separately.

In the first subperiod, during which the Irish economy began to reverse the economic decline of the early and mid-1950s, output and employment in manufacturing grew at unprecedented rates. This performance, which was far more spectacular than anything anticipated by the authors of the First Programme for Economic Expansion, generated considerable expectations of further employment and output growth in manufacturing, and paved the way for increased policy intervention in the manufacturing sector during the 1960s and 1970s. The sector continued to grow rapidly throughout the 1960s and by 1972, the year before Ireland's entry into the European Community (EC) and the first major rise in world oil prices, output in manufacturing was two-and-a-half times its 1957 level, and manufacturing employment was 30 per cent higher.

While manufacturing output continued to grow at over five per cent per annum during the mid-1970s, the growth in manufacturing employment began to slow down. While aggregate employment in manufacturing rose slightly, in the five-year period 1977-82, a downturn in employment was already in train as the considerable growth in the first three years was almost completely offset by a decline in the final two years. The rate of decline in employment peaked between 1982 and 1983 but employment in manufacturing has continued to decline, albeit at a diminishing rate, and employment is now below its 1968 level. Meanwhile the growth in manufactured output continued at over 3.5 per cent in the five years 1977-82, and while this rate was low by the standards of the previous two decades, it was relatively high by international standards, as this period was dominated by the world recession which followed the second major international oil price rise in 1979. The performance of manufacturing output in the post-1982 period has followed the trend in employment, with lower rates of growth in output, and a weaker export performance. While the overall performance is difficult to gauge because there are no reliable data available for 1984,[3] it is markedly weaker than in earlier periods, for, despite the high growth rate in 1983 (which contrasts dramatically with the decline in employment in the same year), the growth rates in 1985 and 1986 were less than three per cent. In subsequent sections, the reasons underlying this change in performance of manufacturing output and employment will be discussed in terms of the apparent diminishing success of the export-led-growth strategy.

While Table 11.1 presents an overall picture for the manufacturing sector, this aggregate view masks a considerable amount of diversity at the subperiod, subsector and plant levels. Ideally, analyses at these levels should be based on net value added in manufacturing, but as such data are not available, absolute employment numbers in manufacturing plants are used as an indicator of value added. Since technological change in some sectors is inherently labour saving, the use of employment as a measure of value added is not perfect; however, employment is the only measure available at plant level on a time-series basis, and in the case of foreign-owned firms, it consititutes the major component of domestic value added. Tables 11.2 to 11.7 use employment data

Table 11.2

Manufacturing Employment by Sector,[1] 1973, 1978 and 1986

Subsector	1973		1978		1986	
	Aggregate employ- ment	Share %	Aggregate employ- ment	Share %	Aggregate employ- ment	Share %
Food	48,116	22.0	51,410	22.0	40,400	19.6
Drink and Tobacco	11,021	5.0	10,685	4.6	9,039	4.4
Textiles	20,530	9.4	17,528	7.5	10,874	5.3
Clothing, Leather and Footwear	28,122	12.8	23,878	10.2	16,781	8.1
Paper and Printing	15,890	7.3	17,126	7.3	13,991	6.8
Non-Metallic Minerals	15,491	7.1	17,163	7.4	13,318	6.4
Timber and Furniture	10,087	4.6	10,521	4.5	9,998	4.8
Chemicals	11,068	5.0	12,933	5.5	13,112	6.3
Metals and Engineering	46,750	21.3	57,544	24.6	62,148	30.1
Miscellaneous	8,347	3.8	10,356	4.4	10,329	5.0
Grant-Aided Non-Manufacturing[2]	3,706	1.7	4,701	2.0	6,537	3.2
Total	219,128	100.0	233,845	100.0	206,527	100.0

Sources: IDA Employment Survey Files.

[1] Data in this table are those collected in the IDA employment surveys taken on January 1, 1973, January 1978 and November 1, 1986. The total survey figures differ from the Central Statistics Office estimates of total employment in manufacturing in two respects. First, they include some non-manufacturing activities which are grant-aided by the IDA. Second, the 1973 figures exclude certain plants in Dublin which were not surveyed in 1973 and which subsequently closed. These employed over 8,000 people in 1973 so that the total reduction in manufacturing employment is approximately 20,000. No sectoral or nationality data are available on these closed plants.

[2] This category includes some 25 jobs which are not yet classified by sector.

from the Industrial Development Authority (IDA) employment surveys taken on and between January 1, 1973, and November 1, 1986, to examine this diversity.[4] The data include virtually all manufacturing firms and a small number of international service firms which have been grant-aided by the IDA.

The most striking feature of Table 11.2 is that all of the so-called 'traditional' sectors, (the first seven subsections listed in the table) witnessed an *absolute* decline in employment over the period 1973-86 and, with the exception of Timber and Furniture, a decline in employment *share*. However, when one looks at the two subperiods 1973-78 and 1978-86, a different pattern emerges. The decline in employment during the 1973-78 period was confined to three sectors (Drink and Tobacco; Textiles; and Clothing, Leather and Footwear) which were in a major state of structural readjustment in the wake of the gradual reduction in tariffs following the Anglo-Irish Free Trade Area agreement and Ireland's entry into the European Community.[5] The decline in these sectors was primarily the result of older Irish firms adjusting to free-trade conditions. By contrast a considerable portion of the decline in employment in the post-1978 period arose in firms which were either established as part of the export-led-growth strategy or which had received financial support to reequip and modernize in anticipation of increased competition under free trade. As will be discussed below, it is the decline in these traditional sectors in the post-1978 period which casts doubts on the success of the export-led-growth strategy.

The growth sectors of the economy (the last five subsections listed in the table), have recorded significant absolute growth in employment, and increases in the share of total manufacturing employment, over the period 1973-86 taken as a whole. In terms of employment, Metals and Engineering is now the largest manufacturing sector and most of the growth has been in domestic and foreign-owned electronics firms in that sector. However, recently there has been a decline in employment even in the Metals and Engineering sectors, from a maximum of over 70,000 in 1982 to a little over 62,000 in 1986. This decline is paralleled in the Chemicals sector, which was the other major sector emphasized in the 1970s as part of the government's export-led-growth strategy. It is this absolute decline in the employment levels combined with lower rates of output growth in the two major exporting sectors which has reinforced widespread concerns about the potential and realized success of the export-led-growth strategy.

The scale of job creation and job loss in the manufacturing sector cannot be fully appreciated without reference to gross job gains and

Table 11.3
Components of Manufacturing Employment Change,[1] 1973-86

	Total employment	Job gains	Job losses	Net change in employment
Jan 1973	219,128	—	—	—
Jan 1974	230,350	18,526	7,304	11,222
Jan 1975	230,244	16,668	16,774	– 106
Jan 1976	222,091	15,290	23,443	– 8,153
Jan 1977	227,187	22,254	17,158	5,096
Jan 1978	233,845	23,346	16,688	6,658
Jan 1979	241,879	22,029	13,995	8,034
Jan 1980	252,012	25,025	14,892	10,133
Jan 1981	245,053	19,571	26,530	– 6,959
Jan 1982	241,672	19,911	23,292	– 3,381
Nov 1982	234,716	16,623	23,579	– 6,956
Nov 1983	223,484	17,704	28,936	– 11,232
Nov 1984	215,675	16,473	24,282	– 7,809
Nov 1985	209,212	16,330	22,793	– 6,463
Nov 1986	206,527	15,702	18,400	– 2,698
Total		265,452	278,066	– 12,614
Subperiod (1973-78)		64,195	49,478	14,717
Subperiod (1978-86)		83,199	110,517	– 27,318
Total period (1973-86)[2]		114,092	126,718	– 12,626

Sources: as for Table 11.2.

[1] The estimate of jobs created in a given year was obtained by enumerating at each survey date those jobs which existed at the current survey date but which had not existed at the previous survey date. Similarly, job losses are those jobs which existed at the earlier survey date but which no longer exist. The same procedure is used for the longer time period; hence jobs gained 1973-86, for example, are jobs which exist in 1986 which did not exist in 1973. All jobs which have been gained but subsequently lost have been netted out.

[2] Estimates for the net change based on the total period and of the net change based on each year differ by a small number (13). This is due to their being calculated on slightly different base figures due to daily updating of IDA files.

losses in the sector. These are shown in Table 11.3 by year, and separately for the whole period 1973-86 and for the two subperiods, 1973-78 and 1978-86. While the change in employment is small over the whole period[6] — a decline of approximately 12,600 or 5.7 per cent — the total number of jobs created in the period was 265,452, while job losses came to 278,066; in other words, the total number of jobs created and lost between 1973 and 1986 exceeded the number in existence in either 1973 or 1986. It is possible to identify the survival rates of the original 219,128 jobs and of the 265,452 jobs which were created since 1973 by reference to the last row in Table

11.3. This row shows that over 114,000 jobs existed in 1986 which had not existed in 1973; in other words, the survival rate of new jobs created since 1973 is under 43 per cent which is scarcely more than the survival rate on the jobs already existing in 1973 (42 per cent). Although a certain level of job turnover is to be expected in manufacturing, the same failure rate in new plants as on the existing plants, many of which were engaged in traditional activities, seriously undermines the notion that the export-led-growth sector is becoming 'self-sustaining'.

Examination of the two subperiods is also revealing. Looking at 1973-78, it appears that almost 50,000 jobs or 22 per cent of the jobs which existed in 1973 were no longer in existence in 1978; in other words, the survival rate of the original 1973 jobs in the 1973-78 period was 78 per cent. It seems reasonable to suggest that many of these job losses were to be expected as the sector adjusted to free-trading conditions. However, comparison of the initial subperiod and the total-period data indicates that a further 77,200 of the original 1973 jobs or 35 per cent were lost during the period 1978-86. As it can be reasonably argued that most of the adjustment to free trade would have taken place by 1978, the further decline needs some alternative explanation.

Looking again at job gains, it is possible to calculate from the data in the table that of the 96,000 jobs created between 1973 and 1978, over 32,000 were lost in the first five years (a survival rate of 66 per cent), while a further 31,000 were lost in the subsequent eight years, yielding an overall survival rate of 32 per cent. In the period 1978-86 almost 83,200 jobs survived out of a total of almost 169,400 created in the period, a survival rate of under 50 per cent. Since 30 per cent of the jobs were created in the most recent three-year period, the outlook for job survival in the recent period does not look very favourable.

As might be expected from the aggregate figures, while net job losses occurred primarily in the traditional sectors, there were significant job losses in the sectors of the economy which were being actively promoted. This pattern is identified in Table 11.4, which lists jobs gained and lost, and net employment change by sector over the fourteen-year period. A striking feature of Table 11.4 is the significant numbers of jobs lost in the 'growth' sectors and especially in Metals and Engineering over the period. In the past five years job losses have run at between 5,000 and 10,000 per year and have *exceeded* job gains in each of those years. While a high rate of job turnover is to be expected in this sector, a net reduction of 8,000 in employment in the past five years does not augur well for self-sustaining growth or the sector's contributing to domestic value added.

Table 11.4

Components of Employment Change by Sector, 1973-86

Subsector	Job gains	Job losses	Net change in employment
Food	15,228	22,944	– 7,716
Drink and Tobacco	1,734	3,716	– 1,982
Textiles	5,020	14,676	– 9,656
Clothing, Leather and Footwear	9,816	21,157	– 11,341
Paper and Printing	5,228	7,127	– 1,899
Non-Metallic Minerals	4,581	6,754	– 2,173
Timber and Furniture	6,387	6,476	– 89
Chemicals	7,478	5,434	+ 2,044
Metals and Engineering	46,467	31,069	+ 15,398
Miscellaneous	7,422	5,440	+ 1,982
Grant-Aided Non-Manufacturing	4,731	1,925	+ 2,806
Total	114,092	126,718	– 12,626

Sources: as for Table 11.2.

In the case of the traditional sectors, a significant amount of the job losses in those sectors took place between 1973 and 1978 in response to the adjustment to free trade. However, this job loss has continued into the 1980s, and the gap between jobs gained and jobs lost has widened rather than narrowed in this period. There is nothing paradoxical *per se* about this phenomenon of gains and losses taking place simultaneously within the same sector, especially in the late 1970s as contracting or closing firms were selling on the decreasingly-protected domestic market while expanding firms were selling on the growing international market. What is of concern, is the low survival rate of many new, government-aided projects and the consequential budgetary implications. The efficiency of such a promotional policy is particularly in question if in both traditional and growth sectors the expansion of certain activities within given sectors or certain subsectors within manufacturing is crowding out other activities.

Using employment data, Table 11.5 shows how the ownership pattern of Irish manufacturing has changed over the period 1973-86. In terms of employment, close to 40 per cent of Irish manufacturing was foreign owned in 1986, compared with 33 per cent in 1978 and

Table 11.5

Manufacturing Employment by Nationality of Ownership of Project, 1973-86[1]

Nationality	1973		1978		1986	
	Aggregate employment	Share %	Aggregate employment	Share %	Aggregate employment	Share %
US	14,760	6.7	25,679	11.0	37,788	18.3
UK	29,243	13.4	25,450	10.9	13,514	6.5
German	5,452	2.5	8,380	3.6	9,904	4.8
Other EC	9,959	4.5	10,005	4.3	6,967	3.4
East Asian	0	0.0	1,406	0.6	2,218	1.1
Other non-EC	3,217	1.5	5,607	2.3	8,971	4.3
Total non-Irish	62,631	28.6	76,527	32.7	79,362	38.4
Irish	156,497	71.4	157,318	67.3	127,103	61.6
Total	219,128	100.0	233,845	100.0	206,465	100.0

Sources: as for Table 11.2.

[1] These figures were provided by the IDA. Note that the aggregate figures differ slightly from those in Table 11.2 and figures based on that table, as they were computed on a different date.

29 per cent in 1973. Some other features are noteworthy; first, over the period, US firms have replaced UK firms as the major non-Irish employers in manufacturing industry — the UK share has halved over the period while the US share has almost trebled. Furthermore, between 1973 and 1978, the UK was the only nationality category in which employment actually fell; again this reduction is in large part due to the adjustment to free trade, as many of the UK firms which closed in that period were older firms which depended on high tariff protection for survival.[7] Second, the share of employment in EC firms, other than the UK, rose slightly over the period, with a steady increase in employment in German firms and an overall reduction in employment in other EC firms. Third, East Asian (Japan, Hong Kong and Malaysia) companies now account for one per cent of jobs in Irish manufacturing; all of the projects involved were established after Ireland's entry to the EC. Finally, of striking significance is the reduction of some 30,000 jobs in Irish-owned firms between 1978 and 1986; this reduction arises in part from modernization of certain sectors, which has proven to be labour saving, but also from a failure of Irish firms to remain competitive on world markets.

Table 11.6

Components of Manufacturing Employment Change by Nationality, 1973-86[1]

Nationality	Job gains	Job losses	Net change in employment
US	31,064	8,036	23,028
UK	3,432	19,161	− 15,729
German	7,472	3,020	4,452
Other EC	4,129	7,121	− 2,992
East Asian	2,218	0	2,218
Other non-EC	6,458	704	5,754
Total non-Irish	54,773	38,042	16,731
Irish	59,289	88,683	− 29,394
Total	114,062	126,725	− 12,663

Sources: as for Table 11.2.

[1] These figures were provided by the IDA. Note that the aggregate change figures differ slightly from those in Tables 11.3 and 11.4, which were computed on a different date.

A similar pattern emerges from an analysis of the employment gains and losses by nationality in Table 11.6. The growth in the number of jobs in US firms is very striking, outweighing the number of job losses over the whole period by a ratio of almost 4:1. However, the growth rate has slowed down over the period and in fact between 1985 and 1986, US firms suffered a *net* decline in employment for the first time, of over 1,200 jobs. Although on a much smaller scale, jobs gained exceeded jobs lost in both the other non-EC and German categories. The table is dominated by the Irish-owned firms which recorded high levels of both gains and losses over the period, but with a net loss of almost 30,000 jobs. Thus while the difference between Irish and non-Irish firms in terms of job gains over the period is only a little over 4,500, the difference in terms of jobs lost is over 50,000. Again some of these job losses undoubtedly reflect the adjustment to free trade, as do those in UK firms, but combining the data here with those in Table 11.4 indicates that a very high proportion of net jobs lost over the period was in new and traditional Irish-owned industry.

The IDA Employment Survey data provide the clearest indication of the dramatic changes which have been taking place in the Irish manufacturing sector since the mid-1970s. Such changes are hidden by data which deal with *net* changes in output, employment and other variables. While closures and redundancies were relatively scarce in the 1960s, they are now commonplace both in older and more recently established industries. A key question which will be raised later in this chapter is whether or not this high rate of job turnover is due in part to the industrial strategy which is being pursued or whether it is simply an inevitable consequence of Irish industry adapting to changing circumstances on international markets. Whatever its source, this rapid rate of turnover has strong implications for the costs and effectiveness of industrial policy generally, and also for regional policy, which until recently has been an integral part of industrial policy. At the regional level the focus of public attention has tended to be on the distribution of new jobs, rather than on job gains and losses. If, however, manufacturing plants in a particular region are concentrated in a depressed sector, as is often the case, the region suffers disproportionately from closures and contractions. Table 11.7 shows how the nine IDA regions have fared in terms of job losses and gains between 1973 and 1986.

Table 11.7
Components of Manufacturing Employment Change by
Region, 1973-86[1]

Region	Job gains	Job losses	Net change in employment
Donegal	4,682	2,553	2,129
North-West	3,220	2,296	924
West	10,355	4,697	5,658
Mid-West	14,274	10,394	3,880
South-West	15,051	20,225	− 5,174
South-East	14,383	12,526	1,857
East	34,310	57,620	− 23,310
North-East	8,478	11,260	− 2,782
Midlands	9,309	5,154	4,155
Total	114,062	126,725	− 12,663
Dublin	26,166	48,782	− 22,616
Kildare, Meath and Wicklow	8,144	8,838	− 694

Sources: as for Table 11.2.
[1] Note that the aggregate change figures in this table are identical to those in Table 11.6 and differ slightly from the figures in Tables 11.3 and 11.4, which were computed on a slightly different date.

In terms of the net change in employment, the western regions, with the exception of the south-west, all experienced increases, with job gains outweighing job losses. The south-west experienced a net decline in manufacturing employment — much of which may be accounted for by the closure of older traditional industries (e.g. the Ford Motor Assembly plant) and by the failure of some large new projects in the Cork area. The impact of these job losses on Cork city has led to the establishment of some specific community-based groups to deal with the crisis which has resulted in unprecedented high unemployment rates in the city.

However, the most striking feature of the data in the table is the net loss of over 22,000 jobs in Dublin, which rises to 30,000 when firms not covered in the IDA survey are included. This loss reflects in large part the decline in many of the protected traditional industries, which were heavily concentrated in Dublin. While the western counties suffered in the 1960s from the lack of an industrial base, the Dublin area suffered throughout the 1970s from having a large proportion of the country's declining industries. The decline also reflects a low level of job gains which were sustained over the period — given the size of Dublin's population, 26,000 represents a very low level of net jobs created. The total number of jobs created in the period was 65,000, indicating a survival rate of 40 per cent, compared with a survival rate of 44 per cent for the rest of the country.

3   POLICIES FOR MANUFACTURING INDUSTRY

In Section 1 the general principles underlying the export-led-growth strategy were outlined. The central idea behind the use of this strategy in the Irish context was the promotion of the exporting component of the manufacturing sector, since the import-substituting component, which had expanded considerably during the early years of tariff protection, had become stagnant and increasingly inefficient during the post-war period.[8] In this section the actual policies used to promote export-led growth are discussed, and also the recent changes in policy which are shifting the balance more evenly on to both the exporting and import-substituting components of manufacturing.[9]

There are four key elements to the strategy which was adopted in the 1950s and which has developed since then: first, assistance for the protected import-substituting industries in preparation for free trade, and more recently, assistance to new industries which can hopefully substitute for new industrial imports; second, encouragement of exports by existing and new export-oriented domestic (indigenous) industries; third, promotion of Ireland as an exporting base for direct foreign investment; and fourth, promotion of the depressed regions of the country (referred to as 'designated areas') as locations for new domestic and foreign-owned manufacturing plants. While the policies associated with these four elements are all interrelated, it is useful to consider the set of policies directly associated with each element separately.

Import-Substituting Industry

At the end of the 1950s, the majority of Irish manufacturing firms were selling their output solely on the domestic market. This inward-looking concentration was primarily the result of prolonged protection, which had effectively discouraged exports and ultimately growth, because of the limited size of the domestic market. A series of reports published by the Committee on Industrial Organization (CIO) in the early 1960s found that most existing manufacturers were producing in low-scale, undercapitalized, inefficient units and dependent on the high tariffs for survival. The conclusion was reached that, despite and perhaps because of more than twenty years of protection, Irish industry needed assistance to adjust to free trade.[10]

The major policy response to these findings was the introduction of adaptation or reequipment grants (up to 35 per cent) towards the cost of new plant and machinery. These grants were available to enterprises which, on the basis of the CIO reports, would be viable under free trade. The only additional policies specifically supporting import-substituting firms were occasional 'Buy Irish' campaigns (culminating in the establishment of the Irish Goods Council in the late 1970s), and allowances against the standard rate (45-50 per cent) of corporate income tax.[11] In effect, it was presumed that, after an initial shake out following the adjustment to free trade, these firms would survive, maintaining employment and output, without any of the additional support being granted to exporting firms.

However, the increased rate of import penetration in recent years and consequential job losses have led to a reevaluation of the import-competing sector. In fact, what has finally been recognized is the inappropriateness of subsidizing exports to a greater extent than import substitutes, i.e. of creating a net export bias; such a bias existed once tariff protection had been finally removed in the late 1970s. In association with the recent policy changes in the *White Paper on Industrial Policy* (1984), the status of import substitutes has been recognized for policy purposes as being identical with exports; the elements of the new policy approach accorded to import substitutes, which are now identical to those of exporting firms, will be discussed in the next subsection, and discussion for the remainder of this subsection will be restricted to policies peculiar to import substitution.

The major policies peculiar to import-substituting firms relate to schemes which are intended to encourage the development of sub-supply industries, whose output would substitute for new export-oriented industrial inputs which were previously being imported. The main scheme, the National Linkages Programme (which is directed initially at the electronics sector), contains the following elements:

(i)   a comprehensive data base containing details of the raw material component requirements of large industries together with a capability register of subcontractors and suppliers;
(ii) selective promotion and development of the programme around firms and individuals who have been clearly identified as having potential for success; and
(iii) coordination of State support and assistance for marketing, product and process development, and quality control during the critical initial business development period.

[*White Paper on Industrial Policy*, p. 74]

In effect, this scheme is attempting to fill *selectively* an information gap in the subsupply industry and to directly encourage exporting firms which are importing many of their inputs to have them supplied by local Irish firms. By the end of 1986 over 70 electronics multinationals had participated in the programme, and it is estimated that the net additional business generated for Irish firms was IR£40 million in 1986.

Irish Exporting Industry
Promotion of exporting industry has been the major feature of Irish industrial policy over the past twenty-five years. In the main, this has meant encouraging the establishment of new export-oriented firms, and to a lesser extent, the encouragement of export expansion by existing Irish firms. To this end, a wide range of policies, which can be broadly classified as financial and fiscal, have been introduced and their main elements are as follows:[12]

387

Financial	*Fiscal*
Non-repayable cash grants	Reduced rate of corporate
Labour training grants	income tax
Research and development grants	Allowances against corporate
Rent and interest subsidies	income tax

The main *financial* incentives are administered by the IDA.[13] The most important incentive by far is the non-repayable cash grant,[14] the value of which at certain periods amounted to as much as 60 per cent of the cost of new fixed asset investment and has been typically around 35 per cent. Furthermore, in the mid-1970s, the reequipment grant scheme, designed originally for traditional import-substituting industry adjusting to free trade, came to be widely used by established exporting firms, some of which had been grant aided when originally established, i.e. both initial and replacement investment were grant aided. It is important to note that all of the grant schemes are operated on a *discretionary* basis, i.e. there is no entitlement to a grant and its award and size are determined on an individual project basis by IDA personnel. Because the grant for new projects is paid out in fixed proportion to the value of the firm's new fixed assets, and the grant maximum is expressed in terms of the value of fixed assets, it is typically referred to as a capital grant. However, IDA personnel have always insisted that the grant programmes for new projects did not subsidize capital-intensive projects or techniques of production, because the grant rate depends on certain key variables, e.g. employment generation, linkage potential, etc. Hence, they argue, the link between the grant payment and the acquisition of fixed assets is solely for administrative convenience and therefore creates no bias towards capital intensity.[15]

There were some significant modifications to the grant programme in the White Paper, though much of the programme remained unchanged in essence. A seemingly major change was the abolition of the reequipment grant scheme. However, it is not clear what the eventual impact of its abolition will be on Irish manufacturing industry as the White Paper simultaneously empowered the IDA to give exporting and import-substituting firms technology-acquisition grants (towards 'the costs of acquiring new product or process technology from abroad'), which sound remarkably similar to reequipment grants under a new title. For some existing import-substituting firms this may represent an improvement as the technology grant maximum is actually higher than the reequipment grant (50 compared with 35 per cent). In any event, it seems likely that the technology-acquisition grants will be administered on a more selective basis than the reequipment grants, with firms in subsectors which have rapidly changing technologies being the greatest beneficiaries of the new scheme.

The capital grant programme has remained basically intact with a recommendation of lower grant levels and once again greater selectivity in the choice of projects. The downward adjustment in grant levels has been negligible to date, possibly reflecting a greater reduction in project supply to the IDA rather than a reduction in the funds available. In common with all state agencies, the IDA's expenditure procedures would involve its using all available funds, even if this ran counter to the government's objective of lowering the level of grants. To ensure greater selectivity new administrative procedures have been introduced, involving more clear-cut operational guidelines within the discretionary grant system, and a Company Development Programme for export firms has been established which involves 'the identification of promising firms, which will be prepared to commit themselves to working on a more intensive basis with the appropriate State agencies.' *(White Paper on Industrial Policy,* p. 39*).* The Company Development Programme, which is popularly referred to as 'picking winners', is aimed at building up 'strong Irish based companies which are capable of taking strategic decisions and developing their own R & D programmes here and of achieving a strong market position' (p.38). To date 150 companies have participated in the programme, but there is no measure available of its effectiveness. There will be some further discussion of the merits of this type of scheme in Section 5.

One further significant change in the basic grant scheme was introduced in 1986 for *small* manufacturing firms. Such firms have the possibility of availing of employment grants as alternatives to grants paid towards the cost of machinery and buildings. There is no evidence available yet on how small firms will respond; when such evidence becomes available it may provide some valuable information on employers' perceptions of the grant scheme.

In terms of exchequer cost, the most important of the other schemes administered by the IDA are the rent and interest subsidy programmes, which included for most of the 1970s an 'Advance Factory' scheme, i.e. the building of general purpose units for leasing to potential manufacturing enterprises. This latter scheme became the subject of considerable criticism in the early 1980s because of its high cost (involving almost as much government expenditure as the grant programme in some years) and the low occupancy rate of completed units (despite the very favourable terms on which they are leased to manufacturers). The IDA's justification for continuing its building programme, despite the large surplus of unoccupied factory space, was that the availability of a range of ready-to-occupy units in different locations represented a valuable incentive in enticing foreign companies to locate in Ireland. This policy was finally withdrawn at the time of the policy review which culminated in the publication of the White Paper.

In addition to the IDA, there are several other agencies involved in promoting Irish-owned industry. The most important of these from the viewpoint of Irish exporting firms is Córas Tráchtála (CTT) which has responsibility for promoting industrial exports. Much of CTT's work in the 1960s and 1970s was at an arms-length distance from the individual firm, e.g. trade shows, broad promotional literature, etc. However, under the proposals in the White Paper an export development scheme has been introduced which is specifically designed to address identified weaknesses and to help raise the level of export performance of firms in the following areas: market entry and development, market research, group marketing for small exporters, building marketing strengths in firms, export of services, warehousing, and distributor support programmes.

To date, according to the government, the response to the initiatives taken by CTT has been slight, suggesting that, despite state assistance, manufacturers have not considered it worthwhile and/or possible to launch products on international markets on a large scale.

The other important agencies which are involved directly in providing support to both import-substituting and exporting manufacturing firms are An Comhairle Oiliúna (AnCO), which has responsibility for industrial training; the Industrial Credit Company (ICC) which has responsibility for assisting investment finance; the Institute for Industrial Research and Standards (IIRS), which has responsibility for providing technical support to Irish industry; the National Board for Science and Technology (NBST), which has responsibility for developing and planning science and technology programmes, with special reference to the industrial sector; and the National Development Corporation (Nadcorp) which has a small amount of equity available to invest for limited periods as venture capital in firms in certain key sectors. While these agencies vary in their importance to different companies, collectively they play a key role in determining the institutional environment facing the industrialist, for whom the costs of export promotion, labour training, working capital, new technologies and equity capital have been rising steadily in recent years.

Virtually all of the *fiscal* incentives available to manufacturing industry take the form of relief from taxation of corporate profits.[16] The main policies have recently come through a state of transition, and the incentives for which a firm is eligible depend crucially on whether it is deemed to have commenced production before or since January 1, 1981.[17] Firms established prior to January 1981 were entitled to *complete* relief from Irish taxation on *all* profits generated by new export sales for a maximum of fifteen years, and *partial* relief for a further five years until January 1990. This tax provision, Export Sales Relief (ESR), was available *automatically* to all firms whether new or old, domestic or foreign-owned, on the export component of their output. The main purpose of the incentive, when originally introduced in 1956, was to encourage old, established Irish firms to extend their markets beyond the small, highly-protected domestic market, by counteracting the strong bias in favour of import substitution created by tariff protection. However, for the most part this tax relief has been used by *new* manufacturing projects rather than the older enterprises for which it was intended, and, with the reduction in the tariff wall during the 1970s, it actually created a net *export* bias. Since this bias in favour of exports compared with domestic sales was in breach of EC regulations, the incentive was withdrawn in December 1980.

Firms establishing since 1981 which are not eligible for ESR can avail of a *reduced* rate of taxation on corporate profits which was introduced in January 1981; the rate is 10 per cent, which compares favourably with rates in other European countries and with the 45 per cent rate which applies in the non-manufacturing section of the corporate sector. This special rate, which is guaranteed until the year 2000, applies to all manufacturing firms irrespective of whether they sell abroad or on the domestic market, i.e. while the financial treatment of exporting and import-substituting firms is becoming more similar, the fiscal treatment of exporting and import-substituting firms is now identical.

Finally, exporting firms have been legally eligible for the same depreciation allowances against corporate income tax as import-substituting firms, even when they faced a zero tax rate. This somewhat paradoxical situation has resulted in exporting firms enjoying ESR choosing to lease (rather than purchase) capital equipment from tax-paying institutions, usually banks, which can use the tax allowances associated with this equipment to reduce their tax liabilities. (The firms themselves, with no such liabilities, cannot benefit from these allowances.) The extent to which the benefit of this tax saving is transferred to the manufacturing firms, via the terms of the lease, is determined by bargaining between the firms and the banks, which may actually receive grants from the IDA towards the cost of this equipment. This arrangement, which will be discussed further below, is widely referred to as tax-based lending.[18] It has represented considerable additional support for exporting firms, and consequently has involved a considerable cost to the exchequer in terms of reduced revenue from taxation of bank profits.[19] Though leasing is still common, there are now controls in place to limit its use; these will be discussed further in Section 4.

Direct Foreign Investment
The decision to promote direct foreign investment in Ireland in the late 1950s and early 1960s represented a change of policy similar in spirit and perhaps as important in impact as the move from an import-substitution to an export-led-growth strategy. The change represented a major shift in attitudes in favour of foreigners, from one of virtual xenophobia to one of positive enthusiasm, with extensive international campaigns promoting foreign investment in Irish manufacturing.

Foreign firms are eligible for all of the financial and fiscal incentives which are available to Irish-owned exporting firms. Furthermore, double taxation agreements have been negotiated to ensure that foreigners can enjoy maximum benefit from Ireland's generous tax concessions when profits are repatriated. In terms of financial and fiscal incentives, these policies have resulted in Ireland being the most attractive location for foreign investors in Europe.[20]

While direct foreign investors have been given the same investment incentives as domestic exporting industry, there are several important issues which arise in the case of foreign firms which mean that the policies, though identical, operate differently. First, the initial set-up decision for domestic companies is different from that for foreign companies: the foreign entrepreneur is typically deciding between investment in Ireland and in other countries which are competing for investment projects, while the Irish entrepreneur is typically deciding on whether or not to invest in Irish manufacturing or elsewhere in the economy. This means that while the reference point for a foreign entrepreneur considering an investment in manufacturing in Ireland is the attractiveness of alternative locations in terms of incentives and natural advantages, the reference point for the Irish entrepreneur is the net rate of return in manufacturing compared with other sectors in the economy. In practice, the IDA says that this means that grants to foreign firms are set by their next best offer rather than by what the projects need to become profitable, while grants to domestic firms are determined by what is essential for profitability.

Second, the nature of the market for foreign investment projects, characterized by well-established companies and tried-and-tested products, allows the IDA to be reasonably selective in choosing foreign projects. Such selectivity is not usually possible with new and untested Irish exporting companies. This may explain the emphasis on direct foreign investment projects in IDA operations over the 1970s. Ex ante a simple comparison of Irish and foreign projects would certainly tend to favour the latter, especially from a risk viewpoint.

Third, for many foreign companies, production in Ireland is just one stage in the production process, with firms typically buying from and selling to their own subsidiaries. This gives foreign firms the opportunity to engage in transfer pricing, i.e. by buying from and selling to their own subsidiaries, they can adjust the declared prices of inputs (downwards) and outputs (upwards) to increase the value of the profits they declare as being generated in Ireland. Because of the double taxation agreements, which imply that corporate tax is deemed to have been paid at the official corporate tax rate, the potential for transfer pricing greatly increases the value of the ESR incentive and probably explains why, according to the IDA, ESR possibly outweighed all the other incentives offered, including the cash grants, in encouraging new foreign industry to locate in Ireland during the 1970s.

Finally, in the context of changes in industrial policy, the focus of IDA activity (in terms of its allocation of personnel and financial resources) is clearly shifting towards indigenous industry and it seems that increasingly the *actual* grant rates for foreign investment projects are well below the allowable maxima. Indeed, while the reallocation of resources between fixed-asset incentives and the new technology and export development incentives may still be slight since the publication of the White Paper, the reallocation of resources from foreign to domestic industry seems likely to be much larger.[21] The likely effects of the shift in emphasis on the supply of such projects to the Irish economy is difficult to gauge, because of the increased international competition for foreign investment projects and the greater relative, but declining, importance of the automatic fiscal incentives to foreign investors compared with the discretionary financial incentives.

The White Paper states that IDA efforts should be concentrated on securing foreign-owned projects with the following characteristics:

(i) stand-alone projects which can survive without significant reliance on the parent company;

(ii) projects which form a significant market for potential sub-supply linkages, particularly those in potentially traded businesses and in businesses requiring high-skilled labour;

(iii) projects with a real commitment to skilled employment; and

(iv) projects which can substitute for imports where there is no possibility for Irish firms to enter the business.

[*White Paper on Industrial Policy,* p. 64]

However, despite the undeniable desirability of projects with such characteristics, as will be shown in the next section, the actual incentives offered do little if anything to encourage foreign firms to forge subsupply linkages, employ skilled labour, or develop stand-alone projects in Ireland.

Regional Dispersal

The regional dispersal of industrial employment was one of the key features of Irish industrial policy in the 1960s and 1970s. In fact, the IDA grant scheme was initially introduced as a regional policy, with grants being offered for new manufacturing projects in the depressed areas of the country, where low levels of income and high levels of emigration were attributed to the absence of an industrial base.[22] While the grant scheme was very quickly extended to all parts of the country, the regional dimension persisted in the higher maximum grant rate (grant as a percentage of fixed asset investment) which applied in these depressed (designated) areas.[23]

During the 1960s there was considerable debate on the direction of Irish regional policy — whether it should support general dispersal of economic development (as implicit in the policy of higher grants for regions of declining or stagnant populations) or whether it should support a growth-pole strategy, i.e. the concentration of resources for development in a small number of large centres.[24] From the perspective of manufacturing industry, this debate culminated in the publication of the IDA's Regional Industrial Plan in 1973, which effectively rejected the growth-pole strategy in favour of a general dispersal strategy, based on groups of towns rather than on the simple binary (designated/non-designated) classification.[25] This strategy was implemented through the discretionary grant system (higher grants being offered to compensate for locational disadvantages) and through the general promotion of certain locations, especially for foreign investment projects. For example, foreign industrialists contemplating investment in Ireland were brought to specific locations selected by IDA personnel on the basis of the firms' production requirements and the relative priority of the location for new projects.

However, in the White Paper, the Government announced that there would no longer be a close formal link between regional and industrial policy. Instead of offering higher grant rates to permanently designated areas and attempting to allocate mobile projects to meet particular town-group job targets, there will be a flexible system (based on objective criteria) 'of designating areas for higher grant rate purposes for clearly defined industrial sectors and limited periods' (p. 47). A further change in the industrial strategy which has implications for regional dispersal is the centralization of all state services to *small* industry at a single location in each region, in order to reduce the costs they incur in applying for state assistance from a variety of state agencies. The change recognizes the significant role which small firms have played in employment creation. If effective, this rationalization of services at regional level should increase the response rate of small indigenous firms to the existing incentive package.

As mentioned at the beginning of this section, the policies associated with the four elements of industrial strategy are interrelated in practice, as many firms are involved both in import substituting and exporting, some are jointly owned by Irish and foreign enterpreneurs, and others have plants located in different regions. Naturally, this interaction complicates the manner in which the policies affect the environment facing manufacturing industry. Furthermore, other policies which are not associated with the industrial strategy have a major impact on the manufacturing sector in Ireland (see Chapter 8). For example, the competitiveness of manufacturing is *directly* affected by the government's energy pricing policy, by the Pay-Related Social Insurance (PRSI) scheme, by labour legislation, etc., and *indirectly* affected by income taxation, which is passed on in the form of wage demands, and by the quality of Irish infrastructure.[26] There has been a tendency in the past to ignore these other policies, as they do not form part of the industrial strategy *per se*. In fact, the White Paper was the first major government document to recognize explicitly the influence of non-industrial policies on the performance of the manufacturing sector.

Because these policies are outside the control of the Minister for Industry, Trade, Commerce and Tourism, no specific changes in them were proposed in the White Paper, although the direction in which some such changes might be made was indicated, e.g. personal taxation and energy pricing. However, it is noteworthy that no mention was made of the penalty which is placed on industrial employment by employers' PRSI contributions, which have been raised rapidly in recent years, in spite of the government's stated intention of attempting to reduce unemployment.

4   IMPACT OF POLICIES

It is not possible to measure precisely the impact of industrial policy on the growth of the manufacturing sector, because there is no appropriate reference point with which to compare its actual growth performance. In other words, it is not known how differently the manufacturing sector would have performed had there been no fiscal or financial incentives. Despite the impossibility of such precise measurement, attempts are made to evaluate policies in terms of the performance of the sector and these attempts merit some discussion.

The measures of the overall impact of the policy package most frequently cited are the positive changes in such sectoral indicators as employment, investment, output and exports. Such aggregate data on the manufacturing sector are inadequate indicators, as they imply that the variables would have been unchanged had there been no industrial policies in operation.[27] Such an assumption is clearly most unrealistic in the Irish context, where exogenous changes such as EC membership, oil price increases, etc. during the 1970s dramatically affected the performance of the manufacturing sector.

An alternative measure of the impact of policies often used is the performance of firms which have availed of the discretionary policies (e.g. the grant programme) administered by the IDA. However, this measure tends to *overstate* the effects of the policies, since it seems likely that a fair proportion of the projects which receive grant assistance are in fact intramarginal (i.e. projects which would have been undertaken in the absence, or with lesser amounts, of government subsidy). Indeed, the IDA's description of its own method of project evaluation definitely implies that the payment of some grant has been the norm for all projects,[28] and this, together with the claim that Irish incentives for direct foreign investment are very generous by international standards, increases the likelihood that some projects are intramarginal.[29]

Even if it were possible to isolate the effects of policies by eliminating both the changes arising from exogenous factors and the intramarginal cases, the choice of variable or set of variables appropriate to measuring the impact of policies is not clear cut. Ideally the impact of policies should be measured in terms of changes in an index of economic welfare. Unfortunately no such index exists, and because of the emphasis on reducing unemployment, direct employment on new and expanding manufacturing projects has been the main indicator used.[30] However, more recently, IDA personnel have argued that direct employment understates the gross benefit of such projects to the economy, and they have suggested that changes in *net domestic value added* be used instead.[31] Net domestic value added is defined by the IDA as sales less imported inputs, the import content of all domestic inputs and repatriated profits. Despite the difficulties of measurement and dangers of double-counting[32] this concept has been endorsed by the government and is used operationally in the evaluation of projects. Unfortunately there are virtually no data available as yet on net domestic value added, but such evidence as is available suggests that between 1983 and 1984, when real output in manufacturing was growing, real domestic value added was declining.[33]

Despite the difficulties of measuring precisely the impact of industrial policies on the growth of the manufacturing sector, it is possible to gauge their impact on its *pattern* of development by analyzing the incentives which they create within the sector. While the broad orientation of policies is clear — they seek to encourage the expansion of employment and output in domestic and foreign export-oriented and more recently, import-substituting industry — the precise focus tends to be blurred by the complex structure of the financial and fiscal policies described in Section 3. Since the manufacturing sector is guided rather than controlled by government, the incentives created by these policies should promote the expansion of the sector by enhancing its relative attractiveness to potential entrepreneurs, and by reducing any constraints on its self-sustaining development. In Ireland, important impediments have been identified as arising in such areas as management skills, technical expertise, marketing experience, product design and development, research and development, the availability of equity finance, etc.[34] It is argued that these constraints are reflected particularly in the small relative size of employment in the manufacturing sector in Ireland, the low level of intersectoral linkages, the low export ratios of most domestically-owned manufacturing companies and the concentration of these exports on the UK market.[35]

The main focus of the *financial* policies promoting manufacturing industry has been on reducing the cost and hence the risk of fixed asset investment in manufacturing. In the process, the major policies (cash grants, rent and interest subsidies, advance factories) have had several other effects, which are important for the development of manufacturing industry.[36] First, their emphasis on capital rather than labour or other factors of production, tended to generate a bias towards the use of capital in production. This bias, which has been long recognized by industrialists and economists but only recently by government,[37] has been especially evident with reequipment grants. These grants, which were initially intended for older industry adjusting to free-trade conditions, came to be used eventually for replacement capital by virtually all firms, even export-oriented firms which had already been grant-aided.[38] Obviously any such bias is inappropriate in the Irish economy, especially with its serious structural unemployment problems; furthermore, in the case of foreign projects, it tends to reduce the potential level of net domestic value added.

Second, the policies although nominally discretionary, have effectively been automatic at a minimum level, creating an undesirable 'handout mentality' in the manufacturing sector, as firms seek IDA assistance for each and every expansion.[39] This 'handout mentality' is not conducive to manufacturing becoming a self-sustaining, growing sector. In fact, it is arguable that the widespread availability of free investment funds in the form of non-repayable cash grants has seriously undermined the development of an Irish equity market.[40] Third, the grants have also lowered the required commitment of foreign firms to their Irish investments, by reducing the amount of capital they needed to bring into the economy. (Foreign-financed capital is estimated to be only one-third of the capital employed in new foreign-owned projects.) Thus, in terms of establishing a strong industrial base, this policy also does not create the correct incentives. Indeed, given the benefits to foreign firms generated by the tax system and given that such firms were unlikely to have been seriously capital constrained, these grants may in the past have been unnecessarily generous.

The main focus of *fiscal* policies, operating through the reduced rate of corporate tax on all or part of manufacturing profits, has been on increasing the reward for investing in the manufacturing sector in Ireland, relative to the manufacturing sector abroad and the domestic non-manufacturing sector.[41] In effect, such policies have conveyed greatest benefit to the most profitable firms, i.e. those firms which, in principle, needed least assistance. (It is not, however, true to say that such fiscal incentives only benefited profitable firms; they benefited any firm making profits, even if at standard tax rates the rate of profit in such firms was inadequate to make the firm profitable.) ESR for example, has undoubtedly greatly assisted successful exporting firms, but has been of little help to the small firm for which the substantial initial costs of establishing an export market may prohibit survival long enough to generate profits. In general, foreign rather than Irish firms have been in a position to benefit from ESR, as the former typically have established markets for the output which they produce in Ireland. Indeed, as already mentioned in Section 3, many foreign firms have been and still are in a position to reap enormous benefits from ESR through transfer pricing, which allows them to associate the bulk of their profits with Irish production, even though there may be little value added in Ireland.[42] This incentive clearly does not encourage export-led growth, since one of the important elements necessary for an export-led-growth strategy to operate is that the promoted sectors link with other sectors in the economy. In effect, ESR not only discourages forward linkages, by being only available to exporting firms, but also by generating a strong and widely-acknowledged incentive to transfer price, effectively discourages backward linkages in production, as importing from own-company branches abroad is essential to maximizing the benefits of transfer pricing. This undoubtedly helps to explain the low level of backward linkages of foreign firms in Ireland,[43] and as long as transfer pricing remains commonplace, it questions how effective the White Paper's statement that IDA should promote firms with 'a significant market for subsupply linkages' will be in practice.

Both ESR and the preferential (10 per cent) corporate tax rate have created a strong incentive for firms to engage in leasing agreements with banking institutions, which can obtain greater value from the generous allowances associated with the purchase of fixed assets in manufacturing. Such leasing agreements have drastically reduced the cost of fixed-asset investment to manufacturing industry, and when combined with the dramatic increase in the rates of PRSI in recent years, have resulted in a strong bias in favour of capital rather than labour in production.[44] In addition, as the firms best placed to avail of leasing agreements are the larger ones (both domestic and foreign), the banking sector is effectively encouraged to discriminate against smaller firms by these tax provisions. Furthermore, such leasing agreements combined with Section 84 loans[45] have created a strong incentive for Irish firms to finance investment by debt rather than equity, leaving them highly vulnerable to any temporary reduction in sales revenue. Indeed, it is arguable that the problems of many Irish firms in the early 1980s have been generated by their excessive dependence on debt, which has been indirectly encouraged by fiscal policy. While changes in tax policy have reduced the value of tax-based financing in recent years, and while the IDA has imposed some controls on the extent of its use by grant-aided firms, strong incentives for tax-based financing still remain. In effect, like the financial policies the fiscal policies, and ESR in particular, seem to have created incentives which are *incompatible* with the promotion of a strong export base, although they have certainly increased the attractiveness of investment in the manufacturing sector.

Broadly speaking, the approach taken by Irish industrial policy-makers has been to identify the constraints specific to individual firms and to assist these firms in attempting to surmount the adverse effects of these constraints by giving 'handouts', which at best have no *direct* impact on the constraints and at worst reinforce the resource allocation biases created by the constraints. For example, the major financial and fiscal policies have focussed on the provision of cheap fixed asset capital although it is not apparent either that this is a major constraint, or that non-repayable cash grants and tax-based leasing agreements are the most efficient methods of dealing with it.[46] In practice, the emphasis on fixed asset formation more than likely reflects administrative preference rather than economic sense, viz. grants for visible fixed assets and (apparently) costless tax incentives,[47] while at the same time leading the structure of production further from that in which Ireland's endowment ratio of labour to other factors would suggest it has comparative advantage. While there is some evidence of greater economic sense in the policy modifications since the publication of the White Paper, e.g., the recent emphasis on providing finance for manufacturing in forms other than non-repayable cash grants for fixed assets,[48] the overall policy package is still not incentive compatible with the stated objectives of the industrial strategy.

5 INDUSTRIAL PERFORMANCE: A FAILURE OF STRATEGY OR OF POLICY DESIGN?

In the previous section, the analysis showed that the incentives created by the policies used to promote manufacturing industry were not compatible with building strong self-sustaining manufacturing subsectors which would generate growth elsewhere in the economy. Consequently, at least some of the poor performance of the Irish manufacturing sector since 1980 must be attributed to the use of inappropriate policies. Although not all economists share the same views on what the appropriate policies should be, there is widespread agreement on (i) the remaining shortcomings of the basic package, (ii) the improvements associated with recent changes in policy and (iii) the view that the emphasis on foreign investment projects in the 1970s was excessive, because of the relatively low potential value added which might be expected per unit of expenditure cost.

It is perhaps helpful to look at one key element in the industrial policy debate among economists about which there is not yet agreement, i.e. the nature of government intervention.[49] Economists of Neoclassical persuasion tend to be of the view that government policy should have as its aim the creation of a 'healthy economic environment' in which manufacturing industry would thrive. Under this scenario, policies would be oriented towards creating compatible incentives for firms to develop; such incentives would not merely be industrial incentives, but also incentives operating through the personal taxation system, regulatory instruments, etc. In such an environment, it is argued, the economic activities in which Ireland has a comparative advantage would thrive. Economists of what is usually termed the Structuralist school argue that even if the incentives were correct, this would not be sufficient because the scale of Irish industry is too small to overcome the entry barriers to international markets.[50] Thus, the Structuralists argue, that what is required is for the government to identify certain firms in key growth activities, referred to as 'niches', which have the potential to overcome the barriers, and that these firms should be heavily promoted and assisted. Indeed, the company development programme currently being undertaken by the IDA comes close to this concept in the Structuralist model.

In practice, in terms of a specific approach, the major gap between the Neoclassical economists and the Structuralists seems to arise from a difference of view about whether the market (local or international) or the government should identify the key firms, i.e. effectively determine where comparative advantage lies; in reality there is probably some role for both in the process. Certainly both groups of economists would agree that a healthy economic environment is essential, and that if firms require assistance, that such assistance should be related to their symptoms and not merely be 'handouts' given at the initial stage of the project. Structuralists are optimistic about the benefits of close government involvement while Neoclassical economists are pessimistic, citing (i) the dangers of increasing further the already high direct dependence on state assistance, (ii) the political problems associated with government involvement in both project identification and, in some cases, failure in a small community like Ireland, and (iii) the poor performance record of many state-owned companies.

A key issue remains to be discussed; even if the appropriate policies were chosen, would the strategy of export-led growth and more recently, import substitution, actually work?

If by export-led growth, one means the direct promotion of the exporting sector, with corrective policies being introduced as necessary in the economy, the answer is possibly 'yes', but the rate of growth achieved in the long run in the economy as a whole might not be very high. The reason is that although growth may be achieved in the promoted sector, not only may it not lead to growth elsewhere in the economy, it might actually lead to reduced output elsewhere in the economy, even if there is unemployment.

The reasons for the lack of linkages arises from the openness of the economy — even in the absence of a tax incentive which encouraged many firms to import inputs, competitive firms will import if the quality, price or reliability of the domestic alternative does not match that of the import. Furthermore, if an output can be sold at a higher price abroad, a firm will not sell it for further domestic production in Ireland, even if there is a local market. Thus there is no guarantee of production linkages, unless the rest of the economy is internationally competitive. There may of course be consumption linkages, but again these might be expected to be small because of the very high marginal propensity to import, and because, in the case of foreign projects, profits do not add to domestic value added and will eventually be repatriated. Thus the openness of an economy, in terms of commodity and capital markets, tends to reduce the likely impact of linkages, as it does the Keynesian multiplier (see Chapter 6).

The reason why output might actually be reduced elsewhere is because of 'crowding out'. There are three possible sources of crowding out. Crowding out may arise in the first instance because the expanding sector uses a factor which is fully employed elsewhere in the economy, e.g. skilled labour or capital. An example of the former would be where a new project 'poaches' skilled labour from an existing project which consequently is forced to reduce output or even close. In the case of capital, the effect would be less visible, taking the form either of an increased demand for capital which would raise the interest rate, thereby squeezing out a marginal project, or the rationing of a loan to an existing project. Even if there is unemployment and if the factors complementary with labour are in plentiful supply, there may be a second form of crowding out if there is upward pressure on the economy-wide wage as a result of the expansion in the promoted sector. This is most likely to occur the more internationally mobile are the complementary factors, and the higher is the productivity of labour in the promoted sectors.[51] A third type of crowding out occurs in commodity markets, e.g. an increase in one firm's sales leading to a decline in another firm's sales, either on home or foreign markets.

The data in Section 2 are suggestive of crowding out at the factor level in Ireland. There have always been IDA checks on competition between commodities which are likely to ensure a minimum level of crowding out at the commodity level in the home market and as far as possible on international markets. On the other hand, new firms often draw their skilled labour from existing plants and, at certain periods (e.g. with electronics engineers in the late 1970s), this has caused problems for the existing firms. There is no evidence of similar effects on the capital market in Ireland, although the increasing financing of foreign projects on the domestic market since the 1970s must have had some impact on interest terms and/or credit availability. Furthermore, some of the burden of financing the grants for new projects must fall directly or indirectly on existing firms, hence reducing their competitiveness. Finally, rising real wages in the periods of rapid growth (e.g. the 1970s) are supportive of the hypothesis of crowding out. While the value of output of the new firms was almost certainly greater than that of the contracting firms, the domestic value-added content may not have been that much higher since many of the new firms were foreign owned.[52] That this has been achieved in a period of rapid export growth (see Chapter 9) confirms that, whether for reasons of its openness, its structural problems or its use of inappropriate policies, export growth in Ireland has not resulted in export-led growth.

Finally, a brief comment on the outlook for the manufacturing sector. The 'picture' painted in this chapter has been rather pessimistic — declining rates of growth, falling employment levels, minimum linkages, etc. Unfortunately it is not possible to be optimistic about the sector's future performance. The reason for this is that the growth in output in many of the 'growth' sectors (e.g., electronics) has been capacity-led and as the rate of capacity buildup in these sectors has slowed down dramatically, so, it might be expected, will employment and output growth. Furthermore, the outlook for Irish exports on international markets is not promising, especially as there has been a slowdown in growth rates in some of the markets which have been the main source of export growth in recent years. There is one area in which there is some grounds for optimism, namely on the policy front where recent government documents have increasingly recognized the role of incentives and the general equilibrium nature of issues involved in promoting one sector relative to another. If this recognition is harnessed in the policies of the operational agencies, it will at least be possible to ensure that Ireland may develop more according to comparative advantage and be able to make the most of any opportunities which become available to increase manufacturing output and employment.

Footnotes

1 The policy of widespread and ongoing aid to the majority of manufacturing enterprises, which became a feature of the industrial development strategy in the 1970s was never envisaged in the initial period. What was envisaged was selective support to 'seed' projects in key sectors, which would eventually generate their own dynamic and induce growth elsewhere *without* requiring additional government support.

2 An example of a production linkage would be the project's demand for a particular produced input resulting in an additional volume of that input being produced by some other firm in Ireland. A consumption linkage might arise, for example, through the demands for additional Irish outputs generated by individuals employed on the project, which resulted in additional production.

3 See Note 2 to Table 11.1.

4 These are the only employment data available which can be used to track employment changes within subsectors. For a further detailed analysis of employment changes at firm level, using data for the period 1973-81, see P.N. O'Farrell, *Entrepreneurs and Industrial Change*, Irish Management Institute, Dublin 1986. The scale of job losses has increased dramatically since the time period covered in O'Farrell's book; one simple indicator of this is while O'Farrell records job losses in 1973-81 as being 35 per cent of 1973 employment, job losses in 1973-86 are equivalent to 57 per cent of 1973 employment.

5 It seems likely that a considerable portion of the unidentified job losses (over 8,000) referred to in Note 1 to Table 11.2 were in these sectors.

6 In terms of the data here, it amounts to a decline of 12,000 jobs; this increases to 20,000 jobs when the firms not covered in the original IDA sample are included. See Note 1 to Table 11.2.

7 These firms had either been established *before* the Control of Manufacturers Acts (1932, 1934), which controlled ownership of new companies setting up behind tariff boundaries or *after* 1932 by evading these controls. See J.P. Neary and C. Ó Gráda, 'Protection, Economic War and Structural Change: The 1930s in Ireland' (paper read to the Workshop on Recent Economic History at the Centre for Economic Policy Research, London), March 1984.

8 The vulnerability of the import-substituting sector is clear from the loss of an estimated 35,000 jobs due to increased import penetration between 1965 and 1973 before the major

impact of free trade was felt. See John Blackwell, Gerald Danaher and Eoin O'Malley, *An Analysis of Job Losses in Irish Manufacturing Industry* (NESC Report no. 67), Stationery Office, Dublin 1983, Chapter 6; see also Alan Gray and John Kelly 'The Import Dependence of the Irish Economy: Some Implications for Industrial Policy' in Jim Fitzpatrick and John Kelly (editors), *Perspectives on Irish Industry*, Irish Management Institute, Dublin 1985.

9 These changes have been under way since 1980 but have been formalized only since the government's *White Paper on Industrial Policy* was published in 1984; for a complete description of the current state of policy revision, see Department of Industry and Commerce, *Review of Industrial Performance 1986,* Stationery Office, Dublin 1987.

10 For an account of the problems faced by the manufacturing sector in the later protectionist period, see Committee on Industrial Organization, *Final Report*, Stationery Office, Dublin 1965.

11 These allowances were primarily depreciation allowances associated with investment purchases; they were increased over the 1970s (mostly to compensate for the lack of indexation in the corporate tax system) and they applied to the grant-aided as well as the non-grant-aided component of investment in plant and machinery.

12 The incentives change from time to time, and a full list of the current incentives may be obtained from the Industrial Development Authority. For a discussion of how the incentives have developed, see Eoin O'Malley, *Industrial Policy and Development: A Survey of the Literature from the Early 1960s* (NESC Report no. 56), Stationery Office, Dublin 1980.

13 Other agencies are involved at a regional level; these include Údarás Na Gaeltachta in the Gaeltacht, and Shannon Free Airport Development Company (SFADCo) in the mid-west region (Clare, Limerick and Tipperary NR).

14 The grant scheme is important both in terms of exchequer cost (accounting typically for over 50 per cent of IDA non-administration expenditures) and in terms of industrialists' perceptions (see O'Malley, *op. cit.*).

15 The method used by the IDA has gone through a series of adjustments following a somewhat heated debate on the topic in the early 1980s. For reference, see John McKeon, 'Economic Appraisal of Industrial Projects in Ireland', *Journal of the Statistical and Social Inquiry Society of Ireland*, 1979/80, and replies to that paper. See also, the symposium for Industrial Development in *Journal of the Statistical and Social Inquiry Society of Ireland*, 1983/84. Indeed, the present approach is currently under review once again. See Department of Industry and Commerce, *op. cit.*

16 Exceptions are various allowances against personal taxation for individuals undertaking particular investments in new manufacturing enterprises. These include the Business Expansion Scheme which was first introduced in the 1984 budget, and has subsequently been ammended and modified; profit sharing schemes and provisions for a reduced rate of income tax on dividends from companies eligible for the 10 per cent rate of Corporation Profits Tax. While these allowances may prove important in certain instances, their scale of importance is still relatively small.

17 It is sometimes possible for a new project to acquire the status of having been established before January 1, 1981 (and hence the very generous tax provisions which applied prior to January 1, 1981,) by acquiring a company which was granted these provisions when it established prior to 1981.

18 For a straightforward discussion of how tax-based lending schemes operate, see J.L. Deeny, 'The Role of Tax-Based Lending in the Promotion of Industrial Development in Ireland', *Irish Banking Review*, June 1982, pp. 40-49.

19 This issue is discussed in NESC, *A Review of Industrial Policy* (Report no. 64 also known as the Telesis Report), Stationery Office, Dublin 1984, Chapter 9, and was the subject of further analysis in a subsequent NESC Report on the Role of Financial Institutions in Financing the Traded Sectors in Industry.

20 See, for example, D. Yuill and K. Allen (editors), *European Regional Incentives: 1980*, Centre for Study of Public Policy, University of Strathclyde 1980. Of course, this does not mean that Ireland is necessarily the most attractive location overall for foreign investment, since long-term profitability which drives these flows depends on many other factors in addition to such incentives.

21 'In a sense the era of massive foreign investment in Ireland is over'. Statement by John Bruton, then Minister for Industry, Trade, Commerce and Tourism, in an interview with *The Sunday Press*, on July 15, 1984, following the publication of the White Paper.

22 These depressed areas were predominantly in the Donegal, north-west, west and south-west regions.

23 Over the 1960s and 1970s, the grant maximum in the designated areas was 50-60 per cent, compared with 40-50 per cent in the non-designated areas, and during certain periods, with 35 per cent in the Dublin area.

24 For a survey of this debate, which followed the publication of the Buchannan report in 1968, see P.N. O'Farrell, 'Regional Policy in Ireland: The Case for Concentration — A Reappraisal', *Economic and Social Review*, July 1974.

25 For example, employment targets were set for groups of towns and projects were sought for these groups. Both politically and administratively, this approach has obvious advantages over extreme concentration or dispersal.

26 For a discussion of the impact of Irish infrastructure on the manufacturing sector, see C.D. Foster et al., *The Importance of Infrastructure to Industrial Development in Ireland: Road, Telecommunications and Water Supply* (NESC Report no. 59), Stationery Office, Dublin 1981.

27 In fact the logic of attributing the performance of manufacturing industry entirely to the policies being operated would suggest that the IDA policies are disastrous, in that they resulted in a fall in employment between 1973 and 1986!

28 See McKeon, *op. cit.*

29 'In a sense the era of massive foreign investment in Ireland is over. We offer one of the most generous and comprehensive incentive packages available anywhere in the world'. *White Paper on Industrial Policy, op. cit.,* p. 7.

30 For a discussion of the relationship between employment creation and economic welfare, see F.P. Ruane, 'Project Analysis and Industrial Employment in Ireland', *ESRI Quarterly Economic Commentary*, July 1979.

31 See IDA, *Strategic Plan*, 1984.

32 This is especially true given the very high proportion of projects which apply for and receive government assistance at some period. See footnote 37 below.

33 See Department of Industry and Commerce, *op. cit.*, p. 30.

34 One economist, Eoin O'Malley has identified many of these difficulties as symptoms of a specific global problem which Ireland has encountered in trying to develop an industrial base in the latter part of the twentieth century. O'Malley's thesis identifies the key problem as the small size of Irish industrial units which cannot overcome the barriers to entry created by large international companies. See E. O'Malley, 'The Performance of Irish Indigenous Industry: Some Lessons for the 1980s' in Jim Fitzpatrick and John Kelly (editors), *op. cit.*

35 For an evaluation of Irish manufacturing performance from the perspective of successful international firms, see Charles Carroll, *Building Ireland's Business: Perspectives from PIMS*, Irish Management Institute, Dublin 1985.

36 While other incentives (e.g. labour training, export, and research and development grants) may play a significant role in the policy package, quantitatively they are far less important and less focussed than the fixed-asset incentives.

37 The bias is explicitly commented upon on page 11 in the Department of Industry and Commerce, *op. cit.*

38 See F.P. Ruane, 'Government Financial and Tax Incentives and Industrial Employment', *Irish Banking Review*, June 1983.

39 A recent survey of senior executives in Irish industry indicated that over the period 1983-86 three quarters of the firms had received a subsidy or grant from at least one agency and one half had received assistance from two or more agencies. See speech by the Minister for Industry and Commerce to the CII National Council on 10 December 1986.

40 This issue is discussed in the NESC Report on the Role of the Financial System in Financing the Traded Sectors in Industry.

41. See *Direct Taxation: The Role of Incentives* (Second Report of the Commission on Taxation), Stationery Office, Dublin 1984, p. 63.

42 The recent estimates of repatriated projects have provided additional evidence that such transfer-pricing behaviour has taken place.

43 The low level of backward linkages is discussed in P.N. O'Farrell and B. O'Loughlin, *An Analysis of New Industry Linkages in Ireland*, Industrial Development Authority, Dublin 1980.

44 See F.P. Ruane and A.A. John, 'Government Intervention, Debt Finance and the Cost of Capital to Irish Manufacturing', *Economic and Social Review*, 1985. It should be noted that even if the IDA capital grant is neutral in its effects on factor choice, the fiscal policies unambiguously reduce the cost of capital relative to labour facing the manufacturing sector.

45 Section 84 loans are similar to preference share loans where the return to the lender, i.e. the bank, is classified as a tax-free dividend. See *Direct Taxation: The Role of Incentives, op. cit.*, p. 104.

46 Arguably, when the grants were introduced in the 1950s, capital financing was a major constraint on manufacturing.

47 One economist has likened the policy of extensive and almost exclusive support to fixed assets, in the face of rising labour costs, rising taxation and increasingly congested infrastructure, to a medical policy which allocated the bulk of its resources to maternity units!

48 See Department of Industry and Commerce, *op. cit.*

49 For a very good summary of the issues in the debate, see Jim Fitzpatrick and John Kelly, 'Industry in Ireland: Policies, Performance and Problems', in Jim Fitzpatrick and John Kelly (editors), *op. cit.*

50 The government's current position on this debate seems to endorse the Structuralist viewpoint in spirit if not in detail. See Department of Industry and Commerce, *op. cit.*

51 In fact chemicals and electronics are the sectors in which labour productivity is highest.

52 Comparing two identical projects, one foreign-owned and one domestically-owned, the value of the latter will always exceed that of the former, since profits of domestically-owned firms accrue to Irish residents.

12 The Non-Traded Sector: Services and Building and Construction

Kevin O'Rourke*

1 INTRODUCTION

IN THE context of a small open economy (SOE), a non-traded good can most easily be defined as a good the price of which is determined by supply and demand within that economy. It is thus distinguished from traded goods the prices of which are given exogenously to the SOE, being determined by developments in the rest of the world. A good can be non-traded for several reasons, the most obvious one being transport costs. If transport costs are sufficiently high for a commodity, it will not be traded between countries, and its price in, say, Ireland will be determined within Ireland. For example, it would normally be prohibitively expensive to fly hairdressers (or their customers) from London to Dublin; another example is cement, which was long considered too heavy to import into the country.

A second reason why a good or service may be non-traded is government intervention. The most obvious example of this is the case of a prohibitive tariff, or zero quota, which blocks the import of a good into a country. Although the good could in theory be traded, it now plays an economic role precisely analogous to more traditional non-traded goods, such as sewerage or street lighting. More subtle examples might include regulations on quality, which can effectively prohibit imports, or a government procurement policy that links consumption in a country with production in that country.

From the above discussion it can easily be seen that the list of all goods and services which are non-traded for a country will be evolving over time; and that this list will differ between different

*The author is grateful to the following for helpful comments and encouragement: Sean Barrett, Richard Caves, Max Corden, Jim Fitzpatrick Atish Ghosh, Kala Krishna, Ivor Kenny, John McEniff, Sean Nolan, Des Norton, John O'Hagan, Jim O'Leary and Michael Ross. The usual disclaimer applies.

countries at the same point in time. In other words, the boundaries of the non-traded goods sector are endogenous to the economic system. Given the parameters of the system (tastes, technology, preferences, government policies and so on), whether a good is non-traded or not will depend upon the actions of rational economic agents. For example, if transport costs are declining over time, then one would expect some goods which were previously non-traded to become traded. Alternatively, an increase in demand for a good in a country may raise the price of that good within the country so much that it will become worthwhile for foreign entrepreneurs to export the good to that country, whereas previously the existence of transport costs, tariff barriers or other impediments to trade had blocked all trade in the product. A sufficient increase in the domestic cost of production of the product would have the same effect. For one or more of the above reasons, cement has been imported into Ireland in the past few years for the first time ever. One example of a previously non-traded service becoming traded that has attracted particular attention in recent years in Ireland, and aroused serious concern among policy makers, has been the case of retailing in border areas. As is well known, in this case it was changing government policy, and in particular high indirect taxes, that induced individuals to shop in Northern Ireland. This example is particularly striking, first, as retailing has traditionally been considered a typically non-traded industry, and second, as it illustrates the effect that government policy has in shaping the limits of the non-traded sector.

Non-traded sectors will also differ between countries. This is self-evident if one compares say Luxembourg with the US (although not irrelevant, as the non-traded sector can play a crucial role for a government interested in macroeconomic policy making). In Ireland's case, the fact that it is a small island presumably affects the relative size of its non-traded sector vis-à-vis other countries.

One major problem arising in empirical work on non-traded goods is that while it is easy in theory to say whether a *good* is internationally traded or not, it is very difficult in practice to say of a particular *sector* in the real world that it is either traded or non-traded. For example, the banking sector in Ireland clearly contains elements that can best be thought of as non-traded services (e.g. the provision of branch banking); equally clearly, other banking activities occur within an international context. The same is true of the transport and communications sectors, the insurance sector, and others. Another point to bear in mind is that it is crucially important for the analysis of a non-traded industry whether it is in the public or the private sector, since the factors influencing it differ depending on which sector it is in. For example, employment levels in the public sector can be regarded as exogenous in some sense (at least in the short run), while employment levels in the private sector can be regarded as endogenous. As shall be seen later, there are grounds for suspecting that the sustainability of an increase in sheltered sector employment will depend on whether the increase is in some sense exogenous or endogenous. It will be argued that existing analyses of the effects of such an increase are really more concerned with increasing exogenous (i.e. public sector) employment in the non-traded sector.

This chapter is divided into three main sections. The first deals with theoretical approaches to the non-traded sector, and in particular takes issue with the standard view that the sector is a derivative one, as articulated in successive official Irish policy documents and indeed in Chapter 7 of this book. The second section examines the services sector, both theoretically and empirically, while the third section deals with the Irish building and construction industry. As stated in Chapter 7, the non-traded sector is conventionally defined as comprising the two sectors above, plus the public utilities sector. In 1985, service sector employment was approximately 600,000; employment in building and construction was 76,000 and in utilities 15,000. Altogether, 53 per cent of total employment was in the non-traded sector, with the overwhelming bulk of employment being in services and construction. It thus seems reasonable to concentrate on these two industries when studying the non-traded sector as a whole.

2   THE ROLE OF THE NON-TRADED SECTOR

Some Misconceptions

Because it is the traded goods sector which earns foreign exchange, the impression is frequently given that it is this sector on which all other sectors in the economy depend, and that government policy should focus on it. The purpose of this section is to argue theoretically that not only does the non-traded (NT) sector matter, but that in fact government policy can be most usefully directed at it. The argument will have three main strands. First, it will be argued that it is mistaken to equate, as has been done, the real wage with national welfare. Second, Chapter 7 is essentially looking at increases in NT output that one would *a priori* regard as undesirable. However, desirable increases in NT output, which involve changing some fundamental parameter of the economic system, are

410

compatible with balance-of-payments equilibrium. Third, the performance of the non-traded sector is vital to the well-being of the traded sector. Such issues as monopoly power and positive externalities will be considered. The section will also examine what special features one might expect to observe in a sector insulated from international competition.

Chapter 7 has shown that under restrictive circumstances the level of national output depends uniquely on the output of the traded goods sector — and, by implication, that the real wage depends uniquely on technological progress in the traded goods sector. However, it should not be inferred from this that technological progress in the non-traded goods sector is irrelevant. Indeed, if what one is concerned with is real GDP rather than the real wage, technological progress in both sectors is equally important. This is obvious: such progress means that with a given amount of resources, more goods and services can be produced. Thus, technological progress in either sector increases the total of goods and services in the economy, and hence increases GDP.[1] Therefore technological progress in either sector leads to the nation as a whole being better off, so, to attribute a uniquely beneficial role to technological progress in the *traded* sector is quite misguided.

There is another, more subtle, theoretical point to be made about the presentation in Chapter 7 of the role of the non-traded goods sector. The chapter derives a relationship between the sizes of the traded and non-traded goods sectors which must hold in equilibrium. It is then implied, quite correctly, that an attempt to expand employment in the non-traded goods sector by fiat (say by increasing government expenditure on non-traded goods) will run into difficulties. The higher incomes that the extra employment entails will be partly spent on imports; in the absence of increased exports, the country will experience balance-of-payments difficulties. This analysis illustrates the dangers which interventionist bureaucrats face, and holds great relevance for planned economies. In the context of more mixed economies, however, where levels of output are largely determined by demand and supply, it is not the only appropriate thought experiment.

In a Neoclassical market economy, levels of output (and hence the allocation of labour) are determined by the interaction of supply and demand, and depend on the state of technology in a country, on preferences, and on endowments. If all prices (including factor returns) are flexible, an equilibrium will be reached in which all markets clear. In particular, a country's current account will balance (ignoring complications which arise in multi-period models, when countries can lend to or borrow from each other). In such an economy, it is indeed the case that an attempt to artificially expand employment in the non-traded goods sector will lead to current account deficits. It is also the case that attempts to artificially expand employment in any sector are undesirable (assuming that there are no distortions such as production externalities which would lead to the free-market outcome being suboptimal). However, if any of the underlying parameters of the economy are changed (tastes, technology or preferences), or indeed if the institutional framework within which these parameters interact is altered, then the long-run, sustainable equilibrium labour allocation of the economy will change. Under such circumstances, it is perfectly possible for the non-traded goods sector to increase in size, without the country running into deficits. Seen in this light, assertions that the non-traded goods sector cannot on its own provide new employment seem quite misplaced.

Recall that from Equations 3 and 6 in Chapter 7, it follows that

$$L_{nt} = V_t \times (\beta_s/1 - \beta_s) \times (1/W)$$

It is now clear that labour employed in the non-traded sector depends not only on V_t, but also on β_s, a fundamental parameter describing SOE tastes, and the equilibrium wage W. W is determined by supply and demand, and depends on endowments (i.e. the total labour supply in the SOE), and technology (which determines the aggregate labour demand curve, see Figure 7.2 in Chapter 7). In the absence of distortions, labour is allocated efficiently between sectors; optimal (and hence actual) labour allocation will only change if either tastes, technology or endowments change. If this happens then the ratio of L_{nt} to V_t will change; employment in the non-traded sector can indeed rise without traded sector output rising, and without the country running into balance-of-payments problems. By considering the case where L_{nt} increases while β_s (and W) remain constant, it restricts the discussion to examining undesirable increases in non-traded sector employment. In a smoothly functioning market economy, though, desirable increases in employment can and will occur without balance-of-payments problems arising, no matter which sector they arise in.

Unfortunately, the notion that the non-traded goods sector cannot by itself help solve Ireland's unemployment problem has become almost universally accepted dogma in Irish policy thinking. A few examples will suffice. The Telesis Report, speaking of the development of successful non-traded businesses, says that 'while these strategies are understandable from the point of view of the individual companies, from the point of view of the country, the absence of these companies from the effort to build a successful international export base is a serious problem'[2] and recommends that non-traded businesses be discriminated against by reducing grants available to them while increasing grants to export businesses.[3] The standard economic argument against this policy prescription (derived, it is claimed here, from incorrect economic analysis) is, as was made clear above, that any attempt to divert resources from where they would naturally flow reduces national income.

The 1984 ESRI report on unemployment policy stated that 'a primacy attaches to the open or competing sector in that it is the only sector in which expansion will tend to alleviate rather than exacerbate the fundamental balance of payments and fiscal constraints'.[4] A 1986 NESC report claimed that 'those sectors of the economy which exclusively or predominantly serve the domestic market cannot be regarded as an independent source of sustained economic growth...the demand for the goods and services produced by these sectors is a derived demand and the output they produce and the level of employment they provide are ultimately determined by the size of the exposed sector and the strength of the economic linkages between the exposed sector and the rest of the economy'.[5] It has been seen why this view is incorrect and, as shall be seen later, why policy-makers should pay special attention to the non-traded sector; first, however, a brief digression to examine a famous model of the SOE that will help to motivate the discussion that follows.

The Aukrust Model
The discussion so far has stressed the symmetrical way in which both traded and non-traded goods enter into the economy: their output is determined by the interaction of tastes, technology and preferences, and in the absence of distortions the market mechanism produces the optimal mix. Moreover both sectors contribute in an equivalent fashion to GDP. There is however a key distinction between the two sectors: the non-traded goods sector is insulated from international competition. This is the central feature of an influential model of the small open economy (SOE) due to the Norwegian economist Odd Aukrust. It is worth briefly examining the model here, as it helps in clarifying the role of non-traded goods, and it has also been used, with a slight twist, in discussing the Irish economy.

413

Aukrust's model starts by making the standard assumption that the prices of traded goods are determined on world markets, and that the SOE takes them as given. Given productivity levels in the traded goods sector (also assumed exogenous) and given the price of the output, there will be a certain level of wages which firms in the traded goods sector can pay if they are to earn a 'normal' rate of return. It is assumed that on average wages in the traded goods sector will be forced down to this level, given the exposure of the sector to international competition. Trade union solidarity, an inter-sectoral demonstration effect, or some other mechanism is then assumed to generalize the wage level, set in the exposed sector, to the sheltered sector. This nominal wage level, together with productivity in the sheltered sector, determines the costs of non-traded goods producers; these producers are assumed to pass on fully their costs to consumers, using a cost-plus pricing rule. (Demand for non-tradables is left to adjust to price in this model.)

The Aukrust model as outlined above is clearly too simplistic to be satisfactory; for example, it totally ignores the role played by demand. However, it plays a useful role in highlighting the difference in competitive environments faced by the two sectors, and in emphasizing the role of the labour market as a link between the two. Exposed industries have to meet the price set by their foreign competitors; sheltered firms can always pass on higher costs to domestic consumers. One might thus expect the sheltered sector to be less competitive in some sense, as will be discussed later. In the Irish context the model has been neatly turned on its head by reversing the direction of the wage-formation process. It has been argued that wages are set in the sheltered sector (and specifically in the public sector) by trade unions enjoying great monopoly power. The wages determined here, which spill over into the rest of the economy, bear no necessary relationship to what the exposed sector can bear; the result is of course that the exposed sector is squeezed, with consequent job losses. Assuming that the above is roughly true, an interesting question to ask is why union-negotiated wages are set in the exposed sector in some European countries (e.g. Scandinavia) and in the sheltered sector in others (e.g. Ireland). It is interesting that the Irish version of the model to some extent rehabilitates the priority of productivity increases in the exposed sector. If firms in the exposed sector are faced with wage increases they cannot afford, then they need productivity increases to survive. By contrast, in the Scandinavian model, in which inflation was the focus of attention, productivity in the sheltered sector was crucial. Traded goods prices were set abroad; domestic goods prices were positively related to the wage set in the exposed sector (and thus positively related to productivity in the exposed sector), and negatively related to productivity in the sheltered sector.

Another interesting feature to emerge from the model is that the traditional labour-capital conflict over income shares may not be the only, or even the most important one in society. In particular, the interest of both labour and capital in the sheltered sector may be directly opposed to that of labour and capital in the exposed sector.[6] For example, an increase of wages and prices in the non-traded sector may be to the benefit of both partners in this sector; to the extent, however, that non-traded goods are used as inputs in the exposed sector, or enter into the consumption of workers and capitalists in the exposed sector, this will hurt either labour or capital in the exposed sector, or both.

The Non-Traded Sector and Competitiveness: Concentration and Externalities
It was emphasized above that the non-traded sector is in no meaningful way 'derivative' as standard Irish economic analysis suggests; its output is determined simultaneously with that of the traded sector. From this analysis stems a highly relevant but essentially negative policy prescription: in the absence of distortions, firms in the non-traded sector should not be discriminated against by giving preferential subsidies to exposed sector firms. In this section some more positive policy options will be considered (and the arguments will be found to be in close conformity with those of earlier chapters). First, it will be argued that a country's competitiveness depends uniquely on the performance of the non-traded sector. Second, following on from this, it will be argued that there is potentially a highly useful role for anti-trust policy in Ireland. Third, some modern literature concerning the role of externalities in formulating industrial policy will be considered; it will be found that non-tradability plays a key role in such discussions.

First, it is in an important sense the non-traded sector, and the non-traded sector alone, upon which a country's competitiveness depends. (It is probably easiest to think of competitiveness as being the rate of return which factors of production specific to the export sector in a given country can earn, facing given world product prices, relative to such factors in other countries.) The argument is trivial. If a good or factor is internationally traded, then its price will tend to be equalized between countries. If labour was perfectly mobile internationally, then wage differences between countries would vanish; it is only because labour is largely a non-traded factor that low labour costs are a basis for competitiveness. The same is true with all other goods and factors. Therefore, it is only the price at which non-traded inputs are supplied to exposed sector firms that determines how well they can compete against foreign firms. (One factor of production which is non-traded and which may be particularly important is the general institutional environment of a country; its legal and tax systems, for example.)

If this is true, then it is clear that a government interested in strengthening the competitive position of its exposed sector should focus its attentions on trying to improve the supply of non-traded inputs to that sector. This may involve the use of anti-trust legislation against sheltered sector monopolies; it may involve trying to improve the educational standards of the work-force. Most importantly, perhaps, it may involve the government looking at its own activities in the economy. There is then a case for arguing that industrial policy, far from concentrating on the exposed sector itself, as has tended to be the case in Ireland in recent years, should concern itself mainly with the sheltered sector.

In asking whether anti-trust policy may be needed in Ireland, it is of course necessary to ascertain whether firms in the non-traded sector in Ireland have monopoly power in goods markets. It seems intuitively plausible that this could be so; they are operating in a small market insulated from international competition. (Remember also that the Irish version of the Aukrust model assumed that unions had some monopoly power in factor markets.) Note that the question of whether or not these firms have market power is important regardless of whether or not their output is used as an input by traded sector firms. If the prices they charge exceed marginal cost, then this has a direct negative effect on economic welfare (in terms of the familiar optimality criteria of welfare economics, the marginal rate of transformation no longer equals the marginal rate of substitution). (As a digression, it should be noted that if workers negotiate for real, rather than nominal wages, which indeed appears to be so, then it will be the case that all non-traded goods entering into workers' consumption will be indirectly traded. An increase in the price of any such good will lead to an increase of (wage) costs in the exposed sector. In this case, excessive price/cost margins in almost all non-traded industries will adversely affect the position of traded goods firms.)

There is at least some indirect evidence that firms in non-traded goods industries enjoy a higher level of monopoly power than firms in the traded sector. (It would be interesting to do a rigorous study of the question.) O'Malley, in a study using 1964 data,[7] allocated

Irish industries to one of three categories: monopolistic, oligopolistic and perfectly competitive. Hughes,[8] in another study using 1964 data, gave a breakdown of transportable goods industries (i.e. not including building and construction or services) into exposed and sheltered sectors. Comparing O'Malley's classification with Hughes' breakdown of Irish transportable goods industries into exposed and sheltered industries the following results are obtained: in the exposed sector, twelve industries were competitive, two were oligopolistic and four monopolistic. In the sheltered sector, by contrast, seven industries were competitive, seven oligopolistic and ten monopolistic. Obviously the structure of Irish industry has evolved vastly in the past 20 years, but the above numbers at least suggest that there may be some tendency for sheltered industries to be more concentrated than exposed industries. This in turn suggests that if exposed industries are being hurt by this, policy makers should consider the use of anti-trust legislation to break up home goods monopolies in cases where these monopolies are due to factors other than economies of scale.[9]

Finally, some mention should be made of the recent literature in trade theory on the role of positive externalities in the formulation of optimal industrial policy.[10] If there are positive externalities to the production of a good (i.e. benefits arising from the production of the good which accrue to society at large, but not to the manufacturer of the good), standard closed economy theory suggests that there is a case to be made for subsidizing the production of that good. In an open economy context, things are more complicated. Think of a world with two countries. If the positive externality accrues to both countries, then it is not important which country the good is produced in; country A should not try to promote the industry in question (call it industry X) if comparative advantage suggests that country B should produce X's output. Only if the externality is 'non-traded' (i.e. accrues only to the country in which the good is produced) should A try to promote its own X industry.

The typical externality considered is known as a 'linkage' externality. Say industry X uses an input, Y, which is produced under conditions of increasing returns to scale. The externality in the X sector then arises from the fact that if any firm increases its output of X the cost of Y is reduced for all users. Since firms do not take this societal benefit into account, they underprovide X; in a closed economy the X industry should be subsidized. In an open economy context, whether Y is traded or not is crucial. There are three cases to consider. First, if it is traded, all that matters for both countries is that production of Y is concentrated in one country, no matter which (so that all possible economies of scale are reaped). Second, if Y is non-traded, but enters as an input into only one sector X of the economy, then again both countries will want Y to be produced only in one country. This is because even the country not producing Y gains the benefit of having Y production concentrated; in this case, that benefit is simply the lower price of X resulting from the lower price of the input Y. The third case is when Y is non-traded, but is an input into most (or all) sectors of the economy. In this case country A will want to produce a lot of Y, since this increases its overall productivity in some sense, and hence its income (as well as reducing the prices of final, traded goods).[11] This provides a powerful argument for subsidizing the construction of infrastructure, for example.

For all of the above reasons, one can argue that government should concentrate far more on the non-traded sector in formulating industrial policy; in some sense, if you get the non-traded sector right, the traded sector will take care of itself. There have been some signs of an official move to this position; for example, the 1984 White Paper on Industrial Policy spoke of bringing Irish electricity prices down to European levels, of liberalizing road freight haulage and of promoting more competition in professional services. None the less, in speaking of services for example, the report concentrated almost exclusively on exportable services.[12] Clearly, a lot of persuading still has to be done if official thinking on the subject is to change.

3   THE IRISH SERVICES SECTOR

Services: Some General Considerations
There have been several Irish studies on services in recent years, but the sector generally has been a neglected one. One can think of at least two broad classes of reasons why this has been the case.

First, there are problems of definition and measurement associated with the sector. Attempts have been made to provide rigorous definitions for services. The fact that the output of service industries is usually intangible has often been cited as one of their distinguishing characteristics; however, this is not always the case. For example, management consultants produce physical reports as well as knowledge. Another factor stressed by economists is that services are consumed immediately, and cannot be stocked. To consider this potential definition for the service sector it is useful to make a distinction between service products and service functions.

A service product is the output of a service industry, for example attendance at a cinema. A service function refers to the satisfaction of the underlying want giving rise to the demand for the service product. In the case of the admission to the cinema, the service function involved is the provision of video entertainment, which desire could also be satisfied by, say, watching television. Now it can clearly be seen that while service products are generally consumed immediately, the service functions which they provide may be consumed over a period of time, or even a lifetime. In the sense of a service function, a haircut may last for some weeks, while a haircut in the sense of a service product takes around twenty minutes. An education generally continues to provide a service function even longer than does a haircut. Given that most consumer goods are either consumed or become obsolescent eventually (and that they too are only purchased in order to satisfy underlying wants) the difference between physical goods and services would seem to be one of degree rather than kind.[13] The difficulties involved with trying to provide a rigorous definition for services has led to the service sector being most commonly defined as everything other than industry and agriculture (with some controversy over where exactly the boundaries should be drawn). In Ireland the practice has been to include transport, communications and storage with the services sector, but to exclude electricity, gas and water supply, which some authors have suggested belong in the sector.

Furthermore, the very nature of services makes their output difficult to measure. This is especially so given that so many of the services provided in modern economies are non-marketed; that is, they are not purchased by consumers in the usual way, but are instead paid for (usually) by general taxation. This means that one cannot even measure the amount of money that people are willing to pay for them. Empirical discussions of services thus tend very often (and especially in Ireland) to make use of employment data rather than output data.

A second reason for the neglect of the services sector is that historically there has been a view that the sector is unimportant (if not actually harmful) to economic development, a view vestiges of which are still to be found today. This view was particularly prevalent among Classical economists, and is connected with the idea of services being instantly consumed. The Classical economists focussed on accumulation, which depended on saving, reflected in the production of a physical surplus. The value of this surplus represented the country's 'neat revenue' in Adam Smith's terminology, and could be allocated between consumption and investment. Certain occupations constituted unproductive labour:

The sovereign, for example, with all the officers both of justice and war who serve under him, the whole army and navy, are unproductive labourers...In the same class must be ranked, some both of the gravest and most important, and some of the most frivolous professions; churchmen, lawyers, physicians, men of letters of all kinds; players, buffoons, musicians, opera-singers, opera-dancers, &c...Like the declamation of the actor, the harangue of the orator, or the tune of the musician, the work of all of them perishes in the very instant of its production.[14]

Not only did such labourers not produce value; their wages were paid out of the surplus, and thus reduced the amount available for investment. If the Classical system represented an advance on the earlier Physiocratic notion that all wealth derived ultimately from the land, it only considered as wealth-producing the primary and secondary sectors. One present-day legacy of the Classical economists is the practice in Marxist countries of computing Gross Material Product rather than Gross National Product, as is done in the West. Echoes of the old attitude can also be heard in the fears expressed by some American protectionists that America is becoming a 'hamburger stall' economy as its traditional heavy industries decline in the face of foreign competition. In Ireland service companies face a 45 per cent corporation tax rate, as opposed to the 10 per cent tax rate faced by manufacturing industry. The Irish service sector has often been discriminated against in official thinking not just because of the standard Classical bias against services, but because services are seen as being mostly non-traded. The problems with such an attitude have already been discussed above.

To the Neoclassical economists who started writing about a century after Smith, the enjoyment of utility was the end of all economic activity. 'Man cannot create material things. In the mental and moral world indeed he may produce new ideas; but when he is said to produce material things, he really only produces utilities...'[15] Given this, the tertiary sector could not be said to be in any way less productive of wealth, i.e. of utility, than either the primary or secondary sectors. 'It is sometimes said that traders do not produce: that while the cabinet-maker produces furniture, the furniture-dealer merely sells what is already produced. But there is no scientific foundation for this distinction. They both produce utilities, and neither of them can do more: the furniture-dealer moves and rearranges matter so as to make it more serviceable than it was before, and the carpenter does nothing more'.[16]

According to this view, any activity is 'worthwhile' if there exists a purchaser for its output, as the existence of such a purchaser reveals the existence of an underlying demand for the activity.[17] An obvious problem arises when one considers the services sector in an economy such as Ireland's: namely, that many services are non-marketed. For such services the fact that they are provided does not necessarily mean that they do in fact satisfy underlying demands efficiently. Chapter 2 has listed several cases where services can be provided efficiently only in a collective manner; where there exist externalities, for example. That analysis is not at issue here; the point is simply that while privately marketed services will not be sold unless there exists a demand for them, it is at least possible that government may provide services which the community does not really desire (see Chapter 4).

Growth and Structure of the Services Sector in Ireland
It is surely not coincidental that the progression in economic thought from Physiocracy to Classical economics to Neoclassical economics, with the resultant changes in emphasis from agriculture, to agriculture and manufacturing, to all three main branches of economic activity, should have paralleled the development of Western economies from predominantly agricultural societies to more modern mixed economies. The tendency for growing economies to devote an increasing proportion of their resources to the production of services has often been noted, with the share of industry generally rising to a peak and then declining again. The following section examines the growth and evolving structure of the services sector in Ireland. The basic features of the sector will be described; the next section will present some theories regarding the growth of services in modern economies.

Ireland has not been an exception insofar as the growing share of services is concerned (see Chapter 8, Table 8.8). As noticeable, however, as the increase in the share of services is the large absolute share (33 per cent) that services had in the economy as early as 1926. In comparison with other European countries it was disproportionately large, given the role that agriculture still played in the economy. Similarly, industry has never had the importance in Ireland that it has had in other European countries; Ireland seems to have progressed from an agricultural to a service society, without experiencing the intervening phase of industrialization.

The structure of the sector, and how this structure has evolved, is now examined in some detail. Table 12.1 gives a very simple breakdown of services into marketed and non-marketed services, with the former category being further subdivided into producer, distributive and personal services.

Table 12.1

Irish Employment in Services 1971-81

| | Employment ('000s) | | Annual average change |
	1971	1981	(%)
Non-Marketed	111.8	164.0	3.9
Marketed	347.2	419.4	1.9
Producer	70.2	109.7	4.6
Distributive	208.4	235.4	1.2
Personal	68.7	74.3	0.8

Sources: D. Dineen, *Strategy for the Development of the Services Sector in the Mid-West Region of Ireland,* Mid-West RDO, Limerick 1986.

As can be seen, between 1971 and 1981, the growth rate for non-marketed services (largely accounted for by increases in health and education) greatly exceeded that of marketed services. However, employment in the marketed services sector was still far greater than employment in the non-marketed sector. Within the former sector, the largest area of employment in both years was the distributive sector, consisting of transportation, wholesale and retail commerce, etc. However, the area with the most rapid growth in employment during the period was producer services, which grew even faster than the non-marketed sector. This provides confirmation of the theories laying emphasis on intermediate services which will be considered below.

It might be thought that, given the importance of non-marketed services to total service employment growth, the regional distribution of the growth in services would be very lopsided, concentrated on Dublin, the centre of government activity. It is certainly the case that services are very heavily centred on Dublin: in 1985, 71.4 per cent of employment there was in the services sector, as opposed to 49.0 per cent in the rest of the country. Moreover, 39.2 per cent of the country's service jobs were in Dublin. However, the picture is somewhat more complicated than this with regard to growth, as Table 12.2 makes clear.

As can be seen from the table, the percentage increase in marketed services employment between 1971 and 1981 was greater in the East than anywhere else. However, non-marketed service employment grew more rapidly in the rest of the country than in Dublin, as can be seen by comparing the growth rates for the east and the country as a whole. Furthermore, the non-marketed sector in the east contributed less as a percentage of overall service employment growth than in any other region of the country. It would thus appear that although service employment is heavily concentrated in the capital city, the regions are more dependent on government than Dublin for an expansion of their service employment.

Table 12.2
Growth in Service Employment by Region, 1971-81

	Marketed ('000s)			Non-marketed ('000s)			Non-marketed (% share of change)
	1971	1981	% change '71-'81	1971	1981	% change '71-'81	
East	168.2	215.9	28.6	48.4	70.9	46.2	32.1
Ireland	347.2	419.4	20.9	111.8	164.0	46.7	41.2

Sources: as for Table 12.1.

Table 12.3
Service Employment in Ireland by Sector, 1961-85

Industrial branch	1961	1971	1975	1981	1985
Commerce: wholesale	30.3	36.5	37.5	42.6	46.8
Commerce: retail	109.9	110.3	117.1	119.7	121.8
Insurance, finance, business services	13.7	23.6	27.6	42.9	40.4
Transport, communications, storage	53.2	59.5	69.3	70.0	67.7
Public administration and defence	39.9	48.4	60.0	77.0	73.2
Professional services	83.7	108.0	126.8	164.1	171.9
Personal services	62.2	53.9	46.8	49.1	60.8
Other	12.3	14.2	13.2	24.8	17.2
Total	405.2	454.3	498.2	590.3	599.8

Sources: D. Coniffe and K. Kennedy (editors), *Employment and Unemployment Policy for Ireland,* ESRI, Dublin 1984, and CSO, *Labour Force Survey 1985.*

Table 12.3 gives a breakdown of service employment in Ireland into its principal categories. Traditionally, commerce (wholesale plus retail) was the largest of the service sectors in terms of employment. However, by 1981 it had been overtaken in size by the professional services group, consisting largely of the health and education industries, and thus largely a public sector category. In 1981, 58,000 people worked in education and 62,000 in health.[18] Numbers employed in public administration and defence have also dramatically increased in the past 25 years, reflecting the increased role of government in the economy (see Chapter 4). The transport, communication and storage category is also mainly within the public sector: the largest sector within it in 1981 was the postal, telegraph and radio communications sector, employing 28,000 workers. Road transport employed 18,000 workers, rail transport 5,500 workers, and air transport 6,000 workers. The private sector category showing the most rapid increase was the insurance, finance and business services sector, about half of the employment of which is accounted for by banking and finance, and a further quarter by the insurance industry. The residual category, which also showed a substantial percentage increase, largely consists of recreational services, theatre and broadcasting.

In the personal services category development was not as static as the figures suggest. This used to consist predominantly of domestic servants, whose numbers have declined sharply over the past few decades. This fall in employment was offset by an increase in other areas, the most important of which are the hotel and restaurant industries, accounting together for over one-half of the total employment in the category. (These sectors are not, of course, non-traded activities, as they depend largely on tourists for their business. Given official thinking on the importance of the traded sectors, this explains the government efforts that have been made to promote the industries.)

Explanations for Service Sector Growth[19]
The traditional explanation for the relative growth of the service sector over time relied on two stylized facts. First, an 'Engel's Law' of sorts applied to the demand for services; the income elasticity of demand for services was greater than unity, and thus as countries became richer, they spent a greater proportion of their incomes on services. Second, it was argued that the rate of productivity increase in services was less than that in manufacturing. Thus, the increase in the share of service employment was even greater than that of the share of services in final demand. A problem with this explanation is that lower productivity growth in services leads to an increase in their relative price over time, which may lead consumers to substitute away from services to other methods of satisfying their underlying wants (examples include the widespread adoption of dishwashers and washing mashines).

The above argument deals with consumer services, that is services which make up a part of final demand. Another, not incompatible explanation for the growth in services over time focusses on intermediate or producer services, which are purchased as inputs by other firms. It is argued that on balance it is becoming advantageous for production processes to become vertically disintegrated, and for inputs to be provided by specialized intermediate goods and services firms. In part of course this just results in a statistical transference of labour previously employed in the manufacturing sector (but in a service occupation within that sector) to the services sector; however, Smith's dictum that the division of labour depends on the extent of the market implies that an evolving pattern of the division of labour (which is in our case occurring between rather than within firms, and which indeed involves the creation of entirely new industries) will generally take place in a context of growth and innovation.

This would not seem to enable anything to be said *a priori* about the share of services; most of the arguments stressing intermediate services as a source of service sector growth have been primarily empirical. Some researchers have questioned the notion that the income elasticity of demand for services is greater than that for other consumer goods and thus that the growth in services is driven by final demand; others have shown that as much as half of the final demand for marketed services is intermediate in nature or that a disproportionately large percentage of the growth in services occurs in the producer services sector. This has been found to be the case in the Irish context.

Evaluating the Irish Service Sector
Any attempt to evaluate the performance of the Irish service sector will of necessity be patchy, given the disparate nature of the sector and the paucity of information available on it. This section will therefore focus on how in principle the sector could be evaluated, although a few suggestive statistics will be presented.

As seen, the non-traded goods sector is important, both because its own output provides the community with utility directly, and because it is an important source of inputs to the traded sector. For both of these reasons any attempt to evaluate the service sector should be concerned with the price at which services are made available to the public. An excessive price means either that traded sector firms are placed at a disadvantage vis-à-vis their foreign competitors (in the case of indirectly traded services) or that domestic consumers are paying too high a price for services, and consequently are not consuming enough. (In this case it is likely that more employment in the sector could be generated if prices were to fall and quantity produced increased.)

As emphasized in earlier chapters and in the discussion above, excessive levels of concentration may be a problem in the non-traded sector. It is therefore important to examine concentration levels in the Irish services sector. Cogan points out that the services sector in Ireland differs radically from the free market ideal.[20] First, many services have been taken out of the market system altogether and are provided by government (e.g. health and education). This has generally occurred on considerations of equity. Second, industries such as rail transportation and telecommunications, although provided within a market context, are run as monopolies by government proxies. Natural economies of scale are often cited as justifications for this (it must of course be remembered that the rail system was once run by four separate companies, each with a monopoly in their own region). Moreover, in industries such as bus and air transportation, the major 'player' is a government company, and severe restrictions are placed on the ability of potential competitors to enter the market. Third, many privately provided services such as the legal professions restrict entry into the market, thus inhibiting competition and raising the returns to those fortunate enough to be in the industry.

It is difficult to get adequate data on concentration in the services sector in Ireland, but it would appear that inadequate levels of competition are a problem in the sector. Accordingly, at least one commentator has recently suggested that the emphasis of policy directed at the private services sector should be 'emphasis on competition and the dismantling of restrictive practices and price maintenance'.[21] This is of course particularly important for the competitiveness of Ireland's export industries, especially given the increasing role of producer services within the services sector, as highlighted earlier. Norton pinpoints two sectors in particular where increases in competition could be particularly beneficial: the road haulage industry and the legal profession. However, it is difficult to make policy recommendations with confidence when so few reliable data are available; a major study of price-cost margins in the Irish service sector would certainly be warranted.

Such a study would be part of a broader inquiry into the prices at which services are provided in Ireland, comparing these with prices abroad. One factor other than industry concentration which influences prices is the level of labour productivity growth over time. In a major study of the sector, Cogan spoke of 'a dismal picture of labour productivity in service industries'.[22] Using data for the period 1956 to 1971, he found that labour productivity improvements in service industries lagged far behind those in industry and agriculture, with performance in banking, hotels and restaurants being particularly weak. There were however large increases in productivity in transportation. The overall picture, then is not necessarily so dismal given that it is common for productivity increases in services to be lower than in the rest of the economy.[23] It would be interesting therefore to compare Ireland's experience with those of other countries. There are some specific government-provided services for which information on price is available, and here it does appear that Irish firms are being placed at a disadvantage relative to their foreign competitors. For example, domestic postage was more expensive in Ireland than in other EC countries in 1984, as were local telephone calls. International post and telephone charges were also more expensive than in most European countries. Regarding for the moment the provision of electricity as a service (as is often the case), Ireland was estimated to have the most highly-priced electricity in the EC (this is in addition to the fact that various industrial oils are also relatively highly-priced in Ireland, due to the imposition of government taxes).[24] In 1979 output per staff member in the Irish railway system was estimated as joint lowest (with Denmark) in the EC.[25]

A key factor affecting the cost of provision of government services is public sector pay, which is high. Average government sector pay was 136 per cent of the mean industrial wage in 1975, and had climbed to a peak of 149 per cent by 1981. Since then it has fallen to 143 per cent, still an extraordinarily high figure.[26] If one looks at specific areas of government expenditure (excluding transfers), Irish expenditure on health as a percentage of GNP is above the OECD average, and is certainly far above what one would expect given Ireland's relatively low income. Moreover, there are reasons to believe that there are substantial cost inefficiencies in the system. For example, 34.9 per cent of visits to GPs (general practitioners of medicine) funded by the state resulted in return appointments, as opposed to 16.5 per cent of visits not so funded. In education, unit costs rose by 40.6 per cent between 1971 and 1980, a greater amount than costs elsewhere in the economy. As in the health services, increasing levels of pay were largely responsible for the increased cost.[27]

4   THE CONSTRUCTION INDUSTRY IN IRELAND

The Irish construction industry, which in 1985 accounted for nearly

12 per cent of GNP, is the country's second industry after agriculture in terms of share of output. It is noteworthy not only for its size, but for its volatility, and for the role which government plays in it: in 1985, public capital expenditure paid for two-thirds of construction output. It therefore seems worthwhile to briefly examine the main features of the industry.[28]

First, it should be said that not all segments of the industry as commonly defined are non-traded. The industry comprises three sectors: the building sector, the design and consultancy sector, and the building materials sector. The building sector can clearly be regarded as non-traded; the service which it provides (assembling materials in a useful manner) of necessity takes place in the country where it will be 'consumed'; more to the point, while it would in principle be possible for foreign firms to organize the building, it would probably be impractical for them to fly labourers into the country. Thus, costs and prices in the sector are mainly determined by Irish conditions (and especially Irish wage levels), which it will be recalled is the essential attribute of a non-traded activity. (This is not so for all countries; indeed some Irish firms have undertaken work abroad, largely in Africa and the Middle East, and have provided labour for the projects they have been involved in. For such countries, the building sector could indeed be regarded as traded.)

By contrast, there is some foreign involvement in the consultancy sector, and some building materials are traded goods (e.g. cement, as mentioned earlier). (Other building materials include sand and gravel, stone, tarmacadam, timber, and electrical, plumbing and glazing hardware.) In 1983 the building materials sector realized exports of IR£146 million, about 20 per cent of the value of materials used in Irish construction in that year. Exports are largely to the UK. On the import side, it is estimated that the import content of the final product of the construction industry is around 20 per cent.

The Sectoral Consultative Committee for the Construction Sector (SCCCS) has given a useful breakdown of the sector's output into three categories: housing, construction for the market sector, and construction for infrastructure. This is useful conceptually, as the three types of construction activity enter into the economic system in different ways. The output of the first two can be regarded as being determined largely by other economic variables, while that of the third can be regarded as exogenous.

Table 12.4 gives output figures for the three subsectors for selected years. As can be seen, the largest sector of the industry is the housing sector. Long-term trends in the housing sector are obviously strongly influenced by demographic developments. Thus the sector experienced a slump during the 1950s, when emigration was at its peak, but has recovered strongly since then, as the Irish population has expanded rapidly. In 1977, housing accounted for 42 per cent of construction output in Ireland, as compared with only 34 per cent in 16 other European and North American countries.

Table 12.4

Construction Output 1975-84 (IR£million), 1975 prices

Year	Housing	Market sector	Infrastructure	Total	Total/GDP %
1975	253	132	140	525	13.9
1977	267	164	144	575	13.8
1979	359	261	178	798	17.4
1981	288	280	195	763	15.7
1982	254	212	212	678	13.7
1983	275	137	202	614	12.6
1984	275	118	190	583	11.5

Sources: Sectoral Consultative Committee for the Construction Sector, *The Construction Industry*, Dublin 1984.

In the shorter run, both macroeconomic developments and government policy affect the sector. An obvious linkage to the rest of the economy is the interest rate, which determines the cost to house purchasers of availing of mortgages. Government policies affecting the private housing sector include the provision of mortgage tax relief (the value to the average mortgagee of which is estimated at one-third of the value of the typical mortgage), and grants to first time house purchasers. In addition, local authorities provide housing themselves, and also extend loans to private house purchasers. In 1982, for example, out of a total of 26,798 housing completions, 5,711 (21.3 per cent) were public housing units, and a further 6,118 (22.8 per cent) were funded by public loans. The SCCCS estimates that the state provides around 35 per cent of the finance for new housing.

Construction for the market sector consists of construction for the industrial, commercial, agricultural and semi-state sectors. Its level is very volatile, depending largely on the general state of the economy. Moreover, the composition of activity in this sector also fluctuates. During economic downturns, the share of industrial construction might be expected to decrease; and indeed, while in

1979 (a year of expansion) industrial construction accounted for 39 per cent of total market sector construction, in 1984 this figure was only 31 per cent. Related to this phenomenon is the fact that in downturns the share of state financing of construction in the sector increases. State financing in the sector can take the form of grants, loans or direct investment. In 1979, state finance accounted for 57 per cent of total finance in the sector; by 1983, this figure had risen to 75 per cent.

The housing sector responds to long-term demographic trends, interest rates and government policy. Construction for the market sector depends on the general level of economic activity. By contrast, construction for infrastructure has been almost entirely undertaken by government in the past. Thus, construction in this sector can be regarded as exogenous to the system. Of course, when one takes account of the government budget constraint — a binding constraint nowadays — this seems less convincing. However, money has been made available to Ireland from the European Community for infrastructural spending, which enhances the autonomy of this component of construction activity. Roads, sanitary services and educational buildings are its main components.

In evaluating the performance of the sector, it is again appropriate to look at the price of the output, and to examine whether such factors as excessive concentration are raising the price unduly. The Irish construction industry would appear to be competitive in structure, with about 5,000 companies active in it. (It should be noted, however, that the cement industry, supplying one of the industry's main inputs, is heavily concentrated.) Moreover, while the early 1970s saw a trend towards greater scale of operations in the housing sector, this has since been reversed, with many new, small firms entering the industry. In 1983, out of a total of 4,872 firms, only eight firms employed more than 500 people: 90.4 per cent of the firms employed fewer than 20 people. The reaping of excess profits in the industry is therefore unlikely to be a problem; however, there has been some concern that the ease of entry into the industry has led to poor management performance.

Statistics compiled by the EC show that construction costs in the Irish construction industry are lower than in most European Community countries. However, the competitive position of the Irish construction industry has been slipping. In 1975, Irish construction costs in the non-residential building sector (a sector presumably influencing greatly the competitiveness of Irish traded goods industries) were second lowest out of the then nine EC countries; in 1983, Ireland was only sixth lowest out of twelve. As regards civil engineering costs, Ireland came second lowest out of nine in 1975, and seventh lowest out of twelve in 1983. The SCCCS speculates that this may have been in part due to the move towards larger numbers of firms operating at lower levels of production, with subsequent losses of economies of scale; developments in the labour market (increasing wage claims and government employment taxes, for example) may also be to blame. That high levels of PRSI and other taxes may be affecting measured costs is suggested by the spread of the black economy construction industry which may be costing the state up to IR£50 million per year in lost revenue.

5 CONCLUSION

This chapter has argued that much greater attention could be focussed on the non-traded sector by policy-makers, as it is on this sector that the competitiveness of a country's traded industries depends. As stressed in this chapter, the price at which non-traded goods and services are sold both to domestic consumers and traded sector firms is crucial for national welfare. Moreover, it is important to consider these prices relative to what is being charged in other countries. Much empirical work has already been done (e.g. by the Committee on Costs and Competitiveness) on labour costs in Ireland relative to the rest of the world. Unfortunately, there has been no comprehensive survey of the relative costs of non-labour inputs into traded goods industries in Ireland as compared with other countries. Nor has there been a comprehensive study of concentration levels in the non-traded sector. Such a study would greatly help in clarifying what the priorities of government should be in attempting to expand employment in Ireland.

Footnotes

1 The possibility of immiserizing growth, which can occur when the form of growth is such that the country's terms of trade deteriorate sufficiently to offset the direct, positive impact of the growth, is here being ignored. The assumption that the economy is an SOE (i.e. faces given terms of trade), of course, rules out this possibility.

2 NESC, *A Review of Industrial Policy* (Report no. 64), Stationery Office, Dublin 1982, p. 112.

3 NESC, *op. cit.*, p. 36.

4 D. Conniffe and K. A. Kennedy (editors), *Employment and Unemployment Policy for Ireland*, ESRI, Dublin 1984, p. 43.

5 NESC, *A Strategy for Development 1986-1990* (Report no. 83), Stationery Office, Dublin 1986, p. 147.

6 Assuming that there are factors of production specific to the sectors in which they are employed.

7 Patrick O'Malley, *Irish Industry: Structure and Performance*, Gill and Macmillan, Dublin 1971.

8 J. G. Hughes, 'Output, Prices and Productivity in Irish Sheltered and Exposed Transportable Goods Industries, 1953-1967', *Economic and Social Review*, January 1971, pp. 191-208.

9 Breaking up a monopoly where there are economies of scale would of course increase costs to exposed industries.

10 The following discussion draws heavily on Paul Krugman, 'Strategic Sectors and International Competition', in Robert Stern (editor), *US Trade Policies in a Changing World Economy*, MIT Press, Cambridge Mass. 1987.

11 See Krugman, *op. cit*, and E. Helpman and P. Krugman, *Market Structure and Foreign Trade*, MIT Press, Cambridge Mass. 1985.

12 The IDA, CTT and Shannon Development all have programmes to promote internationally traded services based in Ireland.

13 The theory of consumer demand relating tastes for goods to tastes for underlying characteristics is associated with the name of Lancaster, and is widely used in studies of product differentiation.

14 Adam Smith, *The Wealth of Nations*, 1776, Book 2, Chapter 3.

15 Alfred Marshall, *Principles of Economics* (8th edition), Macmillan, London 1920, Book 2, Chapter 3, p. 53.

16 *Ibid.*, p. 53.

17 One key distinction between the Classical and the Neoclassical economists is implicit in their treatment of services: namely, whereas the Classicals thought mainly in terms of the generation of surplus, the Neoclassicals implicitly dealt with economies with fixed endowments of resources, which could be transformed or exchanged, but which remained fixed in quantity.

18 See CSO *Census of Population*, Stationery Office, Dublin 1981.

19 The material in this section draws on Jonathan Gershuny, 'Employment Structure and Post-Industrial Transformation', Chapter 2 in *Services and the New Economy: Implications for National and Regional Development*, Regional Studies Association (Irish Branch), Dublin 1985; D. Norton, 'Public Policy for Private Sector Services', *Journal of Irish Business and Administrative Research,* vol. 6, no. 2, p. 91; J. Gershuny and I. Miles, *The New Service Economy*, Praeger, New York 1983; T. Stanback, *Understanding the Service Economy*, Johns Hopkins, Baltimore 1979; F. Momigliano and D. Siniscalco, 'The Growth of Service Employment: A Reappraisal', *Banca Nazionale Del Lavoro Quarterly Review*, September 1982; and W. O'Riordan, 'Induced Employment in the Marketed Service Sector in Ireland', *Journal of the Statistical and Social Inquiry Society of Ireland*, 1984/85.

20 D. J. Cogan, *The Irish Services Sector: A Study of Productive Efficiency,* Stationery Office, Dublin 1978, Chapter 2.

21 D. Norton, *op. cit.*, p. 100.

22 D. Cogan, *op. cit.*, p. 185.

23 Common but not inevitable: Norton *op. cit.*, cites several studies showing that service sector productivity grew as fast as productivity in other sectors in various countries; a US Department of Labour study showed that, between 1967 and 1979, total factor productivity in the US services sector grew twice as fast as productivity in goods-producing industry. This makes the performance of the Irish services sector appear in a rather unflattering light.

24 On all this, see National Planning Board, *Proposals for a Plan 1984-87*, Dublin 1984.

25 See S. Barrett, *Transport Policy in Ireland*, Irish Management Institute, Dublin 1982.

26 See OECD, *Economic Survey, Ireland 1985*, Paris 1985.

27 See NESC, *op. cit.*, 1986, pp. 209-218.

28 This section draws extensively on Sectoral Consultative Committee for the Construction Sector, *The Construction Industry*, Dublin 1984.

Selected Bibliography

Books
1 J.A. Bristow and A.A. Tait (editors), *Economic Policy in Ireland,* Institute of Public Administration, Dublin 1968.
2 Denis Conniffe and Kieran A. Kennedy (editors), *Employment and Unemployment Policy for Ireland,* Economic and Social Research Institute, Dublin 1984.
3 Raymond Crotty, *Ireland in Crisis: A Study in Capitalist Colonial Undevelopment,* Brandon, Kerry 1986.
4 B.R. Dowling and J. Durkan (editors), *Irish Economic Policy: A Review of Major Issues,* Economic and Social Research Institute, Dublin 1978.
5 P.J. Drudy and Dermot McAleese (editors), *Ireland and the European Community,* Cambridge University Press, Cambridge 1984.
6 Jim Fitzpatrick and John Kelly (editors), *Perspectives on Irish Industry,* Irish Management Institute, Dublin 1985.
7 Norman J. Gibson and John E. Spencer (editors), *Economic Activity in Ireland: A Study of Two Open Economies,* Gill and Macmillan, Dublin 1977.
8 Desmond A. Gillmor, *Economic Activities in the Republic of Ireland: A Geographical Perspective,* Gill and Macmillan, Dublin 1985.
9 Kieran A. Kennedy (editor), *Ireland in Transition: Economic and Social Change Since 1960* (Thomas Davis Lecture Series), Mercier Press, Cork 1986.
10 F.S.L. Lyons, *Ireland Since the Famine,* Fontana, London 1973.
11 James Meenan, *The Irish Economy Since 1922,* Liverpool University Press, Liverpool 1970.
12 John Vaizey (editor), *Economic Sovereignty and Regional Policy: A Symposium on Regional Problems in Britain and Ireland,* Gill and Macmillan, Dublin 1975.
13 T.K. Whitaker, *Interests,* Institute of Public Administration, Dublin 1984.

Journals and Monographs etc.
1 *Administration* (quarterly journal of the Institute of Public Administration of Ireland).
2 *Central Bank of Ireland Quarterly Bulletin* and *Central Bank of Ireland Annual Report.*
3 Commission of the European Communities and Eurostat publications.
4 Economic and Social Research Institute's *Broadsheet Series, Publication Series* and *Quarterly Economic Commentary.*
5 *Economic and Social Review* (quarterly journal of the social sciences published by Economic and Social Studies, Dublin).
6 Government publications, particularly *Economic Review and Outlook* (annual), and *National Income and Expenditure* (annual).

7   *Irish Banking Review* (quarterly).
8   *Journal of the Statistical and Social Inquiry Society of Ireland* (annual).
9   National Economic and Social Council (NESC) publications, especially, *A Strategy for Development 1986-1990* (Report no. 83), Stationery Office, Dublin 1986.
10 Organization for Economic Co-operation and Development, *Economic Surveys* (annual).
11 *Studies* (an Irish quarterly review).

Subject Index